HUMAN RESOURCES ADMINISTRATION

PERSONNEL ISSUES AND NEEDS IN EDUCATION

Fifth Edition

L. Dean Webb
Arizona State University

M. Scott Norton
Arizona State University

Merrill
is an imprint of

Upper Saddle River, New Jersey
Columbus, Ohio

Library of Congress Cataloging-in-Publication Data

Webb, L. Dean.
  Human resources administration personnel issues and needs in
education / L. Dean Webb, M. Scott Norton.— 5th ed.
     p. cm.
  Includes bibliographical references and index.
  ISBN-13: 978-0-13-239771-1
  ISBN-10: 0-13-239771-4
  1. School personnel management—United States. I. Norton, M. Scott.
  II. Title. LB2831.58.W43 2009
  371.2'010973–dc22   2007040038

Vice President and Executive Publisher: Jeffery W. Johnston
Executive Editor: Darcy Betts Prybella
Editorial Assistant: Nancy J. Holstein
Production Editor: Sarah N. Kenoyer
Design Coordinator: Diane C. Lorenzo
Cover Design: Bryan Huber
Cover Image: Super Stock
Production Manager: Susan W. Hannahs
Director of Marketing: Quinn Perkson
Composition/Full-Service Project Management: Christian Holdener, S4Carlisle Publishing Services
Marketing Coordinator: Brian Mounts

This book was set in Palatino by S4Carlisle Publishing Services. It was printed and bound by Courier Westford. The
cover was printed by Phoenix Color Corp.

Pearson® is a registered trademark of Pearson plc.
Merrill® is a registered trademark of Pearson Education, Inc.

Pearson Education Ltd.   Pearson Education Australia Pty. Limited
Pearson Education Singapore Pte. Ltd.   Pearson Education North Asia Ltd.
Pearson Education Canada, Ltd.   Pearson Educación de Mexico, S.A. de C.V.
Pearson Education–Japan   Pearson Education Malaysia Pte. Ltd.

Merrill
is an imprint of

10 9 8 7 6 5 4 3 2 1
ISBN-13: 978-0-13-239771-1
ISBN-10: 0-13-239771-4

Dedicated to the memory of
Madeline K. McDaniel, George N. Norton, and Steven A. Norton.

Preface

Public education in the United States is a labor-intensive enterprise. Personnel costs make up 75 to 85% of the typical school district budget. Because personnel are so important to the achievement of the goals and objectives of an educational system, human resources administration is of central importance. How individuals are recruited, selected, evaluated, motivated, compensated, and aided in their development are factors in determining their personal and professional satisfaction and performance. Human resources administrators can be successful if they have not only gained an adequate knowledge of specifics—such as relevant laws and policies, the application of computer technology, or successful collective negotiation strategies—but also have developed and integrated planning processes and communication systems and, perhaps most important, fostered a relationship of mutual respect and cooperation among the staff, the administration, and the school board.

This edition of *Human Resources Administration* represents a major revision of the previous edition. Important new material on motivation and induction has been included as well as a new chapter on staff development. At the same time, following the suggestion of reviewers, the chapter on historical aspects has been abbreviated and combined with the chapter introducing the human resources function. Also at the suggestion of reviewers, the law and policy chapters have been integrated, with the majority of the chapter on policy eliminated. The chapter on projections for the future also was eliminated and this discussion is included in the context of the relevant material in selected chapters. In all chapters all material included in the previous edition has been thoroughly revised. In addition, new tables and figures have been added to serve as visual organizers for chapter content and to add to the text's visual appeal.

The text consists of 12 chapters that address all the traditional topics in human resources administration along with the most current concern in the field. The chapter in Part I, "Human Resources Administration," describes the development of human resources administration and explores its present functioning in the organizational context of the school system. The chapters that make up Part II, "Shaping the Environment of Human Resources Administration," deal with the environmental and contextual factors within which the human resources function. The chapters in Part III. "Specific Processes in the Human Resources Domain," discuss the various human resources tasks and processes.

Each chapter begins with a list of learning objectives which serves as an advance organizer for the chapter. Discussion questions at the end of each chapter address the topics discussed in the chapter and are designed to allow students the opportunity to demonstrate their understanding of the material presented in the chapter and to apply it in realistic situations and to real-life situations. Case studies in each chapter not only provide students the opportunity to apply chapter concepts to realistic situations in the workplace, but the also provide the stimulus for discussion of complex and controversial issues. Lastly, the text contains numerous charts, figures, and tables which not only serve as visual organizers, but also enrich and illustrate chapter content. In addition, in response to the request of a number of users of the previous edition, a test bank of objective questions (true–false, multiple-choice) is available for the those who adopt the text.

Human Resources Administration is intended for students, human resources administrators, educational administrators, professional educators, policymakers, social scientists, and the interested public. The material in each chapter reflects the most accepted concepts found in the research and literature on that chapter's topic. In addition to establishing a strong research base, consideration has been given to presenting principles that are relevant across all school systems and all states. Where appropriate, actual illustrations and examples from school districts are included.

We wish to express appreciation to the many people who contributed to the publication of this book. We would like to thank our reviewers for their helpful suggestions: Tony Armenta, Southeastern Louisiana University; Joseph Beckham, Florida State University; Lynn Beckwith, Jr., University of Missouri, St. Louis; W. Keith Christy, University of Arkansas, Little Rock; Pamela Harrison, Tarleton State University, Central Texas; and Karen Lieuallen, Marian College.

Finally, we wish to acknowledge our editor, Darcy Betts Prybella, for her support and assistance in the completion of the project.

L. Dean Webb
M. Scott Norton
Tempe, Arizona

Brief Contents

Contents

CHAPTER 9   The Compensation Process   223

CHAPTER 1

The Human Resources Function
ITS ORGANIZATION AND PROCESSES

The information in this chapter will enable you to:

- Define the human resources function and delineate its primary processes.
- Explain the responsibilities of the central human resources unit and the characteristics of individuals in this leadership role.
- Describe line and staff organizational structures and the place of the human resources unit in each.
- Enumerate the major competencies required of human resources administrators.
- Identify the ethics and standards that apply to human resources administration.

This chapter begins with a definition of human resources administration and continues with a brief history of human resources administration in education. The majority of the chapter is devoted to an examination of the major processes that comprise the human resources function. The place of the human resources unit in the overall operation of the school system is also discussed. The competencies required of the human resources administrator are detailed. The chapter concludes with an examination of the ethics and standards that guide professional practices in human resources administration.

WHAT IS HUMAN RESOURCES ADMINISTRATION?

The Society of Human Resources Management (2006) defines human resources administration as the "formal structure within an organization responsible for all the decisions, strategies, factors, principles, operations, practices, functions, activities, and methods related to the management of people" (p. 1). This definition of human resources administration expresses the comprehensiveness of the human resources function in education as well as the basic concept that "organizations are people."

For the purposes of this text, **human resources administration** is defined as those processes that are planned and implemented in the organization to establish an effective system of human resources and to foster an organizational climate that enhances the accomplishment of educational goals. This view emphasizes human resources administration as a foundational function for an effective educational program. The primary elements of the human resources processes implied in the definition are recruiting, selecting, and developing staff, as well as establishing a harmonious working relationship among personnel. Although this definition emphasizes the human element, it also states that the focus of human resources administration is on achieving the goals and objectives of the system. This focus includes a major concern for developing a healthy organizational climate that promotes the accomplishment of school goals and the meeting of the personnel needs of school employees.

THE EVOLUTION OF HUMAN RESOURCES ADMINISTRATION IN EDUCATION

Human resources administration as we know it today did not exist prior to 1900. Prior to 1900 employers assumed responsibility for personnel matters in the business and industrial sectors, in most cases delegating some of this function to front-line supervisors or foremen. The "line boss" generally took charge of such personnel activities as hiring, on-the-job training, rating, and firing. No professional group existed that was concerned with the practice of personnel management.

In the field of education, upthrough the eighteenth century, select lay committees assumed responsibility for personnel duties in the school. Parents and religious groups were reluctant to trust the "proper education" of their children to persons outside the home or church. The title *selectmen* was commonly bestowed on these early control groups that consisted largely of local influential laymen and religious leaders (Lucio & McNeil, 1969). Selectmen exercised tight control over the policies of the school, the supervision of the subjects taught, and the personal habits of the teacher. Although they knew little about education, these select committees were not reticent to criticize, make suggestions, or recommend the dismissal of an "incompetent" teacher.

The slow development of professional leadership in education before the turn of the nineteenth century contributed to the administrative authority of the select committees. The first city superintendent was not appointed until 1837. Even as late as 1870 only 29 districts in the country had appointed superintendents of schools. Initially, these individuals were vested with responsibility for the curriculum and given limited authority for personnel.

While the city or district superintendent had limited authority in matters affecting personnel during this period, the county superintendent had a great deal of influence on personnel activities. The country superintendent was a significant office in most states from 1850 to 1925. Delaware is credited with having the first recorded county superintendent, as early as 1829 (AASA, 1952). By 1879, 34 of the 38 states plus 4 territories had created the office of county superintendent (Newsom, 1932).

Toward the end of the nineteenth century, urban populations increased and the number of public high schools grew and the work of the county superintendent was gradually assumed by local supervisors. At the same time, the growing number of teacher training institutions assumed greater responsibility for the initial and in-service training of teachers. Nonetheless, the county superintendent continued to serve many of the smaller school districts and maintained limited responsibilities for larger districts for several years after 1900.

Teaching staffs in the nineteenth century, and for some years after, were marginally prepared for their tasks. Many elementary school teachers had only a high school education, with no formal teacher training. Although the two-year normal school was well established in the last quarter of the nineteenth century, much of the pre-service and in-service training of teachers was accomplished through other means, primarily the **teacher institutes** operated by the county superintendent. In fact, part of the importance of the county superintendent comes from the fact that the teacher institutes were operated by that office.

During the latter part of the nineteenth century, some specialization in personnel functions began to emerge in business and industry. Such duties as record keeping, preparing salary schedules and rating reports, and other clerical tasks were assigned to one individual (McCoy, Gips, & Evans, 1983). Later, one person became responsible for other, more specialized personnel tasks such as selecting and assigning the needed personnel.

In education, prior to 1900 there was little evidence of an organized central personnel or human resources office in school systems. However, educational institutions began to initiate personnel practices similar to those in business and industry. One common practice was to delegate certain activities, such as compensation and personnel matters, to the business administrator. With the emergence of assistant superintendent positions, more personnel activities related to the professional teaching staff were assumed by these administrators. Building principals did perform some personnel duties, but many were only part-time administrators and had teaching responsibilities as well.

During the first half of the twentieth century, personnel administration in business and education continued to develop. *Personnel administration,* as the term is commonly used today, began with World War I. "The recruiting, training, and paying of masses of workers in war production forced assignment of such responsibilities to specialized personnel" (Moore, 1966, p. 5). In education, beginning in the 1940s, the establishment of personnel departments was encouraged by school surveys conducted by management consultants and by universities, which recommended the establishment of positions charged with the management of personnel (Moore, 1966). As a result, the establishment of central offices to coordinate the human resources function increased significantly during the 1950s and 1960s. By the mid-1960s, approximately 250 human resources administrators were operating in the public schools (Moore, 1966). By 2005 that number had increased almost ten-fold.

The growth of the human resources function was not only a reflection of the growth of the educational enterprise but a growing recognition of the importance of the human resources function on the quality of teaching and learning and to the success of the total education program. This importance has been underscored by the No Child Left Behind Act of 2001, which required that a "highly qualified" teacher be in every classroom by 2006. The success of school districts reaching this goal is determined by the policies and regulations which govern the recruitment, selection, induction, supervision, compensation, and other human resources activities, as well as the competency of those charged with implementing and administering these policies.

In the following sections of this chapter, an overview of the major human resources processes is presented, and the impact of each of these processes on quality teaching and student learning is considered.

THE HUMAN RESOURCES PROCESSES

The processes of the human resources function and their relationships are illustrated in Figure 1.1. These 12 processes within the human resources function are shown as subsets of three major components: human resources utilization, human resources development, and human resources environment.

Human resources utilization is a comprehensive component that encompasses the processes of resource planning, recruitment, selection, induction, assignment, collective bargaining, compensation and welfare, and stability. *Human resources development* includes the processes of staff development and evaluation. The final component, *human resources environment*, includes the processes of organizational climate and protection. Each of the processes is interrelated, and its effectiveness depends directly or indirectly upon the effectiveness of each of the others and working together toward the successful achievement of system goals (see Figure 1.1).

Each of the three processes of the human resources function is described briefly in the following sections and discussed in more detail in the chapters which follow.

Processes of Human Resources Utilization

Resource Planning. *How does the school system determine its direction and priorities? What kinds of data and information are essential for the successful completion of the human resources tasks and responsibilities?*

The resources planning process serves in answering the preceding questions. The purposes of resources planning are to (1) clarify the objectives and mission of the organization; (2) determine in advance what the organization and its parts are to do; and (3) ascertain the assets on hand and the resources required to accomplish the desired results. Effective resources planning is essential in helping the school system determine what it wants to be and provides a blueprint for guiding action. Such a process is essential to avoid guesswork and happenstance, to offset uncertainty, and to ensure efficient accomplishment of goals. Planning constitutes a purposeful set of activities that focus available resources upon the achievement of school district goals.

Figure 1.1 The Human Resources Processes and Relationships

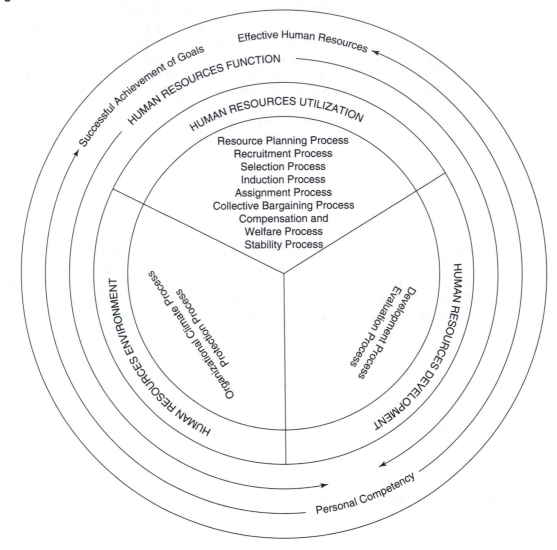

Planning is not synonymous with the plan. A plan is a product of the planning process. Planning, on the other hand, is a continuous, ongoing process characterized by flexibility and subjectivity to change. Effective planning forms a foundation for decision making. It encourages responsive administration and capitalizes on employee talents by establishing goals that elicit the most effective performance from individuals in the organization. Planning is a comprehensive, continuous process that must remain flexible and responsive to changing conditions. Activities within the human resources planning process include developing planning assumptions, determining organizational relationships and structures, inventorying need, assessing labor markets, forecasting resource needs, projecting student populations, participating in policy development, completing position analyses and position descriptions, and evaluating the effectiveness of the process. The human resources planning process is developed in detail in Chapter 2.

Recruitment of Personnel. *How can highly qualified individuals be attracted to the school system for consideration for possible employment?*

The purpose of the recruitment process is to establish a pool of qualified candidates to meet the needs of the school system. It focuses on strategies for attracting and retaining the best qualified persons for the specific positions available. The amount of recruitment necessary to accomplish the goals depends on such factors as enrollment growth and decline, staff turnover, program design, and supply and demand in the labor force. Recruitment is not only a primary responsibility of the human resources function but, when coupled with the selection process, is considered by many practitioners as their most time-consuming responsibility. In fact, 93% of the human resources directors in one state named the recruitment process their highest ranked job responsibility (Norton, 1999). And, 55% of the directors named recruitment, selection, and assignment as consuming the greatest amount of their time.

The demand for highly qualified teachers created by the No Child Left Behind Act, as well as the large number of teachers leaving the profession in their first 5 years and the continuing teacher shortages in many teaching areas (e.g., science and special education), has made an effective recruitment program even more critical to the school district. The recruitment process begins by establishing policy guidelines during the planning process to direct such specific activities as developing recruitment resources, implementing application procedures, establishing formal interview and evaluation procedures, and designing appropriate staff involvement strategies for each of these activities. Although the process of recruitment is one shared by the central human resources unit and personnel in other units of the system, it continues to be administered primarily by the central human resources unit. A major question facing the human resources function is related to the reform/restructuring of school governance. For example, the increase of site-based management has shifted more of the responsibility for recruitment and selection to the local school. Chapters 5 and 12 consider the recruitment process in detail, as related to both professional and support staff personnel.

Selection of Personnel. *How does the school system determine the best person for a specific position? Does selection depend primarily on individual perceptions of an applicant's qualifications, or are there "tools" that lead to staff selection on a more objective basis?*

Selecting the right person for the right job is a basic responsibility of effective human resources administration. Many of the personnel problems of a school district can be avoided through an effective selection process. In addition, effective personnel selection serves to reduce the major costs associated with the retraining of inadequately prepared employees. When asked to cite their most important task, human resources administrators most often mention the selection of personnel. Selection necessitates attention to matters other than merely filling vacancies. And, although placing the right person in the right job is a primary objective, other considerations such as staff load, staff balance, and staff diversity are also important. Moreover, selection often is carried out under complex and confusing conditions. For example, a reduction in force might be taking place in one area while another area is recruiting for additional personnel.

The competition for quality personnel has led to the streamlining of selection procedures. The traditional steps related to the application, background checks, interview, applicant ratings, final selection and offer, and approval by the school board are changing. In the past far too many instances, a quality applicant has been lost to a district because of the time required to complete each step in the lengthy selection process. As a result, more and more districts are giving hiring authority to school officials to offer a position to a candidate in a more expedited process. The teacher is hired in some instances within 1 or 2 days after the interview or perhaps "on the spot." Such hires, as is the case with any newly contracted employee, ultimately are subject to the results of background checks and school board approval.

The selection process is discussed in detail in Chapters 5 and 12.

Induction of Personnel. *How are personnel introduced into the school setting, and how important are such orientation activities to the system and the individual employee?*

Induction often is referred to as *orientation* or *staff development*. We define *induction* as the complex of activities designed to gain congruence between institutional objectives and employee needs. It begins with the initial contact of a prospective employee with the district and continues on an ongoing basis for as long as the employee or the organization views it as necessary. From this perspective, induction is seen as a comprehensive process as opposed to the traditional practice in some schools of scheduling 1 or 2 days of informational sessions for employees at the beginning of the school year; these we consider orientation activities. Induction has gained added attention and importance as a result of the research which has underscored the importance of planned induction activities to employee performance and retention. This is also the time beginning teachers and others are most likely to need help with special problems, and providing novice teachers the assistance and support they need can become the most vital factor in their success and retention.

Chapter 6 includes a consideration of induction and its relationship to other human resources processes.

Assignment of Personnel. *How are personnel assigned so that their talents and interests optimally serve the system and their own self-development?*

Effective employee assignment is a key factor in assuring the effective contribution of individuals to achieving organizational goals. Traditionally, assignment of personnel has centered on the match between personnel and positions, or placing the right person in the right job. Although this view remains operational in most school systems, the concept of competency modeling—the structuring of tasks around the skills or competencies of employees—has gained momentum in many organizations.

Today a comprehensive view of assignment considers the complex of activities related to the talents and interests of the employee and the environment in which the work takes place. These include: the deployment of talent in the best interests of the system, the employee, and the student; effective staff supervision; staff improvement practices; organizational climate; evaluation; and workload. This comprehensive view contrasts with the traditional assignment practice which, with the exception of class size, has given little attention to teacher workload factors. A more comprehensive view of teacher workload considers the number of subjects and levels taught, length of class periods, the number of class preparations, and extracurricular assignments. Although teacher load is only one consideration within the assignment process, it illustrates the need for cooperative efforts among administrative personnel in the school system.

Collective Bargaining. *How do employee groups and school boards decide on matters of salary, working conditions, and other contractual matters? How are negotiation teams formed, and how are negotiations carried out?*

The collective bargaining process has become the primary procedure whereby boards of education and representatives of employee groups decide many of the matters related to terms and conditions of employment. In the opinion of many, no other development in education has had more impact upon the human resources function than collective bargaining. Collective bargaining has come to impact virtually every aspect of human resources administration. Negotiations consume a significant part of the time of the human resources administrator. As discussed in Chapter 10, the human resources administrator often serves as the chief spokesperson for the school board negotiation team and plays a major role in other collective bargaining activities, including negotiation planning and proposal development, strategy development, and implementation of the agreement once negotiated.

While many aspects of the collective bargaining process are regulated by state statutes, more current experiences with the use of **integrative bargaining** strategies, such as **win-win** and collaborative bargaining, suggest that not only has the scope of bargaining become more expanded, but that the competencies required of a successful negotiator have become more specialized. Chapter 10 examines the collective bargaining process in detail, including the role of the human resources administrator and human resource unit.

Compensation and Welfare of Personnel. *What factors determine the levels of compensation for professional and support personnel in the school system? What are the various kinds of compensation and benefits provided employees?*

The compensation of personnel constitutes by far the largest general fund expenditure of any school system; compensation comprises approximately 80% of most general fund budgets. Compensation has a major impact on the ability of the district to attract highly qualified personnel and to retain their services. The compensation and welfare process includes consideration of contract salary agreements, fringe benefits, and other rewards and incentives. The human resources unit in most school districts assumes major responsibility for administering the activities involved in the compensation and welfare processes.

In the last decade the effect of compensation on the school district's ability to attract highly qualified personnel has become a major concern of many states and school districts. In response, new approaches to personnel compensation, including performance-based pay, have been adopted by many school districts. At the same time, teacher shortages and poor student performance have provided the impetus for proposals for increasing teacher salaries in many state legislatures along with proposals for various tax measures to fund the increases.

In an effort to attract and retain quality employees, many organizations are adopting an array of strategies including work life programs, employee assistance programs, and tuition reimbursement benefits, as well as non-monetary methods such as flexible hours. In addition, the growing concern for employee health has led to a new emphasis on wellness programs. Too, extended programs such as child care and elder care are predicated in part on the realization that employees' concerns for their children and aging parents during working hours can serve as an inhibitor to effective work production. Compensation and welfare of certificated personnel are considered in Chapter 9. Chapter 12 discusses compensation for support personnel.

Stability of Personnel Services. *How does the school system maintain a viable workforce over a long period of time? What conditions and programs promote the stability of the school system, and what conditions militate against the continuation of high-level service?*

Once the human resources function secures the personnel needed by the school system, the maintenance of an effective workforce to ensure continuous, high-level service becomes vitally important. Stability encompasses a wide variety of program provisions, including managing teacher and staff absenteeism, securing substitutes to replace absent employees, operating employee assistance programs, separating from service, and perhaps most important, retaining a stable workforce.

Teacher absenteeism and a scarcity of qualified substitutes are common problems in many school districts. The shortage of substitute teachers has resulted in a lessening of certification requirements in some states. For example, in Maricopa County, Arizona, substitute teachers are no longer required to hold a college degree. Rather, a high school graduate who completes a 16-hour, 5-day seminar at a specified university can receive an emergency teaching certificate. Such emergency measures underscore the severity of the teacher shortage problem.

Another important part of the stability program is an the **employee assistance program (EAP)**. An estimated 10% to 20% of the labor force utilizes mental and other health service counseling annually. And, more than half of the nation's school districts have implemented some form of an EAP to work with troubled employees. In addition to the services provided through the EAP, human resources administrators are often called upon to provide counseling to employees concerning family problems, grievances, or other personnel or employment concerns. In fact, human resources administrators report that these activities require as much of their time as recruitment, selection, and assignment.

A growing concern of human resources administrators is teacher retention. Studies of teacher loss indicate that 50% of new teachers leave the profession by the end of the fifth year (College Board, 2006). Such turnover is costly both monetarily and intellectually. It is estimated that it costs at least 50% of a teacher's salary to replace him or her (College Board, 2006); the cost of replacing a school principal or mid-management supervisor is estimated to be much higher. Costs include the administrative costs associated with the separation of the leaving employee, costs to recruit and process all candidates, interview costs, candidate travel costs, severance pay, training for new employees, and other "hidden costs." A conservative estimate for replacing a mid-management administrator in a typical school district (principal, central office supervisor, etc.) would be $25,100. This figure is based on fees for the talent search by a contracted firm or individual and advertisement costs, $7,500; related search expenses including interviewee costs for travel and per diem, $3,600; employee time spent in clerical work and participation in the selection process, $2,500; loss of work due to the necessary involvement of teachers and others in the replacement activities, $3,500; time spent on the "induction" of the new hire, $3,000; and expenses related to hiring the new administrator such as moving costs, travel expenses, temporary housing, and so forth, $5,000. The preceding costs do not include costs such as signing bonuses, salary increases, and other fringe benefits that commonly accompany the hiring of higher-level school administrators.

The loss of intellectual capital is perhaps even more important than the monetary costs associated with employee turnover. No organization can afford to lose its best personnel and continue to be optimally effective. The result of research involving organizations in a number of fields underscores the fact that the organizations that have established stability within their workforce have a competitive advantage and are more successful in achieving their stated goals.

Although the employee retention problem in education is complex and cannot easily be resolved, changes in practices relating to the human resources function itself hold promise for reducing employee loss. This includes not only the recruitment and selection practices suggested in Chapters 4 and 5, but the more comprehensive programs aimed at induction of employees into the school systems and supporting them in professional and personal development as described in Chapter 7. Many of the monetary solutions being proposed today and discussed in Chapter 9 will, hopefully, also contribute both to employee recruitment and retention.

Processes of Human Resources Development

Development of Human Resources. *What do organizations do to motivate employees to improve personal competency? What personal growth programs tend to be most productive for the system and for the individual?*

Development programs that promote increases in personal knowledge of subject matter and effective methods for delivering this knowledge to students serve to increase teacher confidence and, in turn, professional competence. Professional development activities provide employees the opportunity to increase their knowledge, skills, and abilities in the furtherance of system goals. They are also the primary means for helping personnel to achieve personal goals and to reach their potential.

Staff development is a shared responsibility of several units in an educational system; however, human resources administrators often play a major role in in-service training, internship programs, mentoring, and external training support programs. The human resources development process and the responsibilities of all administrators who supervise personnel have expanded significantly in the last decade. Performance assessment centers, administrator academies and cadre programs, special mentoring programs, clinical supervision, skill labs, peer-assisted leadership programs, local school district internship programs in teaching and administration, and cooperative training programs between local school districts and institutions of higher education represent a few examples of such recent expansions.

The establishment of staff development policies, the determination of growth needs, and the implementation of special development programs are activities that concern all school administrators. Staff development and the concern for the maximization of human resources in the school system are presented in Chapter 7.

Evaluation of Personnel. *What purposes are served through personnel performance appraisal programs? Who benefits? What constitutes an effective personnel appraisal process?*

Although the primary responsibility for the formal appraisal of teachers, administrators, and support staff resides with the immediate supervisor, the human resources unit has a major role in developing evaluation policies, monitoring the appraisal process, and maintaining the appraisal records completed by other units. Thus, formal personnel evaluation is a shared responsibility—one that has assumed increasing importance in education.

The appraisal of personnel is a major issue in education. Performance evaluation is seen by many as a major strategy in improving the quality of the teaching force and, subsequently, student achievement. In the wake of the reform movement of the 1990s and No Child Left Behind, most states have adopted or strengthened policies addressing personnel evaluation in the public schools. Often state mandates have directed school systems to present evidence that viable personnel evaluation programs are in place and that provisions for certifying evaluators for these programs have been implemented.

The need for improvement of evaluation policies and procedures, the continued push for personnel accountability, and the growing acceptance of competency-based performance concepts forecast the continued importance of employee evaluation. Chapter 8 considers this human resources process in detail.

Processes of the Human Resources Environment

Development of the Organizational Climate. *What do school systems do to foster a healthy working environment for employees? How can the school become a better place to work? What effect does organizational climate have on employee performance?*

The complex of personal and organizational relationships within the school system necessarily is a concern of the human resources function. **Organizational climate** is defined as the collective personality of a school or school system. It is the atmosphere that prevails in an organization and is characterized by the social and professional interactions of the people.

The concept of **organizational culture** has become a significant force in educational thought. As stated by Pai and Adler (2001), "There is no escaping the fact that education is a socio-cultural process. Hence, a critical examination of the role of culture in human life is indispensable to the understanding and control of the educative processes" (pp. 3–4). Although the concept of organizational culture differs among authorities, most agree that schools and school systems, like other organizations, develop personalities of their own. As a person has a personality, a group is said to have a **syntality** that reflects its traditions, beliefs, values, and visions. School administrators need to understand the culture of the organization in order to help it become what it can become. The school administrator must be knowledgeable about the beliefs and patterns of the organization; communication, influence, motivation, and other factors depend on such understanding. Additionally, the administrator must have the competencies needed to assess existing climates and understand the theories and practices associated with fostering positive environments to develop harmonious and productive working relationships among employees in the system. The school leader must care about the kind of climate being created in the organization and whether the climate is one that encourages employees to want to remain or want to leave. The most desirable climate is one that sends a message to employees that they are valued workers and important to the achievement of the system's goals. Chapter 3 discusses culture and organizational climate as they relate to the human resources function.

Protection of Personnel. *How are school employees protected from unfair treatment and physical harm?*

Protection of personnel includes grievances, transfers, dismissals, Reductions in Force, employee discipline, and tenure and promotion, as well as those intended to provide a safe and secure working environment. The human resources protection process has received increased attention because of the growing number of issues involving employee rights and security. Protecting employee rights and maintaining a more positive work climate have always been objectives of effective human resources administration. In recent years however, these concerns have broadened in scope and are now reflected in virtually every process of the human resources function.

A rapidly growing area in the protection process is that of security from bodily harm. Incidences of attacks on teachers, administrators, and other school personnel are increasingly commonplace. The growing numbers present a challenge in meeting employees' most basic need—the need for a safe, non-threatening work environment. The responsibility for maintaining a safe, healthy, and secure school environment is basic to the human resources protection process.

The 12 major human resources processes discussed in the preceding sections constitute the central focus of the human resources function in education. Each process plays a significant role in fostering a bond between the employee and the school and promoting a collaborative relationship based on the need to direct the performance of all employees toward the accomplishment of school district goals. The central human resources unit, discussed in the following section, has assumed a significant leadership role in most school districts in the administration of these processes. And, while in some districts site-based management has shifted some of the responsibilities of the central human resources unit in such matters as teacher selection, assignment, evaluation and, staff development to the local school level, the leadership of the central human resources unit continues to be critical to the effective administration and operation of the human resources function for the entire school district and to ensuring that school board policies are properly implemented.

THE CENTRAL HUMAN RESOURCES UNIT

Each of the major human resources processes relates directly or indirectly to virtually every other function in the educational enterprise, making the human resources function a shared responsibility. The organizational arrangements for administering human resources vary widely among school districts. In some instances, school districts delegate various personnel responsibilities among administrators throughout the system. Some school districts place human resources responsibilities under the jurisdiction of the superintendent and/or an assistant superintendent for personnel; while in others the human resources responsibilities are performed by an administrative team headed by a general administrative officer of the school district. Still other districts place the major human resources function within the office of a line administrator, such as an assistant superintendent for business affairs, or a staff administrator, such as a personnel director or specialist.

Figure 1.2 illustrates a traditional line and staff organizational arrangement for a school district. The term **line administrator** refers to a school officer in the hierarchical line of authority. A **staff administrator** is one who is not in the direct line of authority and whose position is created expressly to serve the major line functions of the organization. Thus, staff positions are considered to be advisory and supportive. The solid lines in Figure 1.2 indicate authority relationships. For example, the assistant superintendent for instruction, the assistant superintendent for business affairs, and the director of human resources are subordinate to and supervised by the deputy superintendent for business affairs. Dashed lines indicate staff positions/functions.

Variations in practices and arrangements make it impossible to construct an organizational plan that is applicable to all schools. Most studies of human resources administrators have found that they have major professional responsibilities in addition to personnel administration. In some districts the assistant superintendent or director of business affairs may have responsibility for human resources administration, or if not for all personnel, then for non-certificated personnel, and will thus also have responsibility for building construction and maintance, purchasing, payroll services, transportation, and a host of other areas. School district size, educational philosophy, financial ability, and other such factors influence the organization and place of the human resources unit in it. The size of a school district's enrollment or staff does not seem to be directly related to the designation of a central human resources unit. Some school districts with fewer than 1000 students have a central

Figure 1.2 Typical Line and Staff Organization for a School District

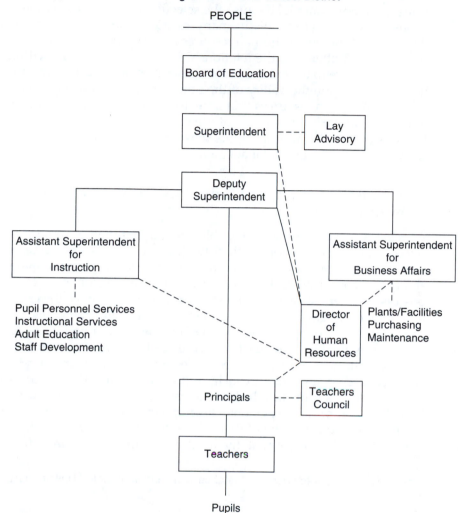

human resources administrator; other much larger districts distribute personnel responsibilities among various units within the system.

Human Resources and Site-Based Governance Structures

Reports indicate that the human resources function in a growing number of school districts nationally has been decentralized in some significant ways with a movement of the responsibility for many of the human resources processes to local schools. While decentralization has brought greater involvement of school administrators in various human resources processes, because the human resources function historically has been to a greater or lesser degree a shared responsibility among various units in most school systems, it is difficult to determine the specific impact of decentralization. For example, because the selection process, has always been a major responsibility of local schools in many districts, the influence, if any, of site-based decision making on this human resources process is difficult to assess.

Figure 1.3 illustrates the relationship of units and groups within the traditional school structure to the central human resources unit. Each individual unit or group has an effect upon the ability of the others to reach their objectives. The success of the central human resources unit in realizing its mission depends upon the support of others. Similarly, the success of each unit or group depends in part on the effectiveness of the central unit. In this sense, the human resources unit is a part of the school district's systems management.

Tasks, Competencies, and Indicators for Human Resources Administration

A **task** is a specific responsibility, obligation, or requirement associated with a professional position or function. Each of the human resources processes discussed earlier includes numerous tasks that require specific competencies. **Competency** refers to the ability to accomplish a task at a satisfactory level of performance. To be competent is to possess sufficient skills to meet a stated purpose or to have the capacity equal to the requirements of the task. Products or behaviors that illustrate one's capacity to perform competently are known as **indicators of competency** or performance specifications.

Identifying the competencies that are needed by human resources administrators and the indicators of those competencies serve two primary purposes. First, identifying competencies provides insight into the nature of the role of the human resources administrator and the human resources function in education. Second, such knowledge points to the personal development required for successful performance.

It is beyond the scope of this text to delineate a complete statement of competencies needed to perform all the tasks of the human resources function. Figure 1.4

Figure 1.3 The Central Human Resources Unit and Interrelated Units and Agencies

Figure 1.4 Selected Competencies for Administering the Central Human Resources Unit

1.1	Ability to communicate with others in the district in regard to current and future staffing needs.
1.2	Ability to evaluate data gathered on staffing needs.
1.3	Ability to identify primary sources of qualified applicants.
1.4	Ability to develop an appropriate screening process.
1.5	Ability to identify the knowledge, competencies, and abilities required for a given position.
1.6	Ability to determine the kinds of information needed by new and continuing personnel.
1.7	Ability to develop programs that enhance employee opportunities for self-improvement and advancement.
1.8	Ability to support and encourage the continuous use of self-evaluation/goal setting as a productive technique for change.
1.9	Ability to utilize effective counseling techniques with personnel.
1.10	Ability to develop and administer a program of employee compensation and benefits.
1.11	Ability to make all necessary preparations for negotiations.
1.12	Ability to develop specific records necessary to meet the needs of the human resources operation.
1.13	Ability to recognize competencies and talents of associates and utilize them effectively.
1.14	Ability to identify the unit's objectives and relate them to budget needs and limitations.
1.15	Ability to understand and interpret statutes, legal opinions, and court decisions relating to contractual relationships and employment conditions.
1.16	Ability to write viable policies and/or regulations; understand systems of codification.
1.17	Ability to assume a leadership role in developing a climate of mutual respect and trust which contributes to a high morale within the district.
1.18	Ability to articulate the human resources unit's objectives, practices, and accomplishments.

Source: From *Competency-Based Preparation of Educational Administrators: Tasks, Competencies, and Indicators of Competencies* by M. S. Norton, 2001, Tempe: Arizona State University, College of Education, Division of Educational Leadership and Policy Studies.

presents a statement of selected competencies for the major tasks related to the work of the administrator of the central human resources unit, although most of them apply equally well to school principals and human resources administrators in other school settings.

Another way of gaining insight into the nature of the work of the human resources unit is by examining the position description. Both the position analysis and position description for the position of human resources administrator are discussed next.

Position Analysis and Position Description for the Central Human Resources Administrator

A *position analysis* examines in depth the nature of a specific assignment and the complex environment in which the assignment takes place. The position analysis includes such considerations as the nature of the assignment itself, the primary work required, the conditions under which the work is performed, the competencies necessary for completing the work at the required level, the physical and mental requirements of the position, the educational preparation needed to perform successfully, the kinds of internal/external contacts required, specific problems encountered in the role, and other related information.

Good personnel practice requires that a position analysis be completed periodically. The position of human resources director should not be an exception. Due to the time involved in conducting a thorough position analysis, as well as the need for objectivity in its completion, outside consultants and human resource specialists often are utilized to complete this task.

The position analysis serves as the source for developing the *position description* of the human resources administrator. As noted throughout this chapter, the administrator of the human resources central unit is not characterized by a single description. Figure 1.5 is an example of a position description for the human resources director that contains many common elements from a general perspective. Note that the position description includes basic information relative to the director's position title, contract time, general responsibilities, position qualifications, immediate supervisor, supervisory jurisdiction, and major duties.

Figure 1.5 Position Description for School District Human Resources Director

Union High School District Position Description

Position Title: Assistant Superintendent of Human Resources
Department/Unit: District Administration
Contract: 12 months, 23 days vacation

General Statement of Responsibilities
To plan, coordinate, and supervise the operation of the department of human resources in such a way as to enhance the morale of school district personnel, promote the overall efficiency of the school system, and maximize the educational opportunities and benefits available to the individual student.

Major Duties
1. Supervises/directs:
   a. The planning and anticipation of human resources needs of the school district;
   b. The recruitment program for certificated and classified personnel;
   c. The screening and processing of all personnel recommendations for submission to the Board of Education;
   d. Those phases of the human resources program that include:
      1) Reports,
      2) Budgeting of personnel needs,
      3) Placement on the salary schedule,
      4) Contracts,
      5) Payroll department,
      6) Employee benefits program,
      7) Certification,
      8) Unemployment compensation,
      9) The Affirmative Action Program for the District (as the officer).
2. Evaluates:
   a. All prospective teacher and administrative applicants;
   b. All prospective classified applicants;
   c. Substitute teacher applicants;
   d. All employment practices and procedures;
   e. Current human resources policies;
   f. Personnel within the division.

3. Coordinates/assists:
   a. In the selection of qualified certificated and classified candidates;
   b. In the review of requests for transfer or promotions of personnel;
   c. As an administrative representative in the Meet and Confer process;
   d. In the counseling of all personnel on matters relating to difficult or sensitive matters;
   e. In research pertaining to human resources management:
      1) Salary and benefits research,
      2) Studies of staff characteristics,
      3) Professional standards,
      4) Other pertinent projects.
   f. In the budgeting process for personnel and employee benefits programs;
   g. As a member of the District Executive Council.
4. Develops/maintains:
   a. A system for personnel records for current and former employees;
   b. An up-to-date application file of prospective candidates for all positions;
   c. Salary schedules for Administrative-Supervisory personnel, Certificated personnel, and Classified personnel;
   d. Position descriptions for all existing and all new staff positions;
   e. Human resources and procedures;
   f. Human resources for employees.
5. Demonstrates:
   a. Knowledge of current administrative procedures and practices;
   b. Ability to provide adequate and timely reports;
   c. The skills to carry through on identified needs;
   d. Written and verbal communication skills with students, staff, and community;
   e. The skills for effective interpersonal relations;
   f. Knowledge and commitment to district policies and procedures.
6. Other assignments:
   a. Special responsibilities (list);
   b. Developmental responsibilities (list).

Qualifications
1. Experience in school administration;
2. Experience in teaching;
3. Knowledge of personnel management and administration;
4. Knowledge of salary and benefit trends in education and industry;
5. Knowledge of theory and practice in discussing salaries and working conditions with various categories of employees;
6. Knowledge of problems of the classroom teacher;
7. Knowledge of office management;
8. Knowledge of school law.

Supervision Received
From the Superintendent.

Supervision Given
The employees assigned to the Human Resources Department.

The many duties and responsibilities assumed by the human resources administrator demonstrate the importance of the training and preparation required for an effective human resources administrator, the need for a better research base for the human resources function, and the need for professional guidelines that direct and support human resources administrators as they carry out their professional responsibilities. The following section focuses on the ethics for school administrators and on the ethical standards for human resources developed at the national level.

ETHICS FOR SCHOOL HUMAN RESOURCES ADMINISTRATORS

The American Association of School Personnel Administrators (AASPA) has been instrumental in advancing human resources administration research and practice. The AASPA has promulgated a statement of ethics to guide school personnel administrators. These guidelines are set forth in Figure 1.6.

Another significant contribution of AASPA has been the development of standards for the ethical administration of the human resources function. The listing of selected standards in Figure 1.7 defines and further clarifies the purposes, processes, responsibilities, and significance of the human resources function. These standards provide both a foundation and a direction for setting policy and guiding the work of human resources administration. As implied by of the AASPA standards, effective human resources administration is based on a strong commitment by the school board and the administrative staff to a planned and comprehensive program of developing human talent within the organization to achieve the goals cooperatively determined for the school district.

Figure 1.6 Statement of Ethics for School Human Resources Administrators

The human resources administrator:

1. Makes the well-being of students the fundamental value of all decision making and actions.
2. Fulfills professional responsibilities with honesty and integrity.
3. Supports the principle of due process and protects the civil and human rights of all individuals.
4. Obeys local, state, and national laws and does not knowingly join or support organizations that advocate, directly or indirectly, the overthrow of the government.
5. Implements the governing board of education's policies and administrative rules and regulations.
6. Pursues appropriate measures to correct those laws, policies, and regulations that are not consistent with sound educational goals.
7. Avoids using positions for personal gain through political, social, religious, economic, or other influences.
8. Accepts academic degrees or professional certification only from duly accredited institutions.
9. Maintains the standards and seeks to improve the effectiveness of the profession through research and continuing professional development.
10. Honors all contracts with fulfillment or release.

Source: From *Statement of Ethics for School Personnel Administrators* (p. 1) by the American Association of School Personnel Administrators, 1988, Virginia Beach, VA: Author. Copyright © 1988 by the AASPA. Reprinted by permission.

Figure 1.7 Standards for Ethical Administration

1. The basic function of the board of education is policy-making and review of the total educational program of the school district.
2. The superintendent of the school district provides the professional leadership necessary for the continuous development of the personnel program to meet the objectives of the school district.
3. The personnel administrator has a clear understanding of the goals, objectives, and processes of the school system and the role which the personnel administration function has in accomplishing those ends.
4. Written personnel policies furnish guidelines for administrative procedures relating to personnel matters.
5. The personnel department is that specific section of the administrative structure established to carry out the personnel activities of the school system.
6. Personnel operations are conducted in a manner that provides for effective and friendly employee relationships and contributes to individual motivation and morale.

7. A well-developed system of personnel accounting and research helps predict staff needs and enables the administration to make sound projections for current and future employment needs.

8. The application form requests information necessary to facilitate screening; contributes to sound decision making on recommendations for appointment; and is in conformity with local, state, and federal laws and regulations.

9. Decisions involving staff selection are based upon a carefully planned program of investigation, screening, appointment, and follow-up support.

10. Placement, assignment, and transfer of personnel is a basic administrative responsibility through which attempts are made to meet the needs of the educational program, implement affirmative action plans, provide balanced staffing, and meet the desires of individual employees.

11. Orientation of teachers is a continuing process based upon a planned program designed to acquaint the teacher with his/her responsibilities toward the student, school, and community, and to acquaint the teacher with the resources in the school system and the community.

12. Appraisal of teaching performance is a cooperative process designed primarily to improve the quality of teaching.

13. The personnel evaluation and supervision system, while directed toward helping employees improve the quality of their performance, provides information which enables evaluators to make objective and fair decisions concerning termination, retention, or discipline when the employee's performance or conduct is marginal or clearly unsatisfactory, and rewards excellent performance.

14. In the interests of promoting high morale and leadership effectiveness, the personnel department will use its influence to assure that individuals on the professional staff are recognized for excellence and promoted on the basis of competency, performance, qualifications, fitness for the job, and probability of future growth and development regardless of age, sex, religion, and natural origin, ethnic heritage, marital status, or handicap.

15. Collective bargaining, as a personnel function, will conclude in an equitable agreement which preserves the board's responsibility to make policy and the administrator's right to manage the school district for the citizens and children and at the same time provide adequate wages, hours, and working conditions for its employees.

16. Compensation plans that place the school board in a favorable, competitive position and salary policies that encourage professional growth and personal improvement in service are essential elements of personnel administration.

17. Job descriptions and classifications include the duties to be performed, the immediate supervisor, educational preparation required, and personal qualifications needed for the position.

18. Regulations governing resignations should provide an orderly termination of service with a minimum of disruption to the school system and inconvenience to the employees.

19. The school district has written and publicized policies for the reduction of staff when needed.

Source: From *Standards for School Personnel Administration* (pp. 5–6) by the American Association of School Personnel Administrators, 1988, Virginia Beach. VA: Author. Copyright © 1988 by the AASPA. Reprinted by permission.

SUMMARY

This chapter discussed the human resources function by examining the major processes that it encompasses, by viewing the organization and relationships of the central human resources unit, by considering the decentralization of the human resources responsibilities, by presenting the concept of competent performance by human resources administrators, and by presenting the ethics and standards to guide the professional practices of human resources administration.

The human resources function is composed of several major processes, each of which is comprehensive and complex. The successful school administrator is aware that an effective educational program depends greatly upon maintaining a high quality of human resources. In this context, human resources administration becomes the most important function of all educational functions. Accomplishment of system goals is inextricably related to the accomplishment of the goals and objectives of the human resources function.

Discussion Questions

1. Examine the definitions and purposes of recruitment, selection, induction, and assignment discussed in the chapter. Illustrate specific ways in which each process is related to another. For example, how does the induction process relate to the assignment process?
2. List several specific problems encountered by teachers today. Discuss the implications of these common problems for the work of the human resources administrator at the district level and for building level administrators.
3. (a) Examine closely the position description and the selected competencies of the central unit human resources administrator. Discuss the type of preparation and experience necessary for effectiveness in such a position, as implied by the requirements of the role. What specific course work and field experiences appear essential?
   (b) Then consider the school principal's role in the human resources function. What specific competencies are necessary for effectiveness in the principal's role?
4. Consider the human resources processes of selection and stability. List several ways in which each of these processes impacts teaching and learning.

CASE STUDIES

—CASE 1.1

Position Descriptions: Fact or Fiction?

Steven Alexander had served as director of human resources in the Union School District for 1 year. The position description for director had been written 4 years ago and listed a comprehensive set of duties and responsibilities. As was the case with other central office administrative roles, however, Steven was involved in several program activities not included in the position description. Some of the responsibilities listed in Steven's position description, and in those of other administrators, actually were being carried out by persons in other units and

employees often were given responsibilities outside those stated in their specific position descriptions.

In Steven's case, the position description stipulated that he was responsible for coordinating the teacher performance evaluation program for the district, yet he admitted that he spent less than 5% of his time on this activity. The instructional unit in the district and local building principals were the ones who performed the evaluation activities. Steven's part was to keep a file of evaluation reports.

Even though the school board policies did call for a position description for every position, and such descriptions did exist, there was a general feeling at the administrative cabinet level that position descriptions were somewhat restraining. As was stated by the superintendent on one occasion, "One way to inhibit individual creativity and incentive is to freeze them in a written position description."

Questions

1. What are the pros and cons of having position descriptions but not using them as intended?
2. Identify two or three specific problems that could develop from practices described in this case.
3. As the human resources director, what actions, if any, might Steven Alexander take in this situation?

—CASE 1.2—

Qualifications: I'd Like to Be Considered

The Columbus School District has 15,220 students and 502 teachers. Personnel responsibilities are divided between the school superintendent, who handles the secondary school personnel, and the assistant superintendent, who is responsible for personnel at the elementary school level. Columbus's student growth has been phenomenal during the last 5 years: student enrollment has increased from 10,400 to the current figure of 15,220. Forecasts are that this suburban area will continue to grow at about the same rate for at least the next 10 years.

The central administrative officials and the school board are convinced that the magnitude of the responsibilities of the human resources function are such that some new organizational arrangement for administering the function is necessary. Both the school superintendent and assistant superintendent agree that the responsibility for personnel needs to be placed elsewhere, especially in view of their increasing workloads over the last few years.

Tyler Scott, a retiring school board member, has expressed an interest in the position of personnel director for the system should it be created. He will leave the board position in June and could assume the role on a full-time basis. Scott has a BS degree in business management and ran a small business for more than 20 years. Although he has never served as an educator, he has served on the school board for 12 years and was board president for 3 years. All of Scott's children are graduates of the Columbus School District.

"I've done most every job a small business requires," stated Scott. "I've kept books, hired sales personnel, trained employees on the job, and have evaluated personal performance. If the board does decide to advertise the position, I'd hope to be a candidate."

Questions

1. Assume that you are Columbus's school superintendent. What recommendations/actions would you make regarding allocation of human resources responsibilities?
2. Consider the matter of qualifications for the central office human resources director. What minimal qualifications do you believe are needed in the position? What specific preparation is important in your opinion? How does Mr. Scott rate in regard to these qualifications?
3. What are the pros and cons associated with Mr. Scott's candidacy?

REFERENCES

AASA (American Association of School Administrators), (1952). *The American school superintendency* (13th yearbook). Washington, DC: Author. American Association of School Personnel Administrators. (1988). *Standards for school personnel administration*. Virginia Beach, VA: Author.

College Board, Center for Innovative Thought. (2006). *Teachers and the uncertain American future*. Princeton, NJ: The College Board.

Fenner, M. S. (1945). *NEA history*. Washington, DC: National Education Association.

Lucio, W. H., & McNeil, O. (1969). *Supervision* (2nd ed.), New York: McGraw-Hill.

McCoy, M. W., Gips, C. J., & Evans, M. W. (1983). *The American school personnel administrator: An analysis of characteristics and role*. Seven Hills, OH: American Association of School Personnel Administrators.

McLaglan, P. (1996, January). Competency models. *Training and Development*, 50(1), pp. 60–64.

Mattern, H. (1996, September 13). Teachers get failing grades. *The Arizona Republic*, p. A1.

Moore, H. E. (1966). *The administration of public school personnel*. New York: Library of Education, Center for Applied Research in Education.

Newson, N. W. (1932). *The legal status of county superintendents* (Bulletin No. 7). Washington, DC: U.S. Department of the Interior, Office of Education.

Norton, M. S. (1999). *The school personnel administrator in Arizona*. Tempe: Arizona.

Pai, Y., & Adler, S. A. (2001). *Cultural foundations of education* (6th ed.). Upper Saddle River, NJ: Prentice Hall.

Society for Human Resources Management. Human resources management. *SHRM Online*. Retrieved October 12, 2006 from: www.shrm.org/hrresources/hrglossary_published/htap .

PART II

Shaping the Environment of Human Resource Administration

CHAPTER 2

Strategic Human Resources Planning

The information in this chapter will enable you to:

- Define strategic human resources planning and discuss its importance to the human resource process.
- Enumerate the six characteristics of strategic human resources planning.
- Discuss the major elements of a strategic planning model.
- Distinguish between external and internal scanning as they relate to strategic planning and the human resources function.
- Define strategic and operational planning and project their use in the human resources administration strategic planning process.
- Explain the importance of a mission statement to the strategic planning process.
- Describe the relationship of the human resources operational plan to the school district strategic plan and how they may best be correlated.
- Explain the major approaches to forecasting student enrollment and personnel needs.

This chapter discusses strategic planning from the perspective of human resources administration. The chapter begins with a discussion of the primary purposes of human resources planning and its importance to the effectiveness of the human resources function. This is followed by a definition of strategic human resources planning and a discussion of the six characteristics of human resources planning. The remainder and majority of the chapter is devoted to a description of a strategic planning model that highlights the integration of human resources planning into the overall strategic plan of a school system.

STRATEGIC HUMAN RESOURCES PLANNING

The aim of planning is to focus the energies and resources of the school system on the right results. When the school system uses proper planning procedures, it encourages accountability on the part of personnel. "Human resource planning (HRP) is the process an organization uses to ensure that it has the right amount and the right kinds of people to deliver a particular level of output or services in the future" (Gómez-Mejia, Balkin, & Cardy, 2001, p. 159). The primary purpose of human resources planning is the same as any other type of organizational planning—to help decide in advance what is to be done and to clarify the school system's expectations of what it envisions the total system and its parts *to be* and *to do*. In this sense, planning is the school system's way of projecting its purposes.

Human resources planning is essential because it can offset uncertainty, can focus the attention of the school system on important objectives, and can serve as a foundation for effective operation of the school system program. **Planning** helps the school district to anticipate and more effectively respond to changes or problems that do occur. Planning also provides (1) a basis for agreement as to the ultimate goals and purposes of the school system, (2) a clear definition of options and alternatives available for decision making, (3) an identification of system strengths upon which an improved program can be built, and (4) a systematized procedure for setting objectives. Planning is the central foci of the human resources function since all of its related processes depend on it.

Strategic planning is a dynamic process for helping a school system shape its future. It is a "rational approach to planned change" (Marion, 2002, p. 263). And through techniques of strategic management, school systems can effectively adjust to the unpredictable demands brought on by environmental changes. Strategic human resources planning serves to tie the specific objectives of the human relations function to the overall purposes and objectives of the school system; it focuses on how the human resources objectives are to be achieved. Strategic human resources planning is concerned with the effective utilization of human resources and their contributions toward the accomplishment of educational goals. Like any good plans, strategic human resources plans are based on assumptions about the future, and *forecasting* is the activity used to develop these basic assumptions (Dessler, 2000). Forecasting serves to anticipate the organization's future, including its internal and external environments.

Strategic human resources planning is not necessarily the making of future decisions; it also focuses upon current decisions and their future implications. Strategic human resources planning produces current decisions about what should be done now to realize desired outcomes in the future. Accordingly, the purpose of **strategic human resources planning** is to ensure the most effective use of personnel resources to move an organization toward its mission and achieve its strategic objectives.

Strategic human resources planning is based on information that justifies conclusions about existing trends, which in turn form a rationale for predicting future events. "Strategic planning, properly done . . . can be the means of moving to the future and determining what that future will provide for children and youth" (Norton, Webb, Dlugosh, & Sybouts, 1996, p. 133).

CHARACTERISTICS OF STRATEGIC HUMAN RESOURCES PLANNING

The professional literature provides numerous definitions and descriptions of strategic human resources planning. First, the strategic human resources planning process should be *comprehensive*. It must include the many subunits of the organization, for example, schools, departments, and divisions. All planning is done so that changes in one unit can be anticipated from planned or observed changes elsewhere in the organization.

Second, strategic human resources planning is a process that is *integrative*. All parts should interrelate to form a whole. It is not simply a collection of plans from the several subunits of the organization, but rather a single plan reflecting personnel recruitment, selection, allocation, compensation, and development for all units.

Third, the strategic human resources planning process is *continuous* and usually conforms to the organization's planning cycle. Data are continuously updated so that decisions can be made with the highest degree of currency and accuracy.

Fourth, a *multiyear planning format* is essential to the continuous process of planning and should reflect activities and developments over a period of 1–5 years. This plan usually becomes less specific as it projects into the latter part of the 5-year cycle. On an annual basis, the plan is updated for each successive year of the planning cycle, and a new year is added annually to maintain the 5-year planning perspective.

Fifth, the many constituencies affected by the plan should have input in the formulation process. Thus the plan must be *participatory* to gain individual commitment to implementation. Involvement in the planning process is a good investment that yields important dividends in commitment.

Last, *flexibility* is integral to the planning process. The plan should provide for modification and change as required by changes in the school system's internal and external environments and the specific needs of its constituencies. This flexibility should also be evidenced in the plan's sensitivity to the evolutionary stage of the school system and changes required in the professional staff mix. For example, a school system on the fringe of a major metropolitan area that is struggling with continuous enrollment increases will be at a different evolutionary stage than a well-established central city district that is trying to retain a quality program in an environment of declining enrollments. The growing system may need leadership that is flexible, innovative, and committed to program development; whereas the city system with a declining enrollment may desire educational leaders who can work with communities in the closing of schools and still maintain high-quality programs. Thus a strategic consideration is to match personnel with the requirements dictated by the evolutionary stage of the organization. This in turn may require that, following established procedures, personnel with specific skills, abilities, and expertise be moved among units of the organization to achieve the organization's strategic objectives.

Developing this professional staff mix involves balancing the best human resources talents with program needs to achieve the strategic objectives of the school system. Similar to the example just discussed, several attendance areas of a school system may be growing rapidly, whereas several others are struggling with enrollment declines. An analysis of the professional staff mix would take into consideration the strategic objectives of both the school system and the individual schools involved to determine the optimum mix of professional staff. This analysis may suggest changes in staffing to help achieve strategic objectives.

Special considerations are frequently given in obtaining the professional staff mix. One special consideration relates to those school districts that are under a court order to provide a particular racial blend of professional staff members in all schools. In other districts obtaining an optimal professional staff mix may require the balancing of professional experiences of faculty members among the schools of the district. Apart from court orders, it is often worthwhile educationally to balance staff on the basis of age, ethnicity, gender, and teaching load.

While it may appear desirable from a strategic planning perspective to improve the professional staff mix by taking certain actions, school board policies, contract agreements, past practices, and traditions can make it difficult to achieve the optimum professional staff mix. And, while policies on transfer and assignment can, often with great difficulty, be modified, traditions and past practices will be more difficult, if not nearly impossible, to change. Thus the human resources administrator must exhibit careful planning, expert leadership, and sensitivity to realize such changes.

INTEGRATING HUMAN RESOURCES PLANNING INTO THE SCHOOL DISTRICT STRATEGIC PLAN

The professional literature is replete with models for applying techniques of strategic planning to education. The model presented in Figure 2.1 was formulated to represent a synthesis of key elements of the strategic planning process rather than an elaboration of the many models found in practice. Figure 2.1 graphically represents the relationship among the various elements of a general strategic planning model for a school system with emphasis on integrated strategic human resources planning (operational planning). The major elements of the model include: 1.0 Environmental Scanning with its subelements 1.1 External Scanning and 1.2 Internal Scanning, and 2.0 Strategic and Operational Planning with subelements 2.1 Strategic Plan and 2.2 Operational Plans. Elements 2.1 and 2.2 in turn contain several subelements. The last major element of the model is 3.0 Implementation.

Strategic human resources planning must be done within a context, and it is this context that forms a basis for establishing a school system's mission and developing its strategic and operational plans. The context is gained from **environmental scanning.** Moreover, it is the interpretation of the environmental scan that will influence a school system's mission and all aspects of the planning process. Information gained from environmental scanning must be analyzed carefully to support the development of a comprehensive plan for administering human resources strategically (Kydd & Oppenheim, 1990). Specifically, the planning process entails the development of human resources operational plans that are consistent with the overall strategic plan (Anthony & Norton, 1991). These operational plans are dynamic because they interact with those of other organizational units. In addition, operational plans

Figure 2.1 Strategic Planning Model

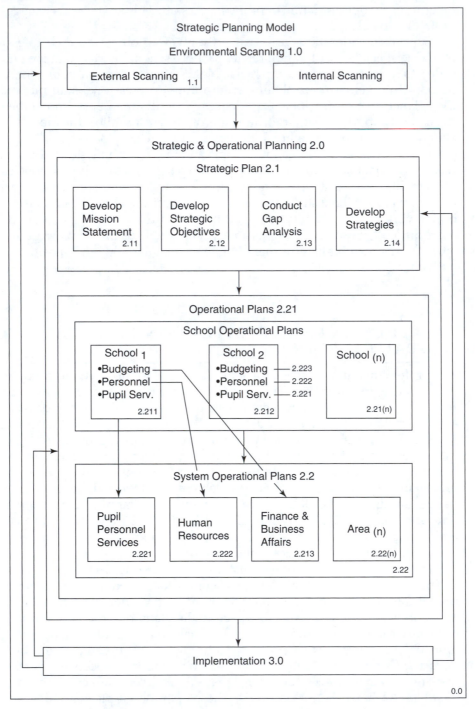

are monitored continuously and can be modified to reflect changing conditions in the school system's environment.

Environmental Scanning (1.0)

One approach to conducting an environmental scan is through an analysis of its Strengths, Weaknesses, Opportunities, and Threats (SWOT). The first phase of the analysis involves an analysis of internal Strengths and Weaknesses. In the next phase, Opportunities and Threats in the external environmental are examined. Based upon an interpretation of the environmental scan, assumptions can be developed to guide all planning efforts. A careful analysis of scanning information provides a school system with information that supports the development of a rationale for operating assumptions. These assumptions are used to assess the viability of the strategic plan. The assumptions relate to the external sociocultural, economic, technological, political-legal domains, and to selected factors of the internal scan, such as human and financial resources.

From a strategic perspective, a school organization must be attuned to its environment.

> Seen from a global viewpoint, the organization exists only as a part of a larger reality, supported and nurtured by the larger system on which it depends: the nation, its culture, and many interest groups, the world economy and political system, and the physical and biological planet itself. To the extent that an organization acts in ignorance of the connections that link it to other parts, and to the whole system of the global environment, it will tend to experience surprise and shock at unanticipated events originating in the larger system. It will experience such events as deficient in meaning, and hence as a threat to its sense of reality and its own identity. (Harrison, 1983, p. 217)

A description of a school system's educational environment includes many considerations that can be viewed simultaneously as constraints and opportunities. In each instance, strategic plans must be developed to minimize the negative effect of constraints and maximize the positive impact of opportunities.

Among the obvious environmental factors are state board policies and regulations, the state aid funding model for education and other state education statutes, relationships with teacher training institutions, services of intermediate service agencies, competition from surrounding school systems that draw from the same teacher pool, the school tax digest, and federal statutes and program regulations. Other environmental factors would relate to the demographic features of the constituencies that the school system serves, including, among others, racial and ethnic composition of the community, age distribution of residents, and their socioeconomic status.

The processes of external and internal environmental scanning are continuous and linked to the school district's planning cycle. Typically, the planning cycle is 5 years. Like the multiyear planning format, this plan is updated for each successive year of the planning cycle. A new year is added annually to maintain the 5-year strategic planning perspective. In each iteration of the planning cycle all elements of the strategic plan are updated to reflect changing conditions, new directions, and emerging basic beliefs about the educational processes. Environmental scanning is included as an integral part of the strategic planning model, and it impacts all elements of the planning process (see Figure 2.1).

External Scanning (1.1). External scanning is the monitoring, evaluating, and disseminating of information from the external environment to key people within the organization. It is a tool used to avoid strategic surprises and to ensure the long-term health of the school district. Typically, the external scan focuses on emerging trends that present opportunities for the school district and potential threats to its continued effectiveness. It also involves "anticipating the future effects of currently made decisions" (Stronge, Gareis, & Little, 2006). Central to the process of the external scan are four focal points of investigation: sociocultural, economic, technological, and political-legal. Milkovich and Boudreau (1991) identified two other important scanning areas: role of government and changing demographics (e.g., age distribution of population, number of immigrants, distribution of workforce by gender, and availability of workers). The scanning of these areas may be done by staff members of the school district or external organizations such as research groups or universities.

Internal Scanning (1.2). The internal scan is usually done by the staff of the district, but it can also be completed by outside groups or organizations. It addresses the questions of strengths that support strategies and weaknesses in the organization that constrain strategies. Specifically, this scan investigates the structure of the organization to determine the extent to which it facilitates the implementation of the strategies the organization has developed. A second area to scan is the organizational culture. An analysis of the culture determines whether organizational behaviors are consistent with planned strategies (Koys, Armacost, & Charalambides, 1990). "Management must constantly be aware of culture in strategic planning. If the culture is antagonistic to a strategic change, plans should include ways to change the culture as well" (Reichrath, 1990, p. 52). To be comprehensive, the internal scan must include an analysis of the financial, human, and facility resources of the district.

Every school system has a unique culture, and the individual schools of a school system often develop subcultures within the system's organization. Moreover, the system's culture is represented by the values, ideology, and goals shared by the members of the organization, including the patterns of behaviors for getting work done.

Ernest (1985) suggested an examination of certain organizational artifacts to gain insight into an organization's culture. This cannot be uncovered simply by an examination of organizational policies. It must also include the informal messages communicated by employee greetings, dress, language, ceremonies, gossip, and jokes. He also indicated that the best understanding of culture can be found in the practices of administrators. The beliefs, values, and philosophies of top administrators influence the practices of upper- and middle-level administrators, who in turn affect the behavior of subordinates (Harris & Harris, 1982). For example, how decisions are made is an indication of culture. Some school organizations value collegiality, working together in groups, and opportunities for participatory decision making. However, others might be characterized by a number of individuals working independently within some formalized decision-making process.

As is discussed in Chapter 3, the rituals of the organization can be a part of the culture and vary greatly from system to system. Some may provide public commendations for exemplary accomplishments or promotions. Others might arrange extraordinary programs of special recognition for retiring personnel (Carlson, 1991). School systems give greater or lesser emphasis to such events by publicizing their importance in both external and internal communications.

Another aspect of the culture is the control of information in the school system. Some control information very tightly; others are more open. Patterns of communication among members of the system also characterize a cultural value. Some exhibit a top-down pattern of communication; a top-down and bottom-up prevails in others. In a similar vein, some school systems tend to operate democratically, whereas others are more autocratic.

Many of these aspects of an organization's culture can be classified into a four-cell matrix representing the two dimensions of people and action, such as that depicted in Figure 2.2. School systems that respond to the external environment are classified as reactive, whereas those that attempt to affect it are proactive. Similarly, systems that encourage interaction and communication are regarded as high in participation. The interactive culture provides good services and focuses on employee and community needs. The integrated culture has a strong people orientation, and the system commits its energies and resources to innovative and creative activities. A systematized culture tends to be rule bound, with low participation of employees and other constituencies. Finally, the entrepreneurial culture tends to be change oriented, with little participation by employees.

Although influenced by the system's overall culture, an individual school often develops its own subculture. Different elements of the system's culture can exist in a similar form at the individual school level. For example, if a school system places great value on the accomplishments of staff members, an individual school may give great recognition to the achievements of students. This system value is transmitted to its organizational members and is evidenced through the emphasis placed on recognizing student accomplishments.

Figure 2.2 The Four Main Corporate Culture Types

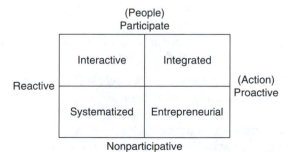

Source: "Corporate Cultures and Effective Planning" by Robert C. Ernest, March 1985, *Personnel Administrator, 30,* p. 52. Reprinted by permission of Sage Publications.

Strategic and Operational Planning (2.0)

Strategic and operational planning are key components of the strategic planning process. The strategic plan is consistent with the assumptions derived from an analysis of the environment, and it forms the bases for relating all operational plans.

Strategic Plan (2.1). A strategic plan is a "long-term plan outlining actions needed to achieve planned results" (Kreitner & Kinicki, 1998, p. 621). The four elements of the strategic plan, as illustrated in Figure 2.1, are 2.11 Develop Mission, 2.12 Develop Strategic Objectives, 2.13 Conduct Gap Analysis, and 2.14 Develop Strategies. The actual strategic plan is published in a relatively brief document (usually 25 pages or less) that gives direction to all operational planning activities. Each operational plan relates to the strategic objectives and strategies in the strategic plan.

Develop Mission Statement (2.11). A critically important factor in the development of a school system's strategic plan is its educational mission statement. A mission statement is the collective response to the question "Why do we exist?" (Stronge, et al., 2006). The mission statement is an expression of the organization's beliefs and vision and becomes the focus for all of the remaining phases of the strategic planning process (Glickman, Gordon, & Ross-Gordon, 2007). A written mission statement helps the system define its vision for the future; it provides a clear focus for the system's personnel; and it identifies a rallying point for committing the human and material resources of the district. Establishing a mission and implementing it through planned strategies permits a school system to shape the organization that it wants to become. It provides a perspective for the future of the system and a vision for the continued existence of the system.

Deciding what function the school system serves within its environment is the first step in deriving a mission. This function focuses upon the current and emerging educational needs of the community. With a vision in mind, the identification of the segment of the population served becomes an essential ingredient of the mission statement. No school system can be everything to everyone. Market segmentation requires a review of the actual population the school system serves as well as whom it might potentially serve. In addition to geographical boundaries, the school system must know the ages of the people it serves; it must know the racial and ethnic makeup of the community; it should have a good sense of the community's financial resources; and it should fully understand the values of the people.

The mission statement is carefully studied by the school system in relation to the realities of the external environment. A careful examination of the mission statement should be conducted to determine if it satisfies the following 10 criteria set forth by Pfeiffer, Goodstein, and Nolan (1986):

1. The mission statement is clear and understandable to all personnel, including rank-and-file employees.
2. The mission statement is brief enough for most people to keep in mind.
3. The mission statement clearly specifies what business the organization is in. This includes a clear statement about
   a. "What" customer or client needs the organization is attempting to fill, not what products or services are offered;

     b. "Who" the organization's primary customers or clients are; and

     c. "How" the organization plans to go about its business, that is, what its primary technologies are.

4. The mission statement should have a primary focus on a single strategic thrust.

5. The mission statement should reflect the distinctive competence of the organization.

6. The mission statement should be broad enough to allow flexibility in implementation but not so broad as to permit a lack of focus.

7. The mission statement should serve as a template and be the means by which managers and others in the organization can make decisions.

8. The mission statement must reflect the values, beliefs, and philosophy of operations of the organization and reflect the organization's culture.

9. The mission statement should reflect attainable goals.

10. The mission statement should be worded so as to serve as an energy source and rallying point for the organization. (p. 82)

The mission statement, once developed, should not become simply a statement to be placed in school district manuals and handbooks or on the district website. It should be shared with all internal and external constituencies and "used as a fundamental consideration for all initiatives of the school district, with attention to how each unit within the organization is striving toward the mission with its goals, plans, and activities" (Stronge, et al. 2006, p. 24).

Over a period of time, all school systems experience changing environmental factors. These environmental shifts can create a need to redefine the general mission of the school system. Usually the mission statement should be reviewed every 5 years to ensure that it meets the needs of the communities it serves. If the leaders of the school system misinterpret or ignore the changing environment and do not refocus the system's mission, obvious conflicts will invariably arise between the system and its constituencies.

Develop Strategic Objectives (2.12). Once articulated the mission statement provides the basis for developing strategic objectives. Objectives are directly related to and flow from the district's mission. Objectives focus on outcomes, not processes, and are client centered and action oriented. Moreover, the strategic objectives should be measurable and related to those indicators against which the school system's constituencies evaluate its success (e.g., improved test scores, low dropout rate, scholarships and awards, employment after graduation, college entrance, etc.). Objectives should be realistic and attainable. Because objectives are accomplished through the various programs and services offered by the district, they should provide enough information to identify and develop such programs and services (Garner, 2004).

Conduct Gap Analysis (2.13). The gap analysis applies reality to the strategic planning process. It involves a review of each strategic objective by comparing the desired outcomes to current outcomes in light of internal scanning information. In other words, the analysis reveals the gap between the outcomes desired and current outcomes in relation to available human and material resources, technologies, and instructional processes. One question frequently raised is whether the objectives provide sufficient challenge to stretch the creative thinking of the organization's members during the development of strategies. A response to this question may suggest that the outcomes sought by the strategic objectives be increased to press for greater challenges or, perhaps, lowered to reflect certain realities.

Develop Strategies (2.14). Strategies are statements about how the proposed strategic objectives will be achieved. If the objective of increasing the reading scores of middle-grade students by a specified amount in a given period of time is established, one strategy might be to evaluate the middle-grade reading curriculum; another may stipulate the creation of an intensive staff development program in reading for middle-grade teachers; and a third strategy might be to create a new screening and selection program for processing applicants to teach in the middle grades to favor those with strength and experience in reading. Strategy selection is dependent upon the expertise of the system's strategic planners, the creativity and competencies of its staff, and their interpretations of both external and internal data from environmental scans.

Strategies are the administrator's most important tools for coping with change, and they provide important bases for mitigating extraneous demands on the school system. Therefore, school administrators must learn to manage strategically; that is, their day-to-day decisions must relate consistently to the strategies adopted for the system's strategic objectives, and their decisions should move the organization in the direction of its mission.

Human resources is an obvious and necessary consideration in the development of strategic objectives and/or strategies. The human resources operational plan is just as important as a curriculum or a financial plan and should be developed in ways that are consistent with objectives of the system's strategic plan. Additionally, system strategic objectives and strategies provide specific direction for the development of individual school operational plans, which also reflect the need for human resource considerations.

Operational Plans (2.2). Operational plans are developed for all functional areas of the school system. These include central office departments or units as well as individual schools. To develop operational plans for the several subunits of the school system (e.g., departments, program divisions, and schools), each subunit engages in crafting plans to achieve the integrating function of the overall strategic plan.

Operational plans are specific to one or more of the established strategic objectives and strategies. The aggregate impact of all operational plans particular to the same strategic objective will contribute to achieving that objective. This concentration of effort is the appeal of strategic planning. It brings important systemwide priorities into focus through operational plans that impact in different ways the achievement of mutually agreed upon objectives. For example, if some area of student achievement is a priority, then the human resources department can develop an operational plan to direct its staffing practices for improving the personnel mix serving this area of the curriculum; the staff development unit could frame operational plans to improve instructional strategies or the knowledge base of teachers in the area; the curriculum unit might map this area of the curriculum to find possible incongruencies; the administration may establish an operational plan to increase public awareness; and the finance unit may work with another unit of the school system to seek external funding to bring additional resources to bear on the problem. Each of these approaches can take the form of operational plans for individual functional units of the system or represent plans of cross-functional areas. This is one of many examples of how many parts of the organization develop operational plans that target a single strategic objective, but use several strategies.

Included in the operational plans are goals to give direction to the overall effort, objectives to establish targets or outcomes sought by the plan, procedures for implementation, policy considerations, time schedules, implementation constraints, and monitoring procedures for control and evaluation. In the end all plans must be reviewed so that a coordinated effort can be used to minimize program overlap.

School Operational Plans (2.21). The school is the primary unit for delivering services in a school system. Each school will have its own operational plan which reflects strategic objectives that are consistent with the system strategic objectives of the school system. At the same time, the individual school plan will focus upon the unique needs of its students and will be in harmony with its immediate environment.

Since operational plans vary from school to school, individuals with different skills and abilities will be required to achieve the individual school's strategic objectives. For example, suppose a primary component of a system's mission is basic skills, and the system has the strategic objective of raising reading scores on a standardized achievement test to the national mean in 5 years. One elementary school might identify reading as a strategic priority. Another elementary school that has maintained a mean achievement score in reading that is well above the national norm may focus its energy and resources on another strategic priority. Accordingly, each school may require a different professional staff mix. Such considerations have important implications for staff development, recruitment, and selection and should be reflected in the strategic human resources plan. In practice, despite its importance to strategic planning, a purely empirical approach to balancing the professional staff mix has not been widely utilized. Personnel policies related to teacher assignments, transfers, and reductions in force have placed limits on the movement of personnel. In the future, strong school board policies that reflect the importance of professional staff mix to strategic planning may help to promote actions to achieve a more balanced mix in the future.

The situation of each of the two elementary schools can serve as another example for understanding a school's operational plan. Certainly, the strategic objective of increasing scores on basic skills tests has implications for site-based budgeting, possible curricular or organizational changes, and of course personnel. Figure 2.1 shows how these considerations become inputs into the operational plans of the system's functional areas.

System Operational Plans (2.22). Each functional area at the system level must have an operational plan for integrating all of the school unit strategies.

If shifts in staff are required to optimize the professional staff mix, the personnel function would incorporate in its operational plan changes that accommodate all school units at an optimal level. Similar changes in the areas of curriculum or budgeting could affect any number of functional areas. Consequently, the specific strategies of each of these functional areas may have implications for an integrated human resources strategy.

Human Resources Operational Plan (2.23). The human resources operational plan reflects an integration of the various school unit plans and the system functional plans. The model does not represent a linear flow of information; on the contrary, there is neither a beginning nor an end. It is a continuous process of integration that supports the school system's strategic plan. Each unit and functional area of the system provides input to the human resources operational plan and has a role in its formulation and subsequent implementation.

The human resources operational plan should accomplish three objectives:

1. It should correlate with the strategic plan of the system and support the implementation of system strategies;
2. It should provide for the collection and analysis of the data needed to develop a master plan for recruiting, selecting, developing, and compensating human resources, including the forecasting of personnel needs; and
3. It should enumerate required changes in personnel, school board personnel policies, and administrative regulations and processes so that the system's strategic objectives can be achieved.

Correlation with and Support of the Strategic Plan of the System. The first task for the human resources administrator in ensuring that the human resources operational plan is correlated with the system strategic plan is to determine how the school system educational strategies are determined. Although all organizations engage in some form of strategic planning, they do so with differing degrees of formality and with varying levels of administrator involvement (Kelleher & Cobe, 2003). The human resources administrator may or may not have been involved in the development of some strategic decisions. Many decisions are based on formal planning procedures that are presented to the superintendent and board of education for approval. At the same time, many other strategic decisions result from a response to a crisis or an ad hoc effort of a temporary task force. Thus the human resources administrator must be aware of both the formal and informal decision-making processes.

A related task for the human resources administrator is to determine how much consideration is given to human resources in the system strategic planning process. Do strategic plans include factors of professional staffing, development, recruitment, and selection? Are appropriate data collected and correctly analyzed? Are these data used to forecast future human resources needs and supply of personnel? Are the results of such analyses used in decision making?

Different district strategies will dictate different levels of human resources involvement. A strategic plan to close several low-enrollment schools may dictate different human resources requirements than a plan for a bond election to renovate school facilities. While both would involve human resources consideration, the former involve more critical human resources considerations than the latter.

The final task for the human resources administrator correlating the human resources operational plan with the strategic plan of the school system is to work toward closing the gap between the amount of consideration that should be given human resources and that actually given to human resources in strategic educational planning. This gap can be closed by continuously giving attention to the credibility of the human resources function. The professional staff must be regarded as competent. They must be knowledgeable about education and educational issues as well as most other aspects of the educational processes in the school system, including curriculum design and development.

Data Collection, Analysis, and Forcasting. Collecting and analyzing valid and current human resources information relative to the school system's strategic objectives can provide a basis for ensuring that the human resources development efforts correlate with strategic educational plans. Human resources information must be collected from the different units of the organization, compared, and reported in a form that supports strategic decisions. Specific data about compensation, professional staff mix, and performance appraisals are important factors around which data must also be collected.

One very important data collection and analysis activity is the *forecasting of personnel needs*. A forecast serves to project future data and activities for purposes of program planning. Personnel forecasts are needed to provide a basis for the recruitment and hiring of personnel and to project future professional staff mixes. Personnel forecasts must include not only considerations of personnel needs associated with enrollment growth or decline but the attrition of personnel. Attrition results from personnel who move to new positions within the organization, leave the organization for positions elsewhere, or retire.

A forecast of changes in personnel provides human resources administrators with information that can be used to guide action to achieve the strategic objectives of the system. Such changes are often studied through the use of cohort analyses, census analyses, or Markovian analysis.

Table 2.1 provides a simplified illustration of the use of Markovian analysis involving six classifications of personnel in a school system. In this example, the hypothetical system has 1,460 professional employees including 300 primary teachers, 250 intermediate-level teachers, 230 upper-level teachers, 500 secondary teachers, 80 supervisors, and 100 administrators. These employee classifications and current employment levels are listed in columns a and b. Data in columns c through h are probability factors for each of the classifications. The factors are based on the mean percentage of personnel changes for the past 5 years, and it is assumed that these transition probabilities remain stable over time. Column c shows a probability of .60 (60%) for primary teachers to remain on the job the next year. This is derived by subtracting from 1.0 the probability of primary teachers moving to an intermediate-level teaching position (.15), the probability of primary teachers moving to an upper-level teaching responsibility (.05), and the probability of primary teachers

Table 2.1 Markovian Analysis of Personnel Attrition

Classification a	Current Employment Level b	Primary c	Intermediate d	Upper e	Secondary f	Supervisors g	Administrators h	Projection i
Primary	300	0.60	0.10					205
Intermediate	250	0.15	0.70	0.10				243
Upper	230	0.05	0.10	0.70	0.05	0.01		227
Secondary	500			0.06	0.75			389
Supervisors	80	0.01			0.01	0.90		80
Administrators	100			0.01	0.01	0.05	0.85	96
Exit		0.19	0.10	0.13	0.18	0.04	0.15	220

becoming supervisors (.01), and the probability of primary teachers leaving the system (.19) [1.0 − (.15 + .05 + .01 + .19) = .60]. In a similar manner, the intermediate-level teachers (column d) have a probability of .70 of remaining next year [1.00 − .10 (those moving to primary teaching) + .10 (those moving to upper-level teaching + and .10 (those leaving the district)].

The projected number of teachers remaining at employment level for the following year is presented in column i. The projected number for each classification is based upon the sum of the products of the probability factors and their corresponding employment level for the current year. For example, a projection of the number of primary teachers available the next year is [(.60 × 300) + (.10 × 250)] = 205. Similarly, a projection of upper-level teachers is (.05 × 300) + (.10 × 250) + (.70 × 230) + (.05 × 500) + (.01 × 80) = 227. Using this procedure for the other classifications, the projection for intermediate-level teachers is 243; secondary teachers, 389; supervisors, 80; and administrators, 96.

A Markovian analysis can easily be performed by the use of spreadsheets such as Excel. The use of a spreadsheet also allows the human resources planner to ask "what if" questions where different assumptions about personnel movement could be investigated.

The *projecting of student enrollments* is the companion to the forecasting of personnel needs. The number of students to be served is the primary determinant of the number and types of staff needed. Most student enrollment projections are made from extensive data sets incorporating 10 years or more of data that may include past school enrollments, current enrollments, parochial and private school enrollments, nonresident enrollments, children per dwelling unit, resident live births, socioeconomic indicators, shifts of population, mobility of families, in/out migration, housing starts, transfer rates, home resales, and student retention rates. Additional factors such as building patterns, types of dwellings, community patterns, transportation changes, integration, and national demographic trends are frequently used to temper the statistical treatment of the historical data for localizing projections.

The cohort survival method has become a popular forecasting technique for a number of years. The cohort survival method is based on certain assumptions, namely that certain statistics (e.g., birth rates, death rates, student migration, grade retention policy, student retention, and other population influx or outflux) will continue to be similar to what they have been in the recent past. Any major fluctuations in population growth do pose problems in the ability of the methodology to accurately predict enrollment data. For this reason projections of 1–3 years are more accurate than those for 5–10 years. In the end, the use of this or any forecasting methods necessitates the application of both the experience and judgment of professionals who can adjust retention ratios based upon their specific knowledge of the school community.

Table 2.2 illustrates the application of the cohort survival technique for forecasting kindergarten enrollments based on annual birth rates over a period of 6 years. In Table 2.2 the cohort retention ratio for each year is calculated by dividing the kindergarten enrollment by the number of births for any one year (e.g., in the year 2000, 3600 divided by 3503 = .9731). The figures for the years 2003 through 2007 represent the actual data for those years. To calculate the projected kindergarten enrollment for the year 2008, first find the average cohort retention ratio by adding the five previous retention ratios and divide by 5. Next, multiply the result, .9826, by the number of births 5 years earlier, 4000. The result, 3930 is the 2008 kindergarten projected enrollment.

Projection Programs. Developments in formulating complex computer algorithms for forecasting student enrollments have increased the reliability of such projections through the inclusion of many more factors than was previously possible. One such software package has been developed by Ecotran Systems. Ecotran's MAPNET system is a basic transportation package that has an enrollment projection module for forecasting population trends and future school district enrollments. The system uses advanced statistical methods and historical data to make projections by grade, school, and geographical area. The module incorporates cohort survival and advanced econometric modeling techniques and uses up to 10 years of historical data. The system has the capability of calculating future populations from birth to grade 12 as well as ethnicity of population. Also, the projection model generated can be displayed on the school district map for further analysis.

Table 2.2 Kindergarten Enrollment Projections

Year of Birth	No. of Births	Kindergarten Year	Enrollment	Cohort Retention Ratio
1998	3400	2003	3380	0.9941
1999	3450	2004	3401	0.9858
2000	3600	2005	3503	0.9731
2001	3701	2006	3650	0.9862
2002	3800	2007	3701	0.9739
2003	4000	2008	3930 (projected)	

Another system with similar capabilities is the ONPASS planning system developed by Educational Data Systems. ONPASS is an online, computer-aided, student demographic system capable of making 5-year projections for the number of students attending schools of the district, percentage utilization of schools, the number of students in each grade level, the number of students in each ethnic group, and the average walk/ride distance of students from each school and from each planning area. Additionally, the system can make projections for the planning area from which students attend school, the number and demographics of students from each planning area, and the number of classrooms that will be required at each school and grade level relative to an established minimum and maximum class size, including combination classes where necessary. All of these projections are based on aging of the student population, in/out migration, new housing construction, cohort survival statistics, and entry-level enrollment projections.

EDULOG, another enrollment projection model, developed by Education Logistics, projects enrollments by grade for the system, individual schools, planning zones, racial/ethnic categories, new attendance boundaries, user-defined student attributes, and other meaningful geographically defined planning areas. The system is based on a modified cohort survival technique that separately identifies the various factors determining enrollment patterns within a district. The model is capable of making enrollment forecasts out to 15 years.

Once projections of enrollment and available personnel have been made, projections of new staff needs can be completed. Projections for the elementary level with self-contained classrooms is relatively easy. For example, a school district with a projected K–6 enrollment of 2500 students, 100 teachers projected to return next year, and board established pupil/teacher ratio of 20:1 will need to hire 25 new teachers (2500 ÷ 20 = 125 teachers needed − 100 returning teachers = 25). Projections for staffing needs at the secondary level are more complex because of the array of courses and unknown student choices but are made easier with accurate data and modeling technology.

Changes in Policies, Regulations, and Processes. As discussed in greater detail in Chapter 11, school policies and regulations are inextricably related to the human resources function in organizations. As a result, the strategic plan of a school system will invariably require that some school board policies and administrative regulations be revised or new ones developed so that strategic objectives can be accomplished. The section of the strategic plan related to human resources should enumerate the need for these changes with specific recommendations.

For instance, to meet the requirements of No Child Left Behind, the human resources plan may include the objective to raise the minimum level of certification or formal preparation of instructional personnel. This objective is to be fully implemented within a specified period of time. An analysis of school board policies may suggest that there are inadequate policies and corresponding regulations for guiding the implementation of the objective. On review, the human resources operational plan would include recommended additions or changes to policies and administrative regulations. Other functional areas, such as finance, may also be affected by such changes and make corresponding changes.

School systems that are experiencing ongoing increases or decline in enrollment provide another example. In the first instance, an analysis of the policies and procedures related to the personnel recruitment program would be suggested. If, on the other hand, the school district's objective is to close a number of schools, then specific human resources objectives that relate to the reduction of professional personnel must be developed. In this regard, a human resources objective might be to establish a program to eliminate a specific number of positions within a time period consistent with the staggered closing of schools. Of course, the plan would require investigations of personnel turnover trends, age distribution of personnel, professional staff mix for the total system, and other relevant considerations, including personnel contract agreements and the legal issues related to teacher rights discussed in Chapter 11. If, for example, the analysis of all important data suggests offering early retirement incentives would be a successful strategy in reducing the teacher workforce, the plan would have to be approved by the board of education. Certain policy areas and regulations would also need to be examined to provide for the plan's implementation. In addition, the plan would require a consideration of system procedures and other personnel changes.

Implementation (3.0)

The results of implementing operational plans provide both product and process data that become feedback to other elements of the model. This feedback gives evidence to support a need for the refinement, modification, or reformulation of other aspects of the plan. In some instances objectives will be changed. On occasion the mission statement will be rewritten, or new strategies will be developed.

SUMMARY

Strategic human resources planning is a process of preparing a school system for activities in the future. The purpose of strategic human resources planning is to ensure that the human resources needed by the school system are available and employed efficiently and effectively in pursuit of identified system goals and objectives.

The effective planning of human resources requires a system for maintaining relevant systemwide data and information. This information is used to forecast trends on which to base decision making; provide for an optimal professional staff mix; and support other functions, such as recruitment, compensation, and affirmative action.

The implementation of strategic human resources planning must be based upon an analysis of the environment. It should be sensitive to the culture of the school system. In addition, the human resources objectives must be consistent with the system's mission and its strategic objectives.

The planning process should be comprehensive and include all subunits of the school system. The plans for each subunit should be integrated to form an overall plan for the total organization. The process is continuous and should conform to the planning cycle of the system, with a multiyear emphasis of 5 years. Finally, the process should be flexible and participatory to accommodate change and expert staff involvement.

Discussion Questions

1. Contact (or obtain from their website) two different school districts in your area and obtain their mission statement. Discuss how they are alike and how they are different. What implications does the mission statement of each have for the personnel requirements of each district?
2. In small groups, make a list of cultural elements that exist in your school or school system. Discuss the differences found on each list and how the several elements affect the behaviors of personnel.
3. One of the important objectives of a human resources operational plan is to provide for the collection and analysis of the data needed to develop the master plan. The master plan should address recruiting, selecting, developing and compensating personnel. Choose one of these functions and describe how you would go about collecting and analyzing the specific data needed to make a 5-year forecast for that functional area.

CASE STUDIES

──CASE 2.1──

Mixed Expectations

Frank Hennessy was filled with excitement as he hung up the telephone. Dr. Brad Richardson, the superintendent, had just asked him to chair the newly created planning committee for strategic planning. As the director of human resources for the Cherryhill School District, he felt that he would now be able to play an important part in shaping the future of the district.

As Frank reflected on the challenges facing the committee, he felt that strategic planning would help the district to become proactive by carefully considering its primary goal. In the past, Frank had argued to narrow the focus of the district. He felt there were so many demands being made on the limited resources of Cherryhill that every program ended up with only limited financial or personnel support.

Now, he hoped that strategic planning would help the school district to narrow its focus by deciding what was important and making a serious commitment to the goals of highest priority.

The community has high expectations for the school district and has been willing to support requests for funds to improve nearly all academic programs. Parents have been very pleased with the apparent rigorous demands made on students. The district has always had a very strong college preparatory program, with 78% of its graduates entering college and a considerable number entering some of the nation's most prestigious colleges.

Despite the fact that the district curriculum has always been geared to the college-bound students, a number of pressure groups have been successful in getting the board of education to enlarge the vocational program, a move that has placed a strain on the district's financial resources and, according to some citizens, is "taking money away from the more important challenge of preparing students for college." Another group of young parents has been working with the coaches to get more emphasis placed on athletics. Some board policies make it difficult for students to fully participate in inter-scholastic competition. Recently, two star foot-ball players were not allowed to participate due to poor grades in the college prep academic program.

The first meeting of the strategic planning committee was held at a country lodge, where Superintendent Richardson welcomed the committee. He also talked about the impor-tance of the committee's work and requested their commitment to the strategic planning process. Frank knew that the superintendent's strong statement showing a commitment to and belief in strategic planning nearly ensured a good kickoff meeting.

After the superintendent spoke, Frank led the group in a discussion of strategic planning by presenting an applied model for school dis-trict planning. This model was the one recom-mended by the State Department of Education in a workshop that Frank had attended last year. This was followed by several group exercises that involved members in a discus-sion of values related to educational issues. All the exercises were focused on consensus decision making and precipitated much more discussion and heated debate than Frank anticipated.

Later, Frank administered a strategic plan-ning readiness instrument and wrote the group's results on the chalkboard. At this point, Frank led a discussion of the results. He was surprised that the scores showed such a high degree of readiness for the team to plan strate-gically. This was the last activity of the day, and the meeting was adjourned.

During the morning session on the next day, Frank explained environmental scanning. He talked about the importance of knowing both the external and internal environments of the school district. This led to a lengthy discussion of many aspects of the district's environment.

Following lunch, Frank introduced the concept of a mission statement and its relation-ship to strategic planning. He emphasized the importance of addressing the questions of What? Who? and How? He asked the planning team members to each develop a written re-sponse to the What question. Frank told the committee to write their statements on the chalkboard, and they would discuss their re-sponses after the coffee break.

As Frank scanned the statements posted, he was surprised to find statements that were very diverse. This concerned him because he feared that a discussion of these statements would deteriorate into serious arguments. Thus he decided to ask the committee members to read only their responses, and he told them that he would make copies of these statements for the next meeting. Frank wanted to give some careful thought to how he might handle the obvious conflicts that would emerge.

Charles Winters read his statement first. He said, "Cherryhill is committed to providing programs that meet the needs of students by developing excellence in both physical and academic abilities through challenge and competition."

Jeannie Crawford followed with, "It is the purpose of Cherryhill to provide quality educa-tion with an emphasis on the basics."

Board member Fredericks followed by very forcefully stating, "Cherryhill School District is committed to providing quality educational programs that will support gainful employ-ment of its graduates."

The Teacher of the Year, Cecilia Cousins, followed with, "It is our purpose to provide a comprehensive educational program that will satisfy the social, psychological, physical, and educational needs of our children."

Sandy Christian read, "The Cherryhill School System is committed to helping students to develop a strong self-concept and a sense of self-esteem."

Principal Joe Tensley offered, "We are committed to providing programs of quality basic education in an environment that supports trust and mutual respect."

Nelson Thomas showed his strong interest in vocational education when he read his statement, "Cherryhill School District will provide a program to support the development of job-related skills that are augmented by skills in basic education."

Terri Moore then read her statement, "Our school system commits itself to providing quality programs that support the educational development and personal interests of all citizens of the community."

Finally, Dr. Richardson stated, "We at Cherryhill commit ourselves to providing the highest quality of education for our students that is focused on student interests and academics."

Frank then thanked the group and told them that he would have the statements reproduced for the next meeting in 6 weeks. At this point he was glad that no discussion followed because he didn't want to end the meeting in controversy. As he drove home, he wondered if any of the statements really reflected what the Cherryhill community wanted. For the next several days, he was preoccupied with thoughts of what to do next.

Questions

1. What problem(s) will Frank have to deal with at the next meeting?
2. What are some symptoms of the problem(s)?
3. What possible actions might Frank take to solve the problem(s)?
4. What consequences should Frank anticipate from implementing each of the actions?
5. What action should Frank not attempt? Give reasons why.

CASE 2.2

The State Mandate

Joan Ellis, a seasoned human resources administrator, attended several workshops on strategic human resources planning that the State Department of Education offered. She tried for several years to convince the superintendent to consider strategic planning in the district because she strongly valued the process and felt that it would greatly help her district. Also, she had reliable information from a friend at the State Department of Education suggesting that it was only a matter of time before the State Board of Education would mandate that all school districts develop annual strategic plans.

Joan knew that the superintendent did not value any type of serious planning. She frequently recalled one of the superintendent's rebuttals to her planning suggestions, "We tried that comprehensive planning once, and it was a waste of time. The governor even had a conference on it. Then we had to submit that huge report that was probably never read."

As expected, the State Board adopted a regulation that required all school districts in the state to plan strategically and submit their plans to the Department of Education for approval.

When the superintendent received notification of the requirement from the State Superintendent of Public Instruction, he asked the assistant superintendent for administrative services, the assistant superintendent for business affairs, and the director of finance to write the plan. Joan was not asked to be involved.

Questions

1. Did the superintendent make a good decision?
2. What problems can be anticipated from the superintendent's decision?
3. What are the possible actions that Joan might take?

4. What consequences can be anticipated from each action?
5. What should Joan do?

—CASE 2.3—

Sara's New Assignment

At the last meeting of the board of education, Sara Olivia was appointed as the new assistant superintendent for human resources. The board's approval was another vote of confidence for Dr. Tyler Woods, who was appointed superintendent only 1 year ago.

Superintendent Woods' decision to recommend Sara was based on her strong background in strategic planning and previous experiences as the director of personnel in a neighboring school system. Previously she directed the strategic planning effort of a large school system in another state.

During her first day on the job, Sara was arranging her personal belongings in a beautifully redecorated office when Dr. Woods stopped by to give her the old "Welcome aboard" greeting. After a few minutes of casual conversation, he said, "Oh, by the way, I need your help. The board is eager to support my suggestions on strategic planning for the district. They asked me to recommend a set of board policies that they can consider for getting this effort underway. This is going to be one of the most important things that this school system has ever done, and the community will be watching it closely. You'll have to be a key player in this effort. So, what I'd like you to do is set up whatever committees you need for developing the policies and get back to me as soon as possible."

Questions

1. What considerations should Sara give to forming the committee? Who should be involved?
2. What should be the committee agenda at the beginning of the committee's work?
3. What policy areas should be reviewed in preparation for making policy recommendations to the board?

REFERENCES

Anthony, P., & Norton, A. N. (1991). Link HR to corporate strategy. *Personnel Journal, 70,* 75–82.

Carlson, R. V. (1991). Culture and organizational planning. In R. V. Carlson & G. Awkerman (Eds.), *Educational planning: Concepts, strategies, and practices* (pp. 49–63). New York: Longman.

Dessler, G. (2000). *Human resources management* (8th ed.). Upper Saddle River, NJ: Prentice Hall.

Ernest, R. C. (1985). Corporate cultures and effective planning. *Personnel Administrator, 30*(3), 49–60.

Garner, C. W. (2004). *Education finance for school leaders: Strategic planning and administration.* Upper Saddle River, NJ: Prentice Hall.

Glickman, C. O., Gordon, S. P., & Ross-Gordon, J. M. (2007). *Supervision and instructional leadership: A developmental approach* (7th ed.). New York: Allyn & Bacon.

Gómez-Mejia, L. R., Balkin, D. B., & Cardy, R. L. (2001). *Managing human resources* (3rd ed.). Upper Saddle River, NJ: Prentice Hall.

Harris, P. R., & Harris, D. L. (1982). Human resources management. Part 1: Charting a new course in a new organization, a new society. *Personnel, 59*(5), 11–17.

Harrison, R. (1983). Strategies for a new age. *Human Resource Management, 22,* 217–223.

Kelleher, E. J., & Cobe, F. S. (2003). Strategic planning for human resources. In J. E. Edwards, J. C. Smith, and N. S. Raju (Eds.). *The human resources program evaluation handbook* (pp. 517–535). Thousand Oaks, CA: SAGE.

Koys, R. L., Armacost, R. L., & Charalambides, L. C. (1990). Organizational resizing and human resource management. *SAM Advanced Management Journal, 55*(3), 30–36.

Kreitner, R., & Kinicki, A. (1998). *Organizational behavior* (4th ed.). Boston, MA: McGraw-Hill.

Kydd, C. T., & Oppenheim, L. (1990). Using human resource management to enhance competitiveness: Lessons from four excellent companies. *Human Resource Management, 29,* 145–166.

Marion, R. (2002). *Leadership in education: Organizational theory for the practitioner*. Upper Saddle River, NJ: McGraw-Hill.

Milkovich, G. T., & Boudreau, J. W. (1991). *Human resource management*. Boston: Irwin.

Norton, M. S., Webb, L. D., Dlugosh, D. G., & Sybouts, W. (1996). *The school superintendency*. Needham Heights, NJ: Allyn & Bacon.

Pfeiffer, J. W., Goodstein, L. D., & Nolan, T. M. (1986). *Applied strategic planning: A how to do it guide*. San Diego: University Associates.

Reichrath, M. R. (1990). *A study of strategic planning readiness in Georgia public school systems*. Unpublished doctoral dissertation, Georgia State University, Atlanta.

Stronge, J. H., Gareis, C. R., & Little, C. A. (2006). *Teacher pay and teacher quality: Attracting, developing, and retaining the best teachers*. Thousand Oaks, CA: Sage.

Chapter 3

Organizational Climate and the Human Resources Function

── **LEARNING OBJECTIVES** ──────────────────────────

After reading this chapter, you will be able to:

- Define school climate and school culture.
- Differentiate between the climate and the culture of a school.
- Delineate the importance of the school climate to the improvement of the human resources function and the achievement of school goals.
- Provide a review of alternative instruments for measuring the climate of a school or school system.
- Describe a school with a positive school climate.
- Describe the impact of climate on student achievement and the commitment of persons in schools.
- Describe a process for climate improvement.

Human resources administration was defined previously as those processes that are planned and implemented in the organization to foster an organizational climate that enhances the accomplishment of district goals. This definition emphasizes the responsibility of the human resources function to foster an environment in which relationships among personnel, students, and others lend support to the work of the human resources function and the achievement of school goals. Human resources administrators throughout the school system must assume a major role in the development of a healthy school environment in which everyone works cooperatively to achieve desired ends.

Terms such as *organizational climate, organizational culture, organizational character, organizational health,* and others are among those found in the literature related to the internal workplace environment. In this chapter the school environment is examined from the perspective of two related concepts—organizational culture and organizational climate. Each of these concepts is intimately related to the human side of the organization, and this is of concern to all those involved the administration of human resources at all levels. The chapter begins with an explanation of the concepts of culture and climate and their importance to the operation of the schools. Next, the research related to the school characteristics associated with a healthy school is reviewed. This is followed by a review of the major instruments used to measure healthy school climate and a discussion of the impact of climate on student achievement, the behavior of school staff, organizational conflict, and organizational change and innovation. In the final section the improvement of school climate is discussed, with attention given to the role of human resources administrators in this process.

SCHOOL CULTURE AND SCHOOL CLIMATE: DEFINED AND COMPARED

The terms *culture* and *climate* are both concepts that address the fact that the behavior of people in an organization "is not elicited by an interaction with proximate events alone but is also influenced by interactions with intangible forces in the organization's environment" (Owens & Valesky, 2007, p. 192). Although the terms are often used interchangeably, they have different meanings. As will be presented more fully in the discussion which follows, *culture* refers to the values, beliefs, customs, and attitudes of an organization, while *climate* refers to the perceptions that individuals hold of that culture.

Organizational culture is commonly defined in the literature as "the unwritten code of conduct that governs the behavior, attitudes, relationships, and style of the organization" (Ortiz & Arnborg, 2005, p. 35). Edgar Schein (1997), one of the experts in organizational culture, has defined it as "the solution to external and internal problems that has worked consistently for a group and that is, therefore taught to new members as the correct way to perceive, think about, and feel in relation to those problems" (p. 12). Over time these solutions become assumptions about human nature, reality, and truth that are eventually taken for granted and eventually operate at an unconscious level (Schein, 1997).

Culture manifests itself at four levels of increasing abstraction (see Figure 3.1): (1) language, symbols, and artifacts; (2) norms; (3) values and beliefs; and

Figure 3.1 Levels of School Culture

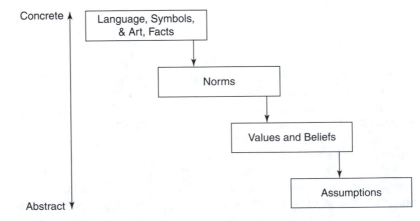

(4) assumptions. *Language, symbols, and artifacts* are the most visible manifestations of culture. It includes such things as language, dialects, sayings, stories, myths, legends, art, heroes, dance, games, rituals, building, and technology. In the school, stories of an alumnus who became a war hero, the rituals associated with the graduation ceremony, or the school mascot and song are all important symbols and artifacts of the culture of the school.

Norms are those standards that are "just below the surface of experience; they have an 'ought to' quality to them" (Sackney, 1988, p. 15) and define acceptable and unacceptable behavior. Norms are communicated by stories as well as by sanctions and rewards. Those who violate norms may be shunned, ignored, or confronted. Examples of norms in the school might include acceptable behavior on the playground, appropriate greetings to administrators (e.g., "Hello, Joe," vs. "Hello Dr. Smith"), and preferences given (or not given) to faculty in parking spaces or the cafeteria line. Norms vary not only from school to school, but over time. One has only to look at student (and teacher) dress in the school to see how norms can change in time.

Values and beliefs define what the organization stands for and what is considered important in the organization. In schools these are typically articulated in the school mission statement and district or school goals. A high level of student achievement, a qualified faculty, quality teaching, and diversity are often mentioned values and, if acted upon, become the rationale for how people are treated (e.g., who gets recognized and rewarded) and what gets done in the organization.

Assumptions are the fundamental presumptions that provide the basis for all actions and decisions in the organization. Assumptions are "abstract premises about the nature of human relationships, human nature, truth, reality, and the environment" (Dyer, cited in Hoy & Miskel, 2005, p. 19). Examples (positive and negative) of assumptions in the school might be "all students are basically good and honest" or "the administration acts to please the school board, even to the disadvantage of teachers."

Culture performs a number of important functions for organizations, including schools. These include but are not limited to

- Culture has a boundary-defining function; it creates distinctions among organizations.
- Culture provides the organization with a sense of identity.
- Culture facilitates the development of commitment to the group.
- Culture enhances stability in the social system.
- Culture is the social glue that binds the organization together; it provides the appropriate standards for behavior. (Hoy & Miskel, 2005, p. 170)

To function effectively as a human resources administrator at any level, one needs to understand the more visible manifestations of the culture of the school as well as the more complex and abstract. It is also important to understand the impact of culture on the climate of the school and the impact of climate on various characteristics of the school.

Organizational climate is related to and a component of culture in that the perceptions of individuals in the organization reflect the values and beliefs present in the organization (Owens & Valesky, 2007). The school climate has been defined as "the set of internal characteristics that distinguish one school from another and influences the behavior of its members . . . the relative stable property of the school environment that is experienced by participants, affects their behaviors and is based on their collective perceptions of behavior in schools" (Hoy & Hannum, 1997, p. 291). School climate is the collective personality of a school or school system. It is the school atmosphere as characterized by the social and professional interactions within it. Climate is a phenomenon that is influenced by both the internal and external environments of the school system. And, while climate is relatively enduring, these internal and external influences can lead to changes in the climate of the school over time.

Table 3.1 illustrates differences between school culture and school climate, as well as those characteristics that serve to link the two. As depicted in Table 3.1, school climate is characterized by the social and professional interactions of people in the school community, while school culture extends beyond the interpersonal life that takes place in the school setting.

Table 3.1 School Culture and School Climate

School Culture	Links	School Climate
Culture is the set of important beliefs and values that members of an organization share. Culture is more normative than climate in the sense that it is a reflection of the shared values, beliefs, and underlying assumptions of school members across an array of organizational dimensions that include but go beyond interpersonal relationships.	People Interpersonal relations Collective phenomena Environmental factors Socialization Shared goals Influenced behaviors	Climate is the collective personality of a school or school system. It is the atmosphere that prevails as characterized by the social and professional interactions of people. Climate is more interpersonal in tone and substance than culture. It is manifested in the attitudes and behaviors of teachers, students, administrators, and community members. Climate is concerned with the process and style of a school's organizational life, rather than its content and substance.

THE IMPORTANCE OF A HEALTHY SCHOOL CLIMATE

Why is school climate such an important consideration? Why does the environmental setting within a school system require the special attention of human resources administrators? And, how can school climate be instrumental in the improvement of the HR function in the school systems?

School climate is important to human resources administrators and to all those who work in and attend their schools. The climate of the school sets the tone for the human considerations of importance to human resources administration. An important part of the work of human resources administrators is to determine the facilitators and inhibitors of school effectiveness, those strengths and weaknesses that impact the climate of the school system. The determination of school climate is a perquisite to a determination of the strategies for school improvement:

Climate provides a reading of how things are going in the school and a basis for predicting school consequences and outcomes. Such a barometer represents an important tool for evaluating present conditions, planning new directions, and monitoring progress toward new directions. Indeed, school climate is a key dimension of human resources supervision. (Sergiovanni & Starratt, 2007, p. 333)

The climate in the school also sets the atmosphere for growth and renewal. Human resources administrators must work to promote a school environment that fosters the positive personnel development needed for the organization to remain vital and alive. The healthy school serves to stimulate the best efforts of people through providing meaningful work, motivating challenges, and continuous opportunities for personal growth and development. Only through an ongoing program of personnel development will the school system have the ability to innovate and change as needed within a changing society.

Climate is also important to maintaining effective communication in schools. Effective communication requires a climate of trust, mutual respect, and clarity of function. Such communication is inhibited in schools where distrust and poor human relations exist. Effective communication is an important component of an open, positive climate; it serves to tie the school community together. Barth (1990) notes several important forms of communication and collegiality that are present in schools with a healthy climate: adults in schools talk about practice, adults in schools talk to each other, adults in schools work together in curriculum, and adults in schools teach each other what they know. In effect, craft knowledge is openly communicated between and among colleagues.

Climate conditions the school environment for creative efforts, innovation, and change. These behaviors serve as foundations for organizational goal achievement. A positive school environment encourages innovative practices that promote the achievement of new goals. And, as has been noted by various authorities, rather than attempting to initiate change and then experiencing failure, school leaders would find it more judicious to examine the school climate first and, if it is not favorable to change, take steps to improve the climate for change before attempting further program innovation.

School climate is important to school systems and to the human resources function because it impacts on all of the important reasons that schools exist. As discussed later in this chapter, research documents the impact of a positive school climate on patterns of human behavior in the school. Human resources leaders have an important role in determining what the school system is and what it might become. In order to have a positive influence, however, they must understand why organizational climate is important to school effectiveness as well as to the effectiveness of the HR function, how it can be assessed, and how to foster a positive environment within the system.

THE MEASUREMENT OF SCHOOL CLIMATE

Numerous climate assessment instruments have been developed and administered in school systems in order to gain an understanding of the nature of school environments, the characteristics associated with different kinds of climates, and the impact of various leadership styles on personnel behaviors. The two most common perspectives of school climate reflected in these instruments are (1) climate as a "personality" of the school viewed along a continuum of open to closed and (2) climate as the "health" of the school (Hoy & Hannum, 1997).

School Climate as School Personality

The first perspective on school climate is reflected in the Organizational Climate Description Questionnaire (OCDQ) developed by Andrew W. Halpin and Don B. Croft in 1962. Halpin and Croft focused primarily on school climate as a function of the relationships between the school principal and the teaching staff. The OCDQ is composed of 64 Likert-type items which assess teachers' perspectives of the climate of the school. The OCDQ yields school mean scores that are averages of the scores for all teachers' responses on eight subtests related to principal and teacher behavior. For example, two of the subtests are disengagement and intimacy. *Disengagement* refers to the teacher's tendency to be uninvolved in the school and to lack commitment to the school. This dimension describes a group that is going through the motions but is not in gear with respect to the tasks at hand. *Intimacy* refers to the social cohesiveness among teachers in the school. Two other subsets, *spirit*, the morale of the group, and *hindrance*, the extent to which rules, regulations, paperwork, and administrators as obstacles to their work, are related to the teacher group. Four others seek the perception of teachers concerning the principal:

Thrust: The extent to which the principal's behavior sets a hardworking example.

Consideration: The extent to which the principal is seen as treating teachers with dignity and human concern.

Aloofness: The extent to which the principal is described as maintaining social distance (for example, cold and distant or warm and friendly).

Production emphasis: The extent to which the principal tries to get teachers to work harder (for example, supervising closely, being directive, demanding results). (Owens & Valesky, 2007, p. 211)

Using the profiles of 71 schools, Halpin and Croft (1962) developed six prototypic profiles to describe climates on a continuum from open to closed. An **open climate** is described as one in which the staff enjoys extremely high morale, works well together, enjoys friendly relations but does not engage in a high degree of socialization, and possesses the incentive to work things out and to keep the school moving. An open climate is further described by Kreitner (2001) as having four characteristics:

1. **Interaction with the environment.** Open systems have permeable boundaries, whereas closed systems do not. Organizations depend on the environment for survival.
2. **Synergy.** An open system adds up to more than the sum of its parts. Only when all parts are in place and working in concert can the winning edge be achieved.

3. **Dynamic equilibrium.** In open systems, dynamic equilibrium is the process of maintaining the internal balance necessary for survival by importing needed resources from the environment.
4. **Equifinality.** Open systems can achieve the same results by different means. (pp. 282–284)

In contrast to the open climate, a **closed climate** is one that is characterized by apathy, low staff morale, limited and inadequate communication, and limited socialization. In addition, closed systems are typified by impermeable boundaries and static equilibrium. Hoy and Miskel (2005) describe a closed climate as one where

> The principal and teachers simply appear to go through the motions, with the principal stressing routine trivia and unnecessary busywork (high restrictiveness) and the teacher responding minimally and exhibiting little commitment (high disengagement). The principal's ineffective leadership is further seen as controlling and rigid (high directiveness) as well as unsympathetic, unconcerned, and unresponsive (low supportiveness). These misguided tactics are accompanied not only by frustration and apathy, but also by a general suspicion and lack of respect of teachers for each other as either friends or professionals (low intimacy and noncollegial relations). Closed climates have principals who are nonsupportive, inflexible, hindering, and controlling and a faculty that is divisive, intolerant, apathetic, and uncommitted. (Hoy & Miskel, 2005, pp. 187–188)

In the years following the development of the OCDQ, the perceived need for instruments more suitable for use at various school levels led to the development of three revised versions, one for use in elementary schools, one for middle schools, and one for high schools. For example, the *OCDQ-RE* was designed by Hoy and Clover (1986) specifically for use in elementary school and addresses climate of the school across six dimensions:

Supportive Principal Behavior: Reflects a basic concern for teachers. The principal listens and is open to teacher suggestions. Praise is given genuinely and frequently and criticism is constructive.

Directive Principal Behavior: Requires rigid, close supervision. The principal maintains close and constant control over all teacher and school activities, down to the smallest details.

Restrictive Principal Behavior: Hinders rather than facilitates teacher work. The principal burdens teachers with paperwork, committee requirements, routine duties, and busywork.

Collegial Teacher Behavior: Supports open and professional interactions among teachers. Teachers are enthusiastic, accepting, and respectful of the professional competence of their colleagues.

Intimate Teacher Behavior: Reflects a strong, cohesive network of social support within the faculty. Teachers know each other well, are close personal friends, and socialize together regularly.

Disengaged Teacher Behavior: Refers to a lack of meaning and focus to professional activities. Teachers are simply putting in time. Their behavior is negative and critical of their colleagues. (Hoy & Miskel, 2005, p. 187)

The *OCDQ-RS* (Kottkamp, Mulhern & Hoy, 1987) is a 34-item instrument designed to assess climate in secondary schools. It focuses on five dimensions of behavior including the supportive and directive behaviors of teacher personnel. Two of the dimensions describe the behaviors exhibited by the principal, and three dimensions center on teacher behaviors, specifically teacher relationships with students, colleagues, and supervisors. Resulting data provide descriptions of the openness and intimacy of the school climate. As previously defined, intimacy refers to the level of satisfaction that teachers obtain from their friendly relationships with other teachers in the school. Similar to the OCDQ-RS is the *OCDQ-RM*, developed by Hoy and Tarter (1997), a revision of the OCDQ for use at the middle school level.

The results of the assessment using any of these instruments can be used to map the openness of the school in terms of four prototypes: open, engaged, disengaged, and closed. Each of the revised instruments has been thoroughly tested for validity and reliability for use at its intended school level. They are available online at www.coe.ohio-state.edu/whoy.

The wide use of the OCDQ and its revisions in hundreds of empirical studies has not only contributed significantly to the foundational concepts of school climate but has served to motivate other researchers to study the topic from a variety of perspectives, including the characteristics associated with positive climates, the impact of climate on personnel, and the climate characteristics associated with effective schools, innovation, and change. Selected research related to these considerations is discussed later in the chapter.

School Climate as School Health

Another way to look at the climate of a school is to look at it organizational "health." The most widely used measure of organizational health is the *Organizational Health Inventory (OHI)*. The Organizational Health Inventory (Hoy & Feldman, 1987) assesses climate in terms of six interaction patterns in schools across the three levels of responsibility and control in the schools:

Institutional Level:
- Institutional Integrity

Managerial Level:
- Principal Influence
- Consideration
- Initiating Structure
- Resource Support

Technical (teaching-learning) Level:
- Moral
- Academic Emphasis

Valid and reliable versions of the OHI have been developed for each school level: elementary, middle, and high school (Tarter, Hoy, & Kottkamp, 1990). Research has determined the OHI is a reliable instrument for measuring the health of a school. Given the established relationship between climate and school achievement discussed in the following section, the OHI can be a useful tool for administrators in identifying problems in the school climate and designing change strategies.

Numerous other instruments have been developed to measure school climate from a variety of perspectives on organizational climate. Among those more widely used is the *High School Characteristics Index* (HSCI), an adaptation of Stern's (1964) *College Characteristics Index*. The *High School Characteristics Index* (Stern, 1964) looked at climate not only from the perspective of the interaction of people with each other, but the interaction of people with their environment. The HSCI measures school climate in terms of six factors. The factors and their implications for school climate are as follows:

Factor 1: *Intellectual Climate.* Schools with high scores on this factor have environments that are perceived as being conducive to scholarly interests in the humanities, arts, and sciences. The staff and the physical plant are seen to be facilitative of these interests, and the general work atmosphere is characterized by intellectual activities and pursuits.

Factor 2: *Achievement Standards.* Environments with high scores on this factor are perceived to stress high standards of personal achievement. Tasks are successfully completed, and high levels of motivation and energy are maintained. Recognition is given for work of good quality and quantity, and the staff is expected to achieve at the highest levels.

Factor 3: *Personal Dignity (Supportiveness).* Organizational climates scoring high on this factor respect the integrity of the individual and provide a supportive environment that would closely approximate the needs of more dependent teachers. The working environment conveys fair play and openness.

Factor 4: *Organizational Effectiveness.* Schools with high scores on this factor have work environments that encourage and facilitate the effective performance of tasks. Work programs are planned and well organized, and people work together effectively to meet organizational objectives.

Factor 5: *Orderliness.* High scores on this factor are indicative of a press for organizational structure and procedural orderliness. Neatness counts, and teachers are pressured to conform to a defined norm of personal appearance and institutional image. There are set procedures, and teachers are expected to follow them.

Factor 6: *Impulse Control.* High scores on this factor imply a great deal of constraint and organizational restrictiveness in the work environment. Teachers have little opportunity for personal expression or for any form of impulsive behavior. (Owens & Valesky, 2007, pp. 213–214)

The CFK School Climate Profile. The Charles F. Kettering School Climate Profile (Phi Delta Kappa, 1973) may be completed by teachers, students, and parents. The CFK has four sections: General Climate (40 items), Program Determinants (35 items), Process Determinants (15 items), and Material Determinants (15 items). Respondents use a Likert-type scale in the General Climate section to assess such climate on eight subscales: (a) Respect, (b) Trust, (c) Morale, (d) Opportunity for Input, (e) Continuous Academic and Social Growth, (f) Cohesiveness, (g) School Renewal, and (h) Caring. Table 3.2 presents each of the three climate determinants and the provisions that accompany them. Originally used primarily at the high school level, the CFK has since been validated for use at the middle school level (Johnson, Johnson, Gott, & Zimmerman, 1997) and has been widely used for organizational development and curriculum revision.

Some of the other instruments used to assess school climate discussed in the literature are the *School Climate Survey* developed by the National Association of Secondary School Principals (Kelley, et al., 1986); *School Climate and Context Inventory* (Bobbett & French, 1992); the *Tennessee School Climate Inventory* (Butler & Albery, 1991); and an Australian import, the *School Level Environment Questionnaire* (Rentoul & Fraser, 1983).

Table 3.2 Summary Form of the CFK Ltd. School Climate Profile

A.	Program Determinants
	☐ Opportunities for Active Learning
	☐ Individualized Performance Expectations
	☐ Varied Learning Environments
	☐ Flexible Curriculum and Extracurricular Activities
	☐ Support and Structure Appropriate to Learner's Maturity
	☐ Rules Cooperatively Determined
	☐ Varied Reward Systems
B.	Process Determinants
	☐ Problem-Solving Ability
	☐ Development of School Goals
	☐ Identifying and Working with Conflicts
	☐ Effective Communications
	☐ Involvement in Decision Making
	☐ Autonomy with Accountability
	☐ Effective Teaching-Learning Strategies
	☐ Ability to Plan for the Future
C.	Material Determinants
	☐ Adequate Resources
	☐ Supportive and Efficient Logistical System
	☐ Suitability of School Plant

Source: Phi Delta Kappa, *School Climate Improvement: A Challenge to the School Administrator* (1973). Robert S. Fox et al. Reprinted by permission.

School-Developed Climate Assessments

In some instances school districts have found it convenient to design their own climate survey instruments for use with teachers and students. Such instruments can serve a useful purpose in gaining feedback from a variety of school stakeholders, but have the disadvantage of lacking state or national norms for comparative purposes. However, results can be used in a variety of ways including a comparison of perceptions of the school climate by students to those of the faculty. Figure 3.2 illustrates a district-designed climate assessment instrument.

There are other assessment strategies for gaining input from staff personnel that are tied closely to one or more of the human resources processes and can result in findings that serve to improve current practices which may in turn lead to climate improvement. For example, valuable information can be gathered from employees who are voluntarily leaving the system by using well-designed exit interviews. Information gained from exit interviews can help to determine the reasons employees are leaving, what the school system might have done to retain them, and suggestions to improve the workplace.

In view of the fact that much more of the time of human resources administrators is given to people management and efforts to make the school system a place where faculty and staff want to be, more attention necessarily will be directed to assessments of the workplace environment and its competitive ability to attract and retain quality personnel.

RESEARCH ON SCHOOL CLIMATE

The focus on the technical aspects of work in fostering productivity, exemplified by Taylor's task system in the scientific management era, was brought into question by Mary Parker Follett (1924) and others. Follett contended that the central problem of any enterprise is the building and maintaining of dynamic yet harmonious human relationships. Her concepts of coordination for refocusing methods of supervisory and personnel practices to achieve organizational harmony were revolutionary. She introduced the concept of *integration* for dealing with conflict and provided the foundation for contemporary practices such as participatory management, commitment to superordinate system goals versus personal vested interests, and integrative approaches to problem solving, including collective negotiations. Follett's work spurred many subsequent investigations which sought a better understanding of the relationship between the human element and organizational health and productivity.

In the decades after Follett, much attention was given to investigations of organizational concepts such as democratic leadership, informal group influences, the school as a social system, and other organizational characteristics now studied in relation to school climate. Much of the contemporary thought relating to organizational climate had its beginning in the research which began in the early 1960s.

Since that time, numerous climate studies have been conducted that center on (1) the characteristics of schools with positive climates, (2) the impact of climate on student achievement, (3) the impact of climate on the behavior of personnel, and

Figure 3.2 Student School Climate Survey Instrument

PEORIA SCHOOLING IMPROVEMENT PRACTICE STUDY
STUDENT SCHOOL CLIMATE SURVEY

School _____

Grade _____

DIRECTIONS:

As you read each statement please circle the number which best describes how you feel about your school. Do not circle more than one number for each statement.

Value of the number: (1) Strongly disagree; (2) Disagree; (3) Neutral; (4) Agree; (5) Strongly agree

I. SCHOOL ATMOSPHERE/MORALE

	1	2	3	4	5
1. Our school has a friendly atmosphere.	1	2	3	4	5
2. Our school is a place where students want to be and a place where they can learn in a pleasant environment.	1	2	3	4	5
3. The students and staff take pride in our school.	1	2	3	4	5
4. School spirit and morale are high in our school.	1	2	3	4	5
5. Students and staff members in our school are usually happy.	1	2	3	4	5

II. STUDENT/STAFF RELATIONSHIPS

	1	2	3	4	5
1. Staff members and students trust and respect one another.	1	2	3	4	5
2. Teachers in our school care about students and go out of their way to help them.	1	2	3	4	5
3. Teachers and other school personnel in our school treat students fairly and as persons.	1	2	3	4	5
4. Students and staff in our school frequently participate in activities that solve problems and improve our school.	1	2	3	4	5
5. The principal of our school is respected by students and staff members and is looked upon as an effective leader.	1	2	3	4	5

III. STUDENT BEHAVIOR/SCHOOL RULES

	1	2	3	4	5
1. There are relatively few discipline problems in our school.	1	2	3	4	5
2. The rules in our school are clearly defined and fair.	1	2	3	4	5
3. Most students in our school obey the school rules.	1	2	3	4	5
4. The attendance is good in our school.	1	2	3	4	5
5. Visitors in our school consider our students well behaved and courteous.	1	2	3	4	5

IV. PEER RELATIONSHIPS

	1	2	3	4	5
1. The students in our school get along well with each other.	1	2	3	4	5
2. The students in our school are treated with respect regardless of race, religion, or physical or mental handicaps.	1	2	3	4	5
3. Students in our school are willing to give a helping hand to other students.	1	2	3	4	5
4. There is little friction or hostility between groups of students in our school.	1	2	3	4	5
5. New students are made to feel welcome and a part of our school.	1	2	3	4	5

V. STUDENT ACHIEVEMENT/LEARNING ENVIRONMENT

	1	2	3	4	5
1. Student achievement is high in our school.	1	2	3	4	5
2. Students feel that our school program is meaningful.	1	2	3	4	5
3. The teachers in our school make learning enjoyable.	1	2	3	4	5
4. I like who I am and feel good about myself.	1	2	3	4	5
5. Students in our school seem to like and feel good about themselves.	1	2	3	4	5

(4) the impact of school climate on school change and innovation. The research studies related to each of these four areas are discussed in the following sections.

Characteristics of Schools with Positive Climates

Many of the studies of climate completed during the late 1970s and 1980s were part of what has become known as the effective school movement. In one often-cited study, Walberg and Genova (1982) found that the use of professional knowledge by teachers was significantly associated with such climate characteristics as equality of staff treatment, integration of staff cooperation, goal direction, and learning orientation. A number of other studies focused on the relationship between high expectations for students and productive school environments. Proctor (1984), after a review of the research on the relationship between teacher expectations and student achievement, maintained that organizational expectations are a critical element of a school's learning environment. A similar finding was reported by Farrar and Flakus-Mosqueda (1986), who found that the one element all successful school improvement programs had in common was the development of a positive climate in which problems and issues could be identified and resolved. A decade later Short and Greer (1997) agreed that "In the healthy organization, challenges are addressed, solutions to problems are found, and new methods and innovations are initiated . . . a healthy organization not only has effective processes but also is likely to have a high trust culture" (p. 63).

A large-scale study by Taylor and Tashakkori (1994) collected data from 9,987 teachers and 27,994 students relative to the factors affecting climate. They found that supportive leadership of the school, the collegiality of the faculty, and student discipline were the major factors associated with a positive school climate (Winter & Sweeney, 1994). Such administrative support is exemplified in the behavior of principals who recognize achievement, back up teachers, encourage teachers, care for teachers, and administer school rules fairly. Bulach and Malone (1994) used three survey instruments to study the impact of the principal's leadership style on school climate and student achievement and reported a significant difference between leadership style and the subscale of school climate. The importance of leadership was also reported in a national study by Sweeney (1992) who reported the results from a study of more than 600 schools. He found that a principal's effectiveness in learning environment administration, instructional leadership, and human resources management correlated highly with a positive climate. In fact, human resources management was the principal behavior most highly correlated with a positive school climate.

Considerable other research in the past two decades has described characteristics that are associated with positive climates in schools and school systems. Among their findings are that schools with healthy climates are schools where

1. Opportunities are provided for active student learning, whereby students perceive the learning process and life of the school to be of high importance.
2. Learning environments give due consideration to individualized performance as related to personal talents, styles, and interests.

3. Programs and activities are designed to reflect the changes in the intellectual, social, and physical development of students.
4. Policies and school regulations are cooperatively developed, clearly written, and effectively disseminated.
5. Reward systems place an emphasis on positive student reinforcement rather than punishment.
6. Leaders work purposefully to effect better systems of communication and to personalize relationships with school personnel and students.
7. A viable set of shared goals with expanded implications for the future has been developed.
8. School leaders give full consideration to the needs of staff and to both their work life and personal life.
9. School leaders give major attention to the general work conditions of the school, including such matters as teacher load, career goals of staff members, and to supervisor/staff relationships.

Collectively the research suggests that a healthy school climate is one that (1) has clear and achievable goals that are accepted by members of the organization (goal focus); (2) transmits needed information relatively distortion-free throughout the organization; (3) distributes power relatively equally; (4) uses resources, particularly personnel, effectively; (5) sustains cohesiveness among members; (6) maintains high morale; (7) grows, develops, and changes rather than remaining routinized and static; (8) acts with a high degree of independence from its environment; (9) adapts and copes to changes in the organization and environment; and (10) has well-developed structures and procedures for identifying and solving problems (Miles, cited in Sergiovanni & Starratt, 2007). In the following section the research and practice relating to organizational climate and student achievement are discussed.

The Impact of School Climate on Student Achievement

The definition of human resources used repeatedly in this text emphasizes the fostering of organizational climate for the purpose of enhancing the accomplishment of school goals. Most people would agree that the No Child Left Behind Act has made student achievement a major goal of most schools. And, as schools have looked to ways to improve student achievement, attention has turned to the large body of research which has examined the relationship between school climate and student achievement. This research has looked at various constructs of climate from the perspective of teachers, administrators, students, parents, or the community. It is beyond the scope of this work to review anything but a small sample of this large body of research.

What had been a limited body of school climate research gained momentum in the 1970s in conjunction with the school effectiveness movement. And, in 1985, Borger, Lo, Oh, and Walberg reviewed 205 studies related to effective schools and reported that in 96% of the studies school climate was found to be directly associated with student achievement. That same year Hopkins and Crain (1985) described efforts in a suburban high school to improve test scores through improvements in the school's climate. Climate improvements included such strategies as student participation in decision making. A 10-year high in ACT scores, improved student attendance, a significant decrease in the drop-out rate, and other positive student outcomes were attributed by the school administrators to the climate changes in the school.

Academic emphasis and teacher expectations have been the focus of a number of student achievement studies. For example, a study by Paredes and Frazer (1992) examined school climate over a 4-year period. Among the study findings were (1) high schools with positive climates had higher student achievement and lower drop-out rates, (2) student achievement was affected most directly by teacher expectations of student success and the instructional goals of teachers, and (3) school climate scores were better predictors of student drop-out rates. Newman and Associates' (1996) report of a 5-year study related to school success and school culture had similar findings. The researchers found that commitment to high student expectations, support for staff innovation and creativity, an ongoing search for new ideas, and a climate of caring and collaboration among staff were among those conditions directly related to school success. And, Goddard, Sweetland, and Hoy (2000) examined the importance of academic emphasis in elementary school—defined as "a climate in which teachers believe that their students have the capabilities to achieve, students work hard to succeed and are respected for their academic accomplishments, and the learning atmosphere is orderly and serious" (p. 699)—and concluded that the academic emphasis was systematically related to student achievement. Similar relationships between academic emphasis and student achievement have been found in middle and high schools (Hoy & Hannum, 1997; Hoy & Sabo, 1998; Phillips, 1997; Shouse, 1998).

While the majority of the studies investigating school climate and achievement have used some form of the OCDQ or the OHI, other climate assessments have been used. The *School Climate Survey* (SCS), unique for having been developed by a professional organization, the National Association of Secondary School Principals, modified for use at the elementary level, was used to study whether climate was an individual-level property (the individual's perception) or a school-level property, as well as the relationship between student achievement and climate ratings by teachers, family, and principals. The study concluded that that climate was a school-level construct and that the ratings by each group were strongly related to academic achievement.

Elementary schools were also the subject of researchers using the Australian-developed School Level Environment Questionnaire. The study found the perceptions of school climate of over 1,100 teachers in 59 elementary schools in the Southwest were positively related to student achievement, with the strongest relationship being in schools in high socioeconomic status communities (Johnson & Stevens, 2006).

The results of the research on the relationship between climate and student achievement have been summarized by Winter and Sweeney (1994):

> For more than a decade, studies have proven that climate makes a difference in secondary school. Climate affects student achievement and behavior independent of student's intelligence or home environment. It is also reflected in the shared attitudes, beliefs, and values of the people of the school. (p. 66)

The Impact of School Climate on the Behavior of Personnel

In their now-famous work of almost 50 years ago, Herzberg, Manser, and Snyderman (1959) proposed that interpersonal relationships with one's superior and the technical aspects of supervision were organizational climate considerations associated with job dissatisfaction. Since that time numerous studies in private and public organizations, including schools, have affirmed the relationship between climate factors and job satisfaction as well as other employee behaviors. Hoy and Clover (1986) used the previously discussed OCDQ-RE climate assessment instrument to describe four prototypes of school climate that result in various teacher behaviors: (1) the open climate, (2) the closed climate, (3) the engaged climate, and (4) the disengaged climate. The previously described open climate features cooperation and respect within the faculty and between the faculty and the school principal. Teacher behavior fosters open and professional interactions among faculty members. The open climate promotes cooperative behavior among faculty members and meaningful engagement in their work. In the **engaged climate,** teachers tend to ignore the principal's attempts to control faculty behavior. Teachers respect each other's professionalism and competence. Attention to tasks is high and the faculty is professionally responsive in spite of the principal's restrictive behaviors. In **disengaged climates**, relationship behaviors in the school are negative. Teachers are not engaged in the tasks, and teacher behaviors are exemplified by divisiveness, intolerance, and noncommitment. Teacher behaviors in closed climates are quite similar to those in disengaged situations. Task commitment is low, intimacy is low, and collegiality also is low.

More recent research using the OCDQ has shown that the degree of openness of the school climate is associated with the level of loyalty and trust faculty award to both colleagues and the principal (Reiss & Hoy, 1998). Studies using the OHI have yielded similar results: the more healthy the climate of the school, the greater the employee trust in colleagues and the principal (Smith, Hoy, & Sweetland, 2001; Tarter & Hoy, 1988). Openness of the school climate has also been associated with a higher level of shared decision making and principal receptivity to teacher input (Barnes, 1994).

The impact of the workplace environment on employee satisfaction, commitment, and loyalty is no longer a matter of debate; virtually every study of employee attitudes and behavior reaches the same conclusion: the workplace environment, in the long run, looms more important to job satisfaction and worker retention than do salary and other monetary incentives. It is clear that success in organizations today depends on a working environment that encourages input of the best ideas from all employees and the collaboration of workers and team efforts to implement these ideas in the most optimal ways. Such working relationships are not possible in school systems with unhealthy school climates.

Dealing with Conflict. Schools with unhealthy climates find it difficult to deal with conflict since personnel do not work well together. Rules and regulations set the manner in which things are done; problems are "resolved" through mandate as opposed to an integration of ideas and alternatives. These systems lack problem-solving capacity; conflict often is resolved in these environments by employee turnover.

In an open school climate, the right to disagree and express other points of view not only is expected, but solicited. That is, the system purposely seeks input from all staff through such means as suggestion systems, the use of "think tanks" for problem solving, and the use of shadow group techniques that place general staff personnel in role-play exercises to examine problems faced by the system and its administrative personnel. Healthy school systems realize that any attempt to discourage disagreement will most likely result in negative outcomes such as poor relationships and lack of confidence in the system's leadership.

In a healthy school climate, the consideration of controversial matters can be useful. Progress in terms of goal achievement and new understandings often are generated through opportunities to reflect on problems and alternative solutions. Thus, the human resources administrator can serve to help make disagreements constructive in a number of ways. One way is for the human resources administrator to broaden the base of stakeholder understanding through purposeful assessment of criticism received by the school or school system. In this way, the human resources administrator is in a much better position to limit unfair criticism since assessment strategies serve to distinguish between constructive and destructive proposals.

Human resource administrators must implement viable methods for learning about the existence and specific concerns of criticism. The advantage of an open climate in this regard is that open channels of communication are most likely already in place; these channels serve as the system's nervous system whereby school leaders are more able to discern conflict at an early stage and make an immediate, appropriate response, as well as keep conflict more manageable. In those instances where criticism is unfair or based on irresponsible behavior, a planned strategy is necessary. The gathering of accurate information concerning the situation at hand, obtaining the participation of knowledgeable groups and individuals on the matter, and strategizing for appropriate counteraction are among the steps needed in such cases.

Public relations personnel have learned that attempts to cover up problems or to use the tired phrase of "no comment" when working with the media and others only tend to exacerbate the problem. Thus the overall task of human resources administrators is to work to maintain integrity and stakeholder confidence in a climate where critics have not only the right to disagree, but to express that disagreement through the school system's open channels of communication. However, conflict need not be avoided. As previously noted, conflict and controversy can be helpful in leading to preferred solutions. Schools that maintain open communications are much more likely to deal effectively with the conflict they will inevitably encounter as a social institution.

School Life and Staff Commitment. Although staff commitment to both other staff and students is the result of various influences, the research suggests that employee loyalty is closely related to school climate: teachers in schools with a healthy climate are more committed than teachers in unhealthy schools (Rosenholtz, 1989; Tarter, Hoy, & Kottcamp, 1990; Tarter, Sabo, & Hoy, 1995). Research has also shown that the biggest driver of employee loyalty was having managers recognize the employees' need to balance work with home life (Aon Consulting, 1995). This climate conditioner differs drastically from earlier views that the worker was never to let family/home life interfere with the job. Now, the importance of *work-life* balance has risen to the top of many employers' and employees' consciousness (Lockwood, 2003). Work life matters are increasingly important to employees. As a result, the structured work schedule for teachers and other school staff members must be reevaluated in view of the changing attitudes of today's employees toward work and life balance. Innovations in work schedules and instructional delivery in schools must be implemented. If not improved, job satisfaction will lessen and school climate will be negatively impacted.

Schools must give full attention to work life benefits in school settings in order to attract and retain quality personnel. Recruiting, selection, and retention processes must give high priority to "advertising" how the school system is giving attention to benefits in the area of work life. Policy decisions and HR strategies must recognize the inextricable relationship between the work and personal life of staff personnel. The HR processes of recruiting, selection, and retention necessarily must place emphasis on the needs of staff members, not only the needs of the school system.

It is increasingly important that HR administrators realize that giving attention to school climate and to staff commitment by recognizing work life balances is not just something they should do, but rather something they must do in order to keep the school system alive and vital.

The Impact of School Climate on Organizational Change and Innovation

A number of investigators have examined the relationship between types of school climate and the rate of innovation in schools. As early as 1972, Christian used Halpin and Croft's OCDQ to study climate in elementary schools relative to the introduction and use of innovative educational practices and found a significant positive relationship between openness and the rate of introduction and utilization of innovations in the school studied. The climate factors of disengagement and esprit (see Table 3.3) were most closely related to the rate of innovative utilization; the characteristics of aloofness and thrust, as related to positive principal behaviors, were most directly related to the degree of school innovativeness.

In the wake of the school reform movements of the 1980s and 1990s, considerable climate research focused on school change as related to school reform. For example, Bulach and Malone (1994) studied the relationship between several school climate characteristics (e.g., group openness and group trust) and the implementation of reform efforts in 13 Kentucky schools and concluded that "school climate was a significant factor in successfully implementing school reform" (p. 7). A similar conclusion was reached by Stevens (1990), who argued that giving attention to important climate considerations is the significant forerunner of school reform.

While noting the important relationship between organizational culture and change, researchers have been cautious in suggesting that changing organizational culture, or even bringing about real change, is simplistic. Other researchers have noted, "something that emerges as an abstract, unconscious, and complex

Table 3.3 A Summary of Climate Types

Climate Type	Group's Characteristics				Leader's Characteristics			
	Disengagement	Hindrance	Esprit	Intimacy	Aloofness	Production Emphasis	Thrust	Consideration
Open	Low	Low	High	Average	Low	Low	High	High
Autonomous	Low	Low	Relatively high	Relatively high	High	Low	High	Average
Controlled	Low	High	High	Low	Somewhat aloof	High	Average	Low
Familiar	High	Low	Average	High	Low	Low	Average to high	High
Paternal	High	Low	Low	Low	Low	High	Average	High but not authentic
Closed	High	High	Low	Average	High	High	Low	Low

Source: The information for this chart was abstracted from *Theory and Research in Administration* by Andrew W. Halpin. New York: The Macmillan Co., 1966, pp. 174–181.

expression of needs and beliefs, it is not a maneuverable or manageable entity" (Norton, Webb, Dlugosh, & Sybouts, 1996, p. 75). Nevertheless, several important conclusions regarding the relationship between climate and organizational change are supported by the research: (1) change in organizations is much more readily realized and effective if personnel understand what the change is all about and why it is necessary; (2) successful implementation of change and innovation requires that attention be given to the special training needed to provide the knowledge and skills necessary to implement new goals and programs; and (3) strategies for recruiting, selecting, assigning, retaining, compensating, and developing personnel must focus on the changes and innovations.

The organizational climate research is also clear that climate can be improved and assessed. The following sections discuss successful programs and practices for improving school climate and the responsibilities of HR administrators in achieving this end.

IMPROVEMENT OF SCHOOL CLIMATE

The improvement of school climate is a complex and challenging process and can succeed only if it is seen as a responsibility of all school personnel. At the district level the superintendent and human resources administrator have major roles and responsibilities in efforts to improve climate. These are discussed in a following section. At the school level, the principal, acting as a human resources administrator, must assume a leadership role in assessing the climate and taking steps to improve the climate using the assessment results. However, before any plan of school improvement is initiated, it is important that school personnel—in particular human resources administrators at all levels—understand what climate is, how it impacts others, how it can be assessed, and what process can be used to improve it.

There is no one change process that can guarantee success in improving the climate of a school. Three general approaches are presented by Hoy and Miskel (2005):

1. *The clinical strategy.* This approach is basically a parallel to the clinical model in health care; (i.e., gain a knowledge of the organization patient history); diagnose; assess the seriousness of the situation (prognosis); prescribe; and evaluate the success of prescriptions.

2. *The growth-centered strategy.* This strategy involves an acceptance of a set of assumptions about school personnel (e.g., change is a characteristic of healthy organizations and school personnel have the potential to plan and implement change), which if acted upon will "allow for a growth policy, which in turn leads to increased opportunities for professional development. From this perspective, administrators would remove obstacles from the path of professional growth and not manipulate people. Finally, the approach should help facilitate a climate of mutual trust and respect among teachers and administrators" (p. 191).

3. *A norm-changing strategy.* One model using this strategy involves employees identifying the organizational norms that influence their actions and attitudes; articulating in what direction the organization should be headed if it is to progress; identifying the norms that will facilitate improvement; identifying the gap between the actual norms and the desired norms; and adopting, monitoring, and enforcing new norms and practice (Kilman cited in Hoy & Miskel, 2005).

Within these three broad categories, a number of approaches to improving school climate have been proposed in the literature. One such example is that presented in Figure 3.3.

Figure 3.3 A Seven-Step Clinical Model for School Improvement

Step One: The district determines those aspects of school climate regarded as most problematic.

Step Two: School climate assessment instruments are developed for the district.

Step Three: The district distributes, administers, and returns surveys, which are then analyzed and reported in written form.

Step Four: School members meet with consultants and others to review survey results.

Step Five: School members break into small groups to pursue selected findings.

Step Six: School members generate multiple explanations for each climate condition identified in Step Five, develop a consensus approach to influencing some of the supposed causes, and construct an action plan.

Step Seven: Follow-through actions are implemented to see that school members pursue the action plans, that the effects of the plans are evaluated, and that the data and working lists of concerns are periodically revisited.

Source: Coladarci, T. C., & Donaldson, G. A. (1991). School climate assessment encourages collaboration. *NASSP Bulletin, 75*, 111–119.

In practice, most schools and school districts take an approach to school improvement that combines elements of the these three strategies. Such an approach might include the following steps:

1. **Recognize the Need for Improvement.** As is true regarding change in individuals or organizations, for sustainable change to occur there must be a recognition that change is needed. Faculty and staff must come to the recognition that the school or school district is not as good as it could be, that it can become a better place to work or learn (Sackney, 1988). "Awareness can come through discussion at staff meetings, reading of the literature, and through in service activities . . . This is the stage for building commitment" (Sackney, 1988, p. 18).

2. **Understand the Organization.** Through ongoing observation, study, and systematic analysis, those with responsibility for the improvement process must come to understand the norms and values of those who work in the organization. The perspective provided by such measures as the previously discussed OCDQ, OHI, and HSCI can be of considerable assistance in gaining this perspective (Hoy & Miskel, 2005).

3. **Identify Areas for Climate Improvement.** The identification of those aspects of the climate where improvement is needed can be informed by the results of a climate inventory by (separate) focus groups of administrators, faculty, staff, students and parents, interviews, or any combination of these and other quantitative or qualitative approaches. Once the areas for climate improvement are identified, faculty, staff, and administration should meet and engage in the conversation necessary to reach agreement upon a prioritized list of climate improvement needs.

4. **Develop Solutions Strategies.** For each area where climate improvement is needed, consensus should be reached on the possible explanations for the condition and alternative improvement strategies developed and prioritized. Some possible solutions may be beyond the ability of the school to correct (e.g., teacher turnover or low morale associated with the low salary offered by a low-income district); others may require changes in school board policy or state statue and may be influenced by political factors beyond the control of school district personnel. To the extent possible, all the internal and external factors bearing on the possible solutions should be identified and factored into the solutions process.

5. **Implement Preferred Climate Improvement Solution.** Implementation of the climate improvement solution in most cases will not be a "quick fix." Administration must be prepared to help others to understand that the change process requires patience and perseverance. The more complex the issue, the more likely the solution will be more long term. Trying to change the direction of an organization can indeed sometimes seem like "trying to turn the Queen Mary around in a bath tub."

6. **Monitor and Evaluate Progress.** An important but often-neglected step in the climate improvement process is the monitoring of success of the intervention in bringing about the desired climate improvement. Since organizations are generally not static, the climate monitoring process is necessarily ongoing. This is not to suggest that a formal climate assessment be conducted annually forever, but that assessment be conducted as frequently and thoroughly as necessary to ensure that improvements have been successfully implemented with the desired results and, perhaps more important, that they are sustainable.

Figure 3.4 The Climate Improvement Process

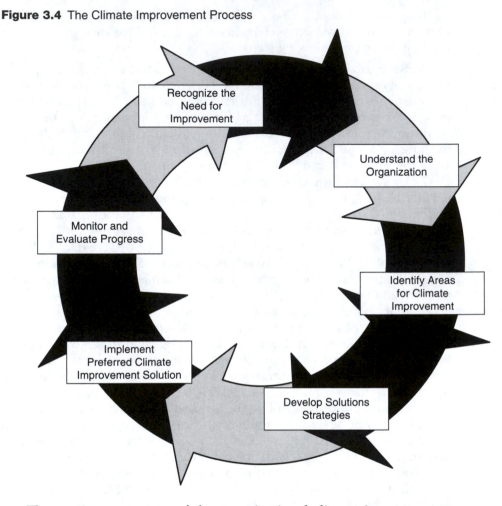

The continuous nature of the organizational climate improvement process is depicted in Figure 3.4.

Human Resources Responsibilities in the Improvement of School Climate

The concept that all school administrators are human resources administrators is emphasized throughout this text. As is true with every human resources process, the organizational climate improvement process is a shared responsibility among school leaders at all levels. These shared responsibilities are most important in the following areas:

1. **The Development of Shared Goals.** The important initial step in the improvement of school climate is the development of a cooperatively determined set of school goals. As was described in Chapter 2, goals are a reflection of the school

district beliefs, values, and traditions and provide a statement of the purposes and aims of the system. The significance of cooperative behavior as an important characteristic of school climate has been well established. And, human resources administrators must assume leadership roles in the development of the shared goals that express the school or school system's important and unique objectives.

2. **The Promotion of Positive Self-Image and High Expectations.** As was previously noted, effective schools, ones with healthy climates, hold high expectations for student and personnel performance. Levels of expectation should be such as to solicit the best performance that each teacher, student, or administrator has to offer. Viable goals provide a focus and give meaning to the people in the school. Such meaning is exemplified by the important work, personal motivations, and commitments of the school system's human element. These meanings, which are viewed as important to the system, comprise the system's self-image. A positive self-image serves as a foundational component of an open, healthy school climate. Human resources leadership must work to develop a positive self-image for the organization, one that reflects the beliefs and values of importance to its stakeholders.

3. **The Provision of Opportunities for Personal Growth and Development.** Healthy organizations understand that they will progress as people in the organization grow and develop. Schools with open, healthy climates tend to attract talented personnel who are motivated by opportunities to contribute and to be recognized for the important roles they play in the achievement of school purposes. Human resources administrators help to develop the school system's full potential by removing obstacles that inhibit growth opportunities, by assigning personnel in positions that allow human potential to be realized, and by establishing an environment that encourages creative activity. Such an environment enables personnel in the school to be innovative, to develop different, more efficient, and more effective methods of achieving school goals and objectives. New and creative ideas must have a chance for implementation as well as to fail under controlled conditions. Otherwise creative ideas will probably not be tried. Human resources leaders must work to provide opportunities for staff personnel to assume the major responsibility for their own personal growth. Such opportunities are more likely to be found and practiced in school systems that encourage the use of individual strengths, and in which staff personnel believe that their ideas and creations are welcome and respected.

4. **The Development of a Viable Set of Personnel Policies and Regulations.** Many persons believe that a school district's personnel policies and regulations are a direct reflection of how it values its human resources. And, since governance policies directly impact on the climate of the workplace, human resources administrators must assume a leadership role in the development of such policies.

School policies and regulations impact the school climate in numerous ways. Policies are the means of implementing the goals that direct programs and influence interpersonal relationships. Policies serve to release human potential by providing opportunities for discretionary action on the part of the professional staff. They also serve an important communication role in helping all persons understand the school system and its purposes. Previously we emphasized the need for the human resources administrator to be directly involved in the development and implementation of all school district personnel policies. Such a responsibility provides human resources administrators an opportunity to have a direct impact on the climate of the schools they serve.

5. **Problem-Solving Capacity.** Schools with healthy climates, like schools with less healthy ones, must face problems on a regular basis. However, a primary difference between the two is that schools with positive climates have an identifiable problem-solving capacity. Climate characteristics that facilitate the availability to meet and resolve problems include open channels of communication, effective suggestion systems, a research posture, and recruitment and selection policies that encourage the hiring of a diversified staff. Human resources personnel must clearly identify ways to increase the effectiveness of communication, educate others about these channels, and facilitate their use. Problem solving requires that the best ideas be heard and that they be considered on the basis of their merit as opposed to their origin. Open systems work diligently to increase the flow of ideas both vertically and horizontally within the system.

Human resources leadership necessitates the development of a research posture within the school system. Problem solving often depends on the development of new knowledge. The effective human resources administrator is a consumer, facilitator, and utilizer of good research, realizing that creative solutions are often the outcome of research efforts that have objectively examined viable alternatives.

6. **Implementation of Climate Improvement Plans.** Human resources administrators must assume leadership in the implementation of specific climate improvement projects. As the school or school system proceed through each step in the climate improvement process, such as one of those described here, the human resources administrator will be called upon to provide specific action. At some stages the role of the human resources administrator may be one of providing guidance or support. In others more direct participation is required. Whatever process the district employs, the implementation and maintenance of a healthy school climate must be seen not as a *product* of a process, but as a continuous search for individual and institutional improvement and change.

SUMMARY

The human resources function by definition has a primary responsibility in fostering an organizational climate that enhances goal achievement. Organizational climate is of paramount importance to the operation of schools and its personnel since it affects every process of the HR function. Early work in the area of organizational climate by Halpin, Croft, and others opened the field for numerous investigations on the topic. Their OCDQ spurred hundreds of empirical studies designed to ascertain the type of climate in various schools and led to major studies to determine the characteristics of various climate types, the effects of climate on people behavior and student achievement, and the extent to which various types of climate influence innovation and change in organizations.

Various field studies have led to the development of frameworks that serve as models for improving climate in schools. Such models hold strong implications for school leaders and especially the school principal. Virtually every study in the area of school climate links the type of climate to the leadership behavior of the school principal.

The improvement of school climate is viewed as the responsibility of all school personnel. Nevertheless, human resources units and administrators have specific responsibilities in the administration of organizational climate, including developing a set of shared goals, fostering a positive self-image for the school system, providing opportunities for personal growth and development, developing a viable set of personnel policies and procedures, working to ensure a problem-solving capacity within the system, and implementing climate improvement plans.

Discussion Questions

1. Consider the climate of the school or school system with which you are most familiar. What climate characteristics can you identify in each situation? After noting several climate characteristics for a particular school or system, attempt to label its climate type according to Halpin and Croft's or Hoy and Tarter's prototypes discussed in this chapter.
2. Discuss the approaches that today's schools are using to change their environments. Which factors tend to foster or inhibit positive climate in educational settings? Are these factors tied closely to monetary provisions or to factors more closely related to conditions of work, such as workload and administrative support?
3. This chapter strongly suggests that school principals have a major influence on school climate. Discuss the most important actions a principal can take to promote a healthy school climate. What changes in school board policies would be necessary to maximize the effectiveness of the role of the principal?

CASE STUDIES

—CASE 3.1—

Making the Worst of a Good Situation

Principal William McChesney was the newly selected principal for Antonio High School. He was following in the footsteps of Art Lown, who had served for 6 years. Under the leadership of Principal Lown, Antonio High School had gained a reputation as one of the best schools in the Southwest region. The teaching staff at Antonio was viewed as highly creative; three on the faculty had been named teacher of the year in the state. Turnover in the high school was

quite low, and Principal Lown was viewed as an administrator who was highly supportive and easily approachable. Faculty and parents regretted his departure to California to head a developing program for at-risk students.

During his first week at Antonio High School, Principal McChesney sent a questionnaire to faculty members asking for their input on what improvements might be made in the school's program and activities. The feedback from the faculty revealed their creativeness; many improvement ideas were presented. One member of the staff suggested that the principal's control over curriculum be lessened and delegated largely to faculty in the respective school departments. Another recommended a representative faculty advisory committee for the purpose of developing school policies and procedures in order to improve faculty involvement in participative management.

Principal McChesney did not act directly on any of the several recommendations received. At the second monthly meeting of the faculty, he commented, "I'll take your ideas under advisement. I must say, however, that I was under the impression that I was entering a school with a happier family than is apparently the case." One faculty raised her hand to speak, but McChesney indicated that he would be following up on this matter soon. Within the next 2 weeks, he talked with faculty members individually about their suggestions. For the most part, he probed the matter about their apparent "unhappiness" with the present school operation. The consensus of faculty responses implied that there were really no major problems at Antonio, but that any school had some room for improvements.

Over the next several weeks, directives from McChesney's office centered on plans for focusing on performance evaluations, his desire to sit in on department meetings dealing with program and activities within the school, and his intention to "flatten the organization" by eliminating the department heads by the end of the first semester. In addition, he sent a newly revised draft of recommended policies and procedures for the faculty's information.

By the close of the first semester, two department heads had asked to be relieved from the role, and three faculty members sent letters requesting transfers to other schools. For the first time in the school's history, Antonio students held a "sit-in" in the school cafeteria; their protest focused on the lack of opportunity for input into the decision-making process. Both student and teacher absenteeism increased significantly as well.

As Principal McChesney sat in his office late one Friday afternoon, he contemplated the school situation with some bewilderment. "How did this situation change in so short a time?" he thought to himself. "What should I do now?"

Questions

1. In view of the somewhat limited information in this case, present your thoughts as to what seems to be happening at Antonio High School.
2. At this point in time, what positive steps might be taken by Principal McChesney to reverse current climate trends? Do you believe that such a reversal is possible in this setting? Why or why not?
3. Discuss the situation in which a new school administrator moves into a school. Are there recommended procedures for entering such a new situation? Name two or more specific actions or behaviors that new administrators would be wise to consider upon moving into a new leadership position.

—CASE 3.2

What's Really Important Around Here?

Virginia Royce was in her second year of teaching at College View High School. Her performance ratings for year one were rated "very good" in all categories. She had gained the reputation as one of the school's most promising new teachers. At the close of school on a Friday in October, Mrs. Royce went to the principal's office and asked if Mr. Henson, the principal, was available. The secretary answered in the positive and indicated that she was certain that he could visit with her.

"Come in, Mrs. Royce," directed Principal Henson. "What's on your mind on this late Friday afternoon?" "Something has been troubling me for several weeks," answered Mrs. Royce. "So far this semester six football players have been absent from my English class for the last period of the day on three occasions, and on two occasions they were absent for the full afternoon to play in out-of-town games, so they had to miss two other teachers' classes as well on those days. Pep rallies generally are held the last class period of the day before games; it all adds up to the question of, What's really important around here?"

Questions

1. Assume the role of Principal Henson. How might you answer Mrs. Royce?

2. Is it sufficient to respond that both subject-matter classes and extracurricular activities are important at College View High School in your opinion? What evidence might you present to support your statement?

3. How should the principal address the problem of absences by student athletes?

REFERENCES

Aon Consulting. (1998). *America @ Work*. Chicago, IL: Aon Consulting Worldwide, Inc.

Barnes, K. M. (1994). *The organizational health of middle schools, trust and decision participation*. Unpublished doctoral dissertation, Rutgers University, New Brunswick, NJ.

Barth, R. S. (1990). *Improving schools from within*. San Francisco, CA: Jossey-Bass.

Bobbett, G. C., & French, R. L. (1992). *Evaluation of climate in 'good' high schools in Tennessee, Kentucky, and North Carolina*. A paper presented at the annual meeting of the Southern Regional Council on Educational Administration, Atlanta, GA.

Borger, J., Lo, C., Oh, S., & Walberg, H. J. (1985). Effective schools: A quantitative synthesis of constructs. *Journal of Classroom Interaction, 20*(2), 12–17.

Bulach, C. R., & Malone, B. (1994). The relationship of school climate to the implementation of school reform. *ERS Spectrum, 12*(4), 3–8.

Butler, E. D., & Albery, M. J. (1991). *Tennessee school climate inventory: A resource manual*. Memphis, TN: Memphis State University. The Center for Research in Educational Policy.

Christian, C. F. (1972). *Organizational climate of elementary schools and the introduction and utilization of innovative educational practices*. Unpublished doctoral dissertation, University of Nebraska, Lincoln, NE.

Farrar, E., & Flakus-Mosqueda, P. (1986). State sponsored schoolwide improvement programs: What's going on in the schools? *Phi Delta Kappan, 67*, 586–589.

Follett, M. P. (1924). *Creative experience*. New York: Longman.

Goddard, R. D., Sweetland, S. R., & Hoy, W. K. (2000) Academic emphasis of urban elementary schools and student achievement in reading and mathematics: A multinational analysis. *Educational Administration Quarterly, 36*, 683–702.

Halpin, A. W., & Croft, D. R. (1962). *The organizational climate of schools*. Contract SAE 543–8639. U.S. Office of Education, Research Project.

Herzberg, F., Manser, B., & Snyderman, B. (1959). *The motivation to work*. New York: Wiley.

Hopkins, W., & Crain, K. (1985). *School climates: The key to an effective school*. Paper presented at the annual meeting of the National Association of Secondary School Principals, New Orleans, LA.

Hoy, W. K., & Clover, S. I. R. (1986). Elementary school climate: A revision of the OCDQ. *Educational Administration Quarterly, 22*, 93–110.

Hoy, W. K., & Feldman, J. A. (1987). Organizational health: The concept and its measure. *Journal of Research and Development in Education, 20*, 30–38.

Hoy, W. K., & Hannum, J. W. (1997). Middle school climate: An empirical assessment of organizational health and student achievement. *Educational Administration Quarterly, 33*, 290–311.

Hoy, W. K., & Miskel, C. G. (2005). *Educational administration: Theory, research & practice* (7th ed.). New York: McGraw-Hill.

Hoy, W. K., & Sabo, D. (1998). *Quality middle schools: Open and healthy*. Thousand Oaks, CA: Corwin Press.

Hoy, W. K., & Tarter, C. J. (1997). *Healthy schools: A handbook for change* (Elementary and Middle School Edition). Thousand Oaks, CA: Corwin Press, Inc.

Johnson, B., & Stevens, J. J. (2006). Student achievement and elementary teachers' perceptions of school climate. *Learning Environment Research, 9*.

Johnson, W. L., Johnson, A. M., Gott, R., & Zimmerman, K. (1997). Assessing the validity of scores on the Charles F. Kettering Scale for the junior high school. *Psychological Measurement, 57*, 858–869.

Kelley, E. A., Glover, J. A., Keefe, J. W., Halderson, C., Sorenson, C., & Speth, C. (1986). *school climate survey (Modified)*. Reston, VA: National Association of Secondary School Principals.

Kottkamp, R. B., Mulhern, J. A., & Hoy, W. K. (1987). Secondary school climate: A revision of the OCDQ. *Educational Administration Quarterly, 23*, 32–48.

Kreitner. R. (2001). *Management* (8th ed.). Boston: Houghton Mifflin.

Lockwood, N. R. (2003). Work/life balance: Challenges and solutions. *SHRM 2003 Research Quarterly.* Retrieved 1/2/2007 from http://www.shrm.org

Newman, F. M., & Associates. (1996). *Authentic instruction: Restructuring schools for intellectual quality.* San Francisco, CA: Jossey-Bass.

Norton, M. S., Webb, L. D., Dlugosh, L. L., & Sybouts, W. (1996). *The school superintendency: New responsibilities, new leadership.* Boston: Allyn & Bacon.

Ortiz, J. P., & Arnborg, L. (2005). Making high performance last: Reflections on involvement, culture, and power in organizations. *Performance Improvement, 44*(6), 31–37.

Owens, R. G., & Valesky, T. C. (2007). *Organizational behavior in education: Instructional leadership and school reform* (9th ed.). San Francisco: Allyn & Bacon.

Paredes, V., & Frazer, L. (1992). *School climate in Austin Independent School District.* Austin, TX: Independent School District, Office of Research and Evaluation.

Phi Delta Kappa. (1973). *School climate improvement: A challenge to the school administrator.* Bloomington, IN: Author.

Phillips, M. (1997). What makes schools effective? A comparison of the relationships of communitarian climate and academic climate to mathematics achievement and attendance during middle schools. *American Educational Research Journal, 34*, 633–662.

Proctor, C. P. (1984). Teacher expectations: A model for school improvement. *Elementary School Journal, 84*, 469–481.

Reiss, F., & Hoy, W. K. (1998). Faculty loyalty: An important but neglected concept in the study of schools. *Journal of School Leadership, 8*, 4–21.

Rentoul, A. J., & Fraser, B. J. (1983). Development of a school-level environmental questionnaire. *The Journal of Educational Administration, 21*(1), 21–39.

Rosenholtz, S. J. (1989). *Teachers' workplace: The social organization of schools.* New York: Longman.

Sackney., L. (1988). *Enhancing school learning climate: Theory, research and practive.* SSTA Research Centre Report #180. Sackatoon, Saskatchewan: School Trustees Association Research Centre.

Schein, E. H. (1997). *Organizational culture and leadership.* San Francisco: Jossey-Bass.

Sergiovanni, T. J., & Starratt, R. J. (2007). *Supervision: A redefinition* (8th ed.). Boston: McGraw-Hill.

Shouse, R. C. (1998). Restructuring's impact on school achievement: Contrasts by school urbanizity. *Educational Administration Quarterly, 34*, 677–699.

Short, P. M. & Greer, J. T. (1997) *Leadership in empowered schools: Themes from innovative efforts.* Upper Saddle River, NJ: Merrill.

Short, P. M., & Greer, J. T. (1997). *Leadership in empowered schools: Themes from innovative efforts.* Columbus, OH: Merrill.

Stern, G. G. (1964). *High school characteristics index.* Syracuse, NY: Psychological Research Center, Syracuse University.

Stevens, M. P. (1990). School climate and staff development: Keys to school reform. *NASSP Bulletin, 74*, 66–70.

Smith, P. A., Hoy, W. K., & Sweetland, S. R. (2001). Organizational health of high schools and dimensions of faculty trust. *Journal of School Leadership, 11*, 135–51.

Sweeney, J. (1992). School climate: The key to excellence. *NASSP Bulletin, 76*, 69–73.

Tarter, C. J., & Hoy, W. K. (1988). The context of trust: Teachers and the principal. *High School Journal, 72*, 17–22.

Tarter, C. J., Hoy, W. L., & Kottkamp, R. (1990). School climate and organizational committment. *Journal of Research and Development in Education, 23*, 236–243.

Tarter, C. J., Sabo, D., & Hoy, W. K. (1995). Multiple school climate, faculty trust and effectiveness: A path analysis. *Journal of Research and Development in Education, 29*, 41–49.

Taylor, D. L., & Tashakkori, A. (1994). *Predicting teachers' sense of efficacy and job satisfaction using school climate and participatory decision making.* Paper presented at the annual meeting of the Southwest Educational Research Association, San Antonio, TX.

Walberg, H. J., & Genova, W. J. (1982). Staff, school and workshop influences on knowledge use in educational improvement efforts. *Journal of Educational Research, 76*(2), 69–80.

Winter, J. S., & Sweeney, J. (1994). Improving school climate: Administrators are the key. *NASSP Bulletin, 73*, 65–69.

PART III

Specific Processes in the Human Resources Domain

CHAPTER 4

Recruitment

LEARNING OBJECTIVES

After reading this chapter, you will be able to:

- Differentiate between a job analysis and a job description.
- List and describe the major recruitment sources/methods used by school districts.
- Describe the major efforts being made to increase the supply of new teachers.
- Discuss the need for and efforts to recruit for diversity.
- Describe the impact of the fiscal resources of the district on the recruitment process.
- Identify the major legal constraints placed on school districts in the recruitment process.
- List the major approaches that may be used to evaluate the recruitment process.

School districts across the nation are facing an unprecedented demand for teachers and administrators at all levels. According to the American Association of Administrators, retirements will create 1,000 superintendent vacancies each year for the next decade (Esparo & Rader, 2001). And, more than half of the nation's 13,000 principals are expected to retire in the next 5 years (Peterson & Kelley, 2001). Even more staggering are the projections that over two million teachers are needed in the next decade (Budig, 2006). This demand has been created by the higher enrollments created by the Baby Boom Echo, the aging teacher population [22% expect to retire by 2010 (National Center for Educational Information, 2005)], the high attrition rate among new teachers [50% of teachers leave the profession within 5 years (Budig, 2006)], and competition from business and industry.

Intercity and rural districts in particular are expected to be hard hit by shortages. The U.S. Department of Education estimates that "hard-to-staff" schools in high-poverty urban and rural districts will require 700,000 new teachers in the next decade (Johnson, 2005). While there is some evidence that, overall, the teacher supply problem is more one of distribution than absolute numbers, the reality is that every year school districts across the country begin the school year without a full-time, fully certified teacher in every classroom.

The recruitment system charged to meet the need for teachers, administrators, and other personnel should be one that is *effective* in terms of recruiting the best candidates, *efficient* in terms of using established, cost-effective procedures, and *fair* in terms of recruiting in a nondiscriminatory fashion (Kempton, 1995). Because recruitment decisions can be for life, the effectiveness of the recruitment program is of great importance. The costs of the recruitment program can be substantial. It has been estimated that the cost of a bad hire is 1.5 times the annual salary for an entry-level employee and over 10 times the annual salary for a senior-level administrator (Davila & Kursmark, 2005). Moreover, the psychological costs to the system in terms of lowered employee morale and productivity and the impact on students in the classroom resulting from a bad hire can exceed the financial cost. And, both can increase the longer it takes to resolve the problem.

The recruitment process is a very visible process. It is one way those external to the district make judgments about the district. The recruitment practices of the district reflect the culture and values of the district. Everything, from the style of the advertising to how the interview is conducted and how promptly and professionally the personnel office responds to applicants communicates what the district expects of these employees and how it treats its employees. In this chapter the steps in the recruitment process—establishment of goals, assessment of needs, job analysis, preparation of the job description, recruitment using internal and/or external recruitment sources, and establishment of the applicant pool—are reviewed. Special attention is given to a discussion of strategies that may be used to increase diversity in the applicant pool and to recruit for hard-to-staff schools. This is followed by a discussion of the fiscal and legal constraints on recruitment. The chapter ends with a section on how to evaluate the effectiveness of the recruitment process.

THE RECRUITMENT PROCESS

The recruitment process involves a number of steps (see Figure 4.1). It begins with the establishment of goals for the recruitment program and the assessment of need. Next is the development of the job analysis and the preparation of the job description. The district may then choose from a variety of recruitment sources to recruit internally and/or externally. The end result is a pool of qualified applicants.

Establishment of Goals

It is important that each year the district review and set short-term and long-term goals for the recruitment process. The goals may address shortages created by the growth or reorganization of the district or the retirement, termination, or transfer of employees. In other cases, goals may address issues related to quality and the need to hire persons with advanced technological skills. The highly qualified requirement of NCLB has made the recruitment and retention of teachers a goal of most school districts nationally. Many districts may have goals related to increasing the diversity of the workforce. The type of goal will be a determining factor in the decision making regarding strategies. For example, a long-term goal to increase diversity might involve a paraeducator "grow your own" program for minority teacher aides,

Figure 4.1 The Recruitment Process

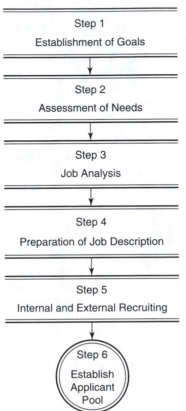

whereas a short-term goal to increase diversity might involve targeted recruiting at traditional minority universities.

Assessment of Needs

Before any action is taken to recruit for a vacant position, an assessment of need must be performed. Perhaps the position is no longer needed, or the position may not be needed as it currently exists. Or, perhaps someone can be laterally transferred from within the district. For example, a third-grade teacher from a school with declining enrollment can be transferred to the same position at a school with growing enrollment. (However, if the move constitutes a promotion for the transferee, then a selection process is required that provides equal employment opportunity to all potential applicants.) As was discussed in Chapter 2, the assessment of need involves an analysis of information and data relative to the staffing or destaffing needs of all schools and other units of the school system, the system's strategic objectives, enrollment forecasts, professional staff mix, and supply-demand data relative to retirements and attrition rates. It will consider "how diverse the teaching staff should be, define what kinds of skills and knowledge new teachers should possess, and specify which grade levels, subject areas, and school buildings are likely to have the most need" (NEA, 2003, p. 4).

It is important that the needs assessment not just address the here and now. A strategic view of recruitment takes a long-term view of what the district wants to look like in 5, 10, or 20 years from now, analyzing the difference between where you are and where you want to be, determining what skills will be necessary to get you there, and then recruiting for those exact skills (Canada, 2001). Use of a continually updated database can provide the information on vacancies, job descriptions, and personnel qualifications that is needed to determine the extent of the "gap." A number of computer programs are also available to provide data (e.g., enrollment programs, retirement projections, etc.) central to projecting personnel needs.

Job Analysis

Once it has been determined that a need exists, the next appropriate step is to consider fully (or reconsider) the knowledge, skills, abilities, and other characteristics (KSAOs) that are needed to perform the duties and responsibilities of the position. This task is referred to as **job analysis**. The job analysis provides information important to many human resources functions:

> A comprehensive, high-quality job analysis provides descriptive (i.e., how a job is done), prescriptive (i.e., how a job should be done), and predictive (i.e., how a job will be done) information about the critical tasks of a job and the KSAOs required to perform these tasks. This information allows HR professionals to engage in competent HR practices. For instance, an HR professional is able to establish legally defensible promotion criteria if required KSAOs for the target position are identified from a well-planned and well-documented job analysis. HR programs developed without an analysis of critical tasks and KSAOs are like skyscrapers built without a solid foundation. (Chen, Carsten, & Krauss, 2003, p. 28)

If the job to be filled is a replacement for an existing or former staff member, then a considerable amount of information likely already exists about the job. If, however, the job is new, the data about the job must be obtained from scratch. Chapter 12 contains a detailed description of the methods used to obtain job analysis data. Whether for a replacement position or a new position, the job analysis should be prepared to meet the following objectives:

- To clarify the details of the position for which recruits are to be sought.
- To provide sufficient detail for the preparation of the job description.
- To provide a base of information from which performance appraisal criteria can be developed.
- To identify where the job fits into the current organizational structure and its relationship to other jobs. (Bolton, 1997, p. 36)

Figure 4.2 provides an outline for a job analysis for a professional position [adapted from Bolton's (1970) work on teacher selection], while Figure 4.3 presents a completed position analysis for a second-grade teacher following this outline.

Figure 4.2 Position Analysis Outline

I. Strategic Nature of the Position
   A. Mission of the school system
      1. Strategic objectives of the school system
   B. Strategic objectives of the subunit
   C. Organizational structure of the subunit
   D. Expectations
      1. At the work site
      2. In relation to other system employees
      3. In relation to members of the subunit
      4. In relation to outside groups, agencies, or individuals
II. Changing Aspects of the Position
   A. At the beginning of the assignment
   B. Anticipated changes
III. Behaviors
   A. At the work site
   B. In relation to other system employees
   C. In relation to outside groups, agencies, and individuals
IV. Screening and Selection Criteria
   A. Interpersonal skills
   B. Oral communication skills
   C. Knowledge and skills base

Preparation of Job Description

Job analysis provides the basis for the next step in the recruitment process, the preparation of the **job description**. The job description not only describes the position and the duties and responsibilities associated with it, but provides information about the school and the school district in which the vacancy exists. The job description serves as an important resource for (1) "describing the job (either verbally by recruiters and interviews or in written advertisements) to potential candidates; (2) guiding newly hired employees in what they are specifically expected to do; and (3) providing a point of comparison in appraising whether the actual activities of a job incumbent align with the stated duties" (De Censo & Robbins, 1996, p. 142). Job descriptions also help to determine compensation, to provide a basis for performance reviews, and to identify the essential functions of the job to ensure compliance with the Americans With Disabilities Act (see discussion in Chapter 12). And, job descriptions play an important role in career development. By providing clear expectations and responsibilities of each position, job descriptions give employees a vision of the opportunities of advancement. Job descriptions provide supervisors the information they need to distinguish between, for example, entry and intermediate level, so they can discuss with employees what they need to do to move up and employees can be prepared for other positions that might become available (Joinson, 2001).

A job description will typically include the following sections:

1. **Heading.** A summary of the open position—the job title, whom the position reports to, job titles reporting to the position, division or

Figure 4.3 Position Analysis for Second-Grade Teacher

I. *Strategic Nature of the Position*

 A. *Mission of the School System*

 The Pine Meadows School System is committed to excellence in elementary and secondary school education. We commit ourselves to working cooperatively with parents and the community to facilitate the growth of our students intellectually, emotionally, socially, and physically, and to create an awareness of our multicultural society. To accomplish this, we will employ the best qualified professional and support personnel available, use innovative materials and technologies, exploit creative methodologies, and enlist community resources.

 1. *Strategic Objectives of School System*
 The mean scores on the State Basic Skills Test (SBST) for elementary students in reading and mathematics will increase to 90% by 2009.
 Computer labs will be installed in all elementary schools by 2009.
 By the end of the 2009 school year, 95% of all seventh-grade students will demonstrate computer skills on a systemwide test.

 B. *Strategic Objectives of the School*

 1. The mean test scores by grade level for each reading subtest of the State Basic Skills Test will increase to 90% by 2009.
 2. The mean test scores by grade level for each mathematics subtest of the State Basic Skills Test will increase to 90% by 2009.
 3. All teachers of reading and mathematics will be able to demonstrate through classroom instruction and the presentation of lesson guides methods for technology integration into their teaching by 2009.

 C. *Organizational Structure of School*

 The grade structure is K–7. Classes are self-contained and are set up heterogeneously. Students are taught material to achieve grade-level objectives. Instruction is supplemented with special remedial reading and mathematics instruction provided by specialists in each area. Leadership staff include the principal, an instructional lead teacher, and a lead teacher for student services. The school provides special classes for four categories of special education. Also, programs for gifted education and speech are provided.

 D. *Expectations*

 1. *At the Work Site*
 The teacher is expected to engage in cooperative planning with other teachers by providing expertise and leadership in mathematics instruction and the integration of technology into classroom instruction in mathematics.

 2. *In Relation to Other System Employees*
 The teacher is expected to work with the system's elementary school coordinator to develop methods for integrating technology into the teaching of elementary school mathematics.

 3. *In Relation to Members of the School*
 The teacher is expected to work cooperatively with all members of the staff on schoolwide committees. Specifically, the teacher will be expected to guide a self-study subcommittee in mathematics that will be convened next year.

 4. *In Relation to Outside Groups, Agencies, and Individuals*
 The teacher is expected to work with the PTA and be a member of professional associations at the state and national levels.

Continued

Figure 4.3 (Continued)

II. *Changing Aspects of the Position*

A. *At the Beginning of the Assignment*

Most teachers will be involved in training for the educational use of the Internet and may call upon this teacher for assistance.

B. *Anticipated Changes*

The Writing Express Program (WEP) will be implemented in the second-year classes. The teacher will be required to participate in an in-service program during the first semester of the school year to be prepared to implement WEP at the beginning of the second semester.

III. *Behaviors*

A. *At the Work Site*

Flexible, cooperative, tactful, helpful, sensitive, empathetic

B. *In Relation to Other System Employees*

Cooperative, willing to assume extra responsibilities, high energy

C. *In Relation to Outside Groups, Agencies, and Individuals*

Professionalism, strong verbal facility and oral communication, enthusiasm

IV. *Screening and Selection Criteria*

A. *Interpersonal Skills*

Shows caring for others; open to the ideas and feelings of others; earnestly seeks candor and openness; maintains a cool and rational approach on a constant basis throughout conflict situations.
Behavioral indicators: empathetic, caring, rational, poised, tactful, flexible, cooperative, helpful, sensitive.

B. *Oral Communication Skills*

Ideas are well organized and clearly presented; effective eye contact; strong voice projection and articulation; easy to understand.
Behavioral indicators: clear enunciation, expressive, poised, self-confident, projects voice, correct grammar and usage, free of distracting mannerisms, effective nonverbal messages.

C. *Knowledge and Skills Base*

General knowledge of elementary curriculum and teaching with specialized knowledge in educational technology.
Behavioral indicators: diagnostic reading skills, knowledge of effective grouping methods, computer operations and maintenance skills, including the educational use of the Internet and the World Wide Web.

department name, geographic location, salary grade, employment status, travel requirements, and date.

2. **Position purpose.** A few sentences describing the objective of the position, major accomplishments, and why the position exists.

3. **Duties and responsibilities.** A list of essential job functions describing what has to be done to achieve the desired results.

4. **Qualifications.** A description of the minimum requirements for performing the essential functions. This section might include required education and experience, special skills, and certifications.

5. **Other.** Some job descriptions include other categories such as the physical requirements of a job, other departments that this employee will be expected to work with, and measurable performance standards. (Davila & Kursmark, 2005, p. 29)

For many classified positions, the job description will also include

- Descriptions of tools and equipment used
- Working conditions and physical environment, including any biological or physical hazards

For many positions, job descriptions may already be written. However, even if job descriptions do exist, they should be reviewed to ensure they are still valid in terms of accurately and completely describing the job to be done and the context in which it is performed. Job descriptions should also be reviewed whenever a reorganizing, downsizing, or restructuring of the unit/department occurs. "The more accurate and current the job description, the better the chance of finding the right person for the position" (Smith, 1997/1998, p. 18). If the position is a new one, job descriptions will need to be prepared. The process for preparing job descriptions typically involves the following steps:

1. Superintendent recommends all or specified positions to be covered by written descriptions.
2. Board approves job descriptions development program.
3. Coordinator assumes overall responsibility for implementation of program.
4. Supervisors and jobholders draft job descriptions.
5. Coordinator reviews draft descriptions in terms of adequacy for meeting management goals and objectives.
6. Job description writer edits descriptions for style and format and returns clean copies to coordinator for routing to supervisors.
7. Supervisors and jobholders review descriptions for currency and accuracy.
8. Superintendent approves final descriptions.
9. Coordinator or job description writer prepares manual of approved descriptions.
10. Board receives copy of job descriptions manual for informational purposes. (National School Boards Association, 1996, p. 157)

Ultimately a procedure should be developed to ensure that each staff member receives a copy of the job description that applies to his or her position (Lawrence & Vachon, 1997).

Figure 4.4 provides a job description for the position of speech and hearing therapist.

A national survey of school districts relative to the development and use of job descriptions found that, overall, the human resources administrator is the person most often responsible for the preparation of job descriptions. The survey also found that the human resources administrator frequently has the primary responsibility of updating job descriptions, and that this role was more significant in larger districts than smaller districts. In smaller districts the superintendent had the more significant role

Figure 4.4 Sample Job Description

TITLE: Speech and Hearing Therapist

QUALIFICATIONS:

1. [Certificate, license, or other legal credential required.]
2. [Degree(s) required and area of major study.]
3. [Kind and amount of prior job experience required.]
4. Such alternatives to the above qualifications as the Board may find appropriate and acceptable.

REPORTS TO:

[Person designated by the Board or the superintendent.]

JOB GOAL:

To help reduce or eliminate speech and hearing impediments that interfere with the individual student's ability to derive full benefit from the district's educational program.

PERFORMANCE RESPONSIBILITIES:

1. Serves as a resource to school staff members in the development of a balanced program for oral communication and speech improvement.
2. Provides a therapeutic program to meet individual needs of speech and hearing handicapped children.
3. Assists and guides teachers in observing, describing, and referring suspected and identified speech and language impairments.
4. Provides a thorough assessment and diagnosis of speech, voice, hearing, and language impairments.
5. Provides screening to identify speech handicapped children at regular intervals and at specified levels.
6. Assists in proper referrals of individuals to agencies and specialists in the community as appropriate.
7. Provides appropriate individualized programs of therapy to meet individual students' needs and correct existing speech or language handicaps.

Source: Job Description: Speech and Hearing Therapist, *The School Personnel Management System*, National School Board Association (Alexandria, VA), 1996: pp. 445–446. Reprinted with permission.

in both preparing and updating job descriptions. Similarly, the involvement of the personnel administrator in approving job descriptions increased with school district size. In 56% of responding districts the board of education had final authority for approving changes in job descriptions. The superintendent had final authority in 26%, and the human resources administrator in 11% [Educational Research Service (ERS), 1994].

According to the same survey (ERS, 1994), the positions for which job descriptions were most frequently used were principals (97%); directors, managers, coordinators, and supervisors (93%); clerical personnel (92%); superintendents (90%); and custodians and teacher aides (88%). The positions for which job descriptions were least frequently used were school nurses (72%) and bus drivers (66%). And, the most frequently revised category of job description was central office administrator.

Internal and External Recruiting

Once the school district has determined that a position needs to be filled and has developed a job description for the position, the decision must be made about the sources and strategies to be used to generate the pool of qualified candidates necessary to provide the needed employee(s). Several factors will influence this decision. The first is whether the need is in the short term, long term, or ongoing. If the need is anticipated to be long term and/or ongoing, in addition to recruiting from existing candidate pools, the district may engage in one or more of the activities designed to develop sources of applicants discussed in the following section.

The second factor in deciding what sources and strategies to use is the actual number of potential applicants that will need to be contacted in order to obtain an applicant pool of the desired size. That is, depending on the position, in today's competitive market, it may be necessary to reach hundreds, if not thousands, of potential applicants in order to obtain a pool of several dozen qualified applicants. Past experience should provide some guidance in determining how extensive the recruitment effort must be (Harvey & Bowin, 1996).

A third factor that will influence the choice of recruitment methods and sources is the type of job. Some sources are more effective than others for filling certain types of jobs. For example, an ad in the *APA Monitor*, a publication of the American Psychological Association, is more likely to be read by a potential school psychologist applicant than a potential applicant for a superintendency.

A fourth factor that will impact on the recruitment methods and sources used is cost. As previously indicated, recruitment can be a costly activity. Needless to say, this cost goes up as the number of advertisements placed increases, as the number and types of media used increase, as the circulation and prestige of the sources increases, as the number of recruitment trips increases, as the advertising materials become more numerous and professionally produced, as the number of mailings increases, and as the amount of internal and external staff time devoted to the effort increases.

Yet another factor influencing the decision relative to recruitment methods and sources is whether the search will be internal or external. The philosophy of some districts is that to the extent possible internal recruiting should be used for positions beyond entry level. **Internal recruitment** has not only the obvious savings of cost associated with external recruitment, but also serves as an important source of employee motivation. Internal recruitment and promotion improve morale among current employees and demonstrate to employees that the district recognizes and rewards effort and competence and that there are opportunities to advance professionally without leaving the district. Additional advantages of internal recruiting are that it is easier to evaluate the strengths and weaknesses of current employees than to evaluate other candidates based on their résumés and interviews (Warren, Gorham, & Lamont, 2000–2001). Hiring from within also reduces the time required for the new employee to become oriented to the job and rise to full productivity. And, perhaps most important, no matter how thorough and careful the recruitment and selection process may be, any external candidate is still an unknown quantity, versus the internal applicant who is a proven entity (Herman, 1994).

Some of the disadvantages of internal recruiting are associated with the limiting of candidate choices. Hiring from within may also limit the introduction of new ideas and perspectives, and can contribute to stagnation or complacency (Warren et al., 2000–2001). Another disadvantage of internal recruitment is that, unless it is handled very carefully, openly, and fairly, jealousies and hostilities can be engendered in those who do not receive the job (Jordan, 1997). And, perhaps the biggest negative associated with hiring from within is that, while one position may become filled, the district will still be left with one unfilled position.

Various recruitment sources and methods are available to school districts. If the district limits itself to informal, primarily internal recruitment, beyond internal job posting to existing employees, its primary sources are retired, previous and part-time employees, and employee referrals. If recruitment is to be a more formal process of **external recruitment**, the district has available to it media advertising, employment agencies, educational institutions, computerized data banks and electronic bulletin boards, and professional organizations and unions. Although not the result of any recruitment effort, another source of applicants is unsolicited applications. Each of these sources is discussed in the following sections.

Retired Employees. Early retirees can be recruited to provide an immediate source of expert knowledge in times of staff shortage or in times of need for emergency or short-term hires. One strategy for enticing retired teachers back that has become common in recent years is to allow them to return to work and retain their full retirement benefits. In fact, all 50 states now allow teachers to return to work full time (34 states) or part time without losing benefits (Jacobson, 2006). Nevada has gone a step further in encouraging retirees to return to the classroom and added additional pay categories to the salary schedule for teachers who have already reached the ceiling ("Nevada balances teacher experience, recruitment," 2006). In some states neither the returning teacher nor the employer is required to contribute to the teacher retirement system, resulting in the district not only gaining an experienced teacher, but saving money. In most states that do allow retired teachers to return to work and keep their benefits, the district must meet certain conditions such as proving that a shortage of qualified teachers in the district does exist (Jacobson, 2006).

Another strategy for recruiting retired employees is **job sharing**. Job sharing of teaching positions involves two teachers each working a 19-hour week to fill one teaching position (Grant, 2001). Again, this provides a savings to the district since no benefits are provided.

Previous and Part-Time Employees. Previous and part-time employees can be an important, but often overlooked, source for recruitment. In fact, former teachers reentering teaching after a break in their teaching career make up 23% of all newly hired public school teachers (Provasnik & Dorfman, 2005).

Part-time employees, including substitute teachers, also represent a very important recruitment source. In fact, among newly hired teachers, 28% of reentrants and 36% of all delayed entrants came from the ranks of substitute teachers (U.S. Department of Education, 2000). Part-time and substitute teachers are considered good recruitment sources for many of the same reasons as are former employees: they are known entities and have had a realistic preview of the job. However, while "encouraging experienced substitute teachers to teach full time is a good idea, some districts find that this practice adds to a growing substitute teacher shortage" (RNT, 2000, p. 20).

Employee Referrals. Present employees are an important and efficient recruitment source for any organization. Numerous studies on recruitment have shown that employees hired as a result of a referral from a current employee typically are higher quality and stay with the organization longer than those who come from other sources (Morehart, 2001). Other benefits of employee referrals (ER) include the fact that they

- Are among the most cost-effective methods for finding qualified candidates.
- Offer another resource for accomplishing recruitment goals.
- Help to reduce the overall cost per hire.
- Can function as team-building devices.
- Provide candidates who are "pre-screened" for cultural fit.
- Make employees at all levels feel they are part of the recruiting process by helping them to contribute to the organization and making them aware of what direction leadership is taking.
- Give current employees a first glance at career advancement opportunities.
- Provide new ER hires with a built-in network and support system on their first day on the job.
- Bring in quality candidates. Most employees won't refer those whose performance would have a negative impact on the operation. (Morehart, 2001, p. 3)

Because of the many advantages associated with hires from employee referrals, districts would be well advised to institute a formal ER program. Such a program would include instituting a reward or incentive program for hires, acknowledging the referral and expressing appreciation, informing the candidate of his or her referral and inviting an application, and publishing the results of the program in appropriate in-house publications and communications (Morehart, 2001).

While most districts encourage employee referrals, almost all districts have policies against nepotism, the hiring or giving of preferential treatment to relatives. Most often these policies bar the person(s) responsible for the hiring decision, or the person who will be supervising the new employee, from being a relative of the new employee. And, a note of warning: by relying on employee referrals, the district must be alert to the possibility of "inbreeding" and violation of Equal Employment Opportunity Commission (EEOC) regulations. Since employees and their referrals will likely be of similar race, nationality, or religion, districts that rely heavily on employee referrals may have a very homogeneous workforce (Kulik, 2004).

Media Advertisements. Advertising, in particular, classified advertising, is a major recruitment tool for most school districts and is often the only source used to fill classified vacancies. Advertising may be through radio, television, bulletins, professional journals, trade publications, newspapers, or even movie theaters. Mass media advertising has the advantage of reaching the largest possible audience. At the same time, aside from its cost, this is its principal limitation. Advertising in any of the mass media results in unpredictable responses. Selectivity may be achieved by careful consideration of where the ad is placed, which in turn is largely determined by the type of job and the labor supply. That is, while ads for unskilled or semiskilled positions could appropriately be placed in the help wanted section of the local newspaper, ads seeking persons with higher-level skills or persons in short supply would be better placed in professional journals, trade or union publications, or newspapers or journals directed toward specific audiences. In general, several factors must be considered when placing recruitment advertising:

- The number and location of potential respondents. For instance, it is likely that unskilled staff will be recruited mainly from a local pool of labor, while the recruitment of senior staff may be from a national . . . pool. This will have implications not only for the amount to be spent on advertising, but also where that advertising will be placed.
- The cost of the advertising must also be considered. It is likely (but not always the case) that the more spent on advertising, the greater the response to that advertising will be. To be efficient, recruitment advertising must aim to attract a satisfactory level and standard of response but at minimum cost.
- The frequency with which the organization wishes to advertise the position must also be considered. If daily or weekly magazines or papers are used, it will be possible to advertise a position several times. If a monthly journal is selected, then it is probable that the position will be advertised only once. (Bolton, 1997, p. 52)

Print Media. The primary avenues for print media advertising are newspapers, association newsletters, trade magazines, and professional journals. Ads placed in newspapers of general circulation, including the so-called "free shoppers," have the advantage of immediacy, a large circulation, a targeted geographic market, and low cost-per-hire but have the disadvantage of eliciting applications from any unqualified applicants. Ads in the special audience publications typically attract candidates with better qualifications but have the disadvantage of a long lag time (Warren et al., 2001). Ads in local newspapers can be effective in securing many of the candidates of support personnel, while trade newsletters and magazines are more effective in recruiting professional candidates from a national or regional pool (Harris & Lasson, 2003).

Wherever the print ad is placed, it is important to attend to certain design considerations: size, amount of white space, type/fonts, wording, and so forth. Design experts state that the "first rule of advertising is to be 'you' oriented rather than 'me' oriented. Think about what the ideal prospect is going to want from a job, and emphasize how the opening can fulfill this person's needs and wishes. Ads have more appeal when they state what the employer has to offer . . . before mentioning what the company needs" (Warren et al., 2000–2001, p. 111:1705). For example, rural and small districts have found that emphasizing the benefits of working in a small district (e.g., small class size, fewer behavioral problems, higher job satisfaction) improves their recruitment efforts (Lemke, 1995).

At a minimum, a good recruitment advertisement should include the following:

- The name of the school district
- A descriptive title of the job
- Some statement about the district that tells why it is a good place to work
- A summary of the major features of the job
- A clear statement of the minimum qualifications for the job
- Conditions of employment (length of contract, working hours, travel requirements, etc.)
- Some statement regarding salary, either a specific figure, a range, or a statement to the effect that "salary is commensurate with training and experience"
- Information about where, how, and to whom to apply
- An equal employment opportunity statement

When the district places an ad in a newspaper, or many professional journals, it is often possible (usually for an additional fee) to have the ad appear in the Internet version of the employment section of the paper or job bulletin board of the journal (Wodarz, 2001). By taking advantage of this option, districts can dramatically extend the research of the print ad at a minimal cost.

Broadcast Media. With two exceptions, school districts do not typically advertise in the broadcast media. The two exceptions are in rural areas where newspaper coverage is poor or on radio or television stations that are aimed at minority audiences. The reasons school districts do not use broadcast media are much the same as those for other organizations: (1) cost, (2) lack of a distinct marketplace of job seekers, and (3) the limits of the amount of information that can be communicated in the limited time frame, as well as the amount interested persons can consume or be prepared or able to take down in the same time frame (Warren et al., 2000–2001). Radio advertising is generally effective only if the district is seeking to fill multiple positions; it is very expensive for just a single hire.

The reason for the high cost is that "one radio spot is more or less useless. Radio advertising requires constant repletion if it is to be effective" (Yate, 2006, p. 50). Radio can be effectively used when free, public service announcements can be made to advertise a job, job fair, or to direct listeners to hiring opportunities posted on the district website. One segment of the broadcast media that is used more by school districts is the "community bulletin board" offered by cable TV companies. Most cable TV broadcasters reserve one or more channels for public service announcements. Very often a designated time slot is provided for employment opportunities. These may be presented as written text, or in some cases recruiters are able to make a personal appearance to present job opportunities. Advertising on the cable TV bulletin boards is often at a free or reduced rate.

Employment Agencies. Sometimes it may be necessary or advantageous for the district to utilize the services of either public or private employment agencies. In addition to supplying job applicants, employment agencies often assist in the employment process by performing employment testing, evaluation, and counseling. A beneficial feature of public employment agencies is that they do the initial screening without cost to the district. In some offices this screening may include the administration of a general aptitude test designed to predict success on a broad range of jobs (Warren et al., 2000–2001).

Private agencies can be of most assistance in filling technical and professional positions. Many private agencies specialize in certain fields. Private employment agencies can differ significantly in the services they provide. Some agencies, so-called "head hunters" or executive search firms, will aggressively seek out and approach prospective employees. Employment agencies differ in whether they charge a contingency fee or a retainer. A contingency fee is paid only if a suitable candidate is hired, where a retainer is paid for the firm to work on the assignment whether a hire is made or not (Yate, 2006). If the school district finds it necessary or desirable to use a private employment agency, care should be taken to select an employment agency that is established, receives recruiter certification through the National Association of Personnel Consultants, and provides multiple services (temporary, full time, and management-level recruitment). Perhaps the best gauge of the caliber of the firm is to ask candidates two questions: What did the agency tell you about the school district and position? and How do you feel about your recruiter? (Falcone, 1992).

Educational Institutions. For all certified positions, as well as for some of the more advanced professional and vocational fields in the classified service (e.g., budget director, dietician, director of food services, director of transportation services, and facilities planner), it would be logical for the school district to recruit at colleges and universities. Almost all colleges and universities operate placement offices through which the school district can recruit and arrange interviews with applicants. In addition, many colleges and universities hold annual job placement days, "career days," job fairs, or "teacher roundups." While these events provide the school district the opportunity to meet a number of candidates in a short period of time, since they operate on the academic calendar of the institution, their schedule may delay the hiring process (Kulik, 2004).

Most successful school district recruiters don't wait until they need employees to contact the college or university. "Good college recruiting is labor intensive and depends on forming close relationships not only with the career placement officials . . . but also with the faculty" (Herman, 1994, p. 60). Some school districts approach recruiting student teachers much the same colleges approach scouting and recruiting student athletes. That is, they encourage professors to identify their most capable students in their junior year, interview students on campus, and then invite them for an all-expense-paid visit to the district where they are given first-class treatment. For minority students, early contact is particularly important: recruiters have found that waiting until the senior year to make contact is often too late (Martinez, 1996).

In planning the campus recruitment visit, it is important to work closely with the college placement office to schedule various recruitment efforts, to send ahead videos and literature describing the district and its various employment opportunities, and to involve alumni of the institution as recruiters or recruiter partners. Lastly, rather than spreading your resources thin by attempting to recruit at all the colleges or universities in your region or state, a better practice is to concentrate on the schools your best employees have come from (Herman, 1994). And, if recruiting out of state, target states and areas with a known surplus of teachers, and, if increasing the diversity of the teaching pool is a goal, target predominantly minority colleges and universities. Non-targeted recruiting out of state is generally not very cost effective. As is discussed later in this chapter, research shows that the majority of candidates tend to stay within their geographic area.

In addition, instead of visiting numerous college recruitment officers, some districts have tried the reverse strategy and invited recruitment officers to visit them. For example, once a year the Decatur, Georgia, district invites about 30 college placement directors to visit them for two days. The directors meet with the superintendent, school board members, and teachers and administrators who are alumni of their institutions. They visit the schools and dine in the school cafeteria. The visit concludes with a trip to a major league baseball game (Grant, 2001).

For a number of classified positions, the district can recruit applicants from vocational and technical schools. The school district is also in the unique position to recruit the very best of the graduating seniors in the district. Personal references of students can be readily checked, and school records can provide some indication of on-the-job performance (Jordan, McKeown, Salmon, & Webb, 1985). Rather than letting its best graduates go elsewhere, the school district can hire them.

International Recruiting. The shortage of teachers has led many districts to recruit foreign teachers to fill their classrooms. In fact, a national survey of human resources directors found that 43% did recruit applicants from other countries (Murphy & DeArmond, 2003). By offering special visas to foreigners to teach in areas of greatest need, Chicago Public Schools was able to attract math and science teachers from all over the world, including some from the best universities (Trapps, 2001). Connecticut, Philadelphia, and New York City have recruited Spanish teachers from Spain, while Houston and Los Angeles has recruited Spanish teachers in the Philippines and Mexico. Philadelphia has also turned to India to fill jobs, mostly in math and science. Dallas has also turned to Mexico to find bilingual math and science teachers, while New York City has sought science teachers in Puerto Rico, hired 24 Austrians via teleconference, and has even extended its recruitment efforts into Eastern Europe (RNT, 2000; "Schools seeking teachers overseas," 2001).

To recruit teachers internationally, districts have turned to a variety of sources. Working through foreign governments, recruitment agencies, and personal contracts are common approaches. Other districts have used EdJoin, an internationally based website where the districts can advertise positions and post applications that can be submitted via the Internet (Rodda, 2000). In most states foreign teachers are required to have classroom experience, speak English fluently, and undergo a background check to become employed ("Schools seeking teachers overseas," 2001).

Internet Recruiting. The Internet has become an essential recruitment tool for school districts nationally. The vast majority of new hires today grew up using a computer. Most applicants from this generation do not first look in the newspaper or professional journals for positions, but on online databases and websites. These individuals are also likely to post their résumés online and are comfortable with online applications. The Internet can serve as a recruitment tool in two major ways: (1) allowing the district to create a website for informing potential candidates about the district, employment opportunities in the district, and application information, including application materials; and (2) providing the district with access to national, state, and job banks for education where jobs can be posted and candidate databases searched. The Internet provides a relatively inexpensive way to reach and be reached by applicants worldwide.

The District Website. Almost every school district has a website. However, despite their potential to reach audiences worldwide at minimal expense, many districts underutilize the website for recruitment. A well-designed website is one that includes a listing of employment opportunities, applicant requirements, and an online application process. The district site should have a professional look and be easy to navigate. The most important navigation features are a "home" button, an Internet search engine for users who want to find specific information on the site, and a site map (Swann, 2006). The following recruitment information should be included on the website:

- Information about the district: But don't get so caught up in posting student test scores, school calendars, team schedules, and press releases that you forget to provide the school district contact information;
- Photographs of classrooms and special programs;
- The district mission statement (but not "front and center" on the home page. Provide a link from the home page or move it to an "About Us" page);
- Information about the city/region;
- Current openings;
- Salary ranges and benefits;
- The selection process;
- The contact person(s), including names, titles, phone numbers, and e-mail and mailing addressees;
- Licensure information;
- Access to an online application form (or a statement as to whether the standard application forms provided at USTEACH and similar sites are accepted): and
- Links from career placement offices. (Head, 2001, p. 20; RNT, 2000, p. 16; Wohlleb, 2006)

The effectiveness of the site will be improved if the tools on the site can instantly notify visitors whenever a suitable position is posted on the website (Yate, 2006). Finally, as important as what information is included on the website is that it be updated on a regular basis and let users know when it was updated. "An up-to-date website is an easy way to promote a positive image of your school or school district. An inactive, out-of-date website doesn't necessarily mean a neglected school, but it will raise the question in people's minds" (Wohlleb, 2006).

Job Banks and Education Employment Databases. In addition to posting jobs on its own website, the district can post jobs and search for candidates on an almost endless number of databases worldwide including the largest job bank, America's

Job Bank, and many, many teacher job applicant databases. The specific position will determine which of the many job banks the district will utilize. Most sites allow the district and the applicant to customize the data they import as well as the searches they perform. Among the largest and the more established education databases are

- The American Association for Employment in Education (www.aace.org)
- USTEACH (www.usteach.com)
- CALTEACH (www.CalTeach.com)
- National Teacher Recruitment Clearinghouse (www.recruitingteachers.org)
- REAP (www.reap.net)
- www.K12jobs.com
- www.edjobsite.com

Professional Organizations and Unions. Many professional organizations and labor unions provide placement services to their members. Placement activities often are conducted in connection with the organization's state, regional, and national conferences. In addition, advertisements are carried in publications of the organization and on the association's website. For certain select positions, therefore, the district may want to place an advertisement in the trade journal and/or its website. For others it might be more economical for the district to send a recruiter to a conference to interview a number of applicants than to bring applicants to the district.

Labor unions, through their apprenticeship programs, are the primary source of applicants for certain types of jobs. In fact, in districts in which some or all of the classified personnel are unionized, the district must rely on the union in its recruitment efforts.

Unsolicited Applications. Almost every school district will receive numerous unsolicited applications each year. The number of unsolicited applications received depends to a large extent on economic conditions and the school district's image as an employer. Unsolicited applications provide an excellent source of stockpiled applicants (De Cenzo & Robbins, 1996). In fact, it is often believed that applicants who contact prospective employers on their own initiative may be better employees than those recruited through newspaper advertisements or college placement offices (Sherman & Bohlander, 1992). All unsolicited applications should be handled with respect and courtesy. If there is no chance of employment now or in the future, the applicant should be honestly and tactfully informed of this fact (Sherman & Bohlander, 1992). Maintaining a computerized database of unsolicited applications allows easy updating and purging of files. More important, it facilitates the matching of qualified candidates with specific positions as the need arises.

Recruitment Incentives. In an effort to attract teachers, especially in hard-to-fill disciplines or in certain geographic areas, a number of states and districts have turned to providing financial or other incentives. Thirty-one states offer financial incentives addressed at subject-area shortages, 17 offer incentives for hard-to-staff schools, and 14 states have policies to address both kinds of shortages (Johnson, 2005). These take the form of student loan/tuition assistance, tax breaks, relocation assistance, and housing assistance, to name a few. One increasingly popular incentive is the signing or hiring bonus. For example, Massachusetts has instituted a program offering $20,000 spread over 4 years to career changers and recent college graduates, especially those with expertise in areas such as math and science, and will also pay for them to go through concentrated summer training (Hartigan, 2002). Another state-level incentive is offered by Arkansas, which pays a $4,000 signing bonus to teachers who begin teaching in a high-poverty district and agree to do so for 3 years and $3,000 in each of the next 2 years Examples of hiring bonuses at the district level are numerous. Most are in the $1,500 to $2,500 range, although there are also examples as far ranging as Houston and Los Angeles and Tuba City (AZ) on the Navajo Nation, which provide $5,000 bonuses to teachers in high-demand areas.

Other incentives offered to prospective employees are aimed at helping with relocation or real estate costs. For example, the state of Maryland provides low-interest loans to teachers who buy homes in "smart growth" areas, defined as urban and older suburban areas (www.ncsl.org). At the district level, Baltimore offers new teachers $5,000 toward the purchase of a home in the city. Other districts have provided low-interest mortgages, subsidized rent, or low-rent housing. Other districts offer subsidies for day care, or even in the case of one rural district, providing bird-hunting rights on private property (ECS, 2006).

While increasingly popular, there is also some question as to the effectiveness of signing bonuses, especially in the long term. For example, one study of both experienced and prospective teachers found that a signing bonus of 10% of annual salary was not enough to increase their attraction to a teaching vacancy (Winter & Melloy, 2005). Even when signing bonuses have been effective in attracting candidates, "it is not clear that they have the desired long-term benefit of keeping good teachers in the classroom, especially in hard-to-staff schools" (ECS, 2006).

Recruiting for Diversity

Recruiting for diversity involves finding teachers, counselors, and administrators that reflect the cultural, racial, and ethnic diversity of their classrooms. The need to recruit a workforce which better reflects the student population is made strikingly clear by the comparative demographics of students and educators (see Figure 4.5). The minority enrollment of the public schools, which currently comprises 38% of the student population, is projected to reach 50% by the year 2020. The greatest increase has come among Hispanics: the percentage of Hispanic students has tripled over the past three decades. However, at the same time that the minority student population is growing, the percentage of minority teachers and administrators, which is already significantly disproportionately less than the student population, is projected to decline from 14% in 1999 to 5% in 2010 (U.S. Department of Education, 2000). These disparities are even more acute in urban districts which not only have difficulty attracting staff and higher percentages of teachers teaching out of field, but have high turnover rates. Unfortunately, in many school districts in this country, the only people of color a student will see in their 12 years of school are the custodial and food service workers.

A school district can take a number of steps to enhance the success of its diversity recruitment program. To begin with, the school district recruitment policies

Figure 4.5 Diversity of Student and Teacher Populations

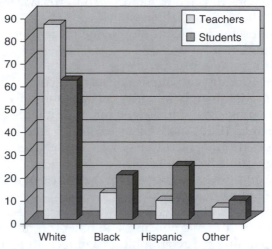

Source: National Center for Education Statistics. (2007). *Condition of Education 2007.* Washington, DC: U.S. Department of Education.

must reflect a commitment to diversity in the workforce. And, this commitment must be reflected in a diverse recruitment team and administrative staff. It is also important that training programs be provided to all those involved in the recruitment and selection process to provide them with the specific skills and knowledge that will enhance their minority recruitment efforts. In addition, all recruitment practices and policies should be continually reviewed to ensure they are not only non-discriminatory but support the stated commitment to diversity. For example, an advertisement or brochure which features photographs of only Anglos, even if it also states the district is an "Equal Opportunity Employer," delivers a powerful subliminal message that the district only pays lip service to being such an employer. "Advertisements that positively depict visible minorities attract significantly larger numbers of minority applicants than those that do not" (Herman, 1994, p. 67).

In addition to attending to these "housekeeping details," school districts can use a variety of proactive recruitment strategies to try to reach qualified minority candidates. Among the recruitment activities districts can utilize in recruiting for diversity are the following:

- Advertising in print and non-print media focused on minorities;
- Networking with minority professional organizations. These organizations can be found by looking in the phone book under "associations" or checking with a college or university that offers a major in the area of interest. These professional organizations offer various types of help. As already noted, many have newsletters that accept advertisements. In addition to the minority professional organizations, national professional

organizations in the field of interest might also be contacted, as many have divisions devoted to minority concerns (Warren et al., 2000–2001);

- Providing financial incentives;
- Identifying and using employment agencies that specialize in minority candidates;
- Hiring a minority recruiter;
- Networking with minority churches, community organizations, and alumni of predominantly minority colleges and universities to identify and encourage individuals who might be interested in pursuing a career in teaching (Education Alliance, 2004);
- Concentrating recruitment visits on schools, colleges, and universities with high minority populations;
- Encouraging and supporting the efforts of minority employees to recruit at their alma maters;
- Working with banks and other local businesses to provide low-interest loans, affordable housing, and other incentives (RNT, 2000); and
- Expanding the geographic area of recruitment.

In addition to these strategies, the strategies described in the following section to increase the overall teaching pool can be used with a focus on minority recruitment. For example, at the high school level, special attention can be given to encouraging minority students to become involved in future educator clubs. Alternative certification programs have also been successful as a minority recruitment strategy (Education Alliance, 2004). And, college scholarships for teacher education students can be earmarked for minority students. Scholarships are particularly important to minority students, many of whom lack the financial ability to attend college.

Other efforts to encourage college students to choose teaching involve presentations to traditionally minority sororities and fraternities and at the various campus racial and ethnic centers and academic studies departments. Many students are undecided on a major when they enroll as freshmen. Many others change their majors one or more times. In fact, a National Conference of State Legislatures (NCSL) (n.d.) study found that 38% of new teachers did not decide to teach until they were in college.

A proven recruitment strategy designed to attract minority teacher education students is to both encourage student teacher coordinators to place student teachers/interns in the district and teacher education students to practice teach or do their internships in the district. That way, the district has the opportunity to identify the most promising future teachers and will have an edge on recruiting these teachers: research indicates that a high percentage of student teachers are interested in remaining in the district where they did their student teaching.

Recruiting for Hard-to-Staff Schools

The term *hard-to-staff schools* generally refers to those schools in highly urban and rural areas, especially those schools serving low-income, minority, and low-achieving students. Hard-to-staff schools face challenges over and above those faced by other schools in attempting to recruit the teachers they need. For example, the research literature suggests four primary challenges faced by rural school districts: (1) low/uncompetitive pay; (2) geographic and social isolation; (3) difficult working conditions (lack of basic resources and materials, lack of a strong professional community, ineffective leadership, large classes, and discipline issues); and (4) NCLB requirements related to subject area proficiency, degree attainment, and certification. There are few incentives to choose to teach in these schools. As a result, "[T]eachers in at-risk (hard-to-staff) schools often tend to have temporary or emergency certification, teach in fields for which they lack strong subject-matter preparation (out-of-field), or are in the first or second year of their careers" (Rowland & Cable, 2005, p. 2). States and school districts have explored a number of policies and programs to recruit teachers for hard-to-staff schools. However, many of these are available to anyone willing to teach in public schools in the state, are too generic to meet the specific challenges faced by hard-to-staff schools, and most have little or no research base or have yet to be proven successful (Rowland & Coble, 2005).

One of the most popular strategies targeted to recruit teachers for hard-to-staff schools is financial incentives. Most of these are loan forgiveness programs. As previously discussed, there is some debate as to the effectiveness of financial incentives (other than higher salaries) in attracting teachers to hard-to-staff schools. In fact, in a national survey of almost 600 rural district superintendents, offering targeted incentives and housing and relocation assistance were identified as among the least successful recruitment strategies (see Figure 4.6).

One recommendation to increase the effectiveness of incentives, including financial incentives, that is increasingly being made in the professional literature is to offer flexible incentive packages to meet different local needs. Teachers choose to teach in specific districts for different reasons, so having packages of financial incentives from which to choose is a highly responsive way to recruit teachers (Rowland & Coble, 2005). Just as there is no single solution for recruiting teachers for hard-to-staff schools, there can be no "one size fits all" preferred incentive: "the incentives needed to recruit and retain an outstanding 22-year-old novice are not the same as those needed to recruit and retain a 45-year-old, National Board certified teacher or a 58-year-old retired teacher who could be lured back into service" (Berry & Hirsch, 2005, p. 11).

Among the array of incentives suggested to give recruits a menu of choice are

- Specialized scholarships for learning to teach in hard-to-staff schools;
- Retention bonuses if teachers go to, and stay in, hard-to-staff schools for at least 5 years;
- Pay for performance and bonuses for teaching hard-to-staff subjects (pilot programs);
- Relocation reimbursement;
- Tuition-free advanced degrees at state universities;
- Housing subsidies (mortgage reduction, teacher housing villages, etc.);
- State income tax credits;
- State university scholarships for children of recruited and retained teachers;
- Early retirement incentives or incentives for retirees to return;
- Targeted professional development;

Figure 4.6 Percentages of Rural Districts Reporting Strategies as Most Useful for Teacher Recruitment

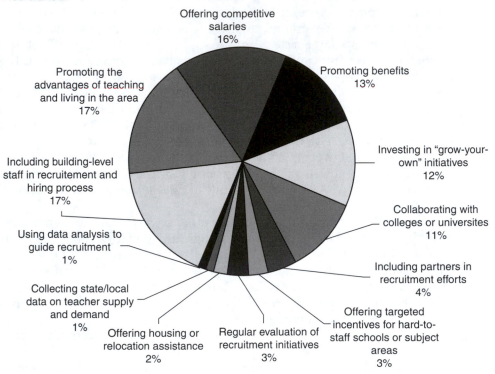

Source: Hammer, P. C., Hughes, G., McClure, C., Reeves, C., & Salgado, D. (2005). *Rural teacher recruitment and retention practices: A review of the research literature, National Survey of Rural Superintendants, and case studies of programs in Virginia.* Charleston, WV: Edvartin, Inc.

- Reduced teaching loads and nonteaching duties;
- Additional teaching assistants. (Berry & Hirsch, 2005, p. 11)

In addition to providing various inducements to prospective candidates there are a number of proactive practices that have been suggested in the literature as promising for hard-to-staff schools. These include

- Investing in grow-your-own initiatives;
- Collecting state/local data on teacher supply and demand;
- Using data analysis to guide recruitment;
- Including partners in recruitment efforts;
- Regularly evaluating recruitment initiatives;
- Collaborating with colleges or universities;
- Including building-level staff in recruiting and hiring processes;
- Promoting the advantages of teaching and living in the area. (Hammer, Hughes, McClure, Reeves, & Salgado 2005, p. 75)

Perhaps the best strategy for districts attempting to recruit teachers and administrators for hard-to-staff schools is that they pursue a strategic approach to responding to the shortage of quality teachers. This requires that they follow the strategic planning process discussed in Chapter 2 in analyzing their personnel needs, analyze the factors contributing to the shortage of personnel, develop alternative solutions, and evaluate the alternative solutions on the basis of the costs and benefits associated with each.

Building the Supply of Future Educators

With the teacher shortage, particularly the shortage of minority teachers, projected to continue into the unforeseeable future, and fewer individuals choosing teaching as a career, school districts must assume a major role in developing the educational workforce for the near and the long-term future. As Dean Grant (2001), past president of the American Association of School Personnel Administrators, explains: "You can not reap what you have not sown" (p. 18). Efforts to increase the pool of qualified educators typically fall into four categories: (1) precollege recruitment, (2) college recruitment and support programs, (3) alternative certification programs, and (4) "grow your own" programs that recruit paraprofessionals and teacher aides into teaching or teachers into the principalship.

Precollege Recruitment. According to the NCSL (n.d.) study, 52% of all new teachers made the decision to become a teacher before they entered college. Therefore, human resources administrators should take the lead in encouraging their districts to sponsor such programs as Future Educators of America or some other locally devised program. The ideal would be to have a program operating in every middle and high school in the district (Grant, 2001). The purpose of such a club is to provide students the opportunity to explore careers in education and to expose them to "meaningful experiences that allow them to understand what teaching is and the rewards of teaching so that in the future they are able to make career choices based on actual experience" (O'Laughlin, 1999, p. 32).

Future teacher clubs or teacher cadet programs can be found in every state. Many are local affiliates of the national FTA. Others are state sponsored. One of the most successful and well-known programs designed to attract middle and high school students to teaching is the South Carolina Pro Team and Teacher Cadet Program (TCP) sponsored by the South Carolina Center for Teacher Recruitment. Pro Team, which serves 1,000 students annually,

> aims to interest middle school students in the education profession before they become "turned off" to the possibility of a career in teaching. Its goals are to make potentially successful students aware of the skills they need to complete college and pursue a teaching career, and to expand the pool of minority and male teachers available to the public schools of South Carolina. The Pro Team Program consists of either a semester- or year-long hands-on course that provides students the opportunity to grow as learners. The Pro Team curriculum includes self-discovery, goal setting, and career exploration activities as well as teaching-like experiences. (NEA, 2003, p. 7)

The Teacher Cadet Program is designed to engage high school juniors and seniors in learning about teaching through both classroom activities and actual teaching experiences in early childhood centers, elementary and middle schools, or classes in their own schools (150 of the state's high schools participate in the TCP). The TCP is making a special effort to enlist largely minority high schools and to provide counseling and scholarship information to minority students. As a result it has proven to be more successful than any other recruitment effort in the state in attracting top-quality minority students to teaching. Contributing to the success of the TCP is that 23 of the 30 colleges and universities in the state with education programs provide support to Teacher Cadet sites and more than two-thirds give college credit (NEA, 2003).

In addition to sponsoring such groups as future teacher clubs, school districts should encourage their guidance counselors to highlight education as a career, invite speakers from colleges of education to speak to the student body (Polansky, 1999), and take advantage of every opportunity to encourage its students to consider education as a career.

College Recruitment and Support Programs. In addition to supporting programs for middle and high school students, an increasing number of states and districts have established scholarship programs to encourage high school graduates to pursue teaching careers. For example, the state of Georgia provides full scholarships to individuals who promise to teach in the state. And, the North Carolina Teaching Fellows Program awards $6,500 per year loan forgiveness scholarships to 700 outstanding high school seniors who are interested in becoming teachers. Teaching Fellows attend teacher education programs in one of 14 state institutions that have developed academically and culturally enriched teacher education programs for Fellows. North Carolina also funds a Principal Fellows Program to attract qualified individuals into careers in educational administration. The program provides a 2-year scholarship of $20,000 per year to support full-time study leading to certification and a master's degree in educational administration. The loan is forgiven if the recipient practices full time as an administrator for 4 years within 6 years of completion of the programs.

A number of other states fund programs similar to these. A few are directed specifically to minority students. For example, the Florida Fund for Minority Teachers awards up to 1,000 scholarships of $4,000 each to students in 29 colleges and universities "with special consideration to community college graduates, since many minorities attend them" (Duarte, 2000, p. 23).

Alternative Certification Programs. More than 40 states now recognize alternative routes to certification. **Alternative certification programs** are designed to attract and train mid-career persons with a baccalaureate degree in a non-teaching field for a career in teaching. Alternative certification programs are typically 1 or 2 years in duration and include a year of internship or close supervision. The most successful programs include not only an internship, but intensive mentoring and substantial coursework in teaching methods (NEA, 2003).

Some alternative certification programs target returning Peace Corps volunteers or retired military personnel. The Peace Corps has sent more than 1,500 of its returning volunteers into community service positions—most in teaching—in return for scholarships to earn a master's degree (Schuerman, 2000). Districts can contact the Peace Corps or Troop to Teachers (www.troops.org) for help in identifying individuals in the local area who are potential candidates for an alternative certification program. Another good source for identifying candidates is current employees. Many teachers may have a friend or relative who needs only a little encouragement to consider teaching. Another alternative, Teach for America, though "small and far from perfect, provides able and enthusiastic (if inexperienced) novice teachers for some difficult school settings" (Budig, 2006, p. 116).

A number of districts have entered into collaborative arrangements with area institutions of higher education to produce alternative certification teachers. Such jointly developed programs provide the district the opportunity to train teachers specifically for the needs of their district—teachers who often come from the community and are familiar with the background of their students. These teachers are also more likely to stay in the profession than other alternatively certified teachers, 60% of whom leave the profession by their third year (Fenwick & Pierce, 2001). However, district involvement in an alternative certification program does place an additional burden on school district personnel, a burden the school district must carefully consider before initiating such a program.

Grow-Your-Own Programs. **Grow-your-own programs** have become an increasingly popular strategy for districts, especially urban districts, to address the teacher shortage, especially the shortage of teachers interested in working in hard-to-staff schools and shortage of minority teachers. However, many rural districts are also developing grow-your-own programs. They, like urban districts, are interested in hiring teachers who are familiar with the strengths and weakness of the district and the culture and background of the students. Research showing that "individuals often choose to become teachers because they want to work in the area where they were raised" has given credence to grow-your-own programs ("School staffing solutions may be around the corner," 2006, p. 8).

While each grow-your-own program has its unique features, they share some basic features: (1) they require the collaboration of the school district and a college or university to recruit and select participants; (2) they offer participants a range of financial and academic support services; (3) they offer flexible course scheduling to accommodate the work schedules of participants; (4) they provide student cohort arrangements; and (5) they offer preparation programs. These preparation programs have "adopted elements of nontraditional teacher education models—field-based learning; adult degree low residency; competency-based assessment; continuing education; summer and weekend course work (distance learning); intern/mentoring; integrated learning; and links to community" (Haselkorn & Fideler, 1996, p. 49). Districts typically do not have any difficulty recruiting participants into paraeducator-to-teacher programs. Moreover, once they are trained, they tend to remain in the district.

ESTABLISHMENT OF APPLICANT POOL

The creation of the applicant pool is the ultimate objective of the recruitment program. To establish an applicant pool of qualified persons, the human resources administrator must give careful attention to the process of handling all applications and supporting materials. This task is made easier by the use of an **electronic document management system (EDMS)**. Most EDM systems provide for applications to be received via the Internet and an immediate e-mail sent acknowledging receipt of the application. More sophisticated software may also "evaluate or filter the credentials of the applicant . . . route applications to the personnel administrator with hiring authority, send out electronic evaluation forms to the references listed, order transcripts or college placement files, electronically order copies of teaching certificates . . . (all) without human intervention" (Grant, cited in Murphy & DeArmond, 2003, p. 52).

Through use of an electronic document management system, all documents received on a candidate are electronically scanned into a computer file or converted into alphanumeric characters using intelligent character recognition, which can then be processed into the applicant's electronic portfolio. The EDMS also allows for instant retrieval of all information on any candidate. Overall, the system is far more secure than traditional paper files being transferred from one used to another. Moreover, once the information on an applicant is entered into the system, it becomes permanent, and if the applicant is hired can be transferred to the master file in the human resources database.

As each application is received, whether an EDMS is used or not, a letter of acknowledgment thanking the applicant for interest in the position should be sent along with a description of the selection process and information regarding persons to contact for additional information. At the same time, applicant information should be entered into the applicant database and a computer or hard copy created for the placement of transcripts, letters of reference, copies of reference checks, copies of licenses, or whatever other documentation in support of the application is required of applicants. As each required document is received or completed, the applicant database should be updated.

At this point in the recruitment process, it is also appropriate to send to each applicant a card or form asking the applicant to indicate if he or she belongs to one or more of the minority groups listed on the card or form. It should be stressed when making this request that the submission of this information is voluntary and will in no way impact the selection process. The form should be returned unsigned to the district affirmative action officer, not to the personnel office.

As the recruitment process proceeds, it is extremely important to have a well-established procedure for keeping applicants informed. A good procedure will help to maintain the interest of qualified applicants and minimize the number of inquiries received by the personnel office. A good EDMS can make this communication task an easy chore. Integrated word processing software can be used to generate letters to applicants advising them of receipt or need of additional documents. Once all application materials have been received, dated, and filed, the screening process described in Chapter 5 can begin.

FISCAL AND LEGAL CONSTRAINTS ON RECRUITMENT

Fiscal Constraints

The fiscal condition of the school district can have a direct impact on the recruitment process. Recruitment can be an expensive process. It is estimated (conservatively) that this process costs a district a minimum of $12,000 in recruiting, processing, interviewing, and training to replace a teacher (Center for Teaching Quality, 2006). Private employment agencies charge fees as much as 30% of the first year salary. The fiscal condition of the district will affect how much the district can afford to expend in terms of recruiters, recruitment trips, advertising, use of professional search firms, coverage of candidate expenses, and a number of other costs.

More important than the impact on the recruitment process, the fiscal condition of the school district can impact on the ability of the school district to attract and retain personnel. High-wealth suburban districts always have a "glut" of applicants, while, as previously discussed, low-wealth urban and rural districts are the ones that have the most difficulty attracting and retaining teachers and administrators. In particular, the fiscal ability of the district to offer attractive beginning teacher salaries seems to have a powerful impact on recruitment. After a review of the available evidence, Odden and Conley (1992) concluded that "beginning teacher salaries can affect both the quantity and the quality of individuals entering the teaching profession. The higher the salaries, the greater the number of able individuals encouraged to become teachers" (p. 53). For example, 48% of sophomores in one study said they would be attracted to teaching if salaries were 45% higher (College Board, 2006).

School districts must compete not only with other school districts for candidates, but also with other employers in the community. For example, the characteristics that boards and superintendents are looking for in principals are the same that business and industry are looking for in CEOs and middle-level managers. And, unfortunately, most school districts cannot compete with financial incentives and opportunities for advancement provided in the private sector (Malone & Caddell, 2000). And, although a substantial body of research supports the proposition that most educators are in education for reasons other than money, a consistent body of research also indicates that both practicing and prospective educators are influenced by salary differentials: about one-half the teachers who leave teaching indicate salary is a factor, and two-thirds say a higher salary would encourage them to stay in teaching (Ingersoll, cited in Berry & Hirsch, 2005). The effect of salary differentials on career choice decisions is particularly strong for males (Han, 1994). Thus, school districts that offer low salaries, either because their low wealth will not support higher salaries or because of a reluctance of taxpayers to tax themselves to provide higher salaries, will typically be less competitive in recruiting than higher-paying districts and employers.

Legal Constraints

A myriad of state and federal laws designed to prevent employment discrimination and promote equal employment opportunity (EEO) impact on the recruitment process. The major federal EEO laws are summarized in Table 4.1.

Table 4.1 Summary of Major EEO Laws Affecting Recruitment

Executive Order 11246 (as amended by 11375)	Bans discrimination on the basis of race, color, religion, sex, or national origin by federal contractors and subcontractors with at least $10,000 in contracts. Requires federal contractors and subcontractors with at least 50 employees and $50,000 in federal contracts to take affirmative action to increase the utilization of minorities and women.
Equal Pay Act of 1963	Prohibits gender discrimination in pay; requires equal pay for males and females in jobs requiring equal skills and responsibilities.
Title VII of the Civil Rights Act of 1964, as amended	Prohibits discrimination in hiring, compensation, and terms and conditions of employment on the basis of race, color, religion, national origin, or sex.
Age Discrimination in Employment Act of 1967, as amended	Prohibits discrimination in employment against persons aged 40 and over.
Equal Employment Opportunity Act of 1972	Extends race coverage of Title VII to include employees of state and local governments and educational institutions. Created the EEO Commission with authority to prohibit discrimination and file suits against organizations believed to be discriminatory.
Title IX of the Education Amendments of 1972	Prohibits discrimination on the basis of gender in programs receiving federal funds.
Section 504 of the Vocational Rehabilitation Act of 1973	Requires federal agencies and organizations receiving federal funds to take affirmative action to recruit, hire, and promote qualified disabled persons.
Vietnam Era Veterans Readjustment Assistance Act of 1974	Requires federal contractors and subcontractors to take affirmative action to hire and promote veterans and disabled veterans.
Pregnancy Discrimination Act of 1978	Provides EEO protection to pregnant workers and requires pregnancy to be treated like any other disability.
Americans With Disabilities Act of 1990	Extends the antidiscrimination provisions of Section 504 to organizations not receiving federal funds. Prohibits employment discrimination against individuals with physical or mental handicaps or the chronically ill.
Civil Rights Act of 1991	Amended Title VII and strengthened it and other civil rights laws that had been weakened by Supreme Court decisions.
Family and Medical Leave Act of 1993	Provides eligible employees of both sexes the right to take 12 weeks of unpaid leave per year in conjunction with the birth or first year of a child, the adoption or foster placement of a child, or the illness of the employee or the employee's spouse, child, or parent.

Recruitment practices that are most vulnerable in terms of non-compliance with EEO principles and guidelines, and possible areas of non-compliance, are described in the following sections.

Job Descriptions. One particular vulnerable area of job descriptions is the specification of minimum qualifications. Too frequently, arbitrary standards are used. For example, specifying "college degree" for a job that clearly does not require it creates artificial barriers that exclude otherwise capable individuals and is therefore discriminatory (Levesque, 1993). Moreover, the EEOC and the Civil Rights Division of the Department of Justice "recommend that job descriptions focus on the results or outcomes of a job function, not solely on the way it is customarily performed. This is because a person with a disability may be able to accomplish a job function, either with or without a reasonable accommodation, in a manner that is different from the way an employee who is not disabled may accomplish the same function" (Pynes, 1997, p. 77).

Advertisements. Ads can make no direct or indirect reference to race, religion, sex, or national origin. For instance, even ads recruiting "new graduates," "college students," "high school students," or "recent retirees" could cause problems because they indicate an age preference. If the ad contains any job qualifications, the qualifications must be job related. "Even when a job is usually associated with one sex, the ad must indicate either male or female is acceptable" (Harvey & Bowin, 1996, p. 46).

EVALUATION OF THE RECRUITMENT PROGRAM

Since the recruitment process is both time consuming and costly, it is important that the human resources administrator evaluate the effectiveness of the recruitment process in terms of meeting both long-term and short-term goals. Three measures of effectiveness that are commonly used in evaluating recruitment programs are (1) recruitment outcome, (2) applicant predictors/criteria, and (3) subjective recruitment measures (Harris & Lasson, 2003). The three most commonly used recruitment outcome variables in education are cost-per-hire from a particular source, the time between the initiation of the recruitment process and the hire, and the number of applications received from qualified applicants.

The calculation of recruitment costs includes not only the direct dollar expenditures for such things as advertising, agency fees, and travel for recruiters and candidates, but the time spent by various school district personnel on the recruitment process. Some experts suggest that another 10% of these costs be added to total costs to account for miscellaneous costs (Dickmeyer, 2001). The human resources department will need to work with the hiring unit to ensure that accurate records are kept of costs per hire.

With the costs and outcomes attributable to each recruitment activity determined, the human resources department can then calculate and rank each recruitment activity in terms of its relative cost effectiveness and cost per hire. For example:

> [C]alculating the cost of visiting a given campus for each hire from that campus makes it possible to compare this cost figure with that for other institutions. This simplifies decision making about which campus visits provide the greatest return. Determining the cost of a given radio advertisement makes it easy to compare the cost-effectiveness of this advertisement with others. Many such comparisons may be made. (Beebe, 1998, p. 81)

Information important to future recruitment efforts can be obtained from a review of the preceding data. For example, if there are many inquiries about a job, but very few applications, then the content and quality of information disseminated to prospective applicants should be reviewed. If, on the other hand, many applications are reviewed, but very few applicants are suitable, then it is possible the advertisements were inaccurately worded or inappropriately placed (Bolton, 1997).

The second evaluation measure involves a comparison of applicant predictors (e.g., test scores) with test performance ratings, turnover rates, or other criteria. The rationale behind this measure is that if the district is using a valid predictor it would be reasonable to compare alternative recruitment sources to see which provided the better candidates (Harris & Lasson, 2003).

The third evaluation category, subjective recruitment measures, involves gathering applicant perceptions of the positive as well as the negative aspects of the recruitment process (Harris & Lasson, 2003). One district asks its new teachers how they came to hear about the district and why they chose that district and then use the information it gleans as part of its interview "pitch" in selling the district and to fine-tune its recruitment activities (Rodda, 2000).

In the long term, the success of the recruitment effort is determined not by the number of hires, but by the success of the hires. The on-the-job performance of the new hires and the degree to which they fit into the school system are the ultimate measures of the success of the recruitment process. This requires that new hires be tracked and a correlation be made of the sources and methods of recruitment and employee performance and fit.

SUMMARY

Recruitment begins with determining the need for a position, analyzing the duties and responsibilities of the position, and preparing a description of the position which can be used in the actual recruitment process. As districts undertake the recruitment process, a number of factors, including the number of potential applicants necessary to contact in order to obtain an applicant pool of the desired size, the type of job, and the recruitment budget, will influence how extensive and formal the process will become. If it appears a pool of sufficient size can be obtained from internal recruiting, the district may limit its search activities to internal posting, recruiting previous and part-time employees, and employee referrals. If it seems necessary or desirable to engage in more extensive, external recruiting, advertisements may be placed in various media outlets, employment agencies may be used, recruitment contacts and trips may be made to educational institutions, and contacts may be made with professional organizations and unions.

Many school districts throughout the country are faced with the challenge of recruiting qualified minorities and personnel for "hard to fill schools staff." A number of districts, in addition to aggressively recruiting the limited number of available minority candidates, have attempted to build capacity. The most common capacity-building programs are the so-called "grow-your-own" programs, which focus on assisting current employees to become teachers, and programs aimed at encouraging middle and high school students to enter teaching.

The recruitment efforts of the school district are subject to a number of fiscal and legal constraints. The fiscal condition of the district places constraints on how much the district can spend on recruitment. It also influences how competitive the district can be in the salaries paid to employees. Legal guidelines designed to prevent employee discrimination and promote equal employment opportunity also impact the recruitment process. In addition, school board policies not only provide the legal basis for the recruitment program, but also give direction for its activities.

Discussion Questions

1. Interview someone in your school district, organization, or acquaintance that holds a job different from yours and write a job description for that position.
2. What are the advantages and disadvantages of a district policy promoting internal recruiting?
3. Under what circumstance should the district pay for the services of a private employment agency?
4. What strategies can a financially poor district use to make itself more competitive in its recruitment efforts?

CASE STUDIES

—CASE 4.1—

So You're in Charge of Minority Recruitment. Now What?

The Lebenon School District is a school district of 6,300 students. The minority student population is 2% Asian American, 13% African American, and 19% Hispanic. Population projections suggest that the minority student population will increase to over 50% in the next 7 to 10 years. The Lebenon instructional staff contains no Asian Americans, 3% African Americans, and 6% Hispanics. The district has attempted to recruit minority staff by advertising in media outlets that focus on minorities and by sending recruitment materials to all the historically black colleges in the state. The results have been disappointing. Only five minority hires have been made in the last 2 years. At the same time, two minority teachers, a young married couple, moved to a neighboring district where they receive salaries of $4,500 more (each) than they were making in the Lebenon district.

The superintendent has decided to put you, the assistant director of human resources, in charge of minority recruitment and has released you from other responsibilities in order to serve in this capacity. The superintendent has asked that you present her with a preliminary recruitment plan prior to the next cabinet meeting.

Question

1. Prepare a draft of the plan for discussion with the director of personnel prior to submission to the superintendent.

—CASE 4.2—

Who Should Be in the Kitchen?

Arlene Kelley, the assistant food service director of the Mount St. Peters School District, retired at the end of the school year. The food services director, Neil Smith, is eager to hire a replacement and is "bugging" the personnel director, Murray Nordin, to "get things going." He has volunteered to do some recruiting himself, saying he knows some good people who might be interested.

In the last 5 years, Mount St. Peters has closed the kitchens at its elementary schools and now serves these schools from a central kitchen. Over the same period of time, the enrollment of the district has declined by 8%, and the number of meals served at the high school has declined accordingly.

By the beginning of August, Neil is frustrated and insisting that he cannot start the new school year without an assistant director. He suggests that he be allowed to recruit as an "emergency hire" a cousin, Louise Smith, who currently serves as the kitchen manager at Mercy Hospital.

Questions

1. For what reasons might the personnel office have delayed the hiring of a replacement for Arlene Kelley? Is Neil justified in his frustration and insistence on the emergency hire?

2. Should Murray Nordin authorize the emergency hire? What problems are presented by the hiring of Louise Smith?

3. If the emergency hire is made, what further action should be taken by the personnel office? If the hire is not authorized, what further action should be taken? What options other than the emergency hire exist for meeting any need presented by the retirement of Arlene Kelley?

REFERENCES

Beebe, R. J. (1998). Recruiting and selecting new teachers: The recruitment budgeting cycle. *NASSP Bulletin, 82*(602), 77–82.

Berry, B., & Hirsch, E. (2005). *Recruiting and retaining teachers for hard to staff schools.* Issue Brief. Washington, DC: NGA Center for Best Practices.

Bolton, T. (1997). *Human resource management: An introduction.* Cambridge, MA: Blackwell.

Budig, G. A. (2006). A perfect storm. *Phi Delta Kappan, 88,* 114–116.

Canada, B. O. (2001). A strategic view of recruitment. *School Administrator, 58*(1), 51.

Center for Teaching Quality. (2006). Why mentoring and induction matters and what must be done for new teachers. *Best Practices & Policies, 5*(2), 1–5.

Chen, P. Y., Carsten, J. M., & Krauss, A. D. (2003). Job analysis—The basis for developing criteria for all human relations programs. In J. E. Edwards, J. C. Scott, & N. S. Raju (Eds.). *The human resources program-evaluation handbook* (pp. 27–48). Thousand Oaks, CA: Sage.

College Board, Center for Innovative Thought. (2006). *Teachers and the uncertain American future.* Princeton, NJ: The College Board.

Davila, L., & Kursmark, L. (2005). *How to choose the right person for the job every time.* New York: McGraw-Hill.

De Cenzo, D. A., & Robbins, S. P. (1996). *Human resource management: Concepts and practice* (5th ed.). New York: John Wiley & Sons.

Dickmeyer, W. (2001). Applicant tracking reports make data meaningful. *Workforce, 80*(2), 65–67.

Duarte, A. (2000). Wanted: 2 million teachers, especially minorities. *Education Digest, 66*(4), 18–23.

Education Alliance. (2004). *Minority teacher recruitment, development, and retention.* Providence, RI: Brown University.

Education Commission of the States (ECS). (2006). Education Policy Issue Site. Teaching quality—Recruitment/Retention. Retrieved from http://www.ecs.org/html/issue.asp?issueid=129&subissueID+65

Educational Research Service (ERS). (1994). *Job descriptions in public schools* (2nd ed.). Arlington, VA: Author.

Esparo, L. J., & Radar, R. (2001). The leadership crisis. *American School Board Journal, 188*(4), 46–48.

Falcone, P. (1992). Selecting the best employment agency: It's a buyer's market. *HR Focus, 69*(8), 8.

Fenwick, L. T., & Pierce, M. C. (2001). The principal shortage: Crisis or opportunity. *Principal, 10*(10). 24–32.

Grant, F. D. (2001). Fast track teacher recruitment. *School Administrator, 58*(1), 18–24.

Hammer, P. C., Hughes, G., McClure, C., Reeves, C., & Salgado, D. (2005). *Rural teacher recruitment and retention practices: A review of the research literature, national survey of rural superintendents, and case studies of programs in Virginia.* Nashville, TN: Edvantia.

Han, Y. (April 1994). *The impact of teachers' salaries upon attraction and retention of individuals in teaching: Evidence from NLS-72.* Paper presented at the annual meeting of the American Educational Research Association, New Orleans, LA.

Harris, M. M., & Lasson, E. D. (2003). Recruitment. In J. E. Edwards, J. C. Scott, & N. S. Raju (Eds.), *The human resources program-evaluation handbook* (pp. 27–48). Thousand Oaks, CA: Sage.

Hartigan, R. (2002). If you can teach math, you're hired. *U.S. News & World Report, 131,* 35.

Harvey, D., & Bowin, R. B. (1996). *Human resources management: An experimental approach.* Upper Saddle River, NJ: Prentice Hall.

Haselkorn, S. J., & Fideler, E. (1996). *Breaking the glass ceiling: Paraeducator pathways to teaching.* Belmont, MA: Recruiting New Teachers, Inc.

Head, J. S. (2001). Web-based recruiting. *School Administrator, 58*(1), 20.

Herman, S. J. (1994). *Hiring right: A practical guide.* Thousand Oaks, CA: Sage.

Jacobson, L. (March 21, 2006). More teachers lured to stay in classrooms: Efforts target retirees, raise policy concerns, *Education Week,* p. 21.

Johnson, J. (May 2005). State financial incentives policies for recruiting and retaining effective new teachers in hard to staff schools. ECS State Notes. Retrieved from www.ecs.org/html/IssueSection.asp?issueid=129&subissueis=65&ssID=O&S=What+States+are+doing on 9/26/2006.

Joinson, C. (2001). Refocusing job descriptions. HR. *Magazine, 46*(1), 66–72.

Jordan, K. (1997). Play fair and square when hiring from within. HR. *Magazine, 42*(1), 49–51.

Jordan, K. F., McKeown, M. P., Salmon, R. G., & Webb, L. D. (1985). *School business administration*. Beverly Hills, CA: Sage.

Kempton, J. (1995). *Human resource management and development: Current issues and themes*. New York: St. Martin's Press.

Kulik, C. T. (2004). *Human resources for the non-HR manager*. Mahwah, NJ: Lawrence Erlbaum.

Lawrence, C. E., & Vachon, M. K. (1997). *The incompetent specialist: How to evaluate, document performance, and dismiss school staff*. Thousand Oaks, CA: Corwin Press.

Lemke, J. C. (1995). Attracting and retaining special educators in rural and small schools: Issues and solutions. *Rural Special Education Quarterly, 14*(2), 25–30.

Levesque, J. D. (1993). *Manual of personnel policies, procedures, and operations* (2nd ed.). Englewood Cliffs, NJ: Prentice Hall.

Malone, B. G., & Caddell, T. A. (2000). A crisis in leadership: Where are tomorrow's principals? *Clearing House, 73,* 162–164.

Martinez, M. L. (1996). Looking for young talent? Inroads helps diversify efforts. HR. *Magazine, 41*(3), 73–76.

Morehart, K. K. (2001). How to create an employee referral program that *really* works. HR. *Focus, 78*(1), 3–5.

Murphy, P. J., & DeArmond, M. M. (2003). *From the headlines to the frontlines: The teacher shortage and its implications for recruitment policy*. Seattle, WA: Center on Reinventing Public Education, University of Washington.

National Center for Educational Information. (2005). *Profile of teachers in the U.S. 2005*. Washington, DC: Author.

National Conference of State Legislatures (NCSL). (n.d.). *State policies to improve the teacher workforce*. Denver, CO: NCSL.

National Education Association (NEA). (2003). *Meeting the challenges or recruitment and retention: A guidebook on promising strategies to recruit and retail qualified and diverse teachers*. Washington, DC: NEA.

National School Boards Association. (1996). *The school personnel management system*. Arlington, VA: Author.

Nevada balances teacher experience, recruitment. (2006). *What works in Teaching and Learning, 3*(3), 9.

Odden, A. R., & Conley, S. (1992). Restructuring teacher compensation systems. In A. R. Odden (Ed.), *Rethinking school finance: An agenda for the 1990s* (pp. 45–96). San Francisco: Jossey-Bass.

O'Laughlin, J. (1999). Recruiting and hiring high-quality teachers. *ERS Spectrum, 17*(4), 31–39.

Peterson, K., & Kelley, L. (2001). Transforming school leadership. *Leadership, 30*(3), 8–11.

Polansky, H. B. (1999). Combating teacher shortages: Frameworks for minority recruitment. *School Business Affairs, 65*(5), 43–44.

Provasnik, S., & Dorfman, S. (2005). *Mobility in the teacher workforce* (Report NCES 2005–114). Washington, DC: U.S. Department of Education, National Center for Education Statistics.

Pynes, J. E. (1997). *Human resources management for public and nonprofit organizations*. San Francisco: Jossey-Bass.

Recruiting New Teachers (RNT). (2000). *A guide to today's teacher recruitment challenges*. Belmont, MA: RNT.

Rodda, C. (2000). Searching for success in teacher recruitment. *Thrust for Educational Leadership, 29*(3), 8–11.

Rowland, C., & Coble, C. (2005). Targeting teacher recruitment and retention policies for at-risk schools. *Policy Issues, 20.* Naperville, IL: Learning Points Associates.

School staffing solutions may be around the corner. (October, 2006). *What Works in Teaching and Learning, 3*(3), 8.

Schools seeking teachers overseas. (April 23, 2001). *Arizona Republic,* p. A17.

Schuerman, M. (2000). Scrambling for teachers. *American School Board Journal, 187*(10), 30-37.

Sherman, A. W., Jr., & Bohlander, G. W. (1992). *Managing human resources* (9th ed.). Cincinnati, OH: South-Western.

Smith, M. (1997/1998). Expanding the role of the job description to support a growing institution. *CUPA Journal, 48*(3/4), 17–25.

Swann, P. A. (2006). Got web? Investing in a district website. *School Administrator, 63*(5), 24–27, 29.

Trapps, T. E. (August 15, 2001). Teacher shortage expected to worsen, especially in California. *Los Angeles Times,* p. A22.

U.S. Department of Education, National Center for Education Statistics. (2000). *Teacher supply in the United States: Sources of newly hired teachers in public and private schools, 1987–88 to 1993–94*. Washington, DC: Author.

Warren, Gorham, & Lamont. (2000–2001). *HR series: Policies and practices,* (Vol. 1). Boston: Author.

Winter, P. A., & Melloy, S. H. (2005). Teacher recruitment in a school reform state: Factors that influence applicant attraction to teaching vacancies. *Educational Administration Quarterly, 41,* 349–372.

Wodarz, N. (2001). Hiring on-line. *School Business Affairs, 67*(2), 52–54.

Wohlleb, J. L. (2006). Twelve essentials of a school district website. *School Administrator, 63*(5), 20–23.

Yate, M. (2006). *Hiring the best: A manager's guide to effective interviewing and recruiting* (5th ed.). Avon, MA: Adams Media.

CHAPTER 5

Selection and Placement

LEARNING OBJECTIVES

After reading this chapter, you will be able to:

- Identify the candidate information typically being sought by the application form.
- Distinguish between the purposes of the preliminary interview and those of the employment interview.
- Identify the types of background checks that should be conducted on school employees.
- Discuss the importance of the physical setting and the psychological atmosphere to the conduct of the employment interview.
- Describe how the interviewer's interpersonal skills, listening skills, and questioning techniques influence the interview process.
- Describe the process by which employment offers are finalized in education.
- Identify the primary considerations in the placement of school personnel.

The selection process represents one of the quickest ways to initiate change and improvement in a school organization. Every vacancy offers an opportunity to improve the quality and effectiveness of the organization. A well-planned and carefully executed screening and selection procedure can identify individuals who will have the potential to bring new life into the organization. A poorly planned or hasty selection can precipitate a potentially endless flow of personnel problems. The employment of the wrong person can reduce the effectiveness of instruction, jeopardize existing working relationships among staff members, and require costly remedial support. In extreme instances, a poor decision can necessitate an unpleasant termination—for both the school and the individual being dismissed. As Redeker (1989) predicted, "You hire a problem and you will have to fire a problem" (p. 6). Moreover, staffing a position with an inappropriate or ill-prepared person can cause serious professional and personal problems for the individual.

Because of the critical importance of selection decisions, screening and selection must be conducted in ways that ensure the highest probability for success.

The selection process discussed in this chapter was designed to improve the reliability of selection decisions through the use of valid screening and selection criteria and processes. The process begins after the recruiting process has produced the applicant pool discussed in Chapter 4. As discussed in this chapter, the selection process begins with the establishment of selection criteria and ends with the notification of unsuccessful candidates. The process is designed to enable administrators to choose from a pool of applicants the person or persons who best meet the selection criteria established for the position. Following their selection, new employees are assigned to a specific position in the school system. The goal of the selection and placement process is to produce, in a cost-effective manner, a highly productive workforce committed to the attainment of school district goals.

ESTABLISHMENT OF SELECTION CRITERIA

The job analysis and job description described in Chapter 4 provide the basis for the articulation of the specific criteria to be used in the selection process. The purpose of establishing "specifically tailored" selection criteria is to hire "only those candidates who are superior in talent, experience, and potential for growth" (Pandiscio, 2005, p. 92). The processes by which the criteria are developed vary, but the recommended practice is that it begin with current job holders. For example, in the teacher selection process, experts suggest that

> A consensus among a system's finest teachers as to what skills and personal qualities they prize in themselves and others is the best gauge by which to look for new teachers. These consensus-based criteria (CBC) are used to focus the information-getting at each stage of the (selection) process and to evaluate the results of each step. (Smith & Knab, 1996, p. 102)

Others typically involved in the establishment of the selection criteria are the immediate supervisor and human resources personnel. Ultimately the selection criteria will provide the basis for the rating of candidates by those reviewing application materials and conducting interviews. Figure 5.1 provides a sample of the selection criteria for an elementary teaching position.

MANAGING THE APPLICATION PROCESS

The Application Form

An application form must be completed by all applicants for a position in the district. An application form provides the school district with the means and opportunity to gather basic but important data in a cost-efficient and time-saving manner. The application form ensures consistency of information and enables the district to define precisely what is needed. According to human resources experts, not even the applicant résumé provides the same benefits as the completed application form: "a résumé is really a person's own promotional piece . . . (where the application form) helps us get the information about a candidate that we need, to see if he or she really fits what we are looking for" (Woodward, 2000, p. 67).

Figure 5.1 Selection Criteria for a Sixth-Grade Teaching Position

ACADEMIC CRITERIA

1. Has appropriate college or university coursework and degree(s).
2. Has earned a grade point average in undergraduate and/or graduate courses that meets the acceptable standards of the district.
3. Demonstrates through an appropriate interview a working knowledge of the English language in verbal and written context.
4. Demonstrates an understanding and working knowledge of elementary mathematics skills that are compatible with the district's mathematics curriculum guide.
5. Demonstrates the skills necessary to teach reading in a manner compatible with the district's reading curriculum guide.
6. Has had some formal or informal training in music and has developed the skill to perform with a musical instrument.
7. Has completed courses in drama or participated in extracurricular dramatic performances, plays, or musical presentations during high school or college.

PERSONAL CRITERIA

8. Indicates a willingness to interact and communicate in a constructive fashion with district staff and community constituents.
9. Exhibits healthy, considerate, mature attitudes that would promote positive intra-staff and community relationships.
10. Dresses in a manner meeting the expectations of the school district and meets socially acceptable standards of hygiene and health care.
11. Is physically capable of actively participating with minimum proficiency in a sixth-grade outdoor experience that includes rappelling, canoeing, spelunking, and ropes course participation.
12. Expresses a willingness to abide by and implement the district's policies as prescribed by the board of education.

EXPERIENTIAL CRITERIA

13. Has relevant past teaching experience.
14. Has relevant student teaching experience.
15. Has a record of participating in extracurricular activities during high school and/or college (Extracurricular being defined as any organized school approved activity).
16. If applicant has had teaching experience, has demonstrated an interest in ongoing self-improvement by participating in professional workshops, seminars, college/university courses, or other professional programs.

Source: Neely, S. (1993, October). *Personnel recruitment/selection/induction in small/rural schools*. Paper presented at the Rural and Small School Conference, Manhattan, KS.

At a minimum, the application for professional positions will seek information regarding the applicant's educational background, work experience, certifications held, conviction record, and other personal data. In addition, the application form, or the instructions accompanying it, will request that the applicant submit a copy of the professional certificate, unofficial transcripts (official transcripts must be submitted if hired), test scores (if required), and letters of reference or names of references who may be contacted. The application will not be considered complete until all these are received. The application will normally conclude with a sign-off section in which the applicant (1) affirms to the truthfulness of the information given and to an understanding that falsification or misinformation may result in disqualification or dismissal and (2) gives permission for the district to verify all information and to contact references.

It is also common as part of the application process to ask applicants for professional positions to submit a written statement of their personal philosophy of education or to respond to other specific questions (e.g., the "Professional Perspective" section of the sample application form in Figure 5.2), which seek to determine each

Figure 5.2 A Typical Application Form for Certified Personnel

APPLICATION FOR CERTIFICATED PERSONNEL

PERSONAL DATA

NAME _____   SOCIAL SECURITY NUMBER _____
         (LAST)   (FIRST)   (MIDDLE)

PRESENT ADDRESS _____   TELEPHONE _____

CITY _____   STATE _____   ZIP CODE _____

PERMANENT ADDRESS _____   TELEPHONE _____

CITY _____   STATE _____   ZIP CODE _____

HAVE YOU BEEN EMPLOYED BY
PARADISE VALLEY SCHOOLS BEFORE? _____   IF YES, WHEN AND WHAT LOCATION? _____

DID YOU COMPLETE YOUR STUDENT TEACHING WITH PVUSC? _____   IF SO, WHERE & WHEN? _____

HEALTH AND PHYSICAL CONDITION

CONDITION OF GENERAL HEALTH _____   DATE OF LAST COMPLETE PHYSICAL _____

DO YOU HAVE ANY PHYSICAL LIMITATIONS WHICH PRECLUDE YOU FROM PERFORMING CERTAIN KINDS OF WORK? _____

IF YES, PLEASE DESCRIBE SPECIFIC WORK LIMITATIONS. _____

_____

_____

CERTIFICATION

I AM CERTIFIED BY THE STATE OF ARIZONA TO TEACH _____

ENDORSEMENTS _____

TEACHING EXPERIENCE

(LIST FULL-TIME AND PART-TIME PROFESSIONAL EXPERIENCE, BEGINNING WITH THE MOST RECENT.
DO NOT INCLUDE STUDENT TEACHING. ATTACH ADDITIONAL SHEET IF NECESSARY.)

INSTITUTION	LOCATION OF SCHOOL CITY STATE	DATES FROM-TO MONTH–YEAR	GRADE OR SUBJECT	ANNUAL SALARY	REASON FOR LEAVING PERSON TO CONTACT & PHONE NUMBER FOR CONFIRMATION OF EXPERIENCE

Figure 5.2 (Continued)

APPLICATION FOR CERTIFICATED PERSONNEL

EDUCATIONAL AND PROFESSIONAL TRAINING

(PLEASE LIST ALL UNDERGRADUATE AND POST-GRADUATE CREDIT. ATTACH ADDITIONAL SHEET IF NECESSARY.)

NAMES OF COLLEGES/ UNIVERSITIES ATTENDED	LOCATION CITY–STATE	DATES ATTENDED FROM–TO	GRADUATION DATE	DEGREE AND/OR SEMESTER HOURS	MAJOR FIELD OF CONCENTRATION

POSITION DESIRED

HIGH SCHOOL _____   ELEMENTARY SCHOOL _____

MIDDLE SCHOOL _____   OTHER _____

PLEASE LIST SUBJECTS OR GRADE LEVELS IN ORDER OF PREFERENCE: _____

_____

WHAT EXTRACURRICULAR ACTIVITIES ARE YOU WILLING TO SPONSOR OR COACH? _____

ARE YOU PRESENTLY UNDER CONTRACT? _____   IF YES, WHERE? _____

ARE YOU BILINGUAL? _____   WHAT LANGUAGES? _____

ARE YOU QUALIFIED TO TEACH COMPUTERS? _____   WHAT LEVELS? _____

PROFESSIONAL PERSPECTIVE

PLEASE ATTACH YOUR RESPONSES TO THE FOLLOWING QUESTIONS. MAKE SURE 1-4 ARE IN YOUR OWN HANDWRITING.

1. DESCRIBE THE CLASSROOM CONDITIONS THAT BEST FACILITATE STUDENT LEARNING. INCLUDE STRATEGIES YOU WOULD USE TO ASSURE MAXIMUM LEARNING FOR ALL STUDENTS.

2. DESCRIBE YOUR BELIEFS RELATED TO STUDENT BEHAVIOR. INDICATE WHAT YOU HOPE STUDENTS WILL HAVE LEARNED ABOUT BEHAVIOR AS A RESULT OF HAVING YOU FOR A TEACHER.

3. IN WHAT WAYS ARE YOU QUALIFIED TO ADDRESS THE ISSUE OF DIVERSITY AS A PART OF YOUR INSTRUCTIONAL PROGRAM?

4. AT THE END OF YOUR FIRST YEAR OF EMPLOYMENT IN PARADISE VALLEY, HOW WILL YOU DETERMINE WHETHER OR NOT YOU HAVE BEEN SUCCESSFUL?

5. PREPARE A LETTER WHICH COULD BE USED WHEN YOU'RE FIRST HIRED TO INTRODUCE YOURSELF TO THE PARENTS, STUDENTS, AND STAFF IN YOUR SCHOOL COMMUNITY. INCLUDE YOUR BELIEFS ABOUT TEACHING AND LEARNING AND HELP US TO VISUALIZE WHAT LIFE IN YOUR CLASSROOM WILL BE LIKE.

APPLICATION FOR CERTIFICATED PERSONNEL

CONVICTION REPORT

Because of the tremendous responsibility Paradise Valley Unified School District has to its school children and community, the following information is needed from all applicants and employees regarding convictions. A record of conviction does not prohibit employment; however, failure to complete this form accurately and completely can mean disqualification from consideration for employment or can be cause for consideration for dismissal if employed. Applicants and employees must report any convictions that occur subsequent to the time they initially completed this form. Questions regarding this information should be directed to the Director of Employment.

1. Name _____   Soc. Sec # _____

   Other names used/known by _____   Dates of Usage _____

2. Have you ever been convicted of any offense other than a traffic violation(s)?   Yes   No

3. Have you ever been convicted of a felony?   Yes   No

4. Have you ever been convicted of a sex- or drug-related offense?   Yes   No

5. Have you ever been convicted of a dangerous crime against
   children as defined in A.R.S. 13.604.02?**   Yes   No

If any of the boxes above are marked "YES," fill in the information below and attach a letter of explanation.

CONVICTION INFORMATION

1. CONVICTION CHARGE	DATE OF CONVICTION		COURT OF CONVICTION
CITY	STATE	AMOUNT OF FINE	LENGTH OF JAIL TERM
REMARKS:		LENGTH AND TERMS OF PROBATION	
2. CONVICTION CHARGE	DATE OF CONVICTION		COURT OF CONVICTION
CITY	STATE	AMOUNT OF FINE	LENGTH OF JAIL TERM
REMARKS:		LENGTH AND TERMS OF PROBATION	

*CONVICTION means the final judgment on a verdict or a finding of guilty, or a plea of nolo comterdere, in any state or federal court of competent, jurisdiction in a criminal case, regardless of whether an appeal is pending or could be taken. Conviction does not include a final judgment which has been expunged by pardon, reversed, set aside, or otherwise rendered invalid.

**A.R.S. 13.604.01 requires applicants to give notice of any conviction for dangerous crimes against children. These crimes are defined as second degree murder, aggravated assault, sexual assault of a child, sexual conduct with a minor, sexual exploitation of a minor, child abuse, kidnapping, and sexual abuse.

I authorize investigation of all the statements in this application including investigation of previous employment experiences if I am considered for employment. I certify that the above answers are true and complete and understand that falsification of facts on this application shall be considered sufficient cause for disqualification or dismissal. References and personal information which becomes a part of this record are to be regarded as confidential and will not be revealed.

Signature _____   Date _____

Source: Paradise Valley Unified School District No. 69, Paradise Valley, AZ.

applicant's position on various aspects of educational theory or their response to a job-related issue or problem. For example, a district that was experiencing declining reading comprehension scores asked elementary principal candidates to respond to a writing prompt which asked them to describe the actions or steps they would take to improve reading comprehension (Madrid, 2001). Such a writing assignment provides information that can be used to assess not only the applicant's professional values and skills, but his or her communication skills as well.

The application form should be made available to prospective applicants in both traditional and electronic formats. The actual design of the application is critical not only in assuring that the data most relevant to the selection decision be obtained, but that it does not violate EEOC guidelines. While all school districts have eliminated questions related to race, national origin, gender, age, religion, or disabilities from their application forms, it is not uncommon to find seemingly appropriate questions that do, in fact, violate EEOC guidelines. For example, questions that ask for the date of high school graduation and the location of the high school are indirectly collecting data on age and race or national origin (Harvey & Bowin, 1996). A list of job-related, nondiscriminatory questions and contrasting not-job-related, potentially discriminatory questions that cannot and should not be used on an application form are presented in Table 5.1. Last, although the district may have taken great care to design its application form, if the district wants to be "applicant friendly," it will accept the standard applications used by such teacher candidate databases as USTEACH.

Lastly, the application form should be reviewed on a regular basis and revised as necessary. Revisions should be based on information that was needed but not collected or collected and not needed (Pandiscio, 2005).

INITIAL SCREENING OF APPLICANTS

The initial screening of applicants involves the reviewing of the application forms and supporting materials against the selection criteria to determine if the applicants meet the minimum qualifications for the job, and, if applicable, assessing the quality of the written exercise. For teaching positions, especially in medium- or large-sized districts, this initial screening is typically conducted by or through the human resources department. However, in some districts, especially smaller districts, the screening is performed at the department or building level. The screening process is made easier if the district has in place an applicant tracking system, as discussed next.

In some districts the initial screening may also involve some form of assessment that attempts to predict the applicant's potential for teaching or administrative success. One widely used tool is the Teacher Insight from the Gallup Corporation. Replacing the 30-year-old, widely used Teacher Perceiver and Urban Teacher Perceiver Inventories, the web-based Teacher Insight and Principal Insight assessments consist of multiple choice and Likert items (70 on the teacher assessment and 135 on the principal assessment). They are available 24/7, and the results can be recorded into existing applicant tracking systems.

Table 5.1 Unacceptable and Acceptable Personal Questions for Applications and Interviews .

Subject	Unacceptable Question	Acceptable Question
Name	What is your maiden name?	What is your name? Have you ever worked or been educated under another name?
Race	What is your race? What is your parent's race? What color are your eyes, hair, skin?	None
Sex	What is your sexual preference? Are you gay? Straight? Are you a member of a gay or lesbian group? Do you have AIDS? HIV? Or any STD?	None
Religion	What is your religious affiliation? What church do you attend? Are you active in any church or religious group? What religious holidays do you observe? Are you available to work on weekends?	Will you be able to work overtime if required?
National Origins	Are you a citizen of the U.S.? Where were you born? Where were your parents from? What is the origin of your surname? What is your maiden name? What is the nationality of your Spouse? What is the nationality of your parents?	Are you eligible to work in the U. S.?
Residence	Do you own or rent your home or live with relatives? What was your previous address?	What is your address?
Age	What is your age? When were you born? When did you graduate from high school? College?	Are you over _____? (the legal age required for the specific job)
Disability	Do you have a disability or handicap? What is the nature and severity of the disability or handicap? Have you ever been not hired or terminated because of a physical reason? What are your past medical conditions? Have you had any recent hospitalizations or surgeries? How many days were you out sick last year?	Can you perform the essential job related functions?

Continued

Table 5.1 (Continued)

	Have you ever filed a Workman's Compensation claim? Have you been denied health insurance? Have you ever been terminated because of a psychological reason? Do you have an alcohol or drug problem? Have you ever been treated for drug or alcohol abuse? Have you ever been treated for any other psychological problem?	
Marital/Family Status	What is your marital status? Do you plan to get married soon? What is your spouse's occupation? How many children or dependents do you have? Are you pregnant? Do you plan to have a family? What are your plans for child care? Do you live by yourself or with someone? Who?	Have you ever worked or been educated under another name On occasion this job requires evening/weekend/overnight travel. Would that be a problem for you?
Military Experience	Have you served in the armed forces? When? What type of discharge did you receive from the military?	Do you have military experience in the armed forces? Have you received notice to report to duty in the armed forces?
Arrest/Conviction	Have you ever been arrested or convicted of a crime?	Have you been convicted of or pled guilty or no contest to a felony? Explain.
Emergency Contact	Who is the nearest relative we should contact in case of an emergency?	Whom should be contacted in case of an emergency?

Applicant Tracking Systems

A complement to the electronic document management system (EDMS) discussed in Chapter 4 is the **applicant tracking system (ATS)**. An applicant tracking system is a software application that provides an efficient means to process and analyze the applicant data being managed by the EDMS. Candidate data are stored in a database that allows applicants to be quickly and efficiently matched to positions. It permits the district to identify individuals within the applicant pool who meet the multiple selection criteria established for the position. "If a site administrator needs someone who can teach seventh-grade physical science, can speak Tagalog, and can coach girls' basketball, the applicant tracking system will allow that person to be identified immediately and also sorted based on rankings of

1–100" (O'Laughlin, 1999, p. 38). ATS are also used to generate many of the reports that are required of, or are of interest to, hiring officials: e.g., EEO and VETS 100 reports, cost-per-hire reports, and hire by source reports (Dickmeyer, 2001). Most ATS used in education also include the district website, allowing the district to recruit applicants.

A number of different ATS software are commercially available (e.g., Applicant Tracker, Recruit Track Staffing and Recruiting Software, and CATS Applicant Tracking System). Another option is the use of an *application service provider* (ASP) or *software as a service* (SaaS) where the software remains in the provider's network and is accessed by the district via the Internet. The advantage of using an outside provider is that the ATS remains current and is maintained. The major drawback is the security issues associated with having the data housed outside the district (Meade, 2000).

THE PRELIMINARY INTERVIEW

Following the initial screening of applicants, depending on district practice and the number of applicants remaining in the applicant pool, the selection process may move directly to an interview of the candidates identified as most qualified, or a preliminary interview may be used as an additional screening device. That is, if there are only a few applicants and the decision is made to proceed with the hiring process, or if the initial screening produced only a few applicants with the necessary qualifications, all could be granted the employment interview discussed later. If, on the other hand, a number of applicants remain in the pool after the initial screening, the district may use the **preliminary interview** as an additional screening tool.

The function of the preliminary interview is to eliminate from the applicant pool those who do not meet the profile and qualifications the district is seeking and to make some preliminary assessment of the candidate's success in the position. Practicing administrators report "a direct correlation between the candidate's ability to communicate during an interview and their positive performance in the classroom." (Polansky & Semmel, 2006, p. 46). The preliminary interview also provides the applicant an opportunity to receive answers to questions about the position or school system.

The preliminary interview is usually conducted by human resources department personnel and may take place on campus, at job fairs, at district offices, on the telephone, or through the use of interactive video. In fact, telephone and interactive video interviews have become more common as candidates apply for positions in school districts located great distances from their present locale and as a time-saving strategy. As opposed to a personal interview, which may require as long as 30 minutes to get the applicant in the office and settled, interviewed, and then out of the office, a telephone interview can be done in half the time and get the same information (Yate, 2006). After the preliminary interview, only the most viable applicants remain to be evaluated.

BACKGROUND CHECKS

It has been estimated that over one-third of all applicants have lied or misrepresented themselves on their résumé or on a job application. A recent study by the Society of Human Resource Management found that 56% of applicants had lied about their previous employment, 54% about their criminal background, 32% about degrees earned and, schools or colleges attended, and 24% about certificates or licenses ("Living history," 2006). Almost every school district has had at least one experience with counterfeited transcripts, falsified licenses, or distorted work histories. Even more seriously, a number of districts have found out too late that they have in their employ persons with previous convictions for child molestation or substance abuse. And, because of their failure to conduct adequate background and criminal records checks, many of these districts have been found liable for negligent hiring. In fact, according to *Public Personnel Management*, employers lose 72% of negligent hiring suits, and the average settlement is $1.6 million (Vaughn, 2001a). To protect district students and employees, it is important that the credentials, references, and employment histories of candidates be checked and that criminal background checks be conducted. In so doing, the district must maintain the proper balance between the district's need to know and the applicant's right to privacy. The district must also comply with state and federal laws and the guidelines provided by court decisions in performing background checks. In performing background checks, the district is subject to the same restrictions that are applicable to all other aspects of the selection process. That is, information is not to be solicited or used unless valid and job related.

An important consideration for the district in performing background checks is the cost of, and the time required for, the process. Traditionally, backgrounds checking has been a time-consuming process which could delay the selection process. In recent years, as technology has improved, as more and more public records have gone online, it has become relatively simple to do a background check online. Among the major commercial research systems providing access to public records are Accurint, Auto Tracker XP, Lexis Nexis, and Westlaw. Again, if the district does not have the desire or expertise to conduct the Internetbackground check, a number of online services are available to perform the research. Four of the more popular are at www.peoplewide.com , www.knox.com, www.informus.com, and www.confichek.com, (Vaughn, 2001b). A major consideration in conducting background checks is who will do the checking—the human resources department, the immediate supervisor, a member of the selection committee, or an external third party. Doing background checks internally may save the district money, but many districts do not have employees with the expertise or time to perform the necessary checks and therefore use a third party to conduct the background checks. Besides providing specialized expertise, using a third party often gives applicants a greater sense of privacy, especially in regards to possible coworkers, and gives the impression that all applicants are being handled uniformly and objectively (Garvey, 2001). As discussed next, background checks are usually performed in the areas of references, credentials, and criminal background.

Reference Checks

A reference check is "an objective evaluation of an applicant's past job performance based on conversations with people who have worked with the applicant within the past five to seven years" (Barada & McLaughlin, 2004). The employment application will typically require applicants to provide the names and addresses of persons who can serve as references regarding their current and past employment. Applicants may be informed on the application form that by supplying the names of references or letters of reference, they are agreeing that these references may be contacted. More typically, they may be asked to sign a statement that authorizes the employer to contact current or former employers or other references for the purpose of conducting the reference check. This reference check authorization statement "typically specifies that applicants waive their rights to have access to the information provided by current or former supervisors or other references. The statement may also stipulate that applicants will not hold the individual providing the reference or the school district liable for any jobrelated information provided or received" (National School Boards Association, 1996, p. 516). The signed statement does not give the district the right to probe into every aspect of the applicant's life. What the district may do should be clearly defined by the language of the waver and nothing more (Barada & McLaughlin, 2004).

The most commonly used methods of checking references are letters and telephone calls, with preference given to telephone calls because they save time and are more likely to produce more candid responses and allow two-way communication and follow-up questions. At least three references should be contacted, with one being the most recent supervisor, or, in the case of beginning teachers, their cooperating teacher and/or college supervisor. For experienced teachers, the person who taught next door, a parent who worked closely with the teacher, or the secretary or janitor from the previous school should not be overlooked as possible references (Slosson, 1999). Preferably, reference checking should be performed by an individual involved in the interview process. The use of a standardized telephone reference check form such as that presented in Figure 5.3 helps ensure consistency and fairness, while allowing the district to determine the areas to be addressed. If a standardized form is not used, investigators should be supplied with a set of standard questions. The questions must relate only to job performance. Such questions might include the following:

- What is your name and position?
- How long have you been acquainted with the applicant?
- In what capacity did you know the applicant?
- What are the strengths of the individual?
- How would you characterize the applicant's relationship with his/her students?
- If we hire the applicant, in what area would you suggest that we provide additional staff development or training?
- Have there been any investigations concerning unprofessional conduct, incompetency, insubordination, or immorality concerning the applicant?
- Would you rehire this individual if given the chance? (DeMitchell, 1990, p. 10)

Although reference checking can be a time-consuming process, the more time and energy the process is given, the more accurate and useful the information gathered (Bliss, 2000).

Figure 5.3   Kyrene School District Administrative Telephone Reference Check

KYRENE SCHOOL DISTRICT
ADMINISTRATIVE TELEPHONE REFERENCE CHECK

Name of Candidate _____
Name of Reference _____ *Title* _____
Place of Business _____ *Phone #* _____
Reference call made by _____ *Date* _____

1. How long have you known (the candidate)?_____

2. In what capacity have you known (the candidate)?
_____
_____

3. What do you find to be his/her greatest strengths?
_____
_____

4. What special or unique contribution has he/she made to your school or district? _____
_____

5. What do you believe to be his/her most important reasons for being an educator?
_____
_____
_____

6. Please tell me about the relationships he/she establishes and maintains with:
   A. Students? _____
   B. Parents? _____
   C. Coworkers/Staff? _____

7. What are the most common management approaches he/she uses? _____
_____

8. How do students especially benefit from being in (candidate's) building? _____
_____

9. On a scale of 1 to 10 (10 = highest) how would you rate his/her overall effectiveness as an administrator?
_____ Why?
_____

10. How do you believe a supervisor should work with this candidate in order to bring out the best in him/her? _____
_____

Source: Kyrene (AZ) School District.

Confidentiality and Liability.   Present or former employers may sometimes be reluctant to share any information about a present or former employee other than factual information (e.g., dates of employment, salary, job title) because of fear of a defamation charge. In an effort to encourage employers to share information openly during reference checks, 40 states have passed laws to protect employers that provide good-faith references that result in negative employment decisions. Added protections are often provided for educational institutions. Even in the absence of such statutory protection, under the legal theory of qualified privilege, an employer has the right to share job-related information, even if negative, if the purpose is a legitimate business need. However, the qualified privilege is lost if the information is shared with others who have no need to be privileged to the information (Essex, 2005). The employer will be protected from defamation claims if

- The statement was truthful. This is an absolute defense.
- The employer had a qualified privilege to make a false or defamatory statement. For this to be applicable the statement must have been made within a privileged situation—for instance, a call from a new employer or to protect your own interest.
- The employer can show "absence of malice" or lack of spite, intent to harm, or ill will.
- The employee consented to your making a reference statement. This is the strongest defense. (Bliss, 2000, p. 5)

Whatever information is obtained from reference checks, it is imperative that it not be shared with the applicant or with any other person not authorized to have access to the information.

Credentials Checks

An applicant's credentials include such items as high school or trade school diploma, college or university transcript, the teacher or administrator certificate, professional license, or a physician's verification of health. It is common practice not to require the verification of health unless the applicant is selected for the position. Only an applicant can request the transcript, not the school district. Transcripts and health documentation should not be accepted if presented by the applicant but must be mailed directly to the human resources office by the school, college, university, or physician. However, because administrator and teacher certificates, as well as various other professional certificates and licenses, are issued directly to the person, they may be accepted from the applicant. Nonetheless, a call should still be made to the state agency that issued the certificate or license to verify that it is valid, because in some states when a license or certificate has been suspended or revoked, the agency does not require that the actual document be returned to the agency.

Criminal Background Checks

The statutes of most states prohibit individuals who have been convicted of drug- or sex-related crimes from employment in the public schools. Laws are generally not as specific regarding conviction of other felonies. It is permissible to ask on the application form if the applicant has been convicted of (not just charged with) any crime and the nature of the offense. To conduct a criminal background check to verify the accuracy of these responses is both time consuming and controversial. However, the heightened publicity given to cases of school employees involved in illegal conduct, as well as the heightened liability of school districts that have hired such persons, has led to an increase in criminal background checking. The extent of the checking will depend on state statutes and school district policy. The majority of the states have enacted statutes requiring criminal background checks of persons applying for positions in the schools. In some states such checks are required only of prospective teachers, while in other states checks are required for administrators, custodial workers, food service personnel, coaches, substitute teachers, volunteers (other than parents), or any other individuals who have ongoing contact with students. In those states in which criminal background checks have been mandated by statute, the school district should have adopted a policy and procedures that identify the school district's role in adhering to the statute. The policy and procedures will also typically identify the state or federal agency through which the records will be obtained, who will pay the fee required, and the applicant's rights regarding receiving a copy of the report or the opportunity to explain any conviction (NSBA, 1996).

In states where criminal background checks are required, the state generally has allowed districts access to state criminal records. Under the National Child Protection Act of 1993, school districts are also given access to the FBI criminal records for background checks. If the district has an electronic live-scan fingerprint machine, the candidate's fingerprints can be scanned and sent via the Internet to the FBI and the state criminal records center and a response received, possibly within seconds (Grant, 2001).

In states in which criminal background checks are not required by state law, background checks may still be conducted through state and federal law enforcement agencies or with the **Teacher Identification Clearinghouse** (TIC). The TIC is operated by the National Association of State Directors of Teacher Education and Certification and maintains records of all teachers who have been denied certification or have had their certificates suspended or revoked for moral reasons in the last 15 years. The information is provided by the certification officer of each member state and can be accessed only by states, not individual school districts. In addition to the information received from state or federal law enforcement agencies or the TIC, all states maintain registries of known sex offenders which can also be accessed by school districts.

Dealing with Negative Information

A major challenge for human resources administrators is how to deal with any negative information that may turn up as a result of the background checks. The first thing that must be done is to ensure the information is accurate. Unfortunately, just as there are applicants who will make false statements on their applications or résumés, there are references that will make false or misleading statements about an applicant. There are also instances where persons have had their identity stolen or someone with bad credit or a criminal conviction has the same name, resulting in a negative and inaccurate report.

If the school district uses a consumer reporting agency to conduct a credit check as part of the background check, the information generated from the background check must comply with the Fair Credit Reporting Act (FCRA). The FCRA requires that all data based on public records (e.g., criminal charges and motor vehicle records) be accurate and up to date and that information involving civil suits and judgments be no more than 7 years old (10 years for bankruptcies). The FCRA also specifies the procedures that are to be followed if the information provided by the consumer reporting agency leads to a negative employment decision. Specifically, the employer must provide the employee with a copy of the negative report and the FCRA's *Statement of Consumer Rights*. Second, the employer should give the employee a "reasonable period of time" (normally considered to be 3–5 days) to refute the information. If the employee does not successfully responded within the designated time frame, the employer is free to take adverse action. When doing so, the employer must send the applicant a "notice of adverse action," along within another copy of consumer rights under the FCRA, the name, address, and telephone number of the consumer reporting agency that provided the negative report, and a clear statement that the reporting agency "did not make the adverse hiring decision and is unable to provide the applicant with specific reasons why the action was taken" (Garvey, 2001, p. 103).

After all background checks are completed, the screening and selection process moves to the employment interview stage.

THE EMPLOYMENT INTERVIEW

The employment interview is the most widely used selection technique. The employment interview is a process of gathering information about an applicant relative to the predetermined selection criteria. During this process, the interviewer(s) and the applicant engage in a developmental conversation that explores the applicant's qualifications, skills, and experiences relative to the criteria. Both positive and negative aspects of the applicant's background are discussed with equal importance.

For teaching positions, the employment interview is most often conducted by the principal of the school where the candidate will teach. In many districts, team interviews are conducted. Use of interview teams not only eliminates the bias associated with a single interviewer, but helps build cooperative relationships among faculty, between faculty and administrators, and between school personnel and parent and community representatives (Caldwell, 1993). For teaching positions, the team might consist of the principal, the chair of the department (if applicable), a teacher in the department/area, a human resource specialist, the central office administrator responsible for that curricular area, or the central office administrator responsible for that grade level. In some districts, site-based decision-making teams participate in all phases of the selection process, including interviewing. In constituting the interview team, it is important that, to the extent possible, it be balanced by race, ethnicity, and gender. Research also suggests that including on the interview team at least one member of the same gender and age group as the applicant tends to make the applicant more comfortable (Koenigsknecht, 2006). And, whether as the employment interview or as a separate interview, almost two-thirds of all teacher candidates (and virtually all finalists for administrative positions) will meet with the superintendent during this phase of the selection process (Vickers, 1996).

Whoever is involved in the interview process, it is important that they should review the questions ahead of time and be trained in the district's selection policies and procedures and appropriate interview techniques. It is also important that they be made aware of the types of questions that are allowed and disallowed under state and federal non-discrimination laws and the types of innocent remarks that can lead to school district liability (Clark, 1999).

The information collected through the employment interview should be viewed with the same concern for validity and objectivity as any paper-and-pencil test used in the screening processes. Every possible effort should be made to develop a structured, behavioral interview that is valid for the position to be filled. Structured, **behavioral interviews** are characterized by a set of job-related questions that seek to examine a candidate's past job behaviors rather than to identify general traits (e.g., "the candidate is reliable" [a trait] versus "the candidate only missed 1 day of work in 5 years" [a behavior]) (Warren, Gorham, & Lamont, 2001). Behavioral interviews are based on the belief that "an individual will do at least as well on the new job as he or she has done in the past and that "[p]ast behavior can and does predict future actions" (Yate, 2006, p. 109).

The questions used for the behavioral interview are usually ordered to support a developmental approach to the interview (e.g., chronological, career path, professional accomplishments, etc.). The structured behavioral interview is an information-gathering process for bringing objectivity into the screening procedure. When the interview is specifically developed in relation to the selection criteria derived from the position analysis, selection decisions can be made with the assurance that the best available applicant for the position has been selected.

Planning the Interview

The first step in planning for the interview is to read carefully all materials contained in the applicant's personnel file. Next, a general first impression of the applicant is written giving special attention to areas of strength and areas of needed development. The information is recorded on the interview planning form. Figure 5.4 illustrates one section of a completed planning form. It shows how data and information are associated with one of the predetermined selection criteria.

In recording information, the reviewer condenses information and lists only relevant phrases, comments, and data under the corresponding selection criterion. For example, as shown in Figure 5.4, if the criterion *interpersonal skills* is one of the selection criteria, each item of information found in the written materials that shows strength or needed improvement in interpersonal skills is listed below the criterion and includes a reference to its source (e.g., application form, recommendation from academic supervisor, etc.).

The individual processing a personnel file must judge the statements and other information in the file relative to the selection criteria. This is not difficult if the criteria and dimensions have been clearly defined and the reviewer is very familiar with them. One hazard for the beginning reviewer is the tendency to write evaluative statements about the applicant rather than facts from the file. For example, a letter of recommendation might include the statement, "Her single most important strength is relating effectively to the parents of handicapped children." If this statement is judged to be distinctive and related to interpersonal skills, the inexperienced

Figure 5.4 Interview Planning Form

Applicant: <u>Mildred Thomas</u>

Screening Dimension Number 3

On the lines provided, identify the third screening dimension that was derived from the Position Analysis. This is to be followed by a definition of the dimension. Add behaviors that would suggest evidence of strength in the dimension.

Screening Dimension: <u>Interpersonal Skills</u>
             Definition: <u>Shows caring for others; open to the ideas and feelings of others; earnestly seeks</u>
                   <u>candor and openness; maintains a cool and rational approach on a constant basis</u>
                   <u>throughout a conflict situation</u>

Behaviors Suggesting
Strength in Dimension: <u>Empathetic, caring, rational, poised, tactful, flexible, cooperative, helpful, sensitive</u>

In the spaces provided, carefully review all written application information and identify each item of information that relates to the screening dimension; develop non-leading interview questions; after the interview, record responses.

Background Information: (A—application form, T—college transcript, R—reference)
   Developed unit on student self-concept. (A)
   "Children must experience success." (A)
   "On occasion, shows some impatience with other teachers." (R)
   "As a general rule, she is a helpful and sensitive person. She is extremely intelligent, but can be a little abrupt with others who are having some difficulty." (R)
   "Working on ability to be a better listener." "(R)

Interview Questions:

Interview Responses:

reviewer might write a statement such as, "She has very good interpersonal skills," rather than actually quoting or paraphrasing the letter of recommendation. The evaluation of interpersonal skills is not made during the information-processing phase but only after all written information has been recorded and combined with new or corroborating information from the behavioral interview.

   After all written materials in the personnel file have been processed and pertinent information recorded, the entries under each criterion must be analyzed further. An important question must be asked about the information included under each: Is the written information for the dimension sufficient to allow an evaluation of the applicant on this factor? If yes, the dimension need not be pursued in the behavioral interview. Conversely, if more information is needed to substantiate or corroborate existing information, then relevant interview questions must be developed, questions that relate to the applicant's previous experiences. These questions are developmentally ordered and used in the behavioral interview with the applicant. The types of interview questions and the conduct of the actual interview are discussed in the following section. Notes taken during the interview are recorded in the Behavioral Interview Planning Form under the appropriate criteria.

Conducting the Interview

Essentially, the employment interview is an attempt to predict the job performance of an applicant 1 year after hiring. And, since the best predictor of what an applicant will do in the future is what he or she has done in the past, the task of the interviewer is to explore past work experiences with the applicant and record information that provides insight into strengths and areas of needed development relative to the identified criteria. The quality of information obtained has a direct relationship to the following aspects of the interview process (see Figure 5.5): (1) physical setting for the interview, (2) psychological atmosphere, (3) interviewer's interpersonal skills, (4) interviewer's listening and note-taking skills, and (5) quality of interview questions and techniques.

Physical Setting. While interactive video interviewing may be used when time, distance, or cost is a major consideration, the face-to-face interview is still the most common and preferred approach to the conduct of the employment interview. The interview should be conducted in a private location, where the environment can be psychologically supportive and free of physical distractions. Some administrators

Figure 5.5 Factors Impacting on the Quality of the Interview

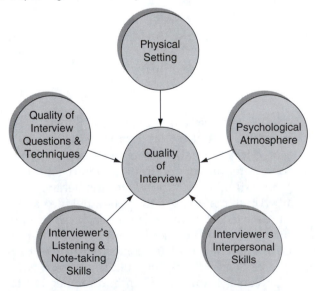

recommend that the interview be conducted in the building, preferably the classroom, where the applicant will teach (Koenigsknecht, 2006). The interview should not be conducted in such public locations as a hotel lobby, restaurant or lounge, or airport. These places have too many distractions, do not offer privacy, and do not support a feeling of confidentiality in the applicant. The best location is a private office.

The interviewer should ensure that all telephone calls and other interruptions are avoided. An interruption during the interview can cause the applicant to lose a line of thought at a time when important information is being communicated. In addition, it is difficult for the interviewer to show interest in the applicant and to record all relevant information if other business is being transacted simultaneously. The interviewer and applicant should not sit across a desk from each other. The desk tends to symbolize authority and may formalize the atmosphere unnecessarily. Similarly, sitting side by side on a sofa is not recommended because it creates a psychological barrier to communication (Martin, 1993). Many experienced interviewers prefer to sit at a table at a right angle to the applicant. Some have conversation areas in their offices with comfortable chairs. Finally, furnishings that cause distractions should be removed from the office (e.g., clocks that chime, fish tanks with bubblers, etc.).

Psychological Atmosphere. The psychological atmosphere must be considered with great care to promote the best conditions for the interview. For the interview to be developmental, the interviewer must minimize the applicant's stress by being friendly and accepting, genuine, open, attentive, and non-judgmental. Stress is particularly great at the beginning of the interview, and careful efforts should be made at that time (and throughout the interview) to put the applicant at ease. The interview should begin with an introduction of committee members and their positions and a review of the job description and responsibilities. The candidate should then be given the opportunity to provide a brief biographical sketch including academic preparation, professional experience, and career goals. Talking about oneself typically promotes confidence (Weller & Weller, 2000).

At the end of the interview, the applicant should feel that the experience was positive and non-threatening. The applicant should also feel that both strengths and areas of needed development for the position were discussed with equal importance. These feelings can more readily occur when the interviewer's beliefs and assumptions about people are positive and supportive. The interviewer should end the interview by thanking the candidate for his or her willingness to be open and honest (Martin, 1993).

Interviewer's Interpersonal Skills. Another aspect of the interview process is the interviewer's interpersonal skills, or manner of dealing with people. Generally, interviewers should not try to use a set of behaviors different from those consistently employed in other settings. The interview is no place to experiment with behaviors. However, it is important for the interviewer to be aware of behaviors that can affect the quality of information gained in the interview.

Body language is one of these considerations. The non-verbal behaviors of an interviewer can significantly affect the interview process. A frown or a smile can communicate meaning to others and serve to increase or decrease the candidate's stress. An authoritative and formal manner on the part of the interviewer will tell the applicant to respond to interview questions in a formal way. On the other hand, a more relaxed manner will tend to put the applicant at ease, and the applicant will respond accordingly. When the interviewer leans toward the applicant with eye contact, it shows that the interviewer is interested and is sincerely concerned about what the applicant is saying. When the interviewer leans back and gives a periodic "ah-ha" or other similar utterance to show understanding and attentiveness, the applicant will know that ample time is available to explore background experiences and qualifications for the position. Conversely, an interviewer's glance at a wristwatch, gaze out the window, or shuffling of papers may tell the applicant that the interviewer is not interested, that a negative decision has been made, or that other, more important things need to be done.

Interviewer's Listening and Note-Taking Skills. One of the most difficult yet important interview skills to learn is listening. Some strategies for improving listening skills are

- Get the respondent to clarify, elaborate, and reflect (e.g., "tell me more," turn a statement into a question, silence).
- Summarize or restate key points (e.g., summary bridges).
- Look at the person (good eye contact).
- Get the main points and test for understanding (e.g., paraphrase).
- Control your desire to mentally agree.
- Avoid making assumptions.
- Recognize your own prejudices.
- Do very little of the talking.
- Be accepting; there are no wrong answers. (Cunningham & Cordeiro, 2006, pp. 286–287)

The task of listening is difficult because the interviewer is trying to record information as it is communicated while thinking about the next question and trying to maintain eye contact with the applicant. For this reason it is best to make brief notes during the interview and then as soon as the interview is over, expand on the notes. When taking notes, stick to the facts; don't interpret the candidate's responses. Ultimately, good notes serve to document the hiring decision.

Quality of Questions and Questioning Techniques. Skill in developing and asking questions is the most difficult yet most important quality for the interviewer to possess. To develop appropriate interview questions, one must be aware of the many considerations that detract from objectivity or contaminate information obtained through positive or negative bias. And, as has been noted, it is extremely important that all questions be totally job related.

To be job related, questions must be centered on previous work experiences, skills, and training in relation to the dimensions established in the position analysis. The questions presented in Table 5.1 as being inappropriate for use on the application form are equally inappropriate for use during the interview. Examples of job-related questions include:

- **Former employment:** What did you like about your former position? What did you like the least? Was your work ever criticized? Did you improve your skills and abilities? In what way? Why did you last your last job? Why do you want to work in this school district?
- **Motivation to work:** Why did you select teaching as a profession? Why did you select this grade level? For non-certificated staff, why did you select this line of work? What do you hope to gain by working here? How do you keep abreast of developments in the profession?
- **Job stability:** What was your original career objective? How has that changed? Why did you leave your last job?
- **Initiative and innovation:** When you ran into a problem you could not solve, what did you do? How did you change your job? What is the most difficult problem you faced and how did you resolve it? What does it take to be a successful teacher? How did you change, create, or work within the parameters of your former employment?
- **Ability to work with others:** How would you supervise others if given the opportunity? How well do you believe your former supervisor did his/her job? What do you believe is the best way for a supervisor/principal to work in this job? How do you manage change? Conflict? Stress?
- **Self-evaluation:** If you had a formal complaint filed against you, how would you handle it? Can you identify a skill that you would like to acquire or that would be appropriate for staff development? What have you found is the best way to handle disputes with parents? Staff? What sets you apart from other candidates? (Clark, 1999, p. 3)

Two types of questions can be used in the interview. First, a direct or **closed question** can be used to obtain factual information. For example, if the applicant omitted information in the application materials, a direct question can be used to complete the record (e.g., "How many years did you teach at Cherryhill Elementary School?"). Closed questions are restrictive in nature and do not provide much opportunity for the interviewee to express opinions or give explanations.

The second type of question, the more commonly used, is the **open-ended question**. This type of question is non-leading, allows the applicant to structure an individual response, and does not suggest an obvious or preferred response. For example, a question such as "We believe in the whole language approach to teaching reading in this district. What do you think is the most effective approach?" is not only leading, it is a closed question. One technique of using non-leading questions involves asking two questions that are considered a polarized pair. If the interviewer wants the applicant to relate an ability to get along with the people in a previous position, the direct question, "Did you get along with the people you worked with at__?" will yield an obvious response. A polarized pair of questions might include the following two questions: "What did you like the most working with the people at__?" would be later followed by "What did you like the least in working with these people?" Both responses may require follow-up questions to gain a greater depth of understanding.

Some words can be quite threatening to the person being interviewed. In the question "What is your most serious weakness for the job?" the word *weakness* can be a threat to the applicant who may view it as a trick question. A less threatening question might be, "What one area do you feel is important for you to develop professionally?" Again, follow-up questions are usually needed to explore fully the applicant's response.

Softening the impact of a question is a useful interviewing technique. When a teacher applicant is being asked about classroom management, it is sometimes helpful for the interviewer to draw on personal experiences to soften the impact of a question. "When I taught mathematics, I did many things that worked well with children. Yet most of us who have taught for a while know that certain situations or types of children give us great difficulty no matter how hard we try. Can you give me an example where you experienced this same feeling?" Usually when this question is asked, the interviewee will give an affirmative, non-verbal nod. If this indication is not given, it might be helpful to first ask, "Have you ever had this experience?" A negative response would raise some obvious concerns about the applicant's veracity. A polarized pair of questions also can work well in pursuing this area of interest.

Avoid hypothetical questions. Quite frequently the interviewer of a teacher applicant will ask, "What would you do if . . .?" A question like this will elicit only a hypothetical or "textbook response." It is far better to ask about actual experiences and accomplishments. If the applicant does not have experience, then it would be better to ask about similar situations that he or she has witnessed rather than ask a hypothetical question. Questions about learning situations and instruction that the applicant observed or participated in as a student would yield far better information than that from a hypothetical question.

One of the most widely used questions with teacher applicants is "What is your philosophy of education?" This is the kind of question that will usually yield a textbook response. If knowing the applicant's philosophy is important, evidence can be found by asking questions about previous teaching strategies, assumptions held, curriculum, and methods of evaluation. An applicant's verbal statement about philosophy may have nothing to do with the ability to teach, manage a classroom, or relate to children. Again, past teaching experiences provide the best guide to what the interviewer can expect of the applicant on the job. This is not to say that exploring the candidate's personal values or perceptions is not important. In fact, questions about the candidate's personal perceptions can tell you a lot about what he or she is like. For example, the answer to the question, "What is the best thing that ever happened to you in education?" has quite a different meaning if the answer relates to an award the candidate won as opposed to a successful student. Other insights can be gained from the responses to such questions as "Who do you admire most?" "Describe the most memorial event that has taken place in your classroom." or "What accomplishment are you most proud of?"

Silence is a very powerful way to ask a question without really saying it. Silence after an applicant's response to a previous question can serve as a prompt that the interviewer wants to hear more. Although this technique can be difficult to master, experience through repeated attempts will minimize the tendency to offer another question after a few seconds of deafening silence. The silence may, in fact, indicate the formulation of a thought or answer. "Let the silence go on for about five to ten seconds before defusing the situation. It will help if you talk about the possibility of silence early on and mention that you understand that coming up with specific situations may take some thought" (Davila & Kursmark, 2005, p. 44).

Several other pitfalls that can affect the interview also should be mentioned. For example, the interviewer should not give the applicant advice. It takes valuable time and is inappropriate in the interview. On occasion, an applicant will say something with which the interviewer will greatly disagree. When this occurs, the interviewer should not argue with the applicant or attempt to "set him straight." It should be remembered that the purpose is to accumulate information about the applicant and not offer another point of view or give evaluative feedback. The best response to negative comments by the applicant is "Ah-ha, I see."

Similarity-attraction is another common pitfall. Research on selection suggests that even well-meaning individuals give subtle advantages to people whose styles and viewpoints are most similar to theirs (Davila & Kursmark, 2005). The **halo effect** occurs when an interviewer's interpretation of the applicant's qualifications are positively skewed when he or she learns that the applicant went to the same college, is from the same hometown, or shares the same hobby (Davila & Kursmark, 2005). Other examples might include belonging to the same fraternity, sorority, or church, or being involved in the same high school or college sport. A negative response can also occur if the applicant speaks very positively about a mutual acquaintance that the interviewer does not hold in high esteem. These examples have the potential of inappropriately tempering the interviewer's understanding of an applicant's qualifications for a position. Every effort should be made to guard against such biases.

In addition to these considerations, experienced interviewers also suggest the following interviewing techniques:

- Pace the interview and apportion interview time approximately. Don't permit the applicant to spend so much time on one area that you must rush to complete the interview in a timely fashion, thus covering other important areas incompletely.
- If there are statements you'd like the applicant to expand on, repeat them in another way. This is called "echoing" and is an effective information-gathering technique.
- Move into the structured part of the interview as soon as you have developed rapport with the candidate. He or she knows the purpose for being there and is eager to get on with the interview.
- Don't interpret the questions for candidates. It is their interpretation that is important.
- Tape record or video the interview if possible. You will often be surprised, upon playback, that what you thought you heard and what was said are not exactly the same. Be sure you have the candidate's permission to use the tape.

- Follow up hunches and unusual statements. If the applicant says, "I don't get along with certain kinds of people," you will want to find out what those kinds of people are.
- Close the interview in a reasonable period of time. Close on a positive note, but don't lead an applicant on or promise anything you can't deliver. ("Conducting," 2001, p. 38. Redeker, 1989, pp. 373–374).

There are innumerable lists of sample questions that can be asked during an employment interview. One commonly used set of questions is the STAR (situation, task, action, and result) Teacher Selection Interview, a structured interview for prospective teachers. The STAR Teacher Selection Interview contains the 36 questions presented in Table 5.2.

ASSESSMENT CENTERS

As described in Chapter 8, the assessment center methodology developed by the National Association of Secondary School Principals (NASSP) is widely used in the preparation and staff development of school administrators. It is also used in administrator selection to observe candidates and assess their performance relative to a variety of tasks considered important to job performance. Individual tasks and exercises, group exercises, in-basket simulations, personality tests, written assignments, and a variety of other assessment techniques may be used to gain performance data on a number of skill dimensions.

Groups of assessors trained and certified in the assessment center methodology rate each candidate on each exercise, compare ratings, and prepare a final evaluation for each candidate for each exercise. The NASSP administrator skill dimensions and the items related to one of these dimensions as presented in the "Observer Assessment for Instructional Leaders for the 21st Century School Administrator Skills" are presented in Table 5.3.

SUMMARY EVALUATION OF CANDIDATES

When the information from both the personnel file and the interview has been recorded, the applicant can be evaluated. A rating form with a point scale where 1 is low and 5 is high, with appropriate descriptors for evaluating each selection criteria, can be used. After this evaluation has been completed, a narrative summary of the evaluation is written relative to each criterion, emphasizing the applicant's strengths and areas of needed development. The written statement should be developed objectively and should include comments that reflect a synthesis of the information from the personnel file and the interview. Some interviewers include a graphic profile depicting the selection criteria on one axis and the numerical evaluation on the other. This provides a quick view of the applicant when reviewing the summaries of several applicants for a position. The graph and the summary statement are particularly helpful if a decision is to be made several weeks after the evaluation is conducted. In the final analysis, a decision must be made to identify the one applicant profile that "best fits" the selection criteria.

Table 5.2 Questions for the Structured Interview of Prospective Teachers

Teacher Relationships with Students

1. What kind of students do you like to work with? What type of students could you teach most effectively?
2. You have an assignment. A student ridicules the assignment, saying it doesn't make sense. What would you do?
3. How do you help students to experience success?
4. A student tells you that he or she is being abused at home. What steps would you follow?
5. How would you individualize instruction for students?
6. What procedures do you use to evaluate student progress besides using tests?
7. How would you challenge the slow learner and the advanced student within the same class?

Teacher Relationships with Colleagues

8. What kind of teachers do you prefer to work with? Why?
9. What activities would you like to work with in our school?
10. What quality or qualities do you have that would enhance our teaching staff?
11. What task would you find most difficult in this position? Why?
12. What are some personality characteristics you find undesirable in people?
13. Who should be responsible for discipline in a school? Why?
14. What needs and/or expectations do you have of the school administration?

Teacher Relationships with Parents

15. A parent walks into your room before the school day begins, yelling and complaining about something you don't even understand. The parent is obviously very upset. What would you do?
16. What do you feel is the most effective way to communicate with parents? Describe how you have used this/these technique(s).
17. Describe the reasons why you would contact parents.
18. What would you include in your Open House presentations to parents?
19. What role do parents play in the education of their children? How would you communicate that to them?
20. What community activities would you like to be associated with? Why?

Instructional Techniques

21. Describe any school experience that you have had, particularly in student teaching (or in another teaching position), that has prepared you for a full-time position at our school.
22. How would you integrate technology into the curriculum that you would teach?
23. Describe any innovative projects that you have been involved in developing.
24. Give an example of how you have used cooperative learning in your classroom.
25. What four words would students use to describe your teaching strategies?
26. What rules do you have for your classroom?
27. Describe your teaching style and how you accommodate the different learning styles of the students in your classes.
28. What do you consider to be your strengths, and how will you use them in your teaching?

A Potpourri of Topics and Background Information

29. Why did you choose to become a teacher?
30. What are your hobbies and Interests?
31. Tell about an experience that has greatly influenced you in your professional development.
32. What are your plans for continuing your professional growth?
33. Tell me about an interesting article that you have read recently in a professional journal.
34. What contributions can you make to our school?
35. What current trends in public education please you? Displease you?
36. Tell me about the three people who have most influenced your own education and educational career.

Source: Pawlas, G. E. (1995). The structured interview: Three dozen questions to ask prospective teachers. *NASSP Bulletin, 79*, 62, 65. For more information concerning NASSP services and/or programs, call (703) 860-0200.

Table 5.3 National Association of Secondary School Principals 21st Century School Administrator Skills

EDUCATIONAL LEADERSHIP

Setting Instructional Direction: Implementing strategies for improving teaching and learning including putting programs and improvement efforts into action. *Developing* a vision and establishing clear goals; providing direction in achieving stated goals; encouraging others to contribute to goal achievement; securing commitment to a course of action from individuals and groups.

Teamwork: Seeking and encouraging involvement of team members. Modeling and encouraging the behaviors that move the group to task completion. Supporting group accomplishment.

Sensitivity: Perceiving the needs and concerns of others; dealing tactfully with others in emotionally stressful situations or in conflict. Knowing what information to communicate and to whom. Appropriately relating to people of varying ethnic, cultural, and religious backgrounds.

RESOLVING COMPLEX PROBLEMS

Judgment: Reaching logical conclusions and making high quality decisions based on available information. Assigning appropriate priority to significant issues. Exercising appropriate caution in making decisions and in taking action. Seeking out relevant data, facts, and impressions. Analyzing and interpreting complex information.

Results Orientation: Assuming responsibility. Recognizing when a decision is required. Taking prompt action as issues emerge. Resolving short-term issues while balancing them against long-term objectives.

Organizational Ability: Planning and scheduling one's own and the work of others so that resources are used appropriately. Scheduling flow of activities; establishing procedures to monitor projects. Practicing time and task management; knowing what to delegate and to whom.

COMMUNICATION

Oral Communication: Clearly communicating when speaking to individuals; small groups; and large groups. Making oral presentations that are clear and easy to understand.

Written Communication: Expressing ideas clearly in writing; demonstrating technical proficiency. Writing appropriately for different audiences.

DEVELOPING SELF AND OTHERS

Development of Others: Teaching, coaching, and helping others. Providing specific feedback based on observations and data.

Understanding Own Strengths and Weaknesses: Understanding personal strengths and weaknesses. Taking responsibility for improvement by actively pursuing developmental activities. Striving for continuous learning

Source: National Association of Secondary School Principals. (2001). *21st Century School Administrator Skills.* Reston, VA: Author.

FINAL SELECTION, OFFER, AND ACCEPTANCE

The final selection of the person to whom the position will be offered depends on the type of position and the specific procedures of the school district. Generally the decision about teaching positions is made by the principal of the school at which the vacancy exists. The decision takes the form of a recommendation through the human resources department to the superintendent. Employment decisions for other types of professional positions are often made by high-level system administrators, also as recommendations to the superintendent. In all cases the human resources department oversees the final selection to ensure the selection is not based on unlawful considerations. In many districts the hiring officials will be asked to indicate why other top candidates were rejected. Because hiring practices are not uncommonly the subject of legal challenge, the human resources department should be sure to document and maintain all records relative to a particular hire.

Once the superintendent has accepted the recommendation of others, if he or she has not participated in the interview process, he or she may wish to interview the finalist(s) before making the final selection. The superintendent will almost always interview the finalists for principalships or systemwide administrator positions. The purpose of this interview is not only to confirm the candidate's qualifications, but to determine which candidate is the best fit for the administrative team (Madrid, 2001). It is also common for the superintendent, before or after the interview, to call references, especially if they are known to the superintendent, to inquire about past performance.

After a decision has been made, it is appropriate to contact the candidate and offer him or her the position, contingent on board approval and the receipt of any required documentation. And, it should be stressed that the offer is not final or legal until all required materials have been submitted and the offer has been approved by the board.

If the candidate accepts the offer, a contract is drafted for approval by the board of education. It is critical that the contract spell out as thoroughly as possible the duties and responsibilities of the position, direct and indirect compensation, and any other terms or conditions of employment or special considerations (e.g., relocation allowance). To be valid, any promises or agreements made during the selection process must be detailed in the contract. For example, if a new principal has been promised secretarial assistance in completing his or her doctoral dissertation, to be enforceable, it must be noted in the contract. Or, if a teacher is to be released from a period to serve as sponsor of an extracurricular activity, that must be noted in the contract. Similarly, the terms of supplemental work assignments and compensation, such as coaching, must be contained in the contract.

It is important that the time between the selection decision and the recommendation to the superintendent, and the time between the superintendent's recommendation to the board and the board's approval, be kept to a minimum. Many good candidates have been lost because someone "dragged his feet," was on vacation, or failed to complete the necessary paperwork in a timely fashion. On the other side of the coin, it is also important that the candidate being offered the position respond to the offer in a timely manner so that if the offer is rejected, an offer can be made to the candidate ranked next in order of preference. For this reason, as noted in Chapter 11, offers normally specify a deadline for notifying the district of the candidate's decision.

NOTIFICATION OF UNSUCCESSFUL CANDIDATES

Only after a position has been filled should all other candidates be notified that the position has been offered to and accepted by another. There are a couple of reasons for doing this as soon as possible after filling the vacancy. First, candidates may want to follow up on other job opportunities with other school districts as quickly as possible. A second consideration is to maintain good public relations with candidates who may want to remain in the pool of qualified persons for future consideration.

The notification is normally made by the human resources department. The notification most often takes the form of a personal letter and may vary depending on whether the candidate was internal, external, or was interviewed but not offered the job. The letter should be written with care so as not to diminish a candidate's candidacy or to communicate to candidates that they are just another number (Pandiscio, 2005). However, in no case should the unsuccessful candidates be told why they did not get the job. To do so could conceivably open the district to unnecessary legal challenge. If any statement is made, it should be a statement about the qualifications of the successful candidate (Weller & Weller, 2000).

EVALUATION OF THE SELECTION PROCESS

The total process of screening and selection should be evaluated on an ongoing basis by the human resources department in cooperation with the hiring departments. The evaluation should include all aspects of the selection process, including the technical quality of selection methods, the psychometrics of selection instruments, as well as the decision-making process (Morris & Lobsenz, 2003).

The evaluation process should also be assessed in terms of the effectiveness of the system in identifying candidates who go on to become successful employees. The performance appraisals of candidates employed should be compared to the screening evaluations to determine their degree of agreement. Where differences exist, a careful analysis of both evaluation procedures should be made to determine ways of improving the screening process. For example, if an applicant was employed for possessing strong organizational skills and the performance appraisal found the opposite to be true, then a careful analysis of the screening process should provide some insight into the screening problem. The involved administrators should try to learn from this experience and make the necessary changes to eliminate the recurrence of such an error. Evaluation of the selection system is important not only for the design of the system, but for refining existing policies and procedures (Morris & Lobsenz, 2003).

PLACEMENT

Human resources authorities agree that one of the most effective means by which human resources administrators can assist the organization to achieve its stated goals and maximize employee potential is through the determination of appropriate placement of personnel. Employees who are appropriately matched to their jobs exhibit higher levels of job satisfaction and performance. An appropriate and productive job match means that the required tasks of the position relate directly to the personal strengths and interests of the employee. One key for helping individuals reach their fullest potential and contribute most toward personal and organizational goals is to assign them to positions in which their knowledge and skills can best be utilized.

Position assignment requires several essential considerations: (1) the specific nature of the position, including role expectations, necessary knowledge and skills, and conditions under which the role is performed, (2) the professional preparation, competencies, and interests of the employee, (3) the relationship of the position and the employee's characteristics and competencies, (4) the extent to which the assignment provides for the personal motivation needed by the employee and the extent to which success can be realized in the position, and (5) consideration of the forces of organizational culture and informal group structure.

Effective placement links closely with effective recruitment and selection. While securing personnel who possess the knowledge and skills needed in the position, recruitment and selection must also be aimed at providing an opportunity for the employee to use the knowledge and skills that are most personally rewarding. Individuals generally have developed personal competence in a large number of task areas. Most persons also have competencies that they most enjoy using and that tend to bring both the highest level of productivity and highest level of personal satisfaction. Position assignment necessitates the careful examination of both the general qualifications of the individual and the specific competencies most rewarding to that person. When a match is found between the competencies required by the job and those most satisfying to the individual, both the school system and the employee are likely to benefit. As Cavanaugh (1984) pointed out:

> When a person's abilities (intelligence, creativity, energy, maturity) are reasonably consonant with the requirements of the job, this will act as a motivating force. When Webb_Ch05.qxd the employee's abilities are significantly higher or lower than those demanded by the job, this typically constitutes a contra-motivational factor . . . . High motivational levels in employees are the result of a good job, by the right person, working for a   competent supervisor, under the banner of positive company philosophy. (pp. 77–82)

Proper position placement is a planned process that uses objective measurements and evaluations of position needs and individual competencies to match positions and individuals. Accurate information about job and employee competencies is necessary for proper position placement. Information about the individual's specific qualifications for the position and his or her specific competencies is gathered through a variety of sources: placement credentials, job application forms, personal résumés, appropriately designed job questionnaires, interviews, examination of job references, and assessment methodology.

Owen (1984) recommended the use of a position and personal profile to enhance the scientific approach to the placement of personnel. His technique is based on the development of a position analysis to evaluate job candidates for respective positions. As described in Chapter 4, the development of the position analysis begins with a thorough consideration of what the position is to accomplish and what primary knowledge and skills are required. Required knowledge and skill levels are quantified to the fullest extent possible and rated on a scale of 0 to 10, or some other appropriate scale. In a similar manner, all available information about the candidate is examined and rated according to the knowledge and skills required. Position and personal profile results are then plotted and evaluated to find the best fit for each candidate.

Several advantages are associated with the profile procedure. It enables the selection activities to concentrate on the requirements of the position as opposed to personality factors, provides continuity to the processes of recruitment and selection, and can be automated to facilitate analyses. In view of the importance of the proper placement of personnel, the technique appears to have significant implications for practice in staff assignments. This is not to presume that position assignment takes place in a vacuum; it takes place in a context. Various aspects of this context must also be taken into consideration in making placement decisions. These context factors include the faculty mix in the schools, the experience and certification of the faculty of the school, anticipated retirements, leavers, and terminations. However, as the process develops within the school system, more objectivity can be established in the process and the instruments used to evaluate individual competency. Although some judgments must be subjective in the job analysis process, its potential for job placement deserves consideration. competency and make placement decisions.

An annual opportunity for teaching personnel to express interest in a change of assignments, both teaching and extracurricular, adds to the effective allocation of personal interests and talents in school systems. Figure 5.6 is an example of an assignment interest assessment questionnaire that might be used by the school principal or other human resources administrators. When there are competing requests for reassignment as discussed in Chapter 11, employee qualifications are the primary consideration, followed by seniority.

School board policies typically provide for a process for employees who are unhappy with their current assignment or proposed reassignment. Such a process typically specifies that (1) an appeal of the assignment/reassignment be made with the administrator responsible for the decision and (2) if not resolved, final appeal to the next highest level.

Figure 5.6 Assignment Questionnaire and Interest Assessment

Name of Teacher: _____

Present Position: _____   _____
                             Location   Grade Level(s)

_____
                             Subjects Taught

Time at President Location: _____

Teaching Assignment Change Being Requested: _____

   Grade Level Change (please explain): _____
   _____
   _____

   Subject-Area Change (please explain):
   _____
   _____
   _____

   Supervisory or Extracurricular Responsibility Change Request: _____
   _____

Comments/Clarifications: _____
_____

Principal's Recommendations: _____
_____

_____   _____
            Signature   Date

The goals, beliefs, traditions, and values of a particular school are important factors in the placement of employees to that school. If an individual employee's personal characteristics and beliefs are significantly incongruent with the culture of the school, personnel problems most likely will develop. The leadership style of the local building administrator and the style of followership on the part of the employee also are important assessments in placement decisions. The time taken to gather information concerning the matter of organizational culture, employee characteristics, and leadership-followership styles will produce positive dividends for the school district and the employee by enhancing job satisfaction and productivity.

SUMMARY

This chapter described a process to be used in the screening and selection of professional personnel. The process included establishing the criteria to be used in the selection process, the application form, the initial screening of applicants, and the preliminary interview; conducting background checks; developing and conducting the employment interview; analyzing and evaluating the personnel file and behavioral interview information; writing summary profile statements; and making the selection decision. The chapter also discussed the final steps in the selection process, job offer and acceptance, and the notification of unsuccessful candidates. The chapter ends with an overview of the consideration of the factors involved in the placement of personnel and the importance of aligning employee interests and talents with the appropriate position.

Discussion Questions

1. Explain the importance of the application form to the selection process.
2. How does the information that can be gathered from the application form differ from that which can be obtained from a résumé?
3. Distinguish between the purposes of the preliminary interview and those of the employment interview.
4. Under what circumstances can background checks become an invasion of privacy?
5. What are the possible advantages and disadvantages of using seniority as a major consideration in placement decisions?

CASE STUDIES

—CASE 5.1———————————

The CEO's Daughter

Sara Mobley leaned back in her chair and reflected on her first year as principal of Finley Elementary School. With a great sense of satisfaction, she thought about the progress that was made in the initial year in implementing a strategic plan for Finley. Two of the school's key strategic objectives related to reading, and Sara was pleased that the school had made great improvement in reorganizing the library media center with the hope of changing the trend in declining reading achievement scores. Sara felt that much of the credit could be attributed to Helen

Monti, one of the finest library media specialists in the system. Helen was instrumental in working with the Library Media Committee to adopt new rules and regulations for library operations that were wholly supported by the entire faculty. She developed a curriculum map of the collection and established critical acquisition priorities for the basic book collection. In fact, the PTA executive council was so pleased with the apparent improvements that it approved a resolution praising the good work of Mrs. Monti and appropriated $3,000 for the acquisition of a CD-ROM system for placement in the media center. Sara thought about how lucky she was to have recruited Helen last summer.

As that thought passed through her mind, Helen appeared at Sara's door and asked to talk with her. After a short period of small talk, Helen told Sara that she would not be returning to Finley next year. Her husband was being transferred to the West Coast and they would be moving in late June. Sara expressed her deep regrets and told Helen that she could count on her for a strong recommendation when she sought employment for next year.

Within a week, Sara met with the Library Media Committee to ask for their assistance in finding a replacement for Helen. Sara told the members that it was important for the school to find a person of Helen's caliber so that the momentum of this year's efforts would not be lost. The selection of the right person for this position was critical to the school's program, and both the faculty and parents had high expectations for the library media program as well.

Sara and the committee worked for several weeks developing a position analysis for the media specialist. Several preliminary screening criteria were sent to the system's department of human resources, and within several weeks, the director of the department sent Sara the credentials of six highly qualified candidates. The committee met to conduct a content analysis of the candidates' files in preparation for the be-

havioral interviews. The committee assisted Sara in preparing the interviews, and during the next 3 weeks, all six candidates were interviewed by Sara. The committee members also met with each applicant to provide an orientation to the school's program and priorities, as well as get to know the applicant. When Sara completed the interviews and subsequent evaluations of the candidates, she called a meeting of the committee to present the findings and decide on the most qualified person. The committee and Sara all agreed that person was John Ashworth. All felt that they had made an excellent choice, and Sara told the members of the committee that she would call John that afternoon.

As Sara returned to the main office, her secretary told her that Superintendent Wilks was on the phone and was anxious to speak to her. Sara picked up the telephone to greet Dr. Wilks. The superintendent expressed his pleasure with the great progress Sara was making at Finley and indicated his hopes and expectations for her long career in the system. He then mentioned that the Chamber of Commerce President, Fran Snell, had been working to assist Henry Mallory, CEO of Albion Manufacturing Corporation, with arrangements for the firm's move of its regional headquarters to the city. Ms. Snell felt that Mr. Mallory would prove to be a strong supporter of the school system and a civic-minded member of the community. Dr. Wilks told Sara that he had assured Ms. Snell that he would do everything he could to gain Mr. Mallory's support.

The superintendent also mentioned that Ms. Snell told Mr. Mallory that she was certain that the school system could find a job for his daughter, Emily, who was graduating from an upstate college as a media specialist this spring. Dr. Wilks then asked Sara to seriously consider Emily Mallory for the media specialist position. In fact, he told Sara that he had already asked the director of human resources to hand deliver a copy of Emily's credentials to her, and the file should be in her hands before the end of the day.

Questions

1. What problem(s) must Sara solve?
2. What are all the possible approaches Sara can use to solve the problem(s)?
3. What are the likely consequences of using each of the approaches?
4. Which approach is the best one to implement?
5. What outcomes can Sara expect from such action?

---CASE 5.2---

Inappropriate Questions

Dr. Anthony Banelli is the assistant superintendent for human resources management in the Pine Valley School District. He recently learned that Frank Honeycutt, a long-time high school principal in the system, was using interview questions related to applicants' age, family, and church membership. He also learned that Frank had been told by the superintendent on two previous occasions to avoid using such questions.

Due to a slowdown in the economy, there was a large pool of well-qualified applicants for all teaching positions in the system. Most recently, Frank received 32 applications for a vacant social science position at his school, and he interviewed 14 candidates. After one of the interviewees was recommended by Frank and hired by the board, Dr. Banelli received a telephone message from the superintendent: "Tony, I just got a call from the EEOC office about Frank Honeycutt. There are three complaints against him. I need to see you right away."

Questions

1. Should Dr. Banelli do anything prior to seeing the superintendent? If so, what should he do?

2. What should Dr. Banelli expect as an outcome of his conference with the superintendent?
3. Is it possible that Dr. Banelli may share some responsibility for the alleged complaints against Frank Honeycutt?
4. What preparations should Dr. Banelli make to remove the possibility of such interview questions being used by other administrators?

---CASE 5.3---

To Lead or Not to Lead?

Middle school principal Pat Kemp prides herself on her ability to interview applicants for teaching positions. She is known to use a lot of tough questions, typified by the following lead-ins: "What would you do if ___?" "How would you go about doing ___?" and "What do you believe ___?"

Despite her confidence in her interview skills, she has an uncomfortable and growing concern that she has not been making the best selection decisions. In fact, the last two teachers she hired are performing differently than she expected. One teacher, Cheryl Hennessy, demonstrated a lot of knowledge about classroom management in her job interview, but now she is having serious behavioral problems with children. Another newly hired teacher, Kevin Smith, articulated many innovative ideas about classroom instruction in his interview, yet parents complain that he uses worksheets as his primary method of instruction. Pat also observed that Mr. Smith does spend most of his time sitting at his desk.

One afternoon, Pat read an article in a personnel journal titled, "The Value of Nonleading, Behavioral Focused Questions in the Employment Interview." She reflected on the content of the article and wondered how she could test such questioning techniques against her own.

Questions

1. Aside from leading questions, what other things could be causing Pat to make poor selection decisions?

2. What could Pat do to test the two approaches to interviewing teacher candidates?

3. What precautions should she make to ensure a fair test of the two approaches?

REFERENCES

Barada, P. W., & McLaughlin, J. M. (2004). *Reference checking for everyone*. New York: McGraw-Hill.

Bliss, W. (2000). Avoiding 'Truth or Dare' in reference. *HR Focus, 77*(5), 5–6.

Caldwell, T. G. (1993). *Hiring excellent teachers: Current interviewing theories, techniques, and practices*. Unpublished master's thesis, California State University-Long Beach.

Cavanaugh, M. E. (1984). In search of motivation. *Personnel Journal, 63*(3), 76–82.

Clark, S. G. (1999). Interviewing job applicants: Asking the right questions. *ELA Notes, 34*(8), 3–4, 6.

Conducting an unbiased job related, stress-free, and predictive interview. (2001). *School Business Affairs, 67*(1), 38–39.

Cunningham, W. G., & Cordeivo, P. A. (2006). *Educational leadership: A problem-based approach*. Boston: Pearson.

Davila, L., & Kursmark, L. (2005). *How to choose the right person for the right job every time*. New York: McGraw-Hill.

DeMitchell, T. A. (1990). Negligent hiring. *The Clearing House, 64*(1), 8–10.

Dickmeyer, W. (2001). Applicant tracking reports make data meaningful. *Workforce, 80*(2), 65–67.

Essex, N. L. (2005). The legal toll of candor in personnel recommendations. *School Administrator, 62*(9), 47.

Garvey, C. (2001). Outsourcing background checks. *HR Magazine, 46*(3), 95–104.

Grant, F. D. (2001). Fast track teacher recruitment. *School Administrator, 58*(1), 18–24.

Harvey, D., & Bowin, R. B. (1996). *Human resources management: An experimental approach*. Upper Saddle River, NJ: Prentice Hall.

Koenigsknecht, S. M. (2006). Stacking the deck during interviews. *School Administrators, 63*(3), 55.

Living history, new employees face more than standard background check. (August 26, 2006). *San Luis Obispo Tribune*, p. J1.

Madrid, M. (2001). The right stuff. *Leadership, 30*(3), 32–34.

Martin, C. (1993). Hiring the right person: Techniques for principals. *NASSP Bulletin*, 79–83.

Meade, J. (2000). Where did they go? *HR Magazine, 45*(9), 81–84.

Morris, S. B., & Lobsenz, R. (2003). Evaluating personnel selection systems. In (pp. 109–129)

National School Boards Association (NSBA). (1996). *The school personnel management system*. Alexandria, VA: Author.

O'Laughlin, J. (1999). Recruiting and hiring high-quality teachers. *ERS Spectrum, 17*(4), 31–39.

Owen, D. E. (1984). Profile analysis: Matching positions and personnel. *Supervisory Management, 29*(11), 14–20.

Pandiscio, H. F. (2005). *Recruiting strategies for public schools*. Lanham, MD: Littlefield Education.

Polansky, H. B., & Semmel, M. (2006). Hiring the best and retaining them. *School Administrator, 63*(8), 46–47.

Redeker, J. R. (1989). *Employee discipline: Policies and practices*. Washington, DC: The Bureau of National Affairs.

Slosson, J. (1999). Hiring right people. *High School Magazine, 7*(2), 27–30.

Smith, M. C., & Knab, K. M. (1996). Designing and implementing teacher selection systems. *NASSP Bulletin, 80*, 101–106.

Vaughn, S. (August 12, 2001a). Background checks are key. *Los Angeles Times*, p. W1–2.

Vaughn, S. (August 12, 2001b). Do your homework in choosing the right person for the job. *Los Angeles Times*, p. W2.

Vickers, N. (1996). Education interviews: Convince districts you can convince their students. In American Association for Employment in Education, *AAEE Job Search Handbook for Educators* (pp. 19–20). Evanston, IL: AAEE.

Warren, Gorham, & Lamont. (1994). *HR series: Policies and practices*. Boston, MA: Author.

Woodward, N. H. (2000). The function of form. *HR Magazine, 45*(1), 67–73.

Weller, L. D., Jr., & Weller, S. (2000). *Quality human resources leadership: A principal's handbook*. Lanham, MD: Scarecrow Press.

Yate, M. (2006). *Hiring the best: A manager's guide to effective interviewing and recruiting*. Avon, MA: Adams Media.

CHAPTER 6

Maximizing Human Performance
MOTIVATION AND INDUCTION

After reading this chapter, you will be able to:

- Describe the three components of motivation.
- Compare the major theories of human motivation.
- Distinguish between the cognitive motivation theories of expectancy, goal-setting, and equity.
- Explain the purpose of a planned induction program.
- List the steps in the induction process.
- Distinguish between induction, mentoring, and orientation.
- Describe the benefits of a mentoring program to the mentee, mentor, and school district.
- Describe the primary elements of the post-orientation phase of induction.

A major responsibility of the human resources function is to maximize employee performance. Previously, human resources administration was defined as the administrative and staff processes planned and implemented for the purpose of establishing a system of human resources that leads to achieving the goals of the school system. This definition emphasizes the purposeful utilization of people, through positive motivation, to achieve both organizational goals and employee self-fulfillment. Maximizing employee performance is critical to achieving the goals of the federal No Child Left Behind Act and other state and local initiatives aimed at improving school performance and is founded on the understanding that organizations progress to the extent that they are able to motivate and develop people.

Individual performance is said to be captured by the following equation:

Performance = motivation × ability.

Given the importance of motivation to both organizational and individual performance, it is essential that school administrators understand the basic concepts of motivation. For this reason the chapter begins with a discussion of the major theories of motivation as applied to the workplace. The discussion then turns to a consideration of the second half of the performance equation, ability. Ability is a function of individual intelligence, personality, knowledge, and skills. While some of these factors are beyond the ability of the human resources unit to affect, others can be affected by the attention given to employee training and development. One component of this, induction, is discussed in the second part of this chapter. The discussion continues in the next chapter with a discussion of staff development.

HUMAN MOTIVATION

Motivation is the set of forces that cause an individual to behave in a particular way (positive or negative) in an effort to achieve a desired end result or goal. The ability to predict, understand, and influence how people will behave is critically important to administrators who seek to improve schools and employee performance and maximize staff potential.

Components of Motivation

Motivation has three dimensions: direction, effort, and persistence. *Direction* is concerned with the pattern of choices a person makes when choosing among possible alternatives. For example, one teacher might choose to take advantage of district paid training to prepare for National Board certification, whereas another might take advantage of a district tuition reimbursement program to take course work at a local college and obtain a master's degree.

In the context of motivation, *effort* refers to behavioral indicators of how hard a person is working on a particular task. However, it should be noted that the amount of effort the employee brings to a task may not be solely a function of motivation, but may be mitigated by environmental factors such as the uncontrolled interruptions common in schools.

The third dimension, *persistence*, is concerned with how long a person pursues a course of action. Persistence is reflected in not only how long one is willing to expand effort on a task, but the extent to which the individual is willing to keep coming back to try again.

Why a person will go in a particular direction, give such an amount of effort, or be more or less persistent is addressed by the various theories of motivation. Those most commonly mentioned in the motivation literature are discussed in the following section.

Theories of Motivation

School administrators who understand human motivation will be much more effective in making positive differences in the school climate and in maximizing human potential. Several theories of motivation hold import to school administrators as they seek to understand what motivates people to perform a job and to persevere until the task is completed. The most commonly discussed theories of motivation in the literature can be grouped into three broad categories: (1) those that are based on the assumption that people are motivated by needs; (2) those that are based on the assumption that people are motivated by rewards or punishments; and (3) those that are based on the assumption that people are motivated by cognitive factors such beliefs, values, and expectations.

Needs Theories. One of the most influential theories of motivation was developed by the psychologist Abraham Maslow. According to Maslow (1970/1954), behavior is motivated by the desire to satisfy unmet needs. These needs are distributed along the hierarchy depicted in Figure 6.1 in order of their urgency to the individual, with physiological needs (need for food, clothing, shelter) being the lowest and self-actualization or self-fulfillment being the highest. According to Maslow, basic lower-level needs serve as potential motivators until they are satisfied or essentially satisfied; then they are no longer motivators. Maslow also maintained that the level of needs, while never completely satisfied, is generally satisfied to the extent that it has little motivational effect. Consequently, in practice, higher-order needs provide greater motivation than lower-level needs. In the school setting one assumes that teachers' physiological needs have been met but that they do have security needs (e.g., tenure, personal safety) that serve as motivators. If they do feel secure in their work environment and feel that they receive adequate compensation, motivators such as a sense of belonging or acceptance become important.

Closely related to Maslow's hierarchy of needs is Alderfer's (1972) ERG theory, which proposed three categories of human needs: existence, relatedness, and growth. *Existence needs* include, in general, Maslow's physiological and safety

Figure 6.1 Maslow's Hierarchy of Basic Needs

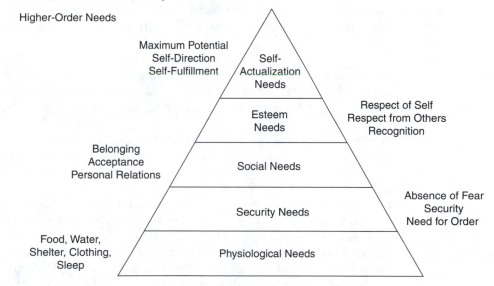

Source: "Hierarchy of Needs" from *Motivation and Personality*, 3rd ed., by Abraham H. Maslow. Revised by Robert Frager et al. Copyright © 1954, 1987 by Harper & Row, Publishers, Inc. Copyright © by Abraham H. Maslow. Reprinted by permission of Addison-Wesley Educational Publishers, Inc.

needs; *relatedness needs* encompass the social needs as they relate to relations with others; and *growth needs* are concerned with self-actualization and esteem needs, as they are reflected in positive self-concepts. ERG views motivation as being present within all of the three levels dependent on the extent to which various needs have been satisfied or remain unsatisfied. In this view, individuals may seek needs at higher levels even though some needs at a lower level have not been met.

Another prominent needs theory of motivation is Herzberg's two-factor model. Herzberg, Mausner, and Snyderman (1959) proposed that individuals have two types of needs: hygiene and motivators. *Hygiene factors* are related to physiological, safety, and social needs. According to Herzberg, hygiene factors (also called maintenance factors) provide little or no motivation, but if not sufficiently present can serve as demotivators or as blocks to motivators. As opposed to hygiene factors, *motivators* are those things that do, in fact, serve to motivate individuals.

Herzberg's theory has been used to explain motivation and satisfaction and dissatisfaction. According to Herzberg's two-factor theory of motivation, satisfaction and dissatisfaction are not opposites of each other but are two distinct conditions. That is, the motivators when gratified tend to generate satisfaction, but when absent do not produce the condition of dissatisfaction, but the condition of no satisfaction. Conversely, the elimination of dissatisfaction does not result in satisfaction, only no dissatisfaction.

According to Herzberg's theory, it is not possible to motivate people with maintenance factors. Reducing class size or providing salary increases can eliminate or reduce dissatisfaction to the level where they can be motivated, for example, by the opportunity to participate in a district-sponsored program to prepare for National Board Certification, but a salary increase in and of itself, is not a motivator. Herzberg has provided three important suggestions for administrators who want to employ his theory:

1. *Enrich the job*, which involves redesigning the work that people do in ways that will tap the motivation potential in each individual. This would include making the job more interesting, more challenging, and more rewarding.
2. *Increase autonomy* on the job. . . it was not suggested that complete autonomy be somehow granted to workers, but that autonomy be increased. This suggests more participation in making decisions as to how the work should be done.
3. *Expand personnel administration* beyond its traditional emphasis on maintenance factors. The focus of personnel administration should be on increasing the motivational factors present in the work. In this view, school districts in which personnel administration focuses almost exclusively on such things as contract administration, the routines of selection-assignment-evaluation-dismissal, and the details of teacher certification and pension plans are attending to important things but not to motivating things. Because 80% or more of the current operating budget of many school districts is allocated directly *to* salaries, wages, and related items, it would seem that the personnel function should be deeply

involved in creating or redesigning jobs that motivate the incumbents and thus increase the effectiveness or productivity of the district's employees. This is the view that, for many, underlies the concept of "human resources administration" in contrast to more traditional views of personnel administration. (Owens & Valesky, 2007, p. 391)

Herzberg's two-factory of motivation is comparable in many ways to Maslow's hierarchy of needs. Maslow's lower-order needs are comparable to Herzberg's maintenance factors, and both theories suggest that job satisfaction is more likely to come from such things as recognition, increased job responsibilities and challenges, and opportunities for professional growth and advancement, which are included among Maslow's higher-order needs or Herzberg's motivators. Herzberg's theory was based on empirical research and has been widely applied in organizations around the world. "Perhaps no other theory of motivation at work has been more extensively researched . . . (and) has been widely influential" in business and industry as well as education. Although some advocate abandoning Herzberg's two-factor theory of motivation in favor of the never and more complex expectancy theory discussed in the next section, "the two-factor theory remains a powerful explanation of motivation in the workplace" (Owens & Valesky, 2007, p. 389, 393).

Reinforcement Theories. Reinforcement theories assert that behavior can be controlled by awarding or withholding of rewards. The concepts of behavior modification, operant conditioning, and behaviorism all reflect the theory that the behavior of an individual can be altered through the reinforcement of desired behaviors. Initially associated with the work of B. F. Skinner (1938), reinforcement theory suggests that an individual's behavior can be modified through immediate rewards to favored responses and by no response to unfavorable behavior. Positive reinforcement, through personal reward, praise, recognition, or extended authority, is used to solidify the continuation of desired behavior. Undesirable behavior is dealt with by use of extinction, whereby the behavior is merely ignored. Skinner's concepts also suggest that desired responses can be learned through shaping. When favored responses are seldom or never demonstrated, initial rewards are given for behavior responses similar to the desired behavior. Finally, only the desired response is reinforced through appropriate rewards (Skinner, 1953, 1969).

Behavior modification suggests that providing careful feedback of positive job performance to an employee would reinforce that behavior. For example, pay incentives or other rewards for exemplary attendance would reduce employee absenteeism, or giving rewards for reaching a desired skill level would lead to a continuation of positive personal development. Behavior modification research provides several suggestions for administrative practice:

1. The kind of behavior desired should be determined as specifically as possible.
2. If the desired behavior is not currently present or is seldom demonstrated, shaping techniques should be utilized to bring about changes in behavior similar to the desired behavior. Similar behavior should be positively reinforced.

3. Desired behavior should be reinforced immediately. Material rewards and "psychic" or "social" rewards, such as benefits, commendations, carefully designed personal feedback, responsibility, and recognition, should be scheduled as reinforcers.
4. Results should be measured and assessed and decisions reached concerning the appropriate schedule of reinforcements needed to ensure the continuation of the desired behavior.

Cognitive Theories. Cognitive theories of motivation address how individuals give meaning to consequences and make decisions based on their beliefs, expectations, values, or other cognitions. Three theories of motivation most commonly associated with the cognitive school are expectancy theory, goal-setting theory, and equity or social justice theory. Each is discussed below.

Expectancy Theory. Expectancy theory was first articulated by Victor Vroom (1964). Expectancy theory is based on the assumption that employees are rational and future-oriented decision makers and will be motivated to behave in a particular way based on their perception of whether that activity will lead to a valued reward (Lawler, 2003). While expectancy theory recognizes that sometimes individuals make mistakes in assessing likely outcomes or misperceive reality, overall the theory sees individuals as generally trying to deal rationally with the world as they perceive it and as rational human beings will behave in a productive way when they see a relationship between their effort and the desired outcome (Lawler, 2003). "Expectancy theory is popular because it is useful for understanding how people are motivated in many aspects of their lives, including relationships, family, and work. The theory accepts the view that there are large differences among people in their needs and as a result in the importance they attach to rewards" (Lawler, 2003, p. 39).

Expectancy theory incorporates three concepts (see Figure 6.2); (1) *valance*, an individual's positive or negative orientation toward a particular outcome; (2) *instrumentality*, the extent to which an individual believes that a specific action will lead to a positive outcome or prevent a negative outcome; and (3) *expectancy*, the extent to which an individual believes that an action or effort will lead to a successful outcome.

The expectancy theory of motivation is based on the proposition that effort, performance, and rewards are inextricable related. Expectancy theory suggests that effort and performance in a particular activity (e.g., obtaining a degree or credential) depend on individuals' perceptions of whether that activity will increase the realization of personal goals. For example, a teacher who wants to become a principal is likely to be highly motivated toward obtaining the credentials needed for the position and will exert the required effort and performance if the individual believes that he or she will obtain a principalship once certified.

Goal-Setting Theory. Following its presentation by Locke and Latham in 1990, goal-setting theory has become the most dominant theory in motivation theory today (Latham & Pinder, 2005). According to Locke and Latham (1990), goals have two dimensions: content and intensity. *Goal content* is the object or outcome sought. Goal content varies from concrete to abstract, from long term to short term, from easy to hard,

Figure 6.2 Expectancy Theory of Motivation

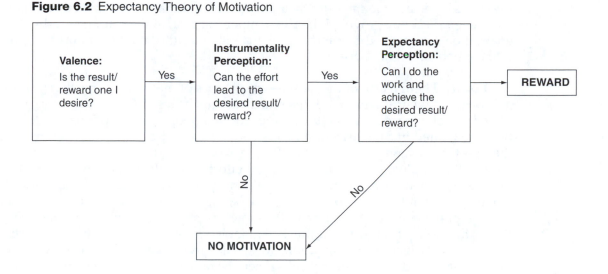

and from few to many. *Goal intensity* is the importance of the goal to the individual and is evidenced by the effort, resources, and commitment given to obtaining the goal.

According to Locke and Latham (1990), if goals are to motivate performance, they must be specific, challenging, and attainable, and be committed to by the individual. Specific goals produce higher performance than vague goals or just "do the best you can" goals. They also suggest that setting high goals "leads to high performance, which in turn leads to rewards. Rewards result in high satisfaction as well as high self-efficacy regarding perceived ability to meet future challenges through the setting of even higher goals" (Latham & Pinder, 2005, p. 497).

Locke and Latham (1990) explain the positive effect of goals on performance in terms of four mechanisms:

> First, goals *increase attention* to the immediate task; that is, they affect choice by helping individuals focus. Second, goals *increase the effort expended* on activities; they help people take action on goal-relevant activities while ignoring others. Third, goals *increase persistence* because there is less temptation to quit once a goal has been clearly established. Once a person decides on a goal, these three mechanisms become relatively automatic. Finally, goal setting increases motivation and performance by encouraging the *development of specific task strategies*, that is, ways of performing the task. Task strategies are conscious and deliberate plans the individual develops to achieve the goals. So whereas attention, effort, and persistence are fairly automatic consequences of goal setting, developing task strategies has conscious, deliberative, and creative consequences. (Hoy & Miskel, 2005, p. 138)

In summary, goal-setting theory suggests that specific, challenging, attainable goals increase motivation because they reinforce effort and persistence and their accomplishment contributes to a sense of accomplishment and self-efficacy. Goal setting is an important aspect of employee evaluation and professional development. As teachers or other staff set goals, individually or in cooperation with their supervisor, it is important that they not only be challenging and attainable goals but that specific measures be detailed to measure their attainment and that feedback on their attainment be periodically provided. It is also important that, in the setting of individual goals, it be remembered that individual goals should inform and support the goals of the school and school district.

Equity Theory. One of the most recent theories of motivation, one that has had a growing influence on motivation research, is equity theory. Equity theory, as articulated by John Stacy Adams (1965), proposes that people's perceptions about how they are treated in comparison to others and in comparison to their effort impacts their motivation and job satisfaction. People expect the ratio of the inputs they provide to the employment relationship (e.g., effort or loyalty) to the outcomes they receive (e.g., salary or recognition) to be fair and equitable. Fairness or equity is evaluated in relation to a *comparison other*. That is, they compare their own ratio to that of a comparison other who performs the same or similar job (Weller & Weller, 2000). When the ratio of input to output is equitable, or nearly so, equity is achieved, contributing to increased motivation and satisfaction. Conversely, a negative effect of motivation and achievement results when the ratio is perceived as being unequal. When this happens, the individual could change the comparison other to someone who is actually more equal with respect to the area of perceived inequity. More commonly, the employee may respond affectively (e.g., decreased commitment) or behaviorally (e.g., decreased helping behavior) (Latham & Pinder, 2005) in an attempt to eliminate the inequity. They may also attempt to improve the input-output ratio by either decreasing inputs (e.g., work less hard) or increasing output (e.g., increase income). They may also choose to leave the position.

A large body of research has documented the importance of equity and justice to workplace motivation. In the school setting, when teachers or administrators feel they are being treated unfairly, not only may their performance motivation decline dramatically, they may even engage in theft, cheating, or other questionable practices to "even the score" or get what they think they deserve (Hoy & Miskel, 2005). Equity theory also explains, in part, why teachers have often opposed performance-based pay, which is seen as based on an inherently subjective process. It also underscores the importance of fair procedures and practices in the awarding of monetary and non-monetary rewards, be they salary, schedule, or honors.

Whatever the different theories of workplace motivation, the relationship between motivation and job satisfaction and performance is clearly established: positively motivated employees are more creative, motivated, and satisfied. The challenge for human resources administrators and other administrators in the school system is to find ways to optimize performance toward the attainment of system and individual goals. This requires that the system of motivation be tailored to the particular employee groups, situation, and organizational culture. At the same time, as previously noted, performance is a function of not only motivation but ability. Thus, in addition to attending to concentrating on motivation, administrators must find ways to increase employee ability through the development of employee knowledge and skills. This can be accomplished by a comprehensive staff development program, one which begins with an induction process such as that discussed in the following section.

INDUCTION

The No Child Left Behind Act of 2001 requirement that schools be staffed by "highly qualified" teachers has brought pressure to increase the supply of teachers and has forced school districts across the country to increase their efforts and strategies to recruit teachers. However, recruiting new teachers will not solve the teacher supply problem if teachers continue to leave the profession in their current numbers. As previously noted, it is estimated that one-half of the new teachers leave in the first 5 years of teaching, with urban and rural schools suffering the greatest losses. While there are many reasons that contribute to this exodus, the reasons most commonly cited by those leaving is lack of support.

In an attempt to stem this flight and to retain professionally skilled professionals, states and school districts have increasingly recognized the importance of staff induction. In fact, 44 states now require some sort of induction program for teachers. Induction is a comprehensive, coherent, and sustained multiyear process designed to train, acculturate, support, and retain new teachers and seamlessly progress them into a lifelong professional development program (Wong, 2004). The induction process begins when a prospective employee seeks employment information, continues through job candidacy and, on an ongoing basis, for as long as the employee or the organization views it as necessary. Although the entry of new employees into the school system requires special orientation considerations, induction is not limited to new employees; nor should it be viewed only as a first-year activity. Rather, the induction process is continuous and serves as an important link to recruitment, selection, and professional development.

If effectively planned and implemented, the staff induction process serves several basic purposes:

1. Encourages individuals with qualifications congruent with district expectations to consider employment in the system.
2. Integrates effectively and efficiently new and experienced staff personnel into their respective roles in the school system.
3. Develops understanding and commitment to the stated goals and objectives of the school system.
4. Reduces and/or removes problems and conditions that tend to inhibit personal effectiveness and job satisfaction.
5. Identifies the specific talents of each employee and builds these abilities into the overall educational team.
6. Acquaints personnel with the important considerations of personal, professional, and community relationships within the school community.
7. Ascertains specific needs of school personnel and analyzes these needs in relation to the school system's expectations.
8. Identifies for each employee those human and physical resources that can enhance personal effectiveness.
9. Provides information and services that promote instruction and learning.

Induction is a purposely planned process that is based on the stated beliefs and goals of the school system and reflects a recognition of the importance of the professional development of every staff member to the realization of these goals. The maximization of human resources serves as the foundation and rationale for induction activities and services.

Characteristics of Effective Induction Programs

Because induction programs are designed to meet the specific character and needs of the school district, they are as varied as school districts and vary in substance and quality. However, research and practice have shown that effective induction programs share a number of characteristics. Such programs:

- Clearly articulate the values they intend to promote.
- Require all beginning teachers and administrators to participate.
- Offer a continuum of professional development that begins prior to the first year of teaching and continues through systematic training over a period of 2 or 3 years.
- Evidence administrative support and involvement.
- Promote practices aligned with recognized professional standards as well as state and local achievement standards.
- Assign every beginning teacher and administrator a highly qualified, experienced practitioner in the same or similar field or grade level to serve as a mentor.
- Provide opportunities for observing and modeling effective practice.
- Incorporate input from new and veteran teachers in program design and structure.
- Provide new teachers a reduced teaching load and stucture time for mentee and mentor to have frequent face-to-face interactions.
- Provide release time for collaboration with other teachers in a learning community.
- Promote learning through a standards-based evaluation process.
  (AFT, 2001; Center for Teaching Quality, 2006; Schlechty, 2005; Wayne, Youngs & Fleischman, 2005; Wong, 2004; Wong, Britton & Ganser, 2005)

Guidelines for establishing an effective induction program from California's New Teacher Center are provided in Figure 6.3.

Induction involves a wide range of support services. Induction is often mentioned in discussions of mentoring; indeed, some use the terms synonymously. This is incorrect. Induction is a component of the staff development process and mentoring is a component, like many others, of induction (see Figure 6.4).

Not only is mentoring too narrow a view of induction, so too is the perception that the aim of induction is to ensure that new employees possess the technical skills to effectively perform their jobs. Effective induction programs also articulate the moral, aesthetic, technical, and other norms and conventions that bring shared meaning and direction to those employed in a particular school and school district (Schlechty, 2005). The description of the Induction Program of the Flowing Wells School District in

Figure 6.3 Guidelines for an Effective Induction Program

1. **Program Vision:** Program leaders must aspire to more than retention; instead, they must seek to promote the highest quality of instruction possible. New teacher programs cannot be preparing teachers for mere survival in the complex and demanding world of today's schools. Instead, these programs must also have as part of their vision, a new image of the successful teacher whose leadership capacity is developed from the moment the teacher enters a classroom.

2. **Institutional Commitment and Support:** School districts and other educational organizations must make teacher learning a priority. Institutional commitment can be demonstrated by designing programs that ensure adequate time and resources for new teacher learning and mentor development; by establishing policies that protect new teachers during the critical stage of induction; and by making teacher development the centerpiece of educational reform across the district.

3. **Quality Mentoring:** The new teacher mentor is the most important feature of any high-quality induction program. No technology, no curriculum, no standardized structures can substitute for the power of a knowledgeable and skillful veteran to move a novice teacher to ambitious levels of teaching.

4. **Professional Standards:** Clearly articulated standards of professional practice are essential in helping both the novice teacher and their mentor communicate effectively about and keep all eyes focused on high-quality teaching and increased student learning.

5. **Classroom-Based Teacher Learning:** Successful induction programs embed opportunities for teacher growth into the daily lives of beginning teachers through observation, collaborative lesson design, model teaching, veteran teacher observation, reflection, analysis of student work, goal-setting, and assessment against professional standards. Effective induction programs help new teachers become on-the-job learners who are constantly questioning and systematically inquiring into their classroom practice . . . Well-balanced programs of new teacher support also provide opportunities for novices to come together with other beginning teachers to learn from each other and to discuss issues with those having similar experiences.

Source: E. Moir & J. Gless, cited in National Education Association (2003). *Meeting the challenges of recruitment and retention.* Washington, DC: Author.

Figure 6.4 The Relationship Between Staff Development, Induction, and Mentoring

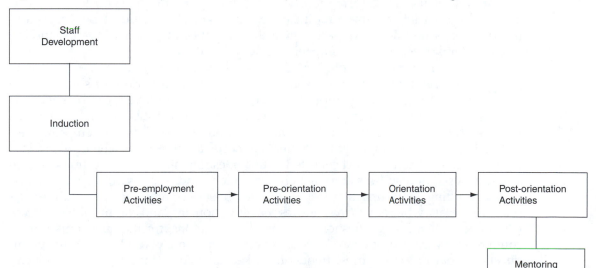

Tucson, Arizona, recognized by the American Association of School Administrators as an Exemplary Staff Development Program captures this prospective:

> The Flowing Wells Induction Program is the transmission of the district and community culture. The major goals of this program are to build a sense of culture and to articulate the district's mission and philosophy. INDUCTION is a structured training program for all teachers new to the district which instructs and models "the way it is done" in the Flowing Wells School District. This program is not merely an orientation to the district's organizational pattern, but a framework of the district's vision for student learning and success. (Institute for Teacher Renewal and Growth, 2003)

Steps in the Induction Process

Pre-employment Activities. Pre-employment induction activities generally are provided during the period between initial contact with the school district and the time the individual assumes a role in the school system. Upon initial contact with the school district, information is provided to a potential employee to communicate: a general understanding of the school district and community; professional expectations and responsibilities; the general working environment; faculty-student information; and professional opportunities within the district, including compensation and benefits.

Pre-orientation Activities. If the potential employee is hired, additional information and assistance, such as help in finding suitable housing, is provided. Commonly the new employee will be provided a district orientation packet and a school orientation packet. The district orientation packet might include (1) the dates and agenda for the orientation program required of all new employees, (2) a copy of the professional development/course offerings handbook for the summer and fall, (3) a list of district and community events a new employee might want to attend, (4) a district calendar, (5) salary schedule and pay periods, (6) a district map, and (7) insurance and real estate information. The building orientation packet, accompanied by a welcoming letter from the principal, would typically include school facts and information, schedules for department and faculty meetings, school events, and the school calendar (Richin, Banyon, Stein, & Banyon, 2003).

A second major pre-orientation activity is the assessment of the needs of new employees. This typically involves gathering data from a variety of sources. One important source is existing employees. School district employees can be surveyed as to what information and personal assistance proved most beneficial to them as well as what communication and assistance should be added prior to employment.

Perhaps the most important statements of needs are those from the new employees themselves. These are best collected with a questionnaire. Some questions may be school focused and address employment regulations and responsibilities such as discipline, grading, extracurricular responsibilities, in-service requirements, and instructional materials, while others may address benefits, housing, and community resources (Weller & Weller, 2000). Questions, or potential questions, for the questionnaire can come from a variety of sources. Various offices and personnel can be asked to submit questions that reflect the most frequently asked questions during pre-employment, major problem areas regarding entry transition, or other school district information considered to be of high priority. A very important source is principals; principals can be asked to provide items that reflect the questions and concerns raised by beginning teachers. The results of the questionnaire are analyzed and induction activities designed to provide the most helpful information and assistance. Administration of the questionnaire to each cohort of new teachers allows the induction program to be "customized" for each cohort of new teachers.

Orientation. Orientation is that component of the induction program that takes place before the school year begins and is designed to provide information about the community, the school district, and the school. The orientation program can also provide the platform to address some activities that later will become routine but often pose considerable frustration for new personnel and detract attention from important position responsibilities. Homework regulations, required records and reports, parental communication, ways of securing instructional materials, and reporting student absence are common administrative problems for beginning teachers. Policies and procedures for student grading, student promotion and retention, student discipline, and parental conferences are other matters significant for induction. The teaching environment, teacher workload, work schedule, position assignment, and other conditions of work also influence the effective transition of personnel into the school system and are also topics to be addressed as part of the orientation program.

Relationships with other staff members and administrators often pose problems for beginning teachers. Orientation activities that establish attitudes of cooperation and team spirit are essential. Position descriptions, communication channels and resources, and an explanation of personnel and office relationships are also helpful.

New personnel also need community information such as educational support services, recreational and cultural opportunities, civic activities, demographic data, medical facilities, governance structure, and community/school support information. Faculty handbooks and planned community tours can be sources for such information.

Personal problems, such as financial need, can inhibit effectiveness on the job. During induction, information should be provided about educational credit associations within the school system or community agencies. In addition, services provided through employee assistance programs (EAPs) should be explained.

It is recommended that orientation take place before the regularly scheduled back-to-school workshops, that attendance be mandatory for all new employees, and that employees be paid for attendance (Clement, 2001).

Orientation activities can be centralized at the district level, decentralized to the school level, or more typically, involve both central office and school-level responsibilities and activities. The Flowing Wells Orientation Program shown in Figure 6.5 is an example of one such program and highlights many of the elements of a successful induction program already noted. (Notice the superintendent acted as a tour guide on a bus tour of the district.)

Post-Orientation Induction

Following initial orientation activities, induction focuses on facilitating an effective, efficient transition of personnel into their respective roles within the school system

Figure 6.5 Flowing Wells School District Induction Overview (8 days)

**FLOWING WELLS SCHOOL
DISTRICT INSTITUTE FOR TEACHER RENEWAL AND GROWTH**

INDUCTION OVERVIEW (8 DAYS)
(refer to attached daily schedules for specific times and topics)

All teachers new to the district are required to attend four days of inservice prior to the return of the continuing teachers. A first-year teacher's contract includes four additional days to meet this expectation. Each new teacher is required to read <u>The First Days of School</u>, by Dr. Harry Wong, prior to the start of the **INDUCTION** training.

DAY 1 – Focus: Team Building and Instruction

A. Welcome by Superintendent and the Governing Board President
   Introduction of all Central Administration, Principals, Directors of Maintenance, Food Services, Transportation
   Welcome by the Educational Association
   The feeling of "family" or "team" is stressed

B. Introduction of all new teachers
   Pictures are taken and displayed
   Organization of cooperative, new teacher groups (K–12)
   Team building and collegial support are stressed

C. Day 1–Content – Instructional Practices

D. Instructors – Staff Development Coordinator, Principals, and "Expert" Level Classroom Teachers

DAY 2 – Focus: Instruction

A. Classroom Instructional Practices

B. Teaching Practicums in small, cooperative groups

DAY 3 – Focus: Flowing Wells Community and Culture

A. Professional Needs (insurance, health care, etc.)

B. Inspirational Video – <u>Flowing Wells Community in Action</u>

C. Bus Tour of District and Flowing Wells Cultural Literacy "Quiz" – conducted by Superintendent

D. New Teacher Luncheon – sponsored by Flowing Wells Education Association

E. New teachers return to respective buildings for planning time with principals. Curriculum, texts, and building-specific procedures are discussed.

DAY 4 – Focus: Classroom Management Procedures and Routines

A. Bell Work, Signal, Dismissal, Homework, etc.

B. Harry Wong Tapes – Discipline Plan, Rules, and Consequences

C. "Expert" level elementary, junior high, and high school teachers share with the new teachers their current, successful classroom strategies.

D. Demonstration classrooms are visited by all new staff. The demonstration teachers model the First Day Procedures and Routines used at the beginning of the year.

E. Slates and markers distributed to all new teachers to encourage the use of student active participation.

F. Follow-up mentoring explained and organized for the school year (five visits per teacher by mentors).

G. During the afternoon, new teachers return to their individual classrooms for preparation.

DAYS 5, 6, 7, and 8 – Focus: Instruction and Classroom Management

A. The days are scheduled throughout the year (October, November, January, and March).

B. Follow-up days include on-site Demonstration Classrooms in Instruction. Also, one-half day is spent on the new Special Education requirements.

C. Day 8 includes:

- Celebration of Learning (Candlelight Luncheon) with Governing Board Members, Central Administration, Principals, and Assistant Principals

- Teacher Awards (framed certificates) presented by Superintendent

Source: Flowing Wells Unified School District. (2003). Retrieved 12/12/06 from http://azk12.nau.edu/ services/ teacherinduction/action/modelDistrict/flowingwells/

and community. Its primary purpose is to assist new employees in the achievement of optimal success as members of the school community. Provisions and practices that add to the induction program following employment include mentor programs, coaching and formative supervision, policy and regulation manuals, and personnel information handbooks.

Mentoring. Mentoring, the pairing of an experienced employee with a new employee, is a crucial component of any induction program. New teachers need the support, advice, and guidance in the use of best practices that only an experienced teacher (mentor) can provide. It is important to emphasize that mentoring should be seen as only one component of an induction program: research has shown that mentoring alone is not an effective strategy (Wong, 2005).

Although mentoring programs for new teachers are required in most states, and 80% of all new teachers participate in a mentoring program, these programs vary considerably in their duration, structure, and intensity. Some consist of only an informal meeting between the mentor and mentee once or twice a term. Others are very structured programs that involve multiple meetings between the highly trained mentor and mentee over 2 or 3 years. Programs also vary as to how much, if any, release time is given program participants, as well as how much, if any, training and monetary compensation is given mentors. They also vary in terms of whether all new employees are required to participate and whether mentors and mentees are matched by grade level and/or subject matter.

Mentor Selection. While there is considerable variation among districts in how mentors are selected, data from effective mentoring programs suggest that mentors should be carefully screened and be required to meet criteria designed to ensure that only high-quality and experienced professionals are selected (AFT, 2001). Ideally mentors should be chosen for their "demonstrated teaching excellence, dispositions toward collaboration and inquiry, commitment to professional growth and change, and expertise in specific district . . . priority areas" (Kelley, 2004, p. 442). The selection of mentors should involve department chairs, principals, and other administrators who have knowledge of the prospective mentors' qualifications. A job description for mentors participating in the Mesa, Arizona, New Teacher Mentor Program is presented in Figure 6.6.

Other practices associated with effective mentoring programs include:

- Participation of all beginning teachers.
- Matching of mentors and mentees from the same grade level or content area.
- Collaboration with other teachers on instructional issues.
- Providing adequate time for mentors and mentees to dialogue and reflect on professional practice.
- Reduced teaching load and fair compensation or in-service or university credit for mentors.
- Training mentors with the knowledge and skills they need to be effective mentors.

Mentoring programs benefit not only the mentee, but the mentor and the school district. The new teacher gains access to an experienced member of the staff for purposes of learning about the school system, its policies and procedures, and effective instructional practices. The mentee also develops a system of personal support and increased self-confidence, develops insight into district purposes, and develops a relationship with a master teacher who can serve as a role model for teaching. The mentor benefits through increased personal self-esteem and recognition as a successful teacher and contributor to the school's program. The mentor also benefits by keeping up-to-date on best practices in teaching and the refinement and improvement of personal knowledge and skills. Mentoring benefits the school system through increases in staff knowledge about the school district, increased confidence and morale of staff, and improved staff effectiveness. Mentoring, as a facilitator of continued professional growth in staff development, is discussed in more detail in the following chapter.

Figure 6.6 Mesa Public Schools New Teacher Mentor Program

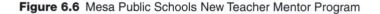

New Mentor Job Description and Application

Mentor Cadre Goal

The New Teacher Mentor Cadre goal is to impact student success by increasing new teacher effectiveness.

Cadre Description

The Cadre is comprised of qualified Career Level educators who provide support to teachers new to Mesa (with no more than two years of approved contract teaching experience). A Career Ladder Specialist coordinates and manages program implementation and establishes mentor and new teacher (mentee) teams with the administrator's approval. Areas of expertise, grade level, assignment, building location, needs of the new teacher, and expertise of the experienced teacher are team assignment considerations. Interaction and communication between the mentor and the new teacher are confidential and teacher evaluation is never a part of the process.

Mentor Responsibilities and Time Commitment

- New mentors are required to attend the following in-service training sessions:

> **Curriculum Services Center**
> **549 North Stapley Drive • Boardroom**
> **4:15–6:15 p.m.**
>
> **Session 1**................. Thursday, September 6, 2007
> **Session 2**.................. Thursday, September 20, 2007
> **Session 3** .... Thursday, September 27, 2007
> **Session 4** ....   Thursday, October 4, 2007

- Experienced mentors may attend training and receive compensation if they have not done so in the previous three years.
- Mentors
  - ✔ orient new teachers to Mesa Public Schools' policies and procedures
  - ✔ individualize the program to meet the new teachers' needs
  - ✔ assist new teachers in increasing skills in management, instructional, and assessment strategies
  - ✔ support new teachers in understanding MPS responsibilities, MPS Curriculum Standards, and Arizona's professional teaching standards
- Meet with the new teacher for a maximum of eight hours off-contract prior to October 15 (compensation provided). Complete and return off-contract log to Career Ladder office by October 22.
- Meet weekly or bi-weekly with the new teacher and maintain documentation and collaboration logs to be submitted by December 3, 2007 (for first semester), and May 5, 2008 (for second semester). These requirements will be clarified when matched with a mentee.

Optional

- Meet with the new teacher for one professional observation day (October–April) in MPS classroom(s) (guidelines provided when matched).
- Participate in professional development opportunities designated for mentors.

Qualifications and Selection Considerations

- Placed Career Level educator with at least 5 years of teaching experience
- Recommendation of site administrator
- Strong interpersonal communication skills
- Professional attitude and demeanor Strong commitment to continuous improvement and a collaborative work ethic
- Student achievement plan and results

Source: Mesa Public Schools New Teacher Mentor Program: MENTOR Job Description from Mesa Public Schools. (2007–2008). Retrieved 9/5/07 from http://www.mpsaz.org/cl/cl/05-06docs/mentor/job_desc.doc

Coaching and Clinical Supervision. In addition to the support provided by mentors, new teachers have consistently reported that what they found most helpful in their professional development is the opportunity to observe master teachers, be observed by others, and be part of a learning community. These and other activities are provided by (1) the induction program throughout Years One, Two, and Three by a continuation of the mentoring program, combined with a (2) program of differentiated and developmentally appropriate workshops focusing on improving instructional effectiveness and on helping new teachers with the myriad problems they face in their first years of teaching, and (3) coaching and clinical supervision. (Coaching and clinical supervision are discussed in the next chapter.)

One example of a Year One Induction Schedule of Activities is included in Figure 6.7. As seen, new teachers have four classroom observations and are required to be videotaped and write a reflection paper based on the taping. Four additional days of induction training focusing on instruction and classroom management are provided, as well as two opportunities to observe master teachers. Finally, monthly support seminars are held at each school site.

School District Policy and Regulation Manual. A properly codified, comprehensive policy and regulation manual can serve as one of the primary induction resources for school personnel. School district policies and regulations are of special significance to the human resources function generally, but contribute to the induction process as follows:

1. By informing school personnel as to what the school district wants to accomplish;
2. By providing a common basis for understanding and a basic reference for effective communication;
3. By clarifying the division of labor between the school board and professional administrative staff;
4. By establishing a basis for action, effective school operations, and meaningful evaluation;
5. By providing information concerning professional responsibilities and opportunities;
6. By setting forth guidelines and procedures for completing specific practices and meeting personal responsibilities that meet the standards of the school system;
7. By providing specific procedures for personnel in such areas as student evaluation, securing instructional resources, community participation, transfer, and professional development.

Personnel Information Handbook. The importance of the personnel information handbook in the induction process demands that its development and dissemination be given high priority by human resources administrators. Although the personnel handbook often includes some information related to school district policy and administrative regulations, the handbook and the policies manual are different documents. The policies manual is the governance document for the district and sets forth

Figure 6.7 Flowing Wells School District First Year Teacher Professional Expectations

FLOWING WELLS SCHOOLS DISTRICT
First Year Teacher Professional Expectations

LEVEL 1 – YEAR 1 CHECKLIST

Name	School
Year	

A. STAFF DEVELOPMENT COORDINATOR OBSERVATIONS (indicate dates)

	Date		Date		Date	Comments by Staff Dev. Coord.
1) Pre-Conf. w/FW lesson plan		Observation		Post-Conf.		
2) Pre-Conf. w/FW lesson plan		Observation		Post-Conf.		
3) Pre-Conf. w/FW lesson plan (optional)		Observation		Post-Conf.		
4) Pre-Conf. w/FW lesson plan (optional)		Observation		Post-Conf.		

B. COMPLETED NEW TEACHER INDUCTION (8 Days)	**Completion Date ⇒**		
	Met Deadline ☑	Date	
C. TWO PEER OBSERVATIONS			
	Met Deadline ☑	Date	
D. 1st VIDEO			
2nd VIDEO			
2nd VIDEO – Post-Conf. + one-page paper			

	Met Deadline ☑								
E. NEW Teacher Support Seminars (at school site)	S	O	N	D	J	F	M	A	M

Signature Verifying Completion: _____

Source: Flowing Wells Unified School District. (2003). Retrieved 12/12/06 From:http://azk12.nau.edu/Services/teacher Induction/action/model District/flowingwells/

the legislative (policy) and executive (regulations) guidelines under which the district is to operate. The personnel handbook is designed to provide information that answers questions relative to (1) the school district's goals, services, and facilities; (2) the community and its makeup; and (3) procedures relating to securing substitute teachers, obtaining curriculum materials, completing grade reports, the school calendar, professional growth activities, insurance plans, and other information that the school district has determined to be of value to employees.

The human resources administrator, school principals, teaching staff, support personnel, and other supervisory staff members need to participate in the development of the personnel handbook, its dissemination, and the evaluation of its effectiveness. The development of the handbook most often is coordinated by the central human resources unit, which also serves as the clearinghouse for needed additions, clarifications, and changes. Such practices as using brief questionnaires to gain feedback from both new and experienced personnel and the various school district units are most useful in assessing the effectiveness of the handbook.

Evaluation of the Induction Program.   Assessment of the induction program is an ongoing process that is both formative and summative. That is, formative evaluation would be conducted during the course of the induction process in an attempt to ensure that the goals are being achieved and to improve the design and delivery of the program if necessary. And, summative evaluation would be conducted at the end of the induction program to assess the outcomes of the program against the intended goals.

The assessment of the induction program should focus on not only individual program components/activities but the overall effectiveness of the program as measured by those outcomes most important to the district. Those outcomes most often deemed important to districts are the effectiveness of the program on the performance of program participants and the effectiveness of the program on the retention of program participants. The performance of program participants is assessed throughout the probationary period. Evaluation of retention should consider not only retention rates but exit interview data from employees who voluntarily leave the district.

SUMMARY

The maximization of human resources in the school system is a primary responsibility of the human resources function. This concern emphasizes the purposeful development and utilization of people within the organization toward the achievement of individual and organizational (school district) goals. An organization's progress depends on the extent to which people are positively motivated and developed.

Motivation is an important consideration of the human resources function generally and of the processes of induction and staff development specifically. Induction is the comprehensive complex of activities designed to gain congruence between institutional objectives and employee needs. Induction begins when the prospective employee makes initial contact with the district. Induction practices, when effectively implemented, enhance employee morale, development, and productivity. Mentoring programs, coaching and formative supervision, policy and regulation manuals, and personnel information handbooks are some of the activities useful in induction programs.

Discussion Questions

1. Examine Maslow's hierarchy of basic needs (Figure 6.1). Discuss the hierarchy of needs as related to teacher personnel generally. For example, what specific provisions and/or activities are important in meeting the safety needs of teacher personnel?
2. Which of the theories of motivation do you or would you find most comfortable using as an administrator? Explain.
3. Describe the induction process in a school district with which you are familiar. To what extent does it compare with the guidelines for an effective induction process presented in this chapter?

CASE STUDIES

—CASE 6.1——

A Question of Low Morale

The Union High School District is experiencing unusually high staff turnover. In addition, general morale throughout the district is low. Teacher absence has increased 20% over the last 3 years and general faculty and support staff complaints have increased substantially as well.

Questions

1. Applying the concepts behind the Herzberg two-factor theory, what specific practices and relationships would you examine to ameliorate the low morale and high turnover?
2. How can a planned induction program contribute to obviating the problems described in the case? A mentoring program?

—CASE 6.2——

The Teacher Transfer

Melvin Schneider was in his third year of teaching at Union Elementary School when parental complaints about his relationships with students started to increase. Calls from parents to Principal Thelma Morton reported that Mr. Schneider was "cold" and that children were afraid of him. Others complained that he didn't work well with the children with learning disabilities, that he lacked the patience to do so.

Principal Morton scheduled a meeting with Human Resources Director Brad Joseph and Superintendent Dorothy Rose. "I observed his classroom twice last week," offered Ms. Morton. "His teaching methods seem satisfactory, but the class atmosphere doesn't come through as a happy one. Maybe we should transfer him next year."

"How do his performance evaluations look?" asked Superintendent Rose.

"As I noted earlier," replied Ms. Morton, "I've given him satisfactory ratings each of his years with me, but he doesn't come off well with parents and I have received more than the usual number of requests from the children themselves to move to Mrs. Martin's fifth-grade class."

Superintendent Rose called her secretary and asked for Mr. Schneider's personal file. Remarks in the record indicated that "parental complaints" and "lack of student rapport" were the primary reasons for these transfers.

"It looks like some specific action is needed again," said Ms. Rose. "This situation cannot continue."

Questions

1. Assume that you are Superintendent Rose in this case. What specific recommendations would you offer at this time?

2. What are your assessments of the history of this case as you can best determine from the given information?

3. In view of the basic concepts of staff orientation what specific steps or programs appear not to have been applied in this case? Is it too late to assign a mentor to Mr. Schneider?

REFERENCES

Adams, J. S. (1965). Inequity in social exchange. *Advances in Experimental Social Psychology, 2,* 267–299.

Alderfer, C. P. (1972). *Existence, relatedness, and growth: Human needs in organizational settings.* New York: Free Press.

American Federation of Teachers (AFT). (2001). *Beginning teacher induction: The essential bridge.* Washington, DC: AFT.

Center for Teaching Quality. (2006). Why mentoring and induction matters and what must be done for new teachers. *Teaching Quality Across the Nation: Best Practices & Policies, 5*(2), 1–5.

Clement, M. (2001). *Finding and keeping high quality teachers.* The Informed Educator Series. Princeton, NJ: Educational Research Service.

Herzberg, F., Mausner, B., & Snyderman, B. (1959). *The motivation to work* (2nd ed.). New York: Wiley.

Hoy, W. K., & Miskel, C. G. (2005). *Educational administration: Theory, research, and practice.* (9th ed.). Boston: McGraw-Hill.

Institute for Teacher Renewal and Growth. (2003). Staff development program description. Retrieved 12/2/06 from http://ark12.nau.edu/service/teacher induction/action/modeldistrict/FlowingWells.

Kelley, L. M. (2004). Why induction matters. *Journal of Teacher Education, 55,* 438–448.

Latham, G. P., & Pinder, C. C. (2005). Work motivation theory and research at the dawn of the twenty-first century. *Annual Review of Psychology, 56,* 485–516.

Lawler, E. E., III. (2003). *Treat people right! How organizations and individuals can propel each other into a virtuous spiral of success.* New York: Jossey-Bass.

Locke, E. A., & Latham, G. D. (1990). *A theory of goal setting and task performance.* Englewood Cliffs, NJ: Prentice Hall.

Maslow, A. H. (1970). *Motivation and personality.* New York: HarperCollins. (Original work published 1954).

Owens, R. E., & Valesky, T. C. (2007). *Organizational behavior in organizations: Adaptive leadership and school reform* (9th ed.). Boston, Allyn & Bacon.

Richin, R., Banyon, R., Stein, R. P., & Banyon, F. B. (2003). *Induction: Connecting teacher recruitment to retention.* Thousand Oaks, CA: Corwin Press.

Schlechty, P. C. (2005). *Creating great schools: Six critical systems at the heart of educational innovations.* New York: Jossey-Bass.

Skinner, B. F. (1938). *The behavior of organisms.* New York: Appleton-Century-Crofts.

Skinner, B. F. (1953). *Science and human behavior.* New York: Free Press.

Skinner, B. F. (1969). *Contingencies of reinforcement: A theoretical analysis.* Englewood Cliffs, NJ: Prentice Hall.

Vroom, V. H. (1964). *Work and motivation.* New York: Wiley.

Wayne, A. J., Youngs, P., & Fleischman, S. (2005). Improving teacher induction. *Educational Leadership, 62*(8), 76–77.

Weller, I. D., & Weller, S. (2000). *Quality human resources leadership.* Lanham, MD: Scarecrow Press.

Wong, H. (2004). Induction programs that keep new teachers teaching and learning. *NASSP Bulletin,* 88.

Wong, H. K. (2005). New teacher induction. Retrieved 12/2/2006 from www.newteacher.com/pdf/corwingallery/pdf.

Wong, H. K, Britton, T., & Ganser, T. (2005). What the world can teach us about new teacher induction. *Phi Delta Kappan, 86,* 379, 384.

Staff Development

After reading this chapter you will be able to:

- Define staff development and its importance to the success of the educational program(s).
- Enumerate the major purposes of staff development.
- Describe the five steps in the staff development process.
- Describe an effective staff development program.
- Compare mentoring and coaching as forms of staff development.
- Define lesson study, assessment centers, learning walks, and clinical supervision.
- Describe the steps in action research.
- Discuss the basic assumptions underlying andragogy.
- Enumerate the unique differences in educating children and helping adults learn.

Staff development is the process of providing ongoing opportunities for employees to improve their knowledge and skills. As important as are the recruitment, selection, and induction processes discussed in previous chapters, the time, effort, and money spent on these activities can be wasted if an effective staff development program is not established for the total school district and its various units (Ray, Condoli, & Hack, 2005). The importance of staff development has increased in the last two decades with the proliferation of technology and the growth of our knowledge base related to cognition, pedagogy, and instructional methodology.

The standards-based reform movement and the requirements of No Child Left Behind have created new performance expectation for students and teachers and have made increasing the effectiveness of every individual in the school system a primary ingredient of school improvement. In this climate, professional development is a major focus of current reform initiatives (Desimone, Smith, & Ueno, 2006). Professional development is the process which "moves a district forward in the culture of high states testing" (Hoyle, Bjork, Collier, & Glass, 2005, p. 5). High-quality professional development is the primary means by which the current teaching force is expected to develop more detailed knowledge and the pedagogical skills necessary to achieve the highly qualified status required by No Child Left Behind (Smith & Rowley, 2005).

It is important for our discussion to make a distinction between professional development and in-service training. Training is directed at imparting information or specific skills. It assumes a deficit in knowledge or skill. Participants in training typically assume a passive role. Training may be part of a comprehensive professional development program, but professional development takes a much broader perspective than skill enhancement. Professional development is an ongoing process that

> focuses on improving the learning of all students, deepens understanding of what is taught and of the powerful ways of teaching it, affects educators' beliefs about teaching and learning, and produces a coherent stream of actions that continuously improve teaching, learning, and leadership. (Sparks, 2005, p. 88)

Staff development must be proactive rather than reactive. The human resources planning process must project and predict as accurately as possible the human skills and talents necessary to meet system needs in the immediate and long term. Armed with this information, staff development joins other personnel processes to recruit, select, and develop the human resources necessary to keep the school system alive and vital. These program activities become cooperative endeavors that account for personal interest as well as for site-level and district-level program needs.

Staff development as presented in this text is based on the following concepts:

1. Effective staff development primarily is a proactive consideration and is developmental in that its emphasis is on an ever-developing individual. It focuses on projected needs and objectives that will help the school system remain creative and productive. Individual growth that meets these projected needs provides employees a personalized opportunity to reach higher levels of self-fulfillment and gratification. Staff development is an important investment in the school system's future.
2. Effective staff development places greater emphasis on the extension of personal strengths and creative talents than on the remediation of personal weaknesses. The major focus of growth is on what the individual can do and how this strength can be further developed and utilized.
3. Effective staff development is self-development. Growth is personal in the sense that what motivates each individual is an individual matter and that each person's self-image is instrumental in determining what incentives will encourage personal growth. Staff development is self-development in that growth begins with a personal need, and individuals develop by taking responsibility for their own growth.

STAFF DEVELOPMENT: PURPOSES AND CONSTRUCTS

The staff development process operates on the basis of several theoretical constructs of human behavior and motivation. For example, the Getzels-Guba (1957) social systems model asserts that each individual employee has unique need-dispositions based on personality factors and that the institution has certain expectations for the purposes of the organization and what it desires from each employee. The areas of agreement between personal needs and institutional expectations constitute areas of high potential for progress. As illustrated in Figure 7.1, as each person realizes new knowledge and skills, new and broadened aspirations of development become possible. Through the use of effective motivation and a system of rewards related to improved performance, personal development becomes an ongoing, continuous process.

Vroom's expectance theory can also be used to explain employees' motivation to participate in professional development. That is, before employees are willing to devote time and effort to a particular professional development activity, they must believe that they will actually acquire specific knowledge and skills (the expectancy perception) and that there is a strong connection between acquiring the knowledge and skills and some positive outcome, be it movement on a career ladder or improved classroom management.

The major purposes of staff development can be summarized as follows:

1. To support planned staff development programs that provide the knowledge and skills necessary to enable the employee to perform at the level of competency required in current and future position assignments.
2. To provide a climate that fosters opportunity for personal self-fulfillment and institutional effectiveness, a climate that facilitates human creativity and system renewal.
3. To provide school personnel with the capacity to implement any changes in the school organization, curriculum, or the instructional program required for school improvement (Glickman, Gordon, & Ross-Gordon, 2007).

Figure 7.1 Agreement Areas for Personal Growth

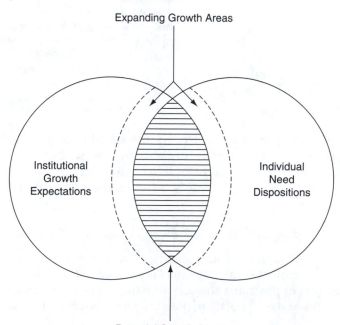

Expanding Growth Areas

Institutional Growth Expectations

Individual Need Dispositions

Potential Growth Areas

4. To save money. It is costly to hire and then dismiss employees who do not work out. It is also costly to lose good employees because they are frustrated by the lack of opportunity for professional growth. And, it is wasteful to accept barely satisfactory work as the norm (NSBA, 1996).

5. To establish viable and meaningful programs that enable system personnel to work cooperatively toward achieving the system's goals and their own personal goals in the areas of achievement, satisfaction, and self-fulfillment.

THE STAFF DEVELOPMENT PROCESS

The staff development process includes five steps: (1) adopt a guiding philosophy; (2) create goals and objectives; (3) plan programs, activities and delivery systems, and determine responsibilities; (4) schedule and deliver plans and programs; and (5) evaluate the process (see Figure 7.2).

Figure 7.2 The Staff Development Process

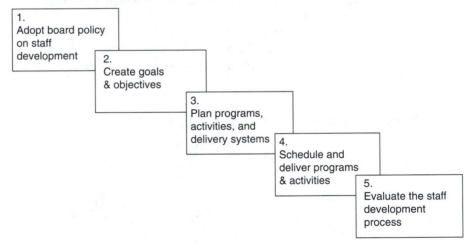

Step 1, the guiding philosophy for staff development, is adopted as official board policy. Such policy is utilized by the school district staff to determine specific procedures through which to implement the program throughout the school system. The following is an example of a board policy relative to staff development.

The board of education supports the principle of continuous personal growth and development for all personnel employed in the school district. Such development programs and activities that serve to enhance the goals and objectives of the school district and to meet the immediate and future needs of district personnel should be made available through cooperative planning and implementation by members of the school district staff.

The general responsibility for the administration of the staff development program belongs to the school superintendent who delegates program responsibilities among the staff as appropriate and who recommends, with proper input from employees, requirements for staff development to meet changing certification requirements, to adjust to program changes, and to gain future knowledge and skills necessary to assure the viability of human resources in the district.

This policy sets the guidelines for the administrative discretion necessary for its implementation. It emphasizes the need for development programs that relate directly to the strategic plans of the school system and its goals and objectives. Such major administrative considerations as certification requirements, needs assessments, program activities, implementation procedures, incentives, and resources are concerns primarily of the school district personnel. Staff development is a shared responsibility, with local school personnel assuming much of the responsibility for program design and implementation. The extent to which the central human resources unit assumes major responsibility for staff development is a function of the individual school district.

Step 2 of the professional development process includes creating goals and objectives for staff development relative to identified system and employee needs. In-service programs that focus on realistic personal needs and local school problems are likely to be more effective than others. Further, programs that consider both the needs of the organization's personnel and the needs of the organization provide an important organizational balance in staff development.

Step 3 links closely with Step 2. Programs, activities, and delivery systems must be planned and programmed. Both school and individual responsibilities must be determined. Ideally, school systems should have a unit or department whose prime responsibility is staff development. School district size, governance structure, and other factors, however, determine the extent to which this is possible. Sometimes the human resources unit or instructional unit serves the purpose of program coordination. In any case, the need for close cooperation and mutual sharing of program activities and responsibilities is important for program success.

Step 4 puts the plans and program options into place. The activities, experiences, and learning programs are scheduled and delivered. Staff development activities are both formal and informal. They include workshops, conferences, peer teaching, mentoring, independent study activities, assessment methodology, internships, job rotation, college courses, and other program pursuits. Selected program options are presented briefly in the next section of this chapter.

Step 5, evaluation of the staff development process, focuses on the assessments necessary to judge the extent to which the stated goals for the program are being met.

RPTIM MODEL OF PROFESSIONAL DEVELOPMENT

One of the most comprehensive models for the administration of staff development is the readiness, planning, training, implementation, and maintenance. (RPTIM) model (Thompson, 1982). This model conceptualizes staff development under five stages and 38 practices. Each stage focuses on several practices. For example, the readiness stage centers on the development of a positive climate before other staff development activities are attempted. Activities associated with this stage might include the collaborative writing of goals for school improvement, the establishment of goals for future program improvement, and the determination of the leadership and support needed. The 38 practices within each stage of the RPTIM model are research based, and the National Development Council and the Council of Professors of Instructional Supervision have endorsed these as practices that should serve as the basis for effective staff development in schools.

CHARACTERISTICS OF EFFECTIVE PROFESSIONAL DEVELOPMENT PROGRAMS

Various professional organizations, researchers, and staff development practitioners, as well as the U.S. Department of Education, have set down principles or guidelines of effective professional development. An analysis by Guskey (2003) of 13 of the better-known lists of characteristics of effective professional development found that the individual characteristics varied widely and that no characteristic was named on all lists. However, a number of characteristics were found on multiple lists. The 10 most frequently mentioned include:

1. Enhances teachers' content and pedagogic knowledge.
2. Provides sufficient time and other resources.
3. Promotes collegiality and collaboration.
4. Includes procedures for evaluation.
5. Aligns with other reform initiatives.
6. Models high-quality instruction.
7. Is school or site based.
8. Builds leadership capacity.
9. Based on teachers' identified needs.
10. Driven by analyses of student learning data. (Guskey, 2003, p. 10)

Another list of characteristics of effective professional development predicated on the "considerable knowledge base" of successful professional development is presented by Glickman, Gordon, and Ross-Gordon (2007):

1. Involvement of participants in planning, implementing, and evaluating programs.
2. Programs that are based on schoolwide goals but that integrate individual and group goals with school goals.
3. Long-range planning and development.

4. Programs that incorporate research and best practice on school improvement and instructional improvement.
5. Administrative support, including provision of time and other resources as well as involvement in program planning and delivery.
6. Adherence to the principles of adult learning.
7. Attention to the research on change, including the need to address individual concerns throughout the change process.
8. Follow-up and support for transfer of learning to the school or classroom.
9. Ongoing assessment and feedback.
10. Continuous professional development that becomes part of the school culture (pp. 353–354).

Finally, the Standards for Staff Development developed by the National Staff Development Council presented in Figure 7.3 are, in effect, statements of what an effective professional development program should look like.

Figure 7.3 NSDC Standards for Staff Development

Context Standards

Staff development that improves the learning of all students:

- Organizes adults into learning communities whose goals are aligned with those of the school and district. (Learning Communities)
- Requires skillful school and district leaders who guide continuous instructional improvement. (Leadership)
- Requires resources to support adult learning and collaboration. (Resources)

Process Standards

Staff development that improves the learning of all students:

- Uses disaggregated student data to determine adult learning priorities, monitor progress, and help sustain continuous improvement. (Data-Driven)
- Uses multiple sources of information to guide improvement and demonstrate its impact. (Evaluation)
- Prepares educators to apply research to decision making. (Research-Based)
- Uses learning strategies appropriate to the intended goal. (Design)
- Applies knowledge about human learning and change. (Learning)
- Provides educators with the knowledge and skills to collaborate. (Collaboration)

Content Standards

Staff development that improves the learning of all students:

- Prepares educators to understand and appreciate all students; create safe, orderly, and supportive learning environments; and hold high expectations for their academic achievement. (Equity)
- Deepens educators' content knowledge, provides them with research-based instructional strategies to assist students in meeting rigorous academic standards, and prepares them to use various types of classroom assessments appropriately. (Quality Teaching)
- Provides educators with knowledge and skills to involve families and other stakeholders appropriately. (Family Involvement)

Source: National Staff Development. (2001). Retrieved 1/6/2007 from: http://www.nsdc.org/standards/index.cfm?printPage=1&

One reason for the lack of agreement on the characteristics of effective professional development is that they are heavily influenced by context. That is, intercity schools that have trouble attracting and retaining highly qualified teachers and with a number of teachers teaching out of field may benefit greatly from a professional development program designed to develop teacher's content and pedagogic knowledge. In contrast, a faculty in a school in an affluent suburb, with all teachers highly qualified, may see little value in such a program (Guskey, 2003). However, whatever the context, the one constant is that, ultimately, the effectiveness of any professional development program, its fundamental benefit, is the extent to which it results in improvement of student outcomes.

STAFF DEVELOPMENT METHODS AND STRATEGIES

The comprehensiveness of the staff development process and the variety of approaches utilized to achieve its purposes have been described in numerous publications. In recent years the approach to professional development has shifted to more interactive and interdependent programs rather than stand-alone technology and to increased staff involvement in planning and implementation (Ray, et al., 2005). A brief description of the major approaches to staff development, including mentoring, assessment centers, learning walks, study groups, clinical supervision, lesson study, action research, individual professional development plans, teacher centers, job rotation, and peer-assisted leadership, is presented in this section. Others not discussed, but somewhat self-explanatory, include college and university course work, sabbaticals, exchange teaching, skills-directed workshops, conferences, conventions, and professional journals and materials.

Mentoring

Webster Online Dictionary (2007) defines the word *mentor* as "A guide, a wise and faithful counselor." Mentoring was previously discussed as it related to staff induction. Mentoring is also a component in a variety of forms of staff development. *Mentoring* and peer coaching are terms often used synonymously, although there are differences between these two strategies. Mentoring generally refers to the art of helping to steer a subordinate or a colleague in the same field. Peer coaching, on the other hand, may be done by a colleague or by an outside specialist and can be one-on-one with an individual or with a group of teachers or administrators. The peer coaching model in teaching is similar to clinical supervision described in a following section: "The teacher meets with his or her teacher coach to agree upon goals; the coach then observes the teacher or the teacher's behavior in the area agreed upon. The coach provides feedback, changes are made, and the cycle begins again with a new goal" (Hoyle, et al., 2005, p. 169).

A mentor in education may use a strategy similar to peer coaching, but it would only be one approach the mentor might use in working with the mentee. Thus the role of the mentor is much broader than the role of the peer coach. The mentor offers advice and guidance across a range of professional issues, helping the individual teacher think through a situation toward the goal of self-resolution of the problem or question. It should be noted that both mentoring and coaching sessions frequently take place through distance methods such as the use of the telephone or online resources.

Assume that a teacher is having serious problems with organizing and presenting effective teaching lessons. The mentor, in this case, might initiate a session by asking the teacher to describe the planning process being used to develop each lesson. The mentor might ask, "How do you determine the objectives for each lesson and how are these objectives supported in follow-up learning activities?" During this time, the mentor serves as a listener and the teacher is the speaker. Clues relative to short-term unit objectives and their relationship to the school's instructional goals can be assessed in regard to the teacher's responses. If it is determined that the development of classroom objectives and learning experiences for students are in need of attention, the mentor can assist the teacher in the process of planning and meeting the requirements of a well-designed daily lesson.

In some cases, depending upon the situation at hand, mentors might go through any number of exercises with the teacher: working on lesson planning, model teaching the actual introduction to a planned lesson, suggesting follow-up activities such as observing other teachers at work, recommending appropriate readings, or critiquing a proposed lesson plan with a follow-up classroom observation.

The emphasis in mentoring should be on providing a positive experience for both the mentor and the teacher. Ultimately, the goal is to have the teacher seek such collaboration and become enthusiastic about the potential of self-improvement. The professional literature is replete with empirical evidence that has shown that individuals can shift from an area of weakness to one of strength, from a lack of confidence to personal self-confidence. Thus mentoring can result in changes of behavior: hesitant innovators can become more creative in their instructional approaches; poor disciplinarians can develop into the classroom authorities that they need to be.

In summary, a mentor is selected to work with an individual staff member or small group of members for the purpose of personal growth. The mentor becomes the primary "coach" and counselor and (1) ascertains the special areas of interest and need regarding the mentee's personal development, (2) works with the mentee to design the most viable plan for individual growth, (3) assesses the most appropriate resources for meeting growth objectives, and (4) serves as a sounding board and constructive critic in evaluating progress and commitment.

ASSESSMENT CENTERS

An assessment center is not a place but a process of using multiple techniques and multiple assessors to make judgments about an individual's performance. Assessment centers were first adopted by the military and business and industry to select and promote administrative personnel. In education the first use of assessment centers was also in personnel selection, the selection of school administrators. As previously noted, beginning in the 1970s the National Association of Secondary School Principals (NASSP) assumed a major leadership role in the development of assessment techniques to select school principals. Since then, assessment center methodology has proven beneficial to assess performance in administrator (and to a lesser extent teacher) preparation programs. And, in recent years it has been increasingly used in staff development. For example, in order to maintain their certification, practicing administrators in Texas are required to participate in an assessment center once every 5 years. One of the options is a Development Assessment Center (DAC) developed by the NASSP. The DAC represents an expansion of the focus of the original NASSP Assessment Center from administrator selection to administrator development.

> In a typical assessment center, participants work through tasks designed to elicit behavior considered important for the job involved. Assessors observe the process and take notes, using specially designed observation forms . . . assessors compare observations and make a final evaluation of each candidate for that exercise. At the end of the process, the assessors develop a summary report on each candidate. (Brown, 1992, p. 35)

Such a center is not viewed as a physical location; rather, assessment activities are conducted in various settings, whenever and wherever a qualified group of assessors meet to assess the performance of an individual or group of individuals for a stated reason. The assessment typically takes a day.

An assessment center is characterized by several activities:

1. Professional standards, such as those developed by the Interstate School Leaders Licensure Consortium (ISLLC), determined to be relevant to a specific job, are assessed through standard methods and activities.
2. Multiple assessment techniques are utilized to gain performance data (e.g., interviews, group discussions, oral presentation, individual task exercises, in-basket simulation, pencil-and-paper tests, personality tests, and other simulation exercises).
3. A group of assessors is used in the evaluation procedures. Such individuals are specifically trained and certified in the methods being utilized and the procedures being followed.
4. Information and individual assessor results are pooled through a process of "jurying" that leads to a final consensus of performance results.
5. If the assessment is for staff development purposes, a system of thorough feedback is provided to the person assessed.

Mentoring, in particular, appears to have considerable potential as a growth model in conjunction with assessment methodology. One major advantage of such a relational approach is its potential for personalizing the growth process by the professional involvement of a specially selected mentor who works with a mentee on the strengths and needs as revealed in assessment results. A major disadvantage of assessment centers is that they are very costly and labor intensive, which may place limits on their use (Hoyle, et al., 2005).

Learning Walks

Learning walks, also known as "instruction walks," refers to an approach to teacher professional development that centers around classroom observation. The procedure involves a team of about five teachers and administrators from the school being observed, or from another school, visiting numerous classrooms in the school where they spend about 10 minutes in each classroom looking for very specific things. Each member of the team is assigned a specific thing to look for. For example, for a learning walk where the focus was on literacy, "one visitor might be assigned to note whether and what type of student writing is displayed in the room, another to write down what is written on the chalkboard, and another to pull aside one or more students to learn what they understood about the writing process" (Richardson, 2001, p. 1). The observers typically sit in the back of the room, but they may walk quietly around the room if necessary to gather the evidence they are looking for. Observers do not talk to each other during the observation. They may talk to students only if the teacher has been previously informed.

After each observation, the observers meet and spend about 5–10 minutes comparing notes. At the end of the day, the observers meet and spend time reviewing and comparing the data they have collected. They then prepare a report that summarizes their overall observation of the school relative to the focus of the observation as well as reports for individual teachers. The individual teacher reports are shared with the teacher; the discussion which follows is a self-learning experience and, as appropriate, serves to focus professional development for individual teachers as well as the faculty as a whole.

According to educators who have had experience with learning walks, learning walks

> produce information in bite-sized pieces that are easier to digest . . . It's easier to attend to a shorter list of things than on a larger list . . . Learning for teachers also occurs when they have a chance to get inside another teacher's classroom . . . Not until teachers get into each other's classrooms and see practice are they actually able to understand what's going on and why there's a need for change and for ideas about how to do that. (Richardson, 2001, p. 3)

A variation of the learning walk is the Data-in-a-Day technique introduced by the Northwest Regional Education Laboratory. Data-in-a-Day involves teams of teachers, parents, community members, and, when appropriate, students, who visit multiple classrooms (or other school areas) in a single day, observing, taking notes, and collecting data relative to a specific theme. The teams then come together and summarize the data collected, share results with the school, and make recommendations. As with learning walks, the goal is that the data will serve to motivate teachers to reflect on practice in their schools and to engage in more focused professional development.

Study Groups

Study groups is another approach to professional development that relies on data analysis to inform professional development. The study group approach, also referred to as Whole-Faculty Study Groups (Murphy, 1999), involves site-based weekly or biweekly meetings of faculty to engage in an in-depth study of a school-based issue. The process begins with the faculty as a whole working together to collect and analyze a wide range of data (e.g., student work, test scores, promotion, retention, attendance, dropout rates, graduate follow-up data, climate surveys, and accreditation reports) to identify and prioritize student needs. Multiple study groups are then formed to examine the highest ranked needs and develop action plans to address the needs. Action plans are then implemented in the classroom of the members of the study group. Members may plan lessons together and even share teaching. They observe each other's classroom and monitor results, including more long-term impact on student performance.

The experience of some districts using study groups with teachers has led them to use this technique for principal professional development. One such district in Springfield, Missouri, expanded by 45–60 minutes what was already the regular principals' meeting to provide for a study session on a particular topic and to provide a unique opportunity for professional learning. "What started out as an attempt to get principals talking with each other eventually led to having more principals working directly with each other in the everyday work of being a leader in the district" (Richardson, 2005, p 4–5).

Clinical Supervision

Clinical supervision is perhaps the oldest, best known, and widely used approach for working directly with classroom teachers (Glickman, Gordon, & Ross-Gordon, 2007). Clinical supervision refers to "face-to-face contact with teachers with the intent of improving instruction and increasing professional growth" (Sergiovanni & Starratt, 2007, p. 233). Clinical supervision involves the study of instructional practice through the collection and analysis of classroom data, with feedback to the teacher in a way that is useful to the teacher and that can provide direction for improvement through professional development. While the clinical supervisor typically holds some type of supervisory relationship—principal or department head to teacher, supervisory teacher to student teacher, mentor teacher to mentee—this need not be the case. The clinical supervisor can be a peer teacher who becomes a partner in inquiry.

Clinical supervision is a cyclical process that involves the following steps:

Step 1 The cooperative relationship between the teacher and supervisor, which is essential to the procedure, is fostered at this phase. At a pre-conference the supervisor and the teacher discuss the nature of clinical supervision, clarify follow-up procedures and responsibilities, specify purposes and focus on development objectives, and discuss the classroom observation.

Step 2 The teacher plans an instructional unit with constructive input from the supervisor. Instructional objectives, teaching methods, instructional materials, monitoring strategies, and other teaching or learning considerations are determined. On the basis of this information, the supervisor and teacher determine the time and procedures to be used with the actual classroom observation.

Step 3 The supervisor makes the actual classroom observation and collects any related instructional material or artifacts of teaching. In this step the agreed-upon methods for collecting information are implemented.

Step 4 Following the observation, the supervisor analyzes the data collected relative to observed instruction and the objectives of the intended lesson. The supervisor incorporates the data collected into the most meaningful and reportable format for the teacher. The specifics to be discussed in the post-observation conference, the approach to be used, and the conference objectives are established in terms of the original planning agreements. Strengths and areas for improvement are analyzed for discussion purposes.

Step 5 The post-observation conference provides the opportunity for the teacher and supervisor to analyze the lesson, review the information collected, and evaluate the results in relation to its predetermined objectives. The supervisor helps the teacher interpret the results of the classroom observation. Through a discussion of actual classroom events, the teacher and supervisor focus on the kinds of changes in classroom practice needed to achieve desired learning objectives. "Throughout the process, the supervisor's role is not to condemn, cajole, or admonish, but to provide information useful to the teacher and to do so in a supportive atmosphere" (Sergiovanni & Starratt, 2007, p. 241).

Step 6 The teacher and supervisor agree on issues to be addressed in this cycle and the behaviors and methods to be implemented in an effort to realize continued instructional improvement. This final step leads to new directions in planning, the reestablishment of the relationship for the future, and the reimplementation of the steps in the clinical supervision cycle.

Unlike traditional classroom observation for evaluation, clinical supervision is ongoing and engenders a climate of shared inquiry and shared responsibility.

Lesson Study

Lesson study is a model for school-based professional development that has been imported from Japan. The process involves a small number of teachers working together to plan a lesson that one of them ultimately teaches while the others observe, looking for evidence of student learning. The group then comes together to critique the lesson and revise as necessary. They may sometimes re-teach the revised lesson. Lesson study can be considered a form of action research, as described in the next section. While appearing relatively simple, lesson study can be complex and time consuming. The steps in lesson study are as follows (Richardson, 2004):

1. Form a lesson study team by recruiting teachers who are interested in the process and work at the same grade level or in the same academic field. One of the teachers or an outside person is appointed to be the facilitator and a second person, a "knowledgeable other," often a university professor, to give a perspective and context.
2. Identify a unit or lesson on which to focus that captures schoolwide goals for students. The lesson need not be unique or overworked with "bells and whistles." This step could take several meetings.
3. Plan the lesson. Lesson planning begins by team members researching the topic of the lesson. This serves as the basis for the creation of a detailed

plan for the lesson and anticipation of student responses to various aspects of the lesson. Planning as a group creates ownership in the lesson.

4. Prepare for observation. In addition to the study team, any other staff from the superintendent on down could also observe. All observers are given a copy of the lesson plan and any instructional materials the students may be using. All observers are expected to collect data to share during the debriefing.

5. Teach and observe the lesson. All observers gather in advance and enter the room together and typically sit at the back of the room.

6. Debrief the lesson. The entire study team along with any other observers meet following the lesson to share their observation and debrief. This is the heart of the lesson study process. The focus is on the goals of the lesson and evidence of student learning. The facilitator ensures that criticism is constructive and that discussion is focused, concrete, and moves forward (Chokshi & Fernandez, 2004).

7. Reflect, revise, and share results. If desired, the lesson may be taught again by a different teacher to test different strategies and studies. A report is written describing the lesson study process, summarizing the data collection, and sharing reflections and lessons learned with respect to the research question.

The lesson study cycle typically takes 3 to 6 weeks to complete, and teachers work on two to three lessons a year (NWRL, 2002). Lesson study presents the opportunity for teachers to learn from each other.

Action Research

Action research is a process in which practitioners identify a problem in their own environment and engage in a process of disciplined inquiry, resulting in a plan for future action. There are several kinds of action research, depending on the participants involved: (1) a single teacher addressing an issue in his or her classroom, (2) collaborative research by a group of teachers investigating a common problem, (3) schoolwide research by a team of teachers and others addressing a schoolwide issue, or (4) districtwide research by a team of teachers and others addressing a districtwide issue (Ferrance, 2000).

The action research process is typically described in terms of the following steps or phases (see Figure 7.4):

1. **Develop the Question.** In this phase of action research, the investigator identifies the problem/issue to be addressed by the research. The question must be one over which the researcher has some control; has not already been answered (just because you do not know the answer does not mean somebody else doesn't); and be able to be done within the confines of the classroom, school, or school district.

2. **Collect Data.** Before the actual collection of data begins, the researcher must answer several key questions: (1) *Why* am I/we collecting this data? (2) *What* specifically will I/we collect? (3) *Where* will I/we collect the data? (4) *When* and over what period of time will the data be collected? (5) *Who* will collect the data? and (6) *How* will the data be collected and presented? (Caro-Bruce, 2002, p. 9). Almost the entire

Figure 7.4 The Action Research Cycle

array of approaches to data collection can be used in action research. Three sources of data should be used (triangulation) to address validity.

3. **Analyze Data.** At this phase the data are analyzed, applying the most appropriate methodology for the type of data collected. The results of the data analysis are reviewed to identify patterns and themes.

4. **Take Action.** Reflecting on the results of the data analysis, and informed by a review of the literature and discussions with knowledgeable others, a plan of intervention or change in practice is developed and implemented. Included in the action plan is the specification of how the success of the action will be measured/determined and what supporting evidence will be used.

5. **Evaluate Results**. Data collected after the intervention are examined to determine if improvement has occurred. If change has not occurred, explanations are discussed and alternative or future actions proposed. Additional action research on the same issue may begin or a new question that arose in the context of the current research can become the focus of a new cycle of action research.

Action research has become an increasingly popular tool for teachers and administrators seeking to expand their knowledge and improve their practice. When working on a problem that is "close to home" and relevant, educators are motivated to examine their own work and consider ways it can be improved—in effect, to develop professionally.

Individual Professional Development Plans

Even the most well-designed school or school district professional development plan cannot meet the diverse professional development needs of the entire staff. The training, experience, and interests of staff vary considerably. Moreover, as discussed in a following section, adult learners want to be actively involved in their own learning. For these and other reasons, a growing number of districts are now requiring that teachers develop individual learning plans as part of the district's professional development program. For example, Ohio requires teachers to develop Individual Professional Development Plans (IPDPs) as part of a revised licensure requirement (Richardson, 2002).

Alternative models of IPDPs are described in the professional education literature. Typically, they incorporate these basic steps: (1) determine focus of professional development efforts; (2) collect data relative to the area of desired improvement (usually various kinds of student data); (3) summarize, analyze, and examine the data; (4) try to make some sense of the data; reflect on current practice and student outcomes in light of the data; (5) design an action plan with strategies (e.g., courses, workshops, action research) for goal attainment; establish meaningful, focused, and achievable goals and determine how their attainment will be assessed; (6) implement action plan; and (7) evaluate results using predetermined indicators.

Teacher Centers

Another effort to place the primary responsibility for personal development on the individual teacher is through the teacher center, an enriched environment of resources, personal involvement, and peer communication. The teacher center concept makes the teacher an active participant in decisions and activities relating to personal growth. A teacher center need not be a permanent site or facility, but conceptually constitutes a teaching resource bank where teachers informally participate in activities that enhance their performance in the classroom. Teachers, alone or in groups with similar interests, examine instructional materials, design teaching aids, read materials related to teaching methods and strategies, develop new lesson plans, and communicate with other teachers and support personnel concerning creative ideas in an area of instructional interest. Based on the proposition that professional staff personnel are best qualified to determine the necessary training needed by their colleagues, the teacher center concept is governed primarily by teachers.

A teacher center might be a temporary site, such as a school district's reading center that is used for a specified period of time for a specific instructional development purpose. It might be a self-contained room with a professional library, audio and visual materials and other resources available for examination and classroom use, and a work area designed for making instructional aids. Some school districts have established a formal learning center with extensive educational facilities for teaching and professional development. Such a center would provide a computer-assisted facility with support staff to assist teachers in the examination of various types of instructional technology and materials while also serving as a meeting place for conferences and workshops.

The positive aspects of teacher centers are numerous. The concept of teachers helping teachers is supported by research. Intrinsic motivation that leads to personal development activities is one important criterion for proactive growth. One concern, however, is the possible absence of research-based development programs.

Conceptual frameworks founded on tested theory, research, and empirical application are essential. If the delivery system for staff development depends exclusively on individual opinions of "effective practice," the potential exists for misdirected effort and practice.

Job Rotation

Industry has experienced success in the practice of moving employees and managers to various positions to enhance organizational effectiveness and employee development. Education has not generally endorsed the practice as it applies to teachers; however, the idea has received some favorable acceptance as a positive growth practice for school administrators. After a certain time period, both the individual and the organization benefit when the employee can exercise personal talents and meet new challenges in a different assignment. Additionally, experience and knowledge of the different educational units and school programs are spread to more persons in the district. Arguments against job rotation in education center primarily on its possible "disrupting" effect on the local school community. Authorities suggest that the practice of job rotation in the future will tie closely to personal competency. That is, the task at hand will determine required skill needs, and personnel will be assigned to such tasks accordingly.

Peer-Assisted Leadership

Peer-assisted leadership (PAL) is a professional development program for principals in which peers help peers in the improvement of their professional skills. Paired principals shadow and observe each other and conduct reflective interviews based on the data collected. The reflective interview requires the principal to reflect on decisions and actions taken or not taken. The program grew out of the Instructional Management Program at the Far West Educational Laboratory in San Francisco. The program was designed to (1) help administrators develop skills that they can use to analyze their own and others' management behaviors, (2) give participants opportunities to learn how other administrators lead in their positions, (3) enable administrators to gain support and insight from colleagues, and (4) provide a means for assisting administrators in the understanding of effective behavior in their specific setting. The PAL program usually lasts 6–9 months with frequent meetings between partner principals.

PAL differs from mentoring in that peer-assisted leadership is not a mentor-protégé arrangement. Rather, peers are placed in dyads or triads and each participant helps others examine and reflect on personal behaviors, skills, and activities in relation to the setting of the school environment, specific skills being implemented, and expected program outcomes. PAL's self-guided approach to professional development reflects professional development concepts of learning communities and learning organizations (WestEd, 1997).

Participants of PAL programs report that it serves to increase awareness of their own behavior, style, and intentions. It serves as an important self-evaluation tool and leads to the learning of new strategies and personal skills.

As previously noted, the field of education has numerous methods and strategies for implementing staff development. Although most of the discussion in this chapter has focused on teacher development, such programs as mentoring, assessment centers, peer-assisted leadership, job rotation, action research, and individual professional development plans apply equally well to administrative personnel. For both teachers and administrators, the underlying importance of staff development in education is reflected in the basic concept that schools will improve as people progress.

ADULTS AS LEARNERS

Professional development is a form of adult learning. Because school system personnel are adult learners, staff development activities must utilize the basic principles that facilitate optimal learning and growth for them. An understanding of adults and how they learn is as vital to successful adult professional development as the knowledge of children and adolescents at the Pre-K–12 level is to their successful learning. "Knowing who is likely to participate in our programs, why adults choose to participate, and what barriers must be overcome before they can participate is knowledge that educators can put to good use in planning and delivering programs" (Merriam & Brockett, 1997, p. 129).

Authorities in the area of adult education point to several important differences between pedagogy, the art of science of teaching children, and andragogy, the art and science of helping adults learn. Knowles and Associates (1984) emphasized four underlying assumptions of andragogy that differ from those of pedagogy and their implications for adult learning.

1. **Regarding the self-concept of the learner.** As the individual grows and matures, his or her self-concept moves from one of dependency to one of increasing self-directedness. The psychological need to be perceived and treated as a person capable of taking responsibility for him- or herself holds important implications for adult learning programs. For example, situations that do not allow the individual to be self-directing tend to produce tension between that situation and the individual's self-concept.
2. **Regarding the role of the learner's experience.** As the adult engages in an ever-expanding variety of experiences, he or she is more able to relate to new learning experiences. Adults enter into an educational activity with both a greater volume and a different quality of experience than youth. Education of adult learners must include an emphasis on experiential strategies that capitalize on the rich resources of experiences of the adult learner. Thus, the use of active, participative activities such as simulation, discussion, problem solving, and team projects are favored over lectures and other more passive instructional methods.
3. **Regarding readiness to learn.** As the individual matures, readiness to learn becomes more dependent on the tasks required for the performance of his or her evolving social role. That is, adult learners are ready to learn because the roles they are approaching or serving set forth the "need."

They become ready to learn when they experience a need to know or to do something in order to perform more efficiently. As Knowles pointed out, the critical implication of this assumption is the importance of timing learning experiences to coincide with the learners' developmental tasks in social roles as teachers, leaders, organizational members, and so forth.

4. **Regarding orientation to learning.** For the most part, adults do not learn for the sake of learning. They learn in order to perform a task, solve a problem, or live in a more satisfying way. Thus, the immediacy of application is a critical learning motivator, and a problem-centered orientation is of primary importance. (Knowles and Associates, 1984, pp. 11–12)

This view of the adult learner has implications for creating structures that support learning for adults. In planning and implementing professional development for education personnel, individuals responsible for human resources administration should consider established guidelines for adult learning to direct the process. These guidelines include:

1. *Set up an environment for adult learning.* Adults, like children and adolescents, can be bored and unproductive in an uninviting environment. In addition to the physical environment, the psychological environment must be one that conveys an interest in and respect for adult learners. "A comfortable physical atmosphere, positive interpersonal climate, and well-prepared organization setting define the . . . correct environment for adult learning" (Terehoff, 2002, pp. 70–71).

2. *Involve adult learners in planning the professional development program.* The research on professional development is unanimous in finding that adults are more likely to support and participate in professional development activities when they are involved in all aspects of the program. This is best accomplished by providing opportunities for teachers to assume responsibility and authority for planning, organizing, facilitating, or conducting various professional development programs or processes. "Mutual planning offers the promise and potential to facilitate developmental growth not only of competencies but also of the capacity to learn from a collective effort of teamwork" (Terehoff, 2002, p. 72).

3. *Pay attention to the interests and needs of the adult learners.* Adults have five basic needs that affect their predisposition toward learning: (a) the need to know that learning will result in a growth in knowledge, skills, attitudes, and interests; (b) the need to feel secure in terms of their self-respect and self-image; (c) the need for new ideas and experiences with new people; (d) the need for appreciation; and (e) the need for recognition (Terehoff, 2002). Adults have different needs at different times during their personal and professional maturation. Staff developers must be aware and sensitive to the varying needs of adult learners as they choose between professional development program options.

Facilitation of learning experiences for adults necessitates a knowledge of the social role development, problems, and needs of the individual. To be able to plan, organize, and implement effective staff development programs for adult personnel, human resources administrators must be prepared to respond in creative ways to the unique needs and interests of the individual learner. Since each adult brings a varied background of experiences and knowledge to any learning situation, knowledge must be personalized, not just individualized. Personalization requires that learning strategies focus on the background and experience unique to the adult learner. To see the value of the learning experiences, adults need to know that the activities and experiences will be applicable to their work and the resolution of problems in their work environment. Moreover, to see tangible outcomes from the learning activities and experiences, adults need to receive some indication of their personal achievement toward learning goals. If necessary remove Discussion Question #4 from the text and renumber question 5 as question 4 to make room for the extra sentence in the Summary.

SUMMARY

The implementation of the staff development process consists of a planned sequence of procedures that begins with commitment by the board of education; continues through cooperative goal setting, program design, program delivery; and culminates in opportunities to practice the knowledge and skills gained in a wide variety of learning activities. Evaluation leads to necessary program changes and ensures continuous program improvement. In all activities, basic principles of adult learning are utilized.

Professional development methods and strategies are virtually limitless and are provided through the local school district, institutions of higher learning, and employee associations. Such developments as mentoring, clinical supervision, teacher centers, assessment centers, lesson study, learning walks, study groups, individualized professional development plans, action research, and peer-assisted leadership are among the viable approaches for meeting the purposes of the professional development process. Attention to the principles of adult learning is essential to the success of any staff development program.

Discussion Questions

1. Examine the most frequently mentioned characteristics of effective professional development programs presented in this chapter. What criteria can be used and should be used to measure their effectiveness?
2. If you were choosing a staff development program that would best meet your professional needs and learning style, which program would you choose? Give reasons why.
3. Identify an educational problem in your discipline that would be suitable for action research. (a) Develop the research question (problem or issue to be researched); (b) explain why, what, where, when, who, and how the data will be collected and presented; and (c) elaborate on the criteria you would use to analyze the results of your findings.
4. Consider a recent professional development program you have participated in. Assess the experience in terms of the extent to which it attended to the guidelines of adult learning.

CASE STUDY

CASE 7.1

Time to Teach

As assistant director of human resources, you receive the memorandum from one of the teachers in your district shown in Figure 7.5. Examine the memo and then present your follow-up ideas in this case. Keep in mind the specific principles of adult learning.

Questions

1. What specific problems do you determine from reading Ms. Petrov's memo?

2. From the somewhat limited evidence provided, what necessary staff development practices appear to have been overlooked in this case in the past?

3. Discuss the alternatives for action at this time. As the school principal, outline a brief action plan that you would recommend in Ms. Petrov's case.

Figure 7.5 Memorandum

To: E. O. Herr, Assistant Director, Human Resources

From: Verna Petrov, Grade 3 Teacher, Union Elementary

Re: Program suggestion

Id like to make a s uggestion for you to consider in planning some of our in-service days. I know that you have run a survey of perceived needs in the district that has given you some general or overall ideas for workshops, but for some of us, surveys don't always capture our needs.

Here are a couple of things I see as concerns:

1. When we test with the battery of the Columbus Test of Basic Skills, and place so much emphasis on it, teachers tend to start teaching to the test, and I'm not sure that is good.

2. I don't want to sound negative, but when I have 27 in my class including two or more who can hardly speak English, it is becoming almost impossible for me to take care of the entire class; the few non-English-speaking students require all my time. This is particularly discouraging because many of the non-English speaking are children of migrant farm workers and will be gone again in a few weeks or months.

Please don't misunderstand me. I'm not saying we need in-service on working with these few children. I want help working with the whole class. Why not set up a training program for children with limited English speaking ability; and when they get up to grade level, place them in appropriate classes?

Thanks!

Verna Petrov

REFERENCES

Brown, M. (1992). Only the best. *The American School Board Journal, 179*(3), 35–36.

Caro-Bruce, C. (2002). Action research: Facilitator's handbook. *The Video Journal of Education, 11*(7), 1–12.

Chokshi, S., & Fernandez, C. (2004). Challenges to importing Japanese lesson study: Concerns, misconceptions, and nuances. *Phi Delta Kappa, 85*, 520–525.

Desimone, L. M., Smith, T. M., & Ueno, K. (2006). Are teachers who need sustained, content-focused professional development getting it? An administrator's dilemma. *Educational Administration Quarterly, 42*, 179–215.

Ferrance, E. (2000). *Action research.* Providence, RI: Northeast and Island Regional Educational Laboratory at Brown University.

Getzels, J. W., & Guba, E. G. (1957). Social behavior and the administrative process. *School Review, 65*(4), 423–441.

Glickman, C. D., Gordon, S. R., & Ross-Gordon, J. M. (2007). *Supervision and instructional leadership: A developmental approach* (8th ed.). Boston: Pearson.

Guskey, T. R. (2003). Analyzing list of the characteristics of effective professional development to promote visionary leadership. *NASSP Bulletin, 87*(637), 4–20.

Hoyle, J. R., Bjork, L. G., Collier, V., & Glass, T. (2005). *The superintendent as CEO.* Thousand Oaks, CA: Corwin.

Knowles, M. S., and Associates. (1984). *Andragogy in action.* San Francisco: Jossey-Bass. 49-51.

Merriam, S. B., & Brockett, R. G. (1997). *The profession and practice of adult education: An introduction.* San Francisco: Jossey-Bass.

Murphy, C. V. (1999). Study groups. *Journal of Staff Development, 20*(3),

National School Boards Association. (1996). *The school personnel management system.* Alexandria, VA: Author.

Northwest Regional Educational Laboratory (NWRL). (2002). *Overview of lesson study.* Retrieved 1/6/2007 from http://www.nwrel.org/msec/lessonstudy/overview.html.

Ray, J. R., Candoli, I. C., & Hsck, W. G. (2005). *School business administration: A planning approach* (8th ed.). Boston: Allyn & Bacon.

Richardson, J. (October/November 2001). Seeing through new eyes: Walk throughs offer new way to view schools. *Tools for Teachers.* Retrieved 1/6/2007 from http://www.nscd.org/library/publications/tools/tools10-01rich.cfrm.

Richardson, J. (2002). Reach for the stars: Individual learning plans allow teachers to take change of their own learning. *Tools for Schools.* Retrieved 1/6/2007 from http://www.nsdc.org/library/publications/tools/tools2-20rich.cfm.

Richardson, J. (February/March 2004). Lesson study. *Tools for Schools.* Retrieved 1/6/2007 from http://www.nsdc.org/library/publications/tools/tools2-01rich. cfm .

Richardson, J. (December/January 2005). Study groups lift Missouri district's teachers, principals, and students. *Results.* Retrieved 1/6/2007 from http:// www. hsdc.org/library/publications/results/res12-04rich.cfm.

Sergiovanni, T. J., & Starratt, R. J. (2007). *Supervision: A redefinition* (8th ed.). Boston: McGraw-Hill.

Smith, T. S., & Rowley, K. J. (2005). Enhancing commitment or tightening control: The function of teacher professional development in an era of accountability. *Educational Policy, 14*, 126–156.

Sparks, D. (2005). *Leading for results: Transforming teaching, learning, and relationships in school.* Thousand Oaks, CA: Corwin.

Terehoff, I. I. (2002). Elements of adult learning in teacher professional. *NASSP Bulletin, 86* (632), 65–77.

Thompson, S. R. (1982). *A survey and analysis of Pennsylvania public school personnel perceptions of staff development practices and beliefs with a view to identify some critical problems or needs.* Unpublished doctoral dissertation. Pennsylvania State University, State College, PA.

West Ed. (1997). *Peer-Assisted Leadership (PAL).* Retrieved 12/27/2006 from www.ed.gov/pubs/triedandtrue/peer.html.

Webster's Online dictionary. (2007). Retrieved 9/5/2007 from www.websters-online-dictionary.org/definition/mentor.

CHAPTER 8

Performance Evaluation

After reading this chapter, you will be able to:

- Match the purposes of a school district evaluation system with the primary types of evaluation.
- Discuss the three major elements of an employee evaluation system.
- Identify the major approach to collecting evaluation data in education.
- Describe the technical standards that must be met by a sound evaluation system.
- List the substantive and procedural due process standards that must be followed in the development and operation of a school district evaluation system.

The accountability movement that began in the later part of the twentieth century became a pressing issue for every public school in the United States as a consequence of the performance expectations placed on students, teachers, and administrators by the No Child Left Behind Act. The attention focused on standards and accountability brought renewed interest in teacher and administrator performance evaluation. "The interest is grounded in the realization that significant improvement in schools and in student learning must have the teacher as a centerpiece" (Tucker, Stronge, Gareis, & Beers, 2003, p. 574). Performance evaluation is important to the internal operation and effectiveness of the school system and to the public's perception of the school system. In response to the school reform movement, two-thirds of the states have passed legislation strengthening their teacher evaluation systems. Almost all states now require the evaluation of teachers, and about half have required the formal evaluation of principals. At the same time, as will be discussed in the next chapter, more and more states and school districts have begun to explore compensation strategies that link compensation to employee skills and performance as well as student performance. As performance expectations have increased, and as efforts to link performance to compensation have increased, so too has the need for every school district to have in place a sound evaluation system. This has become an increasingly complex challenge as the roles and responsibilities of teachers and administrators have expanded along with the definition of what it means to be effective.

A comprehensive and effective evaluation system can be characterized as one that (1) is supported by school board policy; (2) clearly articulates purposes; (3) ensures criteria and data are valid and reliable; (4) uses multiple sources of data; (5) conforms to all federal, state, and local legal standards; and provides for ongoing appraisal and review. In this chapter each of these elements is examined, followed by a discussion of the standards involved in developing and operating a sound evaluation system.

DISTRICT EVALUATION POLICIES

The school district evaluation system is a reflection of the school district's goals, values, and priorities. These goals, values, and priorities are reflected in the policies the school district adopts to govern and direct the evaluation system. A strong policy statement such as that given in Figure 8.1 demonstrates both the board's philosophical position regarding evaluation, the importance of evaluation to the organization, and the board's commitment to the evaluation process. A policy establishing performance appraisal as a school district priority is critical if the evaluation system is to make a meaningful contribution to the improvement of the district and individual employees. Additional policies that clearly articulate the purposes and procedures to be followed in the evaluation of all employees and that emphasize administrative responsibility and accountability for the effectiveness of the system further demonstrate the importance placed on evaluation.

The active participation of all employee groups, school board members, and school patrons in the development of the policies that will guide the evaluation

Figure 8.1 School District Statement of Philosophy for a Teacher Evaluation System

In the Paradise Valley Unified School District the parents, Governing Board members, and staff are committed to the continued growth of the district's strong educational program designed to meet the individual needs of the student. While recognizing the integrity of the teacher's individual instructional style, an effective teacher evaluation system which focuses on the improvement of instruction is essential to this commitment.

While the primary focus of evaluation is to improve instruction, an effective system requires teachers to meet established performance expectations. Therefore, the process for teacher evaluation must clearly state performance expectations (classroom and outside the classroom), must contain criteria for measuring effective teacher performance, and must have an instrument for assessing the competencies relating to the criteria.

It is also vital that the teacher evaluation system allow for and encourage productive dialogue, appropriate commendation, and when required, specific recommendations for improvement including reference to human and material resources. The system must provide for both written and oral communications within designated time lines. The process must be continuous and constructive, taking place in an atmosphere of cooperation, mutual trust, and respect among evaluator, evaluatee, and observer.

Source: Paradise Valley Unified School District. (1997). *Paradise Valley Unified School District No. 69 Teacher Evaluation System*. Paradise Valley, AZ: Author.

system is critical to its success. The district should take care to ensure that policies are written in easily understandable language with clearly defined standards. Lastly, to ensure the continued integrity of the process, the systematic review and revision of evaluation practices and policies should be stipulated in the district policy.

DETERMINING THE PURPOSES OF THE EVALUATION SYSTEM

Determining the purposes of the district's evaluation system and communicating these purposes to all school district constituencies is critical to all aspects of the evaluation process. "The determination of the evaluation purposes influences the design of the evaluation instruments and their administration, as well as the interpretation of results" (Kyriakides, Demetriou, & Charalambous, 2006). Evaluation systems that lack clearly articulated purpose(s) are essentially meaningless and contribute little to the accomplishment of the district's goals (Stronge, 1991).

The stated and actual purposes of evaluation meet a variety of ends. Consider, for example, the following purposes articulated by the Tolleson Elementary School District (n.d.) for the evaluation of professional staff:

- Evaluation shall determine how well the objectives held by the school are being carried out. The success of the educational program is dependent upon the quality of classroom instruction, supervision, and administration.
- Evaluation shall provide the basis for motivation and for self-improvement. Personnel must be aware of their strengths and weaknesses in order to improve.
- Evaluation shall provide the basis for in-service training and supervisory activities. Such activities can be most effective when they are based upon clear evidence of need as shown by evaluation studies.
- Evaluation shall provide the basis for administrative decisions. Such decisions may include the employment of personnel, their assignment, the granting of continuing status, promotion, demotion, or termination. (p. 2)

According to the National School Boards Association (1987), the purposes of teacher performance evaluation are

- To ensure that students are provided high-quality instruction.
- To meet statutory and contractual requirements.
- To recognize outstanding teacher performance.
- To provide opportunities for teachers to develop their professional skills.
- To provide an avenue for two-way communication about school system and individual staff member goals, objectives, and other performance-related concerns.
- To document, in a fair manner, the objective information the board and administrators need when making decisions relative to assignments, transfers, granting of tenure, promotions, or destaffing.
- To provide evidence to the community that proper care is taken to hire, develop, and retain good teachers. (p. 121)

An examination of the policy documents of a number of school systems found the most commonly mentioned purposes for the evaluation of principals were

- To promote professional growth and improvement of principals.
- To provide information for administrative decisions.
- To clarify and communicate role expectation.
- To assess the extent to which expectations are being met.
- To provide evidence for special recognition.
- To identify areas for professional development.
- To improve student performance. (Thomas, Holdway, & Ward, 2000, p. 225)

Other purposes of administrator evaluation, according to Peterson (2000), are to (1) reassure the practitioners of their valuable and competent work; (2) reassure parents, the lay public, and other audiences that good work is taking place; (3) support the teacher evaluation system; (4) recognize and disseminate good administrative practice; and (5) provide opportunities for self-improvement.

From whatever sources, the multitude of reasons for evaluating personnel relate to three broad personnel purposes: (1) staff development; (2) rewarding performance; and (3) retention, tenure, or termination. The first of these purposes is accomplished by formative evaluation, the latter two by summative evaluation.

Summative evaluation is evaluation that is conducted at the end of an activity or period of time and is designed to assess terminal behaviors or overall performance over a period of time. Summative evaluation is used to make employment decisions regarding such matters as contract renewal, tenure, performance pay, and assignment. Summative evaluation is formal, somewhat infrequent, and focuses only on the person being evaluated. Evaluation is conducted by a superior with little input from the person being evaluated. Classroom observation is the strategy most commonly used to conduct summative evaluation.

Unlike summative evaluation, which is a terminal activity, **formative evaluation** is an ongoing evaluation designed to provide continuous feedback to the person being evaluated for the purposes of self-improvement and professional development. Where summative evaluation is externally controlled and judgmental, formative evaluation is employee-directed, individualized, and geared to promote reflection and support professional growth (Black, 2000). Evaluation may involve not only administrators but peers, students, and parents. The major components of formative evaluation are

- **Goal setting** based on a comprehensive self-assessment of practice and feedback from summative evaluations.
- **Selecting supporting resources** to meet these goals.
- **Selecting a method of feedback** (peer coaching, quality colleague, portfolio, etc.) that supports the goal.
- **Evaluating impact on students.**   (Howard, 2005, p. 11)

ELEMENTS OF AN EFFECTIVE EVALUATION SYSTEM

Having decided the purposes of the evaluation, the school district must design an evaluation plan to achieve these purposes. The evaluation plan has three major elements which, in effect, involve the answers to three questions: (1) What will be evaluated? (the criteria); (2) What level of performance is expected? (the standards); and (3) How will evidence be collected? (data collection).

Evaluation Criteria

The **evaluation criteria** are the job-related behaviors expected of the teacher, administrator, or other staff member (Valentine, 1992). A number of sources can be consulted for guidance in determining criteria. The first place that must be consulted is state statutes. As previously stated, in the last decade more and more states have enacted legislation dealing with the evaluation of public school employees. These statutes or state education department policies requiring the evaluation of school personnel vary widely as to their level of specificity. In a number of states not only has teacher or administrator evaluation been required, the criteria that are to be used to define effective teaching or administrative performance are specified. A number of these states, as well as many local school districts have adopted or adapted the 10 core teaching standards developed by the Council of Chief State School Officers' Interstate New Teachers Assessment Support Consortium (INTASC) for use in the evaluation of beginning teachers and the Frameworks for Teaching developed by Danielson (1996), the National Board for Professional Teaching Standards for use in the evaluation of experienced teachers, and the standards for principals developed by the Interstate School Leaders Licensure Consortium (ISLLC). In some states these standards have been used to create tiered licensure designation or career ladder placement designation.

State-adopted criteria for the evaluation of teachers in Bellingham public School (WA) are presented in Figure 8.2. Figure 8.3 show the Oklahoma criteria for evaluating effective administrator performance.

Whether derived from state statute, negotiated employee agreements, or developed by national organizations, what is important is that the criteria be based on recent research about teaching, learning, and leadership. This is important to ensuring

Figure 8.2 Bellingham Public Schools Teacher Observation and Evaluation Criteria

CRITERION I. INSTRUCTIONAL SKILLS – *The teacher demonstrates, in his or her performance, a competent level of knowledge and skill in designing and conducting an instructional experience.*

Indicators:
- Writes and teaches to clear objectives ● Utilizes principles of learning ● Provides a variety of instructional experiences
- Uses appropriate instructional strategies for students, subject, and goals ● Monitors ongoing performance to adjust lessons
- Uses District goals and guide effectively ● Demonstrates creativity in the teaching process

CRITERION II. CLASSROOM MANAGEMENT AND ORGANIZATION – *The teacher demonstrates, in his or her performance, a competent level of knowledge and skill in organizing the physical and human elements in the educational setting.*

Continued

Figure 8.2 Continued

Indicators:
- Provides a classroom climate conducive to learning
- Provides a model in demeanor and appearance that does not detract from teaching effectiveness
- Assess individual differences, provides appropriate student grouping and uses appropriate instructional resources to meet individual needs
- Involves students in planning and evaluating their own work where appropriate

CRITERION III. STUDENT DISCIPLINE AND ATTENDANT PROBLEMS –*The teacher demonstrates the ability to manage the non-instructional human dynamics in the educational setting.*

Indicators:
- Communicates clearly established parameters ● Recognizes conditions that lead to problems ● Assists students toward self-discipline
- Responds reasonably to discipline problems ● Effectively utilizes the assistance of administrators or support personnel

CRITERION IV. KNOWLEDGE OF SUBJECT MATTER –*The teacher demonstrates a depth and breadth of knowledge of theory and content in general education and subject matters specialization(s) appropriate to the grade level.*

Indicators:
- Gives evidence of subject matter competency in area(s) to be taught
- Recognizes the relationship between one's subject matter-field and other disciplines or subjects
- Keeps abreast of new developments in the subject matter area.

CRITERION V. INTEREST IN TEACHING PUPILS –*The teacher demonstrates an understanding of and commitment to each pupil, taking into account each individual's unique background and characteristics. The teacher demonstrates enthusiasm for or enjoyment in work with pupils.*

Indicators:
- Plans educational experiences based on student unique background and characteristics
- Enjoys working with students
- Provide prompt, meaningful communication among parents

CRITERION VI. PREPARATION AND SCHOLARSHIP – *The teacher exhibits, in his or her performance, evidence of having a theoretical background and knowledge of the principles and methods of teaching and a commitment to education as a profession.*

Indicators:
- Keeps abreast of current and effective emerging principles of teaching
- Contributes to school and professionalism
- Maintains professional rapport with colleagues, parents, and community

CRITERION VII. EFFORT TOWARD IMPROVEMENT WHEN NEEDED – *The teacher demonstrates an awareness of his or her limitations and strengths and demonstrates continued professional growth.* **Indicators:**
- Participates in Career Development
- Utilizes self-evaluation as a tool for professional growth
- Responds constructively to recommendations

CRITERION VIII. ASSUMES RESPONSIBILITY FOR DISTRICT, BUILDING, AND CLASSROOM OBLIGATIONS

Indicators:
- Classroom Obligations
- School Obligations
- District Obligations

Source: Bellingham (WA) Public Schools. (2007). Teacher Observation and Evaluation Criteria Retrieved 9/5/07 from www.bham.wednet.edu/departments/clemdept/protdev/observevalcrit.hret

Figure 8.3 Oklahoma Criteria for Effective Administrative Performance

I. Practice
A. Administrator Management Indicators
  1. Preparation: The administrator and staff develop goal statements which are the result of a needs assessment, a written analysis of student test scores and other data as well as community input.
  2. Routine: The administrator uses a minimum of instructional time for noninstructional routines thus maximizing time on task.
  3. Discipline: The administrator works with staff to develop and communicate defined standards of conduct which encourage positive and productive behavior.
  4. Learning Environment: The administrator establishes and maintains rapport with staff and students, providing a pleasant, safe and orderly climate for learning.

B. Instructional Leadership Indicators
  1. The administrator works with staff in collegial and nonthreatening ways to promote and improve instruction.
  2. The administrator sets high expectations for staff.
  3. The administrator provides needed resources for staff.
  4. The administrator works with staff to establish curriculum objectives, sequence and lesson objectives.
  5. The administrator works with staff to assure that all learners are involved in the learning process.
  6. The administrator assists the staff in monitoring student progress.
  7. The administrator works with the staff to develop a program to recognize academic achievement.
  8. The administrator educates the staff to recognize and display the teaching criteria upon which evaluation is conducted.
  9. The administrator observes in the classroom the performance criteria as defined by the district.
  10. The administrator summatively evaluates staff only after classroom observations are made, performance feedback is given, growth goals are set and alternative methods are offered.

II. Products
Administrator Product Indicators
  1. The administrator provides written discipline policies to which students are expected to perform.
  2. The administrator provides a written school building improvement plan that supports the district's four-year school improvement plan describing school goals, objectives and professional development activities.
  3. The administrator provides a written analysis of student test scores and other data to assure that the various student populations are benefiting from the instructional program.

Source: Oklahoma State Department of Education. (2005). *Oklahoma Criteria for Effective Teaching and Administrative Performance*. Oklahoma City: Author.

the validity of the criteria. It is also important that the criteria include all the important domains of the job and not be limited to, for example, just what the teacher does in the classroom or how the superintendent interacts with the school board (Danielson & McGreal, 2000). Lastly, whatever criteria are adopted must be objective, clear, unambiguous, and communicated in advance to the individuals being evaluated.

Standards

Whereas the criteria define the dimensions of performance to be evaluated, **standards** are the indicators of performance required with respect to the criteria. The standards movement has brought a host of performance standards for both teachers and administrators. The choice of standards that are incorporated into the evaluation process can have a significant impact on employee behavior, formalizing expectations of employees, and reinforcing the adage "what gets measured gets done" (Catano & Stronge, 2006).

One or more performance indicators may be related to a specific criterion. For example, the INTASC identified 10 principles or criteria with 53 accompanying performance indicators or standards. The ultimate success of the evaluation system in assessing an employee's performance relative to a particular criterion lies not in how many standards are associated with it, but in how clear and objective the standards are and how effectively they have been communicated to the employee. Vague and subjective standards will only result in disagreements in interpretations later (NSBA, 1996).

For each standard a rubric may be created to distinguish between levels of performance ranging from "unsatisfactory" to "outstanding." Or they may be stated so as to require a more definitive judgment, for example, "exceeds job requirements" or "target for growth." Figure 8.4 provides an example of standards differentiated for four levels of performance associated with one (the appropriateness of a lesson and how the teacher has paced it) of the 22 performance dimensions associated with the evaluation process for experienced teachers in North Carolina.

Data Sources and Collection Procedures

Multiple sources of data should be used when making the value judgments required for the evaluation of education personnel. The use of multiple data sources serves to increase the validity of the evaluations system (Kyriakides, et al., 2006). Moreover, the use of multiple data sources is important because no one source can address all the varied and complex responsibilities of either teachers or administrators. Nor is any single data source appropriate for all employees, all purposes, or all settings (Peterson & Peterson, 2006). Using multiple data sources not only gives a more complete picture of teacher or administrator practice, it allows districts to individualize the evaluation process. In fact, a number of districts have moved to allow teachers choice in the data to present for evaluation. For example, in Utah's Davis School District teachers can choose among a number of data sources, including parent and student survey, student achievement data (e.g., grade-level tests, standardized tests, advanced placement exams, pre- and post-teacher-made tests), documentation of professional activity, and tests of teachers (e.g., the Graduate Record Exam or the PRAXIS series). The only requirement is that

> teachers must present a certain number of data sources at each stage of their evaluation career. For example, beginning teachers must submit a minimum of four data sources per year, whereas veterans use only one to three data sources. (Peterson, Wahlquist, Bone, Thompson, & Chatterton, 2001, p. 41)

More innovative evaluation systems are not only using multiple sources, but are using differential procedures, criteria, and time lines for different groups of teachers. Novice teachers receive more intensive evaluations than experienced teachers. Novice teachers also receive a formal summative evaluation every year where a summative evaluation of experienced, tenured teachers who are meeting or exceeding expectations is conducted only every 2, 3, or 4 years. Experienced teachers often are given the opportunity to engage in formative evaluation designed to contribute to their individual professional growth.

The data used in the evaluation process will vary not only by source, but by the way they are collected. For example, not only will the type of data generated from a

Figure 8.4 Sample Performance Standard and Rubric

Performance Dimension 6: Appropriateness of the lesson and pacing			
Unsatisfactory	**Needs Improvement**	**Competent**	**Accomplished**
The pacing is usually too slow, too rushed, or both, with inappropriate use of instructional time. Students waste time by avoiding work. Most activities do not reflect developmentally appropriate practices.	The pacing is inconsistent. Opportunities for student engagement are limited with inconsistently appropriate use of instructional time. Frequent off-task behaviors observed. Activities are not always developmentally appropriate.	The pacing consistently offers opportunities for active student engagement with appropriate use of instructional time. Activities always appropriate reflect developmentally appropriate practices.	All students are actively engaged in a variety of meaningful ways, with maximum use of instructional time. Activities reflect developmentally appropriate practices that challenge but do not overwhelm students. Activities consistently build on prior knowledge of students.

Source: B. B. Howard & W. H. McColskey. (2001). Evaluating experienced teachers. *Educational Leadership, 58*(5), 48–51. Reprinted with permission from ASCD. All rights reserved.

classroom observation differ from that obtained from a survey of parents, but the classroom observation data may vary as a result of the degree of formality of the observation, the frequency of the observation, the duration of the observation, and whether it is announced or unannounced. Ultimately, whatever process is used to collect data, it is imperative that the procedures be well defined and adhere to any state laws, employment contracts, and school board policies. It is also imperative that all evaluators receive the training necessary to competently perform the evaluation, and that they adhere to all applicable laws, contracts, and policies.

A survey of evaluation practices of the nation's 100 largest school districts found that the most common teacher evaluation methods (and the percent of districts using them) were direct systematic observation of teaching (94%), informal observation of teaching (87%), teacher self-evaluation (46%), student achievement data (25%), teacher portfolio assessment (23%), peer evaluation (16%), and student ratings of teacher performance (9%) (Loup, Garland, Ellett, & Rugett, 1996). Many of these methods are also employed in the evaluation of administrators. Also common to administrator evaluation (but less common to teacher evaluation) are rating scales. A somewhat new approach, 360-degree feedback or full-circle evaluation, can be used in both the evaluation of teachers and administrators. Each of these evaluation methods is described in the following sections, along with some of the major considerations surrounding their use.

Observation. Observation is the most commonly employed methodology in the evaluation of teachers. The observation may focus on a narrow range of behaviors, or it may attempt to encompass all that is being observed (see the sample in Figure 8.5). The duration of the observation may be for an entire lesson or period or for a few minutes. Observations may be spaced throughout the course of the year; in other

Figure 8.5   Observation/conference Form

Date of Observation: _____   Date of Conference: _____

Name of Teacher: _____   Name of Evaluator: _____

School: _____   Assignment: _____

☐ Career Ladder   ☐ Announced   ☐ Unannounced

· ·

This form is to be used for all classroom observations and for conferences with teachers regarding performance. A minimum of one classroom observation is required for *each* evaluation. It is not necessary to observe or comment on all standards.

· ·

Rating

(Optional)   **Quality Standards**

_____   Standard 1: Designs and Plans Instruction
                The teacher designs instruction that develops students' abilities to meet Kyrene and
                Arizona academic standards, including school and district assessment goals.

                ┌──┐
                │ Observations/Comments: │
                │   │
                │   │
                │   │
                └──┘

_____   Standard 2: Creates and Maintains a Learning Climate
                The teacher creates and maintains a learning climate that supports the development of
                students' abilities of meet Kyrene and Arizona academic standards, including school
                and district assessment goals.

                ┌──┐
                │ Observations/Comments: │
                │   │
                │   │
                │   │
                └──┘

_____   Standard 3: Implements and Manages Instruction
                The teacher implements and manages instruction that develops students' abilities to
                meet Kyrene and Arizona academic standards, including school and district assessment
                goals.

                ┌──┐
                │ Observations/Comments: │
                │   │
                │   │
                │   │
                └──┘

Continued

Rating

(Optional)

_____ Standard 4: Assesses Learning and Communicates Results

The teacher assesses learning and communicates results to students, parents, and other professionals with respect to students' abilities to meet Kyrene and Arizona academic standards, including school and district assessment goals.

Observations/Comments:

_____ Standard 5: Collaborates with Colleagues, Parents, and Others

The teacher collaborates with colleagues, parents, the community, and other agencies to design, implement, and support learning programs that develop students' abilities to meet Kyrene and Arizona academic standards, including district and school goals, and transition from school to work.

Observations/Comments:

_____ Standard 6: Engages in Professional Growth and Development

The teacher reviews and evaluates his or her overall performance and implements a professional growth plan.

Observations/Comments:

Additional Comments:

This is a confidential report and the confidential nature of this report is to be respected by all parties. A signature on this report does not necessarily mean that the employee agrees with the opinions expressed, but merely indicates that he/she has read the report and has had an opportunity for discussion with the principal/evaluator. A copy will be placed in the employee's official personnel file. A teacher may add to this record a statement of clarification within 10 working days of receiving his/her copy of the Evaluation Record.

_____ _____ _____
Signature of Employee   Social Security #   Date

_____ _____
Signature of Evaluator   Date

<return>

Source: Kyrene Elementary School District. (1999). *Teacher Evaluation and Growth System Reference Document*. Tempe, AZ: Author.

situations it may be more desirable to conduct the observations several days in a row (Stiggens & Duke, 1988).

Observations may be classified as formal, scheduled, and structured observations or informal, unscheduled observations. According to Murphy (1987) a well-conducted formal evaluation will include the following stages:

1. A preconference in which the substantive focus and procedural conditions for the evaluation are established;
2. An observation during which the supervisor objectively describes and records activities that are occurring in the classroom;
3. A period of analysis and interpretation of the data collected during the observation;
4. A postconference during which the supervisor and the teacher review the analysis of the lesson together for the purpose of planning further efforts at instructional improvement; and
5. A postconference analysis in which the supervisor and teacher analyze the usefulness of the first four phases of the observation cycle. (p. 168)

Critical to the success of the evaluation is that the person being observed be made aware of the requirements and purpose(s) of the observation and that good communication be maintained throughout the process. It is also important that the evaluation be conducted as unobtrusively as possible and that the time and length of the observation be appropriate to ensure that the behavior observed is a representative sample. The actual classroom observation will typically be 30 to 45 minutes. "For most classrooms, four to six observations will provide sufficient coverage of variety in instruction. A few classes having greater variety may require an additional one to two visits. The observation should be scattered over a 30-to-60 day period" (Peterson, 2000, p. 198). Following the observation the data must be analyzed using a conceptual framework that links teacher behavior to student learning. Lastly, those conducting the observations must be trained in observation skills, as well as the purpose and methodology of the particular observation system being used, and the observation instruments themselves must be reliable and valid (Peterson, 2000).

Informal observations referred to as "walkthroughs" lasting 3–6 minutes can often yield more important data than formal observations and are most flexible for focusing specific instructional activities (Peterson, 2004). However, even when observations are considered informal, they should be followed by a brief feedback on what was observed and any appropriate advice. A number of informal observations per class per year may be necessary to provide a complete picture of the teaching and learning that is taking place in the classroom. The time involved is worth the results. In combination with other sources of data, informal observations allow administrators or supervisors to make judgments about teacher performance with a good deal of confidence (Murphy, 1987).

Self-Evaluation. Almost all teachers and administrators engage in some form of informal self-evaluation to assess their performance. In recent years, not only have educators been encouraged to become "reflective practitioners" (Schon, 1987), but self-evaluation has become an increasingly important component of personnel evaluation systems. Although teachers or administrators typically ask themselves what methods or strategies worked well or did not work well, and why, or how they might improve their own or the performance of others, in a formal evaluation system, these reflections "have maximum value when they are undertaken not just as gasps at the end of a working day, but consciously, definitely, and regularly, in a planned approach" (Withers, 1995, p. 269).

For self-evaluation to be successful, several criteria must be met:

- The teacher must have a commitment to practice and to his or her responsibility to understand, evaluate, and improve it. The initiative and desire for self-evaluation have to come from the teacher himself or herself.
- If self-evaluation is to be truly self-evaluation, the teacher must assume control of the self-evaluation process. In particular, the teacher must be the one who carries out reflection and makes the ultimate decision about his or her practice.
- Unless a teacher acknowledges responsibility for or the possibility of being able to improve an area of practice, the self-evaluation process is unlikely to be carried out. (Airasian & Gullickson, 2006, pp. 205–206)

Self-evaluation can be used as part of both formative and summative evaluation. However, because novice teachers are less skilled than experienced teachers in assessing their own practice accurately, when used, it should take the form of self-directed growth for experienced teachers, and guided self-evaluation for novice teachers (Danielson & McGreal, 2000). Self-evaluation can be accomplished by a variety of strategies. Students and colleagues may be surveyed or interviewed by the employee, or self-rating forms similar to the one in Figure 8.6 may be used. Self-evaluation may also be accomplished through the process of journaling or portfolio development. One popular technique for self-evaluation is videotaping a live performance, be it classroom teaching, the conducting of a faculty meeting, or conducting a parent-teacher or administrator-teacher conference. Videotaping allows evaluatees to see themselves as others see them and reduces the subjectivity that is normally involved in evaluating one's own performance. Typically a paper-and-pencil rating or observation form is completed while watching the videotape. It is also common practice for the evaluatee to view the videotape with a supervisor, colleague, or evaluator (Haertel, 1993).

Whatever format is used, if a self-evaluation is one that has been requested by the employer and subsequently conducted by the employee, it must be considered in the employee's overall evaluation. It cannot be ignored by the supervisor because it is perceived as being too self-serving. In order to ensure that self-evaluations are of maximum value and continue to improve, the supervisor should discuss the self-evaluation with the employee without placing value judgments on it, but rather focusing on the basis for the employee's judgments. In areas in which there appears to be a significant difference in the employee's perception of his or her performance and the evaluator's perception, the data that led to each conclusion should be discussed in a nonconfrontational manner. In the end, the validity and reliability of self-evaluations depend on the capacity of teachers or administrators to consistently and accurately judge their own performance (Haertel, 1993).

Figure 8.6 Self-Evaluation Form for Teachers

Name_____ School Year _____ Date _____

Directions: Your job description (performance responsibilities) is shown below. Please review each item and place a check in the appropriate column. "Area of Strength" means you believe your performance in that area is one of your strong points. "Satisfactory" means you are satisfied with your performance. If you are not satisfied with your performance, check "Target for Growth." You may also check "Target for Growth" for performance responsibilities where you also feel you are performing at a satisfactory level. Remember, this is **SELF-ASSESSMENT** and must reflect *your* judgment. We recommend you select or target at least 3 to 5 areas to become the basis for the goals you prepare for the Fall Conference with your evaluator.

Descriptor Applicable	In the left-hand column check each of the descriptors which is applicable to your job responsibilities. **PERFORMANCE RESPONSIBILITY**	Area of Strength	Satisfactory	Target for Growth
	I. *Planning for Classroom Activities:* The teacher A. Consistently plans lessons and activities which incorporate the district's scope and sequence (or other approved curriculum).			
	B. Develops a plan and method for evaluating the students' work.			
	II. *Implementation of the Lesson (the teaching act):* The teacher A. Clearly communicates the objectives of the lesson (in large or small groups, individually, or both).			
	B. Shares with the students the importance of what they are learning (in advance or by discovery, depending on the intent of the lesson).			
	C. Describes for the student how (methods, activities, etc.) the lesson is going to be taught.			
	D. Provides for discovery or acquisition of the information of the lesson.			
	E. Provides for appropriate activities and practice.			
	F. Monitors student progress.			
	G. Provides for summary of key points of the lesson.			
	H. Demonstrates command of the subject matter.			
	I. Uses effective questioning techniques.			
	J. Recognizes different learning styles and employs materials and techniques accordingly.			
	K. Makes reference to and use of other disciplines in order to expand and enrich the learning process.			

Continued

L. Provides for enrichment of the curriculum through the use of a variety of appropriate materials and media.				

M. Other mutually identified responsibilities.
    1.
    2.
    3.				

III. Classroom and Instructional Management Responsibilities: The teacher A. Uses effective classroom and instructional management techniques.				
B. Establishes effective student-teacher and student-student relationships.				
C. Arranges the physical environment to complement the learning atmosphere.				
D. Recognizes the value of time-on-task and demonstrates overall good use of the instructional period.				
IV. Other Duties and Responsibilities: The teacher A. Maintains accurate student records.				
B. Maintains effective communication with parents.				
C. Upholds and enforces school rules, administrative regulations, and Governing Board policies.				
D. Participates in school-related activities.				
E. Maintains a professional attitude in relations with other persons and programs.				
F. Keeps up-to-date in areas of specialization.				
G. Supports the goals and objectives of the district and school.				
H. Provides individual counseling and guidance to students.				

I. Other mutually identified responsibilities.
    1.
    2.
    3.				

Source: Paradise Valley Unified School District. (1997). *Paradise Valley Unified School District No. 69 Teacher Evaluation System.* Paradise Valley, AZ: Author.

Student Performance Data. The focus on student achievement that accompanied NCLB has brought what seems the inevitable focus on the impact of teachers and administrators on student learning. To many policy makers and parents, as well as to many educators, student learning is the primary goal and indicator of teacher quality (Peterson, 2004). However, there are a number of concerns about the use of standardized achievement data, especially in the evaluation of teachers. The major concerns about their use include (1) achievement tests do not exist for all areas of the curriculum, (2) it is virtually impossible to determine the effect of a particular teacher on a student's test score, (3) achievement prior to the time with the teacher being evaluated accounts for 60% of the variance in test scores (Peterson, 2000), (4) valid standardized assessment instruments do not effectively measure what is taught in all classes, (5) so much of what affects learning is beyond the control of the teacher, and (6) variations among students and classes taught does not allow objective comparisons among teachers.

To address these concerns, almost half the states and numerous school districts have adopted or are considering a value-added approach to the consideration of student performance data. That is, student scores on standardized achievement tests at the beginning of the year and at the end of the year are compared, and the difference (i.e., the value added) is attributed to the student's teacher. Evaluations that use value-added use statistical procedures called value-added models (VAMs) that "require data that track individual student's academic growth over several years and different subjects in order to estimate the contributions that teachers make to that (student) growth" (Braum, 2005, p. 3).

The best-known and widely used VAM is the Educational Value-Added Assessment System (EVAAS) developed by William Sanders at the University of Tennessee. The EVAAS has been adopted in several states and is a component of the Milken Foundation Teacher Advancement Program described in the next chapter. An alternative to the EVAAS is the Dallas Value-Added Accountability System that has been in use in Dallas for more than a decade. DVAAS differs from EVAAS in several important ways in that it does use student characteristics to adjust test scores and also considers a number of school variables that may contribute to student achievement.

Some of the same concerns in using standardized test scores apply to the use of VAMs. One is that there are not test scores available in many areas. A more fundamental concern is that in the absence of random assignment of teachers and students, alternative explanations of results cannot be discounted, and a causal interpretation of the relative contribution of a teachers' contribution to student learning is not credible (Braum, 2005). Student progress can be influenced by a host of context variables beyond the control of the teacher, including not only student demographics, but facilities, class size, school and classroom climate, mandated curriculum, and available resources.

In a report for the National Education Association, Stronge and Tucker (2000) examined evaluation systems in several school systems that rely on student learning as a measure of teacher effectiveness. Their examination led them to offer recommendations for districts contemplating linking student achievement and performance. The recommendations have been adopted or adapted by various states (see, e.g., *Guidelines for Uniform Performance Standards and Evaluation Criteria for Teachers,*

Administrators, and Superintendents developed by the Virginia Board of Education) and school districts as guidelines to schools in integrating student learning in the evaluation of educators. The recommendations are as follows:

1. Use student learning as only one component of a teacher evaluation system that is based on multiple data sources.
2. When judging teacher effectiveness, consider the context in which teaching and learning occur (e.g., class size, availability of resources and support, student characteristics, etc.).
3. Use measures of student growth versus a fixed achievement standard or goal.
4. Compare learning gains from one point in time to another for the same students, not different groups of students.
5. Recognize that even gain scores have pitfalls that must be avoided: "In particular, a statistical artifact known as the regression effect needs to be considered. It results in a tendency for students starting with low performance levels to show larger gains than warranted. Conversely, students who start with high performance may show lower gains, or even declines, if the measure of student achievement is not adequately difficult to gauge what those high-scoring students know" (p. 56).
6. Use a time frame for teacher evaluation that allows for patterns of student learning to be documented. "Repeated measures of student learning over time enhance reliability from a statistical point of view and credibility from a decision-making perspective" (p. 56).
7. Use fair and valid measures of student learning.
8. Select student assessment measures that are most closely aligned with the existing curriculum.
9. Do not narrow the curriculum and limit teaching to fit a test (Stronge & Tucker, 2000, pp. 53–58).

Portfolios. It is not uncommon in professions other than education (e.g., art or architecture) for members of the profession to present their credentials for assessment by other members of the profession and the public by means of a **portfolio**. Portfolio assessment in education has been used for many years in student assessment. In recent years it has gained increased favor. Portfolios are increasingly seen as being a more authentic form of assessment and are closely aligned with a constructivist view of learning (Attinello, Lare, & Waters, 2006). Portfolios are used as a central component of the certification process by the National Board for Professional Teaching Standards. Several states also use the development of a portfolio as a component of the certification process, as does the Teach for America program and hundreds of school districts across the country now use portfolios as a component in their teacher or administrator assessment programs.

Basically, a portfolio is a collection of information about a teacher's or administrator's practice. Each item in the portfolio is accompanied by a written explanation of why it is included and a self-reflection on its importance. However, it is more than an elaborate scrapbook or a collection of documents. A portfolio has four distinct characteristics: (1) it has a specific *purpose*, (2) it is developed for a specific *audience*, (3) it contains work samples referred to as *evidence*, and (4) it contains *reflection* on the evidence contained in the portfolio (Bullock & Hawk, 2005).

The specific structure and content of the portfolio can vary depending on how it will be used; for certification, for employment purposes, or part of a formative or summative evaluation. If it is being used as part of the performance evaluation process, the teachers and administrators being evaluated must know the standards by which they are being assessed and be given clear guidelines as to what is to be presented and how the portfolio is to be prepared (Russo, 2004).

For the portfolio to remain manageable for both the person who constructs it and those who review it, the number of artifacts included should be kept to around a dozen. And, being selective about the items to be included in the portfolio does not mean constructing a biased picture, but providing a fair and generous representation. The inclusion of each entry should be supported with a written rationale which describes the artifact, justifies its inclusion in relationship to the standards, and explains what the evaluee has learned about himself or herself and professional practice (Painter, 2001). In the end the artifacts included in the portfolio "may have less importance than the thinking and writing that goes into explaining their importance" (Russo, 2004, p. 37).

A portfolio can be presented in a variety of formats: a binder, a file box, or digitally. The digital portfolio which allows the collection and presentation of material on a CD-ROM or Web server has many advantages. Using the digital portfolio, the evaluatee can not only scan in all written materials, but also present audio and visual evidence of performance or creatively display materials that might not be easily available during a classroom observation or school walkthrough. Digital portfolios also facilitate ease of access (especially web portfolios) and ease of duplication (Wallace, 2005).

Because each portfolio is unique, the evaluation of portfolios does not lend itself to the use of checklists or analytic scoring schemes. In most cases what is involved is the exercise of professional judgment in assessing the extent to which the portfolio documents the teacher or administrator meeting the pre-established criteria. This in turn requires the development of valid and reliable scoring rubrics and training of evaluators in the use of the rubric (Danielson & McGreal, 2000).

In the end the validity of the evaluation process using portfolios depends on the validity of the rubrics (Green, 2004). Guidelines for reviewing artifacts included in a teaching portfolio are presented in Figure 8.7.

The research reported from most districts that use portfolios in the evaluation process is that both administrators and teachers believe the portfolio process helps administrators make finer distinctions about teacher performance, is fair, and that the process itself promotes professional development (Attinello, et al., 2006). Recommendations on the use of performance-based portfolios from the research include the following:

- Develop clear and consistent guidelines for portfolio development and criteria for evaluation.
- Provide adequate and ongoing training for teachers and administrators.

Figure 8.7 Guidelines for Reviewing the Artifacts of Teaching—Conducting a Document Analysis

Artifacts are defined as simple objects, usually a tool or ornament, showing human workmanship or modification as distinguished from a natural object. The artifacts of teaching include any instructional materials or directions employed by teachers to facilitate student learning. Types may vary from commercially prepared textbooks and learning aids, such as maps, software packages, and science kits; to teacher-improvised demonstrations, tests, and worksheets; to the use of educational technology hardware and software.

In considering educational quality, artifacts must be learner oriented and designed to meet a specific outcome or standard. Artifacts are most helpful if they are designed with built-in flexibility permitting updating or adaptation to specific ability levels and uses.

CONTENT

Quality of artifacts can be considered from the point of view of content or essential meaning. Artifacts should be valid, relevant, and current. Some considerations related to quality of content are:

1. *Information:* Is the artifact materially accurate and authoritative?
2. *Areas of Controversy:* If relevant, are alternatives clearly acknowledged?
3. *Appropriateness:* Is the content appropriate for the intended audience? Is it appropriate in detail to the level of the learner and program or lesson objectives?
4. *Relevance and Validity:* Is the content relevant to the purpose of the lesson?
5. *Motivation:* Does the artifact content stimulate interest to learn more about the subject? Does it encourage ideas for using the material?
6. *Application:* Does the artifact serve as a model for applying learning outside the classroom?
7. *Clarity:* Is the content free of regional idioms, jargon, or specialized expressions that would limit its understandability?
8. *Conciseness:* Is the artifact free of superfluous material? Does it stick to the point?

DESIGN AND CONTEXT

Design of artifacts should include characteristics that are conducive to learning. Design should proceed from an analysis of the content of the lesson or local standards or benchmarks. Appropriate artifacts are those that are linked to local standards or benchmarks. The quality of an artifact is the product of its design characteristics, its relevance to identified outcomes, and its application to content.

Objectives for Artifact Design

1. *Meaningfulness:* Does the artifact clearly support the learning outcomes? If so, is this apparent to the learners?

2. *Appropriateness:* Are the artifacts appropriate to the needs of the skill levels of the intended learners? Are time constraints considered in the artifact's design?

Design Characteristics

1. *Sequencing:* Is the artifact itself sequenced logically? Is it employed at the appropriate point in the presentation?
2. *Instructional Strategies:* Is the artifact format appropriate to the students and the teaching approach? Does the artifact's construction incorporate sound learning principles?
3. *Engagement:* Does the artifact actively engage the learner? Does it reinforce the content with appropriate practice and feedback opportunities?

AESTHETIC CONSIDERATIONS

Aesthetic considerations include production and the qualities that enhance or detract from instructional effectiveness of the artifacts.

Quality of Communication

1. *Medium Selection:* Is the best medium used for meeting each specified outcome and presenting each item of content (e.g. motion pictures, videotape, textbook, teacher-prepared handout)?
2. *Economy of Time:* Is the learner's time wasted by such things as verbosity, unnecessary introduction and/or summary, or ad lib conversation without educational substance or purpose?
3. *Pace:* Is the pace appropriate to the intended audience, neither too fast nor too slow, throughout the presentation? Does the pace vary inversely with difficulty of content?
4. *Aids to Comprehension:* Are directions clearly explained? Are unfamiliar terms spelled out?

Technical Production

1. *Visual Quality:* Are subjects adequately illuminated? Do the visuals show all educationally significant details? Is composition uncluttered? Does it help the learner to recognize important content? Are essential details identified through the appropriate use of highlighting, color, tone, contrasts, position, motion, and other pointing devices? Is type size of the text legible at the anticipated maximum viewing distance?
2. *Narration:* Is the pace of the delivery appropriate for the intended audience? Can the audio component be clearly heard?
3. *Physical Quality:* Is the artifact durable, attractive, and simple? Are size and shape convenient for use?

Source: C. Danielson & T. L. McGreal. (2000). *Teacher evaluation to enhance professional practice*. Princeton, NJ: Educational Testing Service.

- Ensure that administrators buy into the process and that sufficient time is devoted in their schedules for portfolio review and comprehensive feedback.
- Use the portfolio process as part of a multidimensional data-gathering system that includes multiple classroom visitations and regular administrative feedback and support. (Attinello, et al., 2006, pp. 147–148)

Peer Review. Peer review is the process by which an employee's performance is reviewed by one or more peers. Given the collaborative nature of education, it does not seem reasonable to ignore peers as a source for performance feedback (Stronge & Ostrander, 2006). The term *peer* means that both the person being reviewed and the reviewer have similar assignments, training, knowledge, and expertise, but are not from the same school or work site and are not socially or politically connected (Peterson, 2000). Peer review typically involves formative evaluation, although in a minority of districts teachers are involved in the summative evaluation of peers. Peer review is more intensive and extensive than traditional administrator evaluation of teachers (Bernstein, 2004). The peer review may be conducted by visitation to the classroom or workplace, by viewing a videotaped lesson, or by an examination of documentary evidence (e.g., portfolios). Peer review provides a method of including "expert" judgment in the evaluation process. Administrators are the ones usually charged with conducting evaluations. Yet administrators cannot be experts in all areas. Who then is more singularly qualified to judge the subject matter or the situation than one's peers? Peer review is being encouraged by both the NEA and the AFT as part of their push to give teachers a larger role in policing their own profession and in the decisions designed to improve teacher quality (Black, 2000) and has been incorporated into the reform of teacher evaluation systems in several states and a number of school systems (Bernstein, 2004).

Most peer review programs do not exist without an accompanying peer assistance program where the consulting teacher serves as a mentor to help the teacher being reviewed to improve his or her knowledge and skills. In fact, the NEA/AFT proposal states that peer review is not to be implemented without a peer-assistance component.

Despite their apparent success, a number of concerns have been expressed about peer review. Perhaps the most significant concern about the use of peer review is that research has shown serious problems with the validity and reliability of peer reviews, especially those involving classroom visitations. Peer review is also fairly expensive to conduct relative to other forms of evaluations. The peers conducting the classroom observations must either be released from their duties and substitutes hired to replace them, or they must have their full-time contract reflect a part-time assignment as a reviewer and a part-time assignment as a teacher, department head, or whatever. In either case, the cost of the peer evaluation system can be significant. Another concern is the absence of a clearly articulated statement of ethical guidelines to frame the evaluations and to address the conflicts and dilemmas that inevitably result from the interactions inherent in peer review (Peterson, Kelly, & Caskey, 2002).

In the peer review process, peer review of materials is seen as having distinct advantages over either peer visits to classrooms or peer surveys of general impressions, primarily because research has shown peer review of materials to have a high inter-rater reliability, and, when conducted by three or more reviewers, to be basically free of bias. Peer review of materials is also logistically easier and less expensive to operate than most other types of peer evaluation. Peer reviewers do not need to leave their classrooms to participate, thereby obviating the need for substitutes or short- or long-term assignments as a reviewer (Peterson, 2000). Among the materials which might be submitted for review are curriculum outlines, sample instructional materials, video- and audiotapes, tests, student achievement data, examples of student work, grade records, lesson plans, handouts and worksheets, classroom rules and discipline procedures, and correspondence with parents.

Peer review and assistance programs have been operating in a few school districts since the early 1980s (Danielson & McGreal, 2000). Supporters of peer review claim that "more teachers have received help and more incompetent teachers have been dismissed under peer review than under traditional methods of evaluation," citing such data as that from Columbus, Ohio, where 20% of the tenured teachers who go through intervention leave the school system and 80% of the new teachers are still on the job 5 years later, compared to only 50% in other urban districts (Hertling, 1999, p. 2). As a result of the passage of California's new Teacher Peer Review & Assistance Act, many more districts are now incorporating peer review into their teacher evaluation program.

Student and Parent Ratings. Student and parent evaluations are central to the concept of 360-degree evaluation, discussed in a following section. And the popularity of this concept in the business world, combined with the continued demand for greater accountability, has led the state of Alaska to request all school districts to include parental input in teacher evaluation, the state of Florida to require it, and a growing number of districts to voluntarily solicit parent or student feedback (Mathews, 2000).

When the district surveys parents, not every parent must be surveyed. However, the sample must be sufficiently large for the return to be representative. Experts recommend either 15 of returned surveys or 50% of parents per class for primary or elementary grades and three classrooms in middle and high school grades is sufficent (Peterson & Peterson, 2006).

In developing parent (and student) surveys or in interviewing parents, care should be taken to ensure that questions are asked only about topics for which the parent can reasonably be expected to have answers. For example, parents would not have direct knowledge of whether teachers presented lessons in a manner students could understand. However, they would know whether their children had the skills they needed to do their homework assignments. And, they would know whether they themselves can understand communications from their child's teacher and whether the teacher promptly returned their phone calls (Danielson & McGreal, 2000).

Sample questions from a parent survey used in the evaluation of building Administrators in Fairbanks (AK) Northstar Borough School District are presented in Figure 8.8.

Unlike parents, students are in the position of observing the classroom performance of the teacher every school day. Students can be a major source of information about the accomplishment of educational goals, methods of instruction, various elements of the classroom (e.g., discipline, homework, textbooks), and relationships with the teacher (Peterson, Wahlquist, & Bone, 2000). Student assessment can provide valuable feedback to the teacher and often can be more effective in changing behavior than administrative evaluation (NSBA, 1996). Student evaluations also can direct teachers to areas in which students hold a perception different from that of the

Figure 8.8 Parent Survey

PARENT/OTHER INPUT FORM
FOR BUILDING ADMINISTRATOR

Neither this input document nor any notes, comments, or other information used in its prepration is a matter of public record

	Building administrator meets the standard:		
Standard A: Provides leadership for our school.	**Agree**	**Disagree**	**NO/NA**
Works with parents, staff, and students in developing a school vision and promoting it. Implements the plan of action to achieve goals. Seeks solutions to problems and appropriately responds to concerns.	☐	☐	☐
Standard B: Guides instruction and supports an effective learning environment.	**Agree**	**Disagree**	**NO/NA**
Has high expectations for the performance of students and staff. Develops and supports programs that improve learning. Ensures that facilities are safe, clean, orderly, and well maintained.	☐	☐	☐
Standard C: Oversees the implementation of curriculum.	**Agree**	**Disagree**	**NO/NA**
Ensures effective delivery of course content. Mointors student grading policy. Promotes the use of technological developments.	☐	☐	☐
Standard D: Coordinates services that support student growth and development.	**Agree**	**Disagree**	**NO/NA**
Effectively coordinates programs that promote student safety, growth, and responsibility; including counseling, special services, and student activities. Administers student discipline fairly and consistently. Acts to ensure safety of students, personnel, and school property.	☐	☐	☐
Standard E: Provides for staffing and professional development to meet student learning needs.	**Agree**	**Disagree**	**NO/NA**
Effectively supervises staff. Makes staff assignments based on student learning needs.	☐	☐	☐
Standard F: Uses assessment and evaluation information about students, staff, and the community in making decisions.	**Agree**	**Disagree**	**NO/NA**
Uses assessment information on student, school, and program performance to implement change where appropriate. Ensures that student progress is monitored and reported to parents in a clear and timely fashion.	☐	☐	☐
Standard G: Communicates with diverse groups and individuals with clarity and sensitivity.	**Agree**	**Disagree**	**NO/NA**
Communicates effectively with the school community. Treats students and adults with respect. Is open to parent comments and is responsive to parent concerns.	☐	☐	☐
Standard H: Acts in accordance with established laws, policies, procedures, and good business practices.	**Agree**	**Disagree**	**NO/NA**
Complies with established laws, policies, procedures, and good business practices.	☐	☐	☐
Standard I: Understands the influence of social, cultural, political, and economic forces on the educational environment and uses this knowledge to serve the needs of children, families, and communities.	**Agree**	**Disagree**	**NO/NA**
Acts with an understanding of social, racial, cultural, political, and economic forces that influence a positive school environment.	☐	☐	☐
Standard J: Facilitates the participation of parents as partners in the education of their children.	**Agree**	**Disagree**	**NO/NA**
Maintains a school climate that welcomes parents and families and invites their participation. Ensures that teachers provide opportunities to engage families to assist in student learning. Involves parents and community in meaningful decision making. Provides information to families in a timely manner to facilitate meaningful participation.	☐	☐	☐

Source: Adapted from Fairbanks North Star Borough School District, Fairbanks, AK.

teacher. Moreover, the very process of soliciting evaluations shows students that their opinions are valued and may encourage them to become more active participants in the learning process (Herbert, 1995).

Student evaluations can be used at all grade levels, with the level of sophistication of the items and the number of items increasing as the age of the student increases. This means care must be taken to ensure that all student surveys used are age appropriate. For example, rating scales such as the one in Figure 8.9 using "smile," "neutral," and "frown" faces can be used with primary grades. "Student comments are not recommended for

Figure 8.9 Sample Elementary Pupil Survey

KINDERGARTEN AND FIRST GRADE PUPIL RATING OF THE TEACHER—FORM A

Note to Teacher: Read items to students, asking them to mark column (face) that describes how they feel about the item. Explain "teacher." Explain any terms as needed.

	Dislike or Not Agree	Neutral or Don't Know	Like or Agree
EXAMPLE:			
A. My teacher lets me choose things.	☹	😐	🙂
1. My teacher treats me fairly.	☹	😐	🙂
2. My teacher uses words I know.	☹	😐	🙂
3. My teacher makes school seem fun.	☹	😐	🙂
4. My teacher lets students tell about things in class.	☹	😐	🙂
5. My teacher shows me what to do.	☹	😐	🙂
6. My teacher helps me learn new things.	☹	😐	🙂
7. My teacher has me do lots of things.	☹	😐	🙂
8. My teacher tells me how well I'm doing.	☹	😐	🙂
9. My teacher praises me for good work.	☹	😐	🙂
10. My teacher never gets mad.	☹	😐	🙂
11. My teacher listens to me.	☹	😐	🙂
12. My teacher expects me to do my work.	☹	😐	🙂

Source: Kyrene Elementary School District. (1986). *Certified Employee Appraisal System Teacher Guidelines* (p. D5). Kyrene, AZ: Author.

student surveys. Individual comments, or even the views of just a few students carry an inordinate and inaccurate weight for teachers' understanding of results" (Peterson & Peterson, 2006, p. 51). Peterson and Peterson (2006) recommend the items in Figure 8.10 for use with middle and high school students.

Parent and student surveys can provide valuable insights into a teacher's or administrator's performance that are unavailable from any other sources. However, because they are based on perception, they should not be considered as completely reliable sources or evidence. "At their best, they can be used for formative feedback and to supplement other indicators of teacher performance" (Danielson & McGreal, 2000, p. 512).

Rating Scales. Rating scales are lists of items that are presumed to constitute effective performance. Items are usually grouped into categories, such as personal traits, knowledge and skills, experience, classroom behavior, and style. Rating scales typically range from 1 to 5 on a scale ranging from, for example, "below expectations" to "exceeds expectations" or "below average" to "excellent." Rating scales are the most popular method used in the evaluation of administrators. Rating scales are popular because they are impersonal, easy to use, and give the appearance of exactness (Cleveland, Peterson, Sharp, & Walter, 2000). Typically the supervisor using the rating scale will have a preconference with the person being evaluated and review the rating scale and the indicators that will be used as evidence. The evaluator may also give the evaluatee a copy of the scale to complete as a form of self-evaluation. After the supervisor completes the evaluation, a postevaluation conference is held where the results are reviewed with the person being evaluated and plans for continuation agreed upon.

A major problem with the use of rating scales is that the judgment regarding any item is purely subjective and may easily be based on personal feelings rather than facts. Another serious threat to the validity of ratings scales when they are used by

Figure 8.10 Recommended Items for Middle and High School Student Survey

	Agree		Not Sure	Disagree	
I know what I'm supposed to do in class	5	4	3	2	1
Teacher shows us how to do new things	5	4	3	2	1
There is enough time to finish class work	5	4	3	2	1
This class is not too noisy or rowdy for learning	5	4	3	2	1
I learn new things I can tell you about	5	4	3	2	1
I know how well I'm doing in class	5	4	3	2	1
This is a good teacher	5	4	3	2	1
We have enough materials and supplies to learn	5	4	3	2	1
At the end of class, I understand well enough to finish the assignment	5	4	3	2	1
I know why we learn what we learn in class	5	4	3	2	1
This class is not too slow or fast to learn well	5	4	3	2	1
The rules in class help me to learn	5	4	3	2	1

Source: K. D. Peterson, C. Wahlquist, & K. Bone. (2000). Student surveys for school teacher evaluation. *Journal of Personnel Evaluation in Education, 14*, p. 151. Reprinted with permission.

a supervisor is the so-called **halo effect**—the tendency of an evaluator to form a strong general impression of the person being evaluated and then to give basically the same rating on every item on the scale (Medley, 1992). Rating scales are not as easy to use as they appear. Terms such as *average* or *excellent* mean different things to different people. And, distinguishing between relevant and irrelevant behaviors and discounting the halo effect require training and practice.

The most serious problem with rating scales is that often the person being evaluated does not find them useful or give them any direction in designing improvement plans (Green, 2004). In addition, the scores derived from the rating scales can also be misleading. That is, "What does it mean when the superintendent gets a high score on 49 out of 50 items? Can that low score outweigh the other 49?" (Cleveland, et al., 2000, p. 17).

Notwithstanding their possible shortcomings, rating scales are used extensively by school districts throughout the nation. If the scale has been cooperatively developed, and if the criteria on the rating scale are legally and professionally defensible, and if different raters arrive at very similar ratings for the same ratee, they can appropriately be used for summative evaluation (MacPhail-Wilcox & Forbes, 1990).

360-Degree Feedback. Known also as team evaluation, multirater feedback, and full-circle feedback assessment (Dyer, 2001), 360-degree feedback evaluation is in common use in business and industry. It involves the systematic solicitation of feedback from the full circle of one's supervisors, subordinates, clients, and others with whom one interacts. The rationale for 360-degree feedback is that "data gathered from multiple perspectives are more comprehensive and objective than data gathered from only one source" (Dyer, 2001, p. 35). Equally important, **360-degree feedback** gives teachers and administrators a full view of their performance and gives them the opportunity to see how their perceptions of their performance compare with that of others (Santeusanio, 1998).

Ultimately the value of 360-degree evaluation depends on who participates in the evaluation and the questions they are asked. Typically the evaluatee is allowed to choose the team of evaluators (except in the case of parents and students who are selected as discussed later). The most common sources for 360-degree feedback for teachers would be principals, curriculum directors, students, parents, peers, aides, support staff, and self-evaluation. Sources for principals would include superintendents, assistant superintendents, peer principals, teachers, parents, site council members, students, support staff, and self-evaluation. Among the evaluators for a superintendent would be school board members, members of the superintendent's cabinet, curriculum directors, principals, teachers, parents, support staff, community members, and self-evaluation. Feedback is obtained from these sources through the use of surveys or questionnaires made up of items that reflect the performance expectations of the position. Different instruments and different questions would typically be asked of each constituent group. Although there are a number of commercially available instruments that can be used for data gathering, many districts have chosen to allow peer design teams to develop the survey instruments that will be used.

The School Improvement Model Center at Iowa State University has worked with a number of school districts in designing and implementing 360-degree feedback systems. They recommend that, for the evaluation of elementary teachers all students be surveyed, that two sections of students be surveyed for a secondary school teacher, and that in surveying parents a random sample of a size that will generate a 25% response be used (Manatt, 2000). For all other categories of raters, the Center for Creative Leadership, another pioneer in the use of 360-degree feedback, suggests that a minimum of three raters be used to ensure confidentiality (Dyer, 2001).

While 360-degree feedback evaluation does offer significant advantages over most single-source assessments which provide only one perspective, it can be time consuming and can create *survey fatigue* (i.e., a principal or even the school secretary could end up completing a survey for every teacher in the school) (Dyer, 2001). It also has been criticized by some who suggest it may yield inflated and biased scores. However, the concerns about 360-degree evaluation, like the concerns about any of the other evaluation sources, can be mitigated by using it as one source in a multisource system.

Appraisal and Review of the Evaluation System

Once in operation, the entire evaluation system should be subjected to ongoing review by the school board, administration, and representatives of employees to ensure that the system is fulfilling its intended purposes and that it is consistent with changes in what we know about instructional and administrative practice and student learning. As a part of this review, the performance of evaluators and the utility of the various instruments and techniques in generating the desired data should be carefully examined (NSBA, 1996). The system should also be continually monitored to verify that it is meeting the technical and legal standards described in the following section.

STANDARDS FOR THE DEVELOPMENT AND OPERATION OF A SOUND EVALUATION SYSTEM

For an evaluation system to be considered sound, it must meet certain technical and legal standards. The technical standards—validity, reliability, utility, and propriety—are primarily concerned with the accuracy of the measurements and ensuring the evaluation system is ethical and fair to all parties. The legal standards are intended to ensure that the system meets substantive and procedural due process requirements and is free from discrimination.

Technical Standards

Validity in personnel evaluation is the extent to which the evaluation measures the performance it is intended to measure. "Validity is perhaps the most important attribute of an assessment system" (Helm, 1995, p. 107). The clarity of the criteria and standards, the data collection procedures, and the competence of the evaluators all affect validity (Ginsberg & Berry, 1990). Among the activities of school districts which can contribute to the validation of the district evaluation system are

- Establish purpose statements.
- Analyze and present empirical data: make comparisons with alternative measures and performance assessments.

- Estimate the empirical reliability of the data.
- Establish multiple data sources, indicators, and judges.
- Establish safeguards to limit the use of data for purposes other than issues of performance that ensures its safe storage and oversees the procedures to ensure its provisions are carried out.
- Conduct studies on current and proposed procedures, relative costs, benefits, and improvement.
- Create archives for reviewing and checking data and as a resource for future development. (Peterson, 2000)

"**Reliability** in evaluation refers to the consistency of measurements across evaluators and observations" (Ginsberg & Berry, 1990, p. 221). Evaluation is by its very nature judgmental. However, if different evaluators using the same criteria and standards to evaluate the same individual produce different results, the evaluation system is not reliable (Helm, 1995). The possibility for such subjectivity is one of the reasons it is important to use multiple sources of data, to train evaluators in the use of the various evaluation instruments and techniques used by the school or school district, and when possible, to use multiple evaluators.

Utility and *feasibility* relate to both reliability and validity and refer to the realistic considerations that must be addressed to ensure each. If the use of a complex evaluation process requires a great deal of training, with associated costs, before evaluators can use it reliably, the utility of the process is compromised. Likewise, even if a particular process or instrument has been judged extremely valid and reliable by measurement experts, but the time required of evaluators and/or evaluatees is excessive, or if it is opposed by the teachers and administrators, its feasibility is reduced.

The Joint Committee on Standards for Educational Evaluation (1988) developed five utility and three feasibility standards for evaluation systems in education. The utility standards state that if evaluations are to be "informative, timely, and influential," they must (1) be constructive; (2) have identified users and uses; (3) be managed and executed by credible evaluators; (4) yield reports that are clear, timely, accurate, and germane; and (5) be followed up so that users and those evaluated understand the results and take appropriate actions. The feasibility standards state that (1) evaluation procedures should produce the needed information with the minimum disruption and cost, (2) the development and monitoring of the evaluation system should involve all concerned parties, and (3) adequate time and resources must be provided to ensure the effective and efficient implementation of the evaluation plan.

Propriety standards require that evaluations be conducted ethically and with regard for staff, students, and other clients. The five propriety standards developed by the Joint Committee (1988) are as follows:

1. **Service orientation.** Evaluations of educators should promote sound education principles, fulfillment of institutional missions, and effective performance of job responsibilities so that the educational needs of students, community, and society are met.
2. **Formal evaluation guidelines.** Guidelines for personnel evaluations should be recorded and provided to employees in statements of policy, negotiated agreements, and/or personnel evaluation manuals so that

evaluations are consistent, equitable, and in accordance with pertinent laws and ethical codes.

3. **Conflict of interest.** Conflicts of interest should be identified and dealt with openly and honestly so that they do not compromise the evaluation process and results.

4. **Access to personnel evaluation reports.** Access to reports of personnel evaluation should be limited to individuals with a legitimate need to review and use the reports so that appropriate use of the information is assured.

5. **Interactions with evaluatees.** The evaluation should address evaluatees in a professional, considerate, and courteous manner so that their self-esteem, motivation, professional reputations, performance, and attitude toward personnel evaluation are enhanced or, at least, not needlessly damaged. (p. 21)

Legal Standards

The legal standards that must be followed in the development and operation of the school district evaluation system are derived from federal and state constitutions and statutes and case law. These standards can be broadly categorized as *substantive due process standards* and *procedural due process standards*. Substantive due process standards are concerned with the objectivity of the criteria, the standards, the evidence, and the results. Procedural due process standards are concerned with the fundamental fairness of the evaluation process. Most legal challenges to personnel evaluation are to the procedural aspects of the process. (See Chapter 11 for a more detailed discussion of substantive and procedural due process.) The following lists of substantive and due process standards are summarized from the discussions of Beckham (1992, 1997) and Tucker and DeSander (2006).

Substantive Due Process Standards

1. The criteria on which the evaluation is based should be
   a. formalized in a written policy;
   b. consistent with state statutes, state department of education regulations, local school board policies, and collective bargaining agreements;
   c. communicated in advance to all employees;
   d. job related, validated, and reflect school district goals;
   e. clear and sufficiently specific to inform a reasonable person of performance expectations;
   f. objective and attainable;
   g. validated, observable, and uniformly applied; and
   h. developed in cooperation with employees.
2. The evaluation process should yield, and decisions should be based on, evidence and documentation that is
   a. representative of the employee's job responsibilities over a period of time sufficient to identify a pattern of performance;

    b. collected from multiple sources and, when possible, multiple evaluators who have been trained to collect data in the manner specified by policy;

    c. sufficient in quantity and depth to support the evaluation conclusions and recommendations; and

    d. credible and noncontradictory.

3. Any deficiencies noted must be consistent with the job-related evaluation criteria.

Procedural Due Process Standards

1. The process should
   a. be conducted in a uniform and consistent manner by trained evaluators;
   b. follow state statutes, state department of education regulations, and school board policies and collective bargaining agreements;
   c. be communicated to all employees in advance of the process;
   d. require that the evaluation results be communicated both in writing and at a postevaluation conference;
   e. provide the opportunity for response to an unsatisfactory evaluation;
   f. provide a written statement of specific deficiencies that are related to the predetermined criteria;
   g. provide clear directions for improvements with a plan of remediation related to the identified deficiencies and assistance in improvement;
   h. provide a reasonable time to remediate; and
   i. provide the opportunity to appeal, including the right to a fair hearing.

2. The evaluation procedures must be applied in a uniform manner.

3. The evaluation process should not be used as a means of retaliating against the employee's exercise of free speech or other constitutional rights.

The courts have traditionally shown a reluctance to attempt to substitute their judgment for that of school administrators or school boards when it comes to evaluative criteria or the methods of evaluation as long as the applicable state and local evaluation procedures or the terms of negotiated agreements are followed. The main concerns of the courts seem to be ensuring that procedural requirements are followed and that the ratings were not subjectively or discriminatorily applied.

SUMMARY

One of the most important and sometimes difficult jobs of the school administrator is the evaluation of personnel. Although evaluation can provide the opportunity for professional growth and school improvement, unless properly conducted, it can also become a source of controversy and low morale. It is imperative that the school district demonstrate its commitment to a sound evaluation system through clearly articulated and publicized board policies and by the adoption of an evaluation system that is technically sound and ensures substantive and procedural due process. Such a system may employ multiple data collection techniques and serve a number of personnel purposes, and if properly designed, perform summative and formative evaluation functions.

Discussion Questions

1. Does your district have written job descriptions for teachers and principals? Do you feel the job descriptions accurately reflect what teachers and principals do?
2. How may a school system combine formative and summative evaluations of its professional staff without damaging morale and effectiveness?
3. How well do you feel your colleagues would be able to evaluate your performance? How well would your students be able to evaluate your performance? Name three ways you use peer input and three ways you use student input to improve your performance. How is this information generated?
4. If you were asked to develop a portfolio of your job-related best works, what would be the six most significant entries?

CASE STUDIES

—CASE 8.1———————————

Evaluation Choice

In the Taylor School District teachers have traditionally been evaluated annually by both the principal and department chair using classroom observation procedures. During the past year the representatives of the teachers' association met with the administration and expressed their concern that the current process was inadequate because it provided only a single source of data. Instead of the sole and uniform use of classroom observations, they recommended that each teacher be able to choose from several techniques or combination of techniques to be used for their annual review. Specifically, they suggested that each teacher be able to choose either portfolio assessment, client surveys, self-evaluation, or the existing classroom observation procedure as the principal method of appraisal.

Questions

1. What are the advantages and disadvantages of using differential appraisal techniques for education personnel?
2. Do you agree with the teachers' association that classroom observation provides too limited a database for appraisal? Why is classroom observation the most commonly employed assessment technique in elementary and secondary schools, whereas peer review and student evaluation of instruction are the commonly used techniques in higher education?
3. If differential performance appraisal techniques were available to you, which of the ones discussed in this text would you choose to be evaluated by and why?

CASE 8.2

Parent Survey

Recently the Mayflower Elementary School District has come under great pressure from the community because of the low achievement test scores of its students. Within the context of criticism of the quality of education provided by the schools, criticism has also been directed at the quality of the instructional staff. In an effort to become more sensitive to parental concerns, Superintendent Ralph Jones decided to survey parents and guardians regarding their perceptions of the effectiveness of instructional staff. He has notified all teachers that the results of the parent survey will become the principal feature of the teacher improvement and evaluation program. The parent survey asked parents to rate their child's teacher on the extent to which the teacher met the following criteria:

1. Monitors the student's progress and provides adequate and timely feedback.
2. Introduces the goals and objectives for the lesson and how they will be obtained.
3. Creates a safe environment conducive to learning.
4. Gives clear directions for tasks.
5. Uses appropriate teaching strategies.
6. Checks regularly for comprehension and understanding.
7. Provides for active student participation.
8. Adapts the content to meet the varied needs of students.

Questions

1. Which of the listed criteria are inappropriate for inclusion on a survey of parents and guardians? Why?
2. Choose three items from the survey and reword them so that they are more appropriate and useful for evaluating the quality of instruction.
3. In addition to including surveys of parents and guardians in the annual evaluation of teachers, what other methods might the school district employ to respond to community concerns regarding the quality of instruction?

REFERENCES

Airasian, P. W., & Gullickson, A. (2006). Teacher self-evaluation. In J. H. Stronge (Ed.), *Evaluating teaching* (2nd ed.) Thousand Oaks, CA: Corwin.

Attinello, J. R., Lare, D., & Waters, F. (2006). The value of teacher portfolios for evaluation and professional growth. *NASSP Bulletin, 90*(2), 132–152.

Beckham, J. C. (1992, November). *Evaluation.* Paper presented at the annual meeting of the National Organization on Legal Problems of Education, Scottsdale, AZ.

Beckham, J. (1997). Ten judicial "Commandments" for legally sound teacher evaluation. *Education Law Reporter, 117*, 435–439.

Bernstein, E. (2004). What teacher evaluation should know and be able to do: A commentary. *NASSP Bulletin, 88*(639), 80–88.

Black, S. (2000). Evaluation for growth. *American School Board Journal, 187*(4), 58–61.

Braum, H. I. (2005). *Using student progress to evaluate teachers: A primer on value-added models.* Princeton, NJ: Educational Testing Service, Policy Information Center.

Bullock, A. A., & Hawk, P. P. (2005). *Developing a teaching portfolio: A guide for preservice and practicing teachers* (2nd ed.). Upper Saddle River, NJ: Pearson.

Catano, M., & Stronge, J. H. (2006). What are principals expected to do? Congruence between principal evaluation and performance standards. *NASSP Bulletin, 90*(3), 221–237.

Cleveland, P., Peterson, G. J., Sharp, W. M., & Walter, J. K. (2000). A three state examination of school board evaluations of superintendents. *Educational Research Quarterly, 23*(3), 3–21.

Danielson, C. (1996). *Enhancing professional practice: A framework for teaching.* Alexandria, VA: Association for Supervision and Curriculum Development.

Danielson, C., & McGreal, T. L. (2000). *Teacher evaluation to enhance professional practice.* Alexandria, VA: Association for Supervision and Curriculum Development.

Dyer, K. M. (2001). The power of 360-degree feedback. *Educational Leadership, 58*(5), 35–38.

Ginsberg, R., & Berry, B. (1990). The folklore of principal evaluation. *Journal of Personnel Evaluation in Education, 3*, 205–230.

Green, J. E. (2004). Principals' portfolios: A reflective process for displaying professional competencies, personal qualities and job accomplishments. *School Administrator, 61*(9), 30–33.

Haertel, G. D. (1993). *A primer on teacher self-evaluation.* Livermore, CA: EREAPA Associates.

Helm, V. M. (1995). Evaluating professional support personnel: A conceptual framework. *Journal of Personnel Evaluation in Education, 9*, 105–121.

Herbert, M. (1995). Student evaluation of teachers: Variables and value. *Business Education Forum, 9*(3), 15–17.

Hertling, E. (1999). Peer review of teachers. *ERIC Digest (126)*. Eugene, OR: ERIC Clearinghouse on Educational Management, College of Education, University of Oregon.

Howard, B. B. (2005). *Teacher growth and assessment process: Procedural handbook.* Greensboro, NC: SERVE Center at the University of North Carolina-Greensboro.

Joint Committee on Standards for Educational Evaluation. (1988). *The personnel evaluation standards: How to assess systems for evaluating educators.* Newbury Park, CA: Sage.

Kyriakides, L., Demetriou, D., & Charalambous, C. (2006). Generating criteria for evaluating teachers through effectiveness research. *Educational Research, 48*, 1–20.

Loup, K. S., Garland, J. S., Ellett, C. D., & Rugett, J. K. (1996). Ten years later: Findings from a replication of a study of teacher evaluation practices in our 100 largest school districts. *Journal of Personnel Evaluation in Education, 10*, 203–236.

MacPhail-Wilcox, B., & Forbes, R. (1990). *Administrator evaluation handbook.* Bloomington, IN: Phi Delta Kappa.

Manatt, R. P. (2000). Feedback at 360 degrees. *School Administrator, 57*(10), 10–11.

Mathews, J. (2000). When parents and students grade staff. *School Administrator, 57*(10), 6–9.

Medley, D. M. (1992). Teacher evaluation. In M. C. Alkin (Ed.), *Encyclopedia of educational research* (Vol. 4, pp. 1345–1352). New York: Macmillan.

Murphy, J. (1987). Teacher evaluation: A comprehensive framework for supervisors. *Journal of Personnel Evaluation in Education, 1*, 157–180.

National School Boards Association. (1987). *The school personnel management system.* Alexandria, VA: Author.

National School Boards Association. (1996). *The school personnel management system.* Alexandria, VA: Author.

Painter, B. (2001). Using teaching portfolios. *Educational Leadership, 58*(5), 31–34.

Peterson, K. D. (2000). *Teacher evaluation: A comprehensive guide to new directions and practices.* Thousand Oaks, CA: Corwin Press.

Peterson, K. D. (2004). Research on school teacher evaluation. *NASSP Bulletin, 88*(639), 60–79.

Peterson, K. D., Kelly, P., & Caskey, M. (2002). *Journal of Personnel Evaluation in Education, 16*, 317–324.

Peterson, K. D., & Peterson, C. A. (2006). *Effective teacher evaluation: A guide for principals.* Thousand Oaks, CA: Corwin.

Peterson, K. D., Wahlquist, C., & Bone, K. (2000). Student surveys for school teacher evaluation. *Journal of Personnel Evaluation in Education, 14*, 135–153.

Peterson, K. D., Wahlquist, C., Bone, K., Thompson, J., & Chatterton, K. (2001). Using more data sources to evaluate teachers. *Educational Leadership, 58*(5), 40–43.

Russo, A. (2004). Evaluating administrators with portfolios: Principals report mostly positive experience when used as part of a performance review. *School Administrator, 61*(9), 34–38.

Santeusanio, R. (1998). Improving performance with 360-degree feedback. *Educational Leadership, 55*(5), 30–32.

Schon, D. (1987). *Educating the reflective practitioner.* San Francisco: Jossey-Bass.

Stiggens, R. J., & Duke, D. L. (1988). *The case for commitment to teacher growth: Research on teacher evaluation.* Albany, NY: State University of New York Press.

Stronge, J. H. (1991). The dynamics of effective performance evaluation systems in education: Conceptual, human relations, and technical domains. *Journal of Personnel Evaluation in Education, 5*, 77–83.

Stronge, J. H., & Ostrander, L. P. (2006). Client surveys in teacher evaluation. In J. H. Stronge (Ed.), *Evaluating teaching: A guide for current thinking and best practice.* (2nd ed.) (pp. 125–151). Thousand Oaks, CA: Corwin.

Stronge, J. H., & Tucker, P. D. (2000). *Teacher evaluation and student achievement.* Washington, DC: National Education Association.

Thomas, D. W., Holdaway, E. A., & Ward, K. L. (2000). Policies and practices involved in the evaluation of school principals. *Journal of Personnel Evaluation in Education, 14*, 215–240.

Tolleson Elementary School District. (n.d.). *Teacher evaluation handbook.* Tolleson, AZ: Author.

Tucker, P. D., Stronge, J. H., Gareis, C. R., & Beers, C. S. (2003). The efficacy of portfolios for teacher evaluation and professional development: Do they make a difference? *Educational Administration Quarterly, 39*, 572-602.

Tucker, P. D., & DeSander, M. K. (2006). Legal considerations in designing teacher evaluation systems. In J. H. Stronge (Ed.) *Evaluating teaching* (pp. 69–97). Thousand Oaks, CA: Corwin.

Wallace, I. (2005). Digital portfolios. In A. A. Bullock & P. P. Hawk (Eds.), *Developing a teacher portfolio: A guide for preservice and practicing teachers* (pp. 143–161). Upper Saddle River, NJ: Pearson.

Withers, G. (1995). Getting value from teacher self-evaluation. In A. J. Shinkfield & D. Stufflebeam (Eds.), *Teacher evaluation: Guide to effective practice* (pp. 261–271). Boston: Kluwer Academic Publishers.

CHAPTER 9

The Compensation Process

LEARNING OBJECTIVES

After reading this chapter, you will be able to:

- Identify the major determinants of school district compensation.
- Describe the major approaches to compensating teachers and administrators.
- Discuss the methods used by school districts to compensate teachers for extracurricular activities.
- List the major categories of indirect compensation of school district employees.
- Distinguish between the two major types of flexible benefit plans.

One of the most difficult processes of the human resources function is compensation administration. Compensation decisions demonstrate what a school district values in terms of personnel characteristics, competencies, and behaviors (Stronge, Gareis, & Little, 2006) and have significant consequences for both the school district and its employees. Between 80 and 90% of the current operating budget of a typical school district is allocated to personnel salaries, wages, and benefits. Compensation affects the district's ability to attract, motivate, and retain qualified employees. Moreover, compensation of educational personnel is increasingly viewed as an integral component of efforts to improve teacher quality and student performance.

In this chapter the compensation program is described in terms of two broad components: direct compensation (wages and salaries) and indirect compensation (employee benefits and services). The opening sections of this chapter deal with the development of school district compensation policies and the major determinants of school district salaries. The discussion of direct compensation in this chapter will focus on the compensation of certificated teachers and administrators. Direct compensation of classified personnel is discussed in Chapter 12. The discussion of direct compensation centers on the predominant approach to compensating teachers—the single salary schedule—as well as the major alternatives to this approach that reflect the broader reform initiatives in education—competency-based pay, job enhancement pay, performance-based pay, and school- or group-based pay.

ESTABLISHING DISTRICT COMPENSATION GOALS AND POLICIES

Decisions about school district compensation and incentives should begin with a determination of the goals that the district wishes to achieve with the compensation program. These might include such goals as

- Attract and retain competent teachers
- Improve teacher productivity
- Develop teachers professionally
- Improve student performance
- Provide a fair and equitable compensation system
- Improve teacher morale and satisfaction
- Reward outstanding performance
- Reinforce accountability

Once the goals of the compensation system have been determined, the district must develop policies that are consistent with the achievement of these goals. The development of such compensation policies is central to the effective administration of the compensation program. Written compensation policies provide assurance to the community that sound procedures will be followed in employee compensation and assurance to staff that recognized policies will be followed in their compensation.

Equally important, written compensation policies provide guidance to those responsible for compensation administration in the development of acceptable compensation procedures (Johns, Morphet, & Alexander, 1983). Among the guidelines that should be considered by school districts in developing and implementing compensation policies are the following:

1. A teacher compensation system should align with the school district's mission and goals.
2. All personnel in the district, certificated and noncertificated, should be included in the compensation policies.
3. The compensation system should be concerned with attracting, motivating, and retaining personnel at all levels.
4. Quality of performance should be recognized. Performance appraisal and accompanying differential reward structures should provide the basis for advancement in income and overcome the limitations of the single salary schedule.
5. The salary system should be equitable. This requires that each position be evaluated in terms of its relative importance to other positions, that a hierarchical arrangement be established, and that salary be awarded accordingly.
6. The compensation program should be nondiscriminatory, defensible, and legal.

7. The compensation plan should be competitive at all stages of career development with other school districts and, to the extent possible, with other employers in the district.
8. Employee benefits should reflect the school district's obligation to provide for the welfare of employees and should be competitive and attractive.
9. The compensation program must be constantly monitored and reviewed to ensure its internal consistency and equity and competitiveness.
10. The compensation system should be flexible, allowing the district to respond to changing needs and allowing individuals choice in compensation options.
11. The compensation program and process should be openly derived, clear, and effectively communicated to all employees and interested citizens (Foster, 1960; Foulkes & Livernash, 1989; Young & Castetter, 2005).

DETERMINANTS OF COMPENSATION

A number of internal and external factors directly or indirectly determine the compensation program established by the school district. As illustrated in Figure 9.1, these include (1) supply and demand, (2) the district's ability and willingness to pay, (3) cost of living, (4) prevailing wage rates, (5) collective bargaining, and (6) government regulations. Each must be considered as a part of a collective force that is referred to as the wage mix (Sherman & Bohlander, 1992). Each of these factors is discussed in this section.

Figure 9.1 Determinants of Compensation

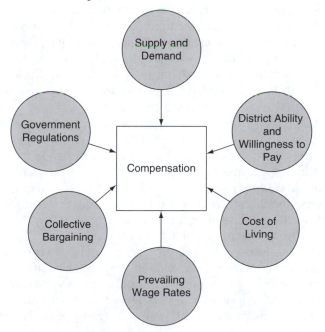

Supply and Demand

All employee compensation, including that of school employees, is a reflection at least in part of the forces of supply and demand. The economic concept of supply and demand states that "value (compensation) is shaped by the balance or imbalance between supply, or the degree of availability of some quantity or quality, and demand, or the extent or need for some quantity or quality" (Chambers, 1996, pp. 53–54).

The *demand* for teachers is in large part determined by three market considerations: (1) the number of students to be served; (2) the number of teachers leaving through death, retirement, dismissal, and so on; and (3) pupil-teacher ratios. Demand is also influenced by nonmarket considerations. The state and federal governments and departments of education and local school boards can greatly influence both the supply and the demand for teachers and other education professionals through such actions as the establishment of certification and accreditation standards, the decision to offer certain types of programs, or the offering of retirement incentives. Because of the influence of federal, state, and local policy decisions, demand can vary greatly from one geographic location to another and from one academic discipline to another. For example, the No Child Left Behind requirement that every teacher be "highly qualified," and what that means, has many districts recruiting teachers who meet these criteria, especially middle school certified and fully certified secondary math and science teachers.

The demand for teachers is expected to continue through the first decade of the twenty-first century. The K–12 enrollment of 55.5 million in 2006 is expected to grow to 58.1 million by 2015, the highest enrollment in the nation's history (Hussar & Bailey, 2006). This enrollment increase will add to the demand for teachers and administrators created by the record retirements discussed in Chapter 4 and the growing number of teachers, both new and experienced, who leave the profession each year. As noted in Chapter 4, more than 50% of teachers leave the profession in the first 5 years. The demand for teachers is also fueled by legislation adopted in a number of states offering full-day kindergarten, universal preschool, and lower pupil-teacher ratios. As was also noted in Chapter 4, the demand for teachers is expected to exceed 2 million in the next decade. The demand is expected to be greatest in the western states with the fastest-growing enrollments.

The *supply* of teachers comes from four groups: (1) first-time teachers; (2) delayed entrants (first-year teachers who engaged in other activities between graduating from college and entering teaching); (3) transfers from other schools, districts, or states; and (4) former teachers. In recent years the percentage of new public school teachers that were newly prepared was 25%, 12% were delayed entrants, 51% were transfers, and 23% were reentrants (Provasnik & Dorfman, 2005). Projecting the supply of teachers is far more difficult than projecting the demand. Although projections of the supply of new teacher graduates are available, only about half of newly prepared teachers actually enter teaching. It is also difficult to project how many former teachers currently unemployed or in other positions are considering reentering teaching, or how many persons in other professions are willing to enter teaching. However, projections by the U.S. Department of Labor suggest that the supply of teachers is anticipated to increase as a result of both state policies that encourage more students to become teachers and more people entering education in response to reports of improved job prospects, higher salaries, more involvement of teachers in decision making, and higher public interest in education (Bureau of Labor Statistics, 2006). As discussed in Chapter 4, the increasing demand and declining supply of both teachers and administrators have made recruiting quality educators one of, if not the, most serious challenges facing school districts today.

Ability and Willingness to Pay

A fundamental determinant of school district compensation is the district's financial ability and willingness to pay (Cohn & Geske, 1990). Differences in salaries among school districts can largely be explained by variations in local fiscal capacity (assessed valuation of property per pupil or per capita income) and community willingness to tax and spend for education (effort). Ratios in school district wealth within a state can be in the order of 1000:1 or even larger. For example, the assessed value of property per student in Texas rages from $27,617 in Boyles ISD to $6,133,640 in Kennedy Countywide CSD. While most state aid formulae are designed to reduce the impact of local school district wealth, it can still be a major factor in determining teacher salaries.

Whereas a district has little control over its tax base, unless there are statutory tax or expenditure limitations to the contrary, it does have control over the effort it makes to support education. In fact, in the process of collective bargaining, unions have often justified their demands for increases in compensation or have been awarded increases by arbitrators because the district's tax rate was substantially below that of its neighbors or below the state average.

Cost of Living

Historically, the most common method of determining salary increases has been the **cost-of-living adjustment** (COLA). Cost-of-living adjustments are based on the consumer price index (CPI), a U.S. Department of Labor index which measures the change in the costs of goods and services over time. COLAs do not reflect judgments about the economic value of persons holding positions or their performance. Rather, they reflect the sentiment that unless personnel compensation keeps pace with the cost of living, the resulting decline in purchasing power has the same effect as a salary cut. As a result, a COLA clause is commonly included in bargaining agreements. The three most common types of COLA clauses are (1) the *escalator clause*, which provides for periodic adjustment during the contract year without additional negotiations if changes in the CPI reach or exceed a certain limit; (2) the *reopener clause*, which provides for negotiations to begin immediately or at the end of the contract year if changes in the CPI reach or exceed a certain limit; and (3) the *end-of-year clause*, found only in multiyear contracts, which automatically, without further bargaining, translate changes in the CPI into salary adjustments (Educational Resource Service, 1987).

The cost of living (COL) differs not only over time but also among states and school districts in a state. Costs associated with land prices, energy services, construction, consumer goods, and personnel services vary among rural, suburban, and urban areas and among geographical regions in the state. For example, intercounty cost-of-living indexes in Illinois ranged from 91.5 in rural counties to 113.8 in suburban DuPage County (McMahon, 1994). In New York State the difference in the COL between Binghamton (99.6) and New York City (149.5) is greater than the difference in the COL between New York State and any other state (Nelson, 1994). If a school district is to maintain the purchasing power of its employees, it must consider these differences in making compensation determinations.

Prevailing Wage Rate

The second most important determinant of current wage increases is the comparability of current rates of pay with those of other potential employers. It would be difficult for a school district to attract and retain competent personnel if its compensation levels were significantly below those paid by other school districts in the community. Data pertaining to prevailing wage rates may be obtained from state and national departments of labor, from surveys conducted by the school district human resources department, and from data supplied by employee organizations. It is not an uncommon practice for employee groups (or school boards) to gather such data and, when supportive, to use it in collective negotiations (Young, Dell, Miller-Smith, & Buster, 2004). Although the veracity of data supplied by the union need not be automatically suspect, because of the possibility of selectivity in collection (i.e., collecting data primarily from those districts known to pay higher salaries), good practice dictates that the human resources office systematically collect wage and salary data. The data collected should include not only direct compensation but also, because of its impact on the attractiveness and value of the total compensation package, benefits.

Collective Bargaining

If school district employees are unionized, wages and other conditions of employment may be largely determined through the process of collective bargaining. In the negotiation process, both the union and the district will focus on those factors that support their bargaining positions (e.g., supply and demand data, ability to pay, cost of living, and prevailing wage rates). Research indicates that collective bargaining is associated with higher salaries of both teachers and administrators (Hill, 2006; Johnson & Donaldson, 2006).

Government Regulations

Like many other areas of human resources administration, compensation administration has become the subject of an increasing number of laws enacted by federal, state, and local governments. The majority of states have statutes providing minimum salaries for teachers. In a number of states, provision is also made for minimum salaries for administrators and other personnel. In addition, numerous state and federal laws address issues related to the compensation of support personnel.

The major piece of federal legislation dealing directly with compensation is the Fair Labor Standards Act (FLSA) passed in 1938 and amended many times. The major provisions of the FLSA are concerned with minimum pay, overtime pay, child labor, and equal pay. The Equal Pay Act of 1963 has become one of the most significant amendments to the FLSA. It states that

> No employer having employees subject to any provisions of this section shall discriminate between . . . employees on the basis of sex by paying wages to employees . . . at a rate less than the rate at which he pays wages to employees of the opposite sex . . . for equal work on jobs the performance of which requires equal skill, effort, and responsibility, and which are performed under similar working conditions. (sec. 206 [d] [1])

According to the provisions of the Equal Pay Act, any difference in pay because of sex must be rationally justified and be the result of a job evaluation study. The Equal Pay Act is enforced by the U.S. Department of Labor and has been the basis for numerous suits in the field of education seeking to eliminate discriminatory compensation practices.

A number of other federal laws have had a significant impact on the compensation practices of school districts. For example, the Social Security Act of 1935, the Health Maintenance Organization (HMO) Act of 1973, the Family and Medical Leave Act of 1993, the Health Insurance Portability and Accountability Act of 1996, and several of the civil rights statutes are intended to protect the welfare and wages of employees. Title VII of the Civil Rights Act of 1964 and the Civil Rights Act of 1991 also protect against discrimination in compensation, as do the Equal Employment Opportunity Act of 1972, the Age Discrimination in Employment Act Amendments of 1978, the Pregnancy Discrimination Act of 1978, and the Americans with Disabilities Act of 1992. In the last quarter century, legislatures and the courts have increasingly concerned themselves with questions of equity and discrimination in employment.

DIRECT COMPENSATION: TEACHER COMPENSATION

The compensation of teachers has proven to be one of the most intransigent aspects of the educational system. In fact, since the 1880s there have been only three major approaches to the payment of teachers: the initial rural tradition in which teachers were primarily paid by "boarden' round" at the homes of students; the move to a grade-based schedule that accompanied the shift to larger, multigrade schools; and finally, under pressure from the growing teachers' unions, the shift to today's **single salary schedule** (Protsik, 1995). By the middle of the twentieth century almost all districts in the United States were using the single salary system. The adoption of the single salary schedule represented the culmination of a century-long struggle by teachers to overcome pay differences between elementary and secondary teachers, between men and women, and between minorities and nonminorities that characterized the profession until 1940. Teachers also saw the single salary schedule as providing objective criteria (preparation and experience) for the determination of pay that would not be subject to the whims of administrators (Firestone, 1994). The education component of the single salary schedule also provided an incentive for teachers, the majority of whom had only 2 years of training from a normal school, to earn a full bachelor's degree, or even a master's or doctorate (Odden, 2001).

The single salary schedule has remained popular with boards of education because it is easy to understand and administer and because it allows for a rather simple budgeting process and for projecting and awarding salaries. Twenty states mandate the single salary schedule (Olson, 2005). However, despite the historic popularity of the single salary schedule, it has fallen under serious attacks in recent years as not being in step with the efforts to improve student performance or the realities of the teacher marketplace: "as expectations for student performance rise, experts wonder if that system still makes sense—either to attract talented people into the profession or to recognize teachers who actually improve student learning" (McCabe, 2005, p. 24). The single salary system is also criticized for fostering a culture of mediocrity; satisfactory performance becomes the norm and most evaluations fail to distinguish between performers and nonperformers (Murray & Brown, 2003).

As policy makers have sought ways to improve teacher quality and student achievement, there has been a growing interest in compensation schemes that link pay to performance. However, while public officials recognize that teacher salaries are a critical variable in recruiting and retaining the highly qualified teachers required to meet the mandates of NCLB, they are unwilling to increase teachers' salaries without some demonstration of increased teacher competence or improved student results. As a consequence, a number of states and school districts have adopted policies linking compensation to teacher acquisition of knowledge and skills or student performance. Eleven states have adopted some type of pay for performance programs: five based on teacher acquisition of knowledge and skills and six based on student achievement (Olson, 2005). (See the website for the Center for Policy Research in Education, www.wcer.wics.edu/cpre, for information on various performance-based and knowledge-and-skills programs across the country.)

As school districts consider the implementation of any teacher compensation plan, a primary consideration should be the extent to which the plan is likely to promote the compensation goals established by the district. In addition, before any plan is selected, it is important that a thorough review of alternative plans be conducted, with particular attention given to those that have proven successful in districts most like the deciding district. The following compensation plans are those presently in use or under consideration by school districts today: (1) the single salary schedule, (2) knowledge- and skills-based pay, (3) job enhancement plans, (4) group-based performance pay, and (5) individual performance-based pay.

Single Salary Schedule for Teachers

The single salary schedule pays equivalent salaries for equivalent preparation and experience. Assumptions underlying the single salary schedule include the following (Greene, 1971):

1. Teaching of all grade levels and subjects is of equal importance and equally difficult.
2. The more professional preparation and training the teacher has, the more effective the teacher.
3. The more experience a teacher has, the more effective the teacher.

4. Salary variations are unnecessary and undesirable motivations for teachers.
5. The single salary schedule minimizes frictions and dissatisfaction among teachers.
6. The single salary schedule is the easiest to administer.

The single salary schedule may be considered a version of knowledge-based pay in that it treats years of experience and degrees or courses taken as proxies for knowledge. The implicit assumption is that as teachers become more experienced and receive additional training, the better their skills and practice should be, and the better their students' test scores (Wilson, quoted in MCabe, 2005, p. 24). The single salary schedule has two basic dimensions: a horizontal dimension made up of columns generally referred to as lanes, scales, or classes, which correspond to levels of academic preparation (e.g., bachelor's degree, master's degree, master's degree plus 30 hours, doctoral degree) and a vertical dimension of rows of "steps" that correspond to the years of teaching experience. A teacher's salary schedule does not have a standard number of columns or rows, although there are usually more rows than columns so that the schedule tends to form a vertical matrix. (See Table 9.1).

Table 9.1 Glenbard Township High School District 87 2007–2008 Salary Schedule

YEARS	BA	BA+15	MA	MA+15	MA+30	MA+45
1	$44,369	$45,700	$48,806	$49,250	$51,024	$52,355
2	$46,144	$47,475	$50,581	$51,912	$53,686	$55,018
3	$47,919	$49,250	$53,686	$54,574	$56,349	$57,680
4	$50,137	$51,468	$56,349	$57,680	$59,011	$60,342
5	$52,355	$53,686	$59,011	$60,342	$62,117	$63,004
6	$54,574	$55,905	$61,673	$63,004	$64,779	$66,110
7		$58,123	$64,335	$65,666	$67,441	$68,772
8			$66,997	$68,328	$70,103	$71,434
9			$69,659	$70,990	$72,765	$74,096
10			$72,321	$73,653	$75,427	$76,758
11			$74,984	$76,315	$78,089	$79,421
12			$77,646	$78,977	$80,752	$82,083
13			$80,308	$81,639	$83,414	$84,745
14			$82,970	$84,301	$86,076	$87,851
15			$86,076	$87,407	$89,182	$90,956
16			$88,294	$89,625	$91,400	$94,062
17			$88,294	$89,625	$93,619	$97,168
18			$88,294	$89,625	$93,619	$100,274
19			$88,294	$89,625	$93,619	$103,380
20			$90,513	$96,281	$100,274	$106,486

Source: Glenbard Township High School District 87, Glen Ellyn, IL.

The Horizontal Dimension. There are two basic ways to establish the professional preparation scales: (1) complete or full schedules and (2) additive schedules. The complete or full schedule, the more common of the two, normally recognizes at least two academic degrees, the bachelor's and the master's, as well as intermediate lanes that recognize a specified number of college credits beyond the academic degree (e.g., BA + 15 hours, MA + 30 hours, MA + 60 hours). Many such schedules also have columns for educational specialist degrees and doctorates. An example of a variation of this schedule is one which provides a bonus of $2,500 or more to teachers who have received National Board Certification.

The additive schedule is not based on several academic degrees, but on the bachelor's degree and the number of college credit hours beyond it. Each salary scale represents a certain number of credit hours beyond the bachelor's. If an advanced degree is earned, however, a fixed amount or an amount related to a percentage of base is added beyond the salary figure represented on the schedule. The payment of the advanced degree additives creates, in effect, scales paralleling the established ones. A variation of the additive schedule establishes similar scales based on the master's degree. The major difference between the two schedules is that in the full or complete schedule, all possible salaries are represented, whereas in the additive schedule, salaries above those specified on the established schedule can be included.

The Vertical Dimension. The vertical steps on the salary schedule provide salary increases based on the number of years of teaching experience. An upper limit generally is placed on the number of steps, usually around 15. A common practice is to offer more steps in the higher academic preparation scales than in the lower. This provides incentive for teachers to attain additional education.

Several factors determine the initial placement of a new teacher to a specific vertical step on a scale, but the most common factor is previous teaching experience. To receive credit for any previous year's teaching, the teacher usually must have taught 75% of the school year. Most school districts place a limit on the number of years of teaching experience that will be credited toward initial placement on the salary schedule. This means that teachers who do not stay in one district for their entire careers—the typical behavior—might never reach the highest step in the salary schedule.

Other considerations in making the initial placement are credit for related experience, credit for military service, and credit for other experience. Some districts recognize related experience such as public library experience for librarians or recreational experience for physical educators. Others grant full or partial credit for military service or for experience in the Peace Corps, VISTA, or the National Teachers Corps.

Vertical advancement from one step to the next within the scale is normally automatic after a stipulated period of time, usually 1 year, although longer periods may be required for advancement to the higher steps. Teachers' groups have continued to advocate automatic advancement, but in an increasing number of districts certain restrictions are being placed on vertical advancements. These include (1) advancement at specified points contingent on additional units of academic credit or completion of in-service training programs, (2) annual advancement contingent on satisfactory performance, and (3) advancement based on merit.

To provide for teachers who have reached the maximum number of steps in a particular scale, some salary schedules also provide for supermaximum or long-term service increments beyond the highest step in the scale. Although in most instances the awarding of this increment is based solely on the attainment of a specific number of years of experience above the highest number recognized on the schedule, in some cases a performance or merit evaluation is required before the award is made.

Establishment of Salary Increments and Increases. An increment is the difference between two points on a salary schedule and may be either horizontal or vertical. The actual dollar difference between points on scales or points on steps can be established by

1. A fixed dollar amount whereby each scale or step is the same dollar amount higher than the previous one;
2. A variable dollar amount between scales or steps;
3. A fixed ratio schedule whereby each step in all scales is determined by applying a ratio to some base amount (index), usually the BA minimum, and the specific ratio at each step varies from the ratio at the previous step by a fixed value (e.g., 1.03, 1.06, 1.09, etc.);
4. A variable ratio schedule that operates the same as a fixed ratio schedule, except the value of the ratio from one step to the next is not fixed but varies.

Both the actual dollar increments and the increases (raises) may be determined as a result of collective negotiations and may not follow any discernible pattern; however, most salary schedules are not haphazardly constructed but reflect some methodology. The most common salary schedule changes that provide for salary increases are (1) changes in the index or ratio base, (2) changes in the index structure, (3) across-the-board changes, and (4) variable changes. If a schedule is based on the indexing method, a change in the index or ratio base (e.g., BA minimum) on which all other salaries are based increases all salaries by the same percentage without altering the existing index structure. Alternatively, holding the base constant while modifying the index figures by fixed index points (e.g., 1.03 increased to 1.05, 1.06 increased to 1.08, 1.09 increased to 1.11, etc.) results in varying percentage increases at each step. Indexing is no longer the predominant method of scheduling salaries, however, so these two approaches for determining salary increases are not commonly used.

The most common method of providing salary increases is by fixed, across-the-board increases in either dollar amounts or percentages. Across-the-board dollar raises, although the more common of the two, are probably the most unfair because those at the lower end of the salary schedule receive the largest percentage increases. Those who have been with the district for a number of years or have sought additional education may feel penalized by a raise that percentage-wise is less than half that received by those at the lower levels of the schedules. Across-the-board percentage raises, on the other hand, while appearing to be a fair way of increasing salaries, especially if based on some index such as the CPI or cost-of-living index, can create another type of inequity that results from the fact that, mathematically, when using the percentage increase method, salaries at the top of the salary schedule will increase faster than those at the middle or bottom of the salary schedule. And, over time, "the difference in value relationship between the top and bottom steps is destroyed" (Plauny, 1994, p. 42). If the district does not use a percentage, it can maintain the spread between the top and bottom salary steps, as well as the value relationship between the top and bottom steps, by applying the percentage increase to a specific base salary and then applying that dollar amount to each salary (Plauny, 1994). However, this approach may be opposed by teachers' unions who view the "unfairness" created by awarding experienced teachers a lesser percentage increase than less experienced teachers as more important than the maintenance of the salary spread or the value relationship.

The variable change approach to salary allows different dollar increases to be added to different salary levels. These variable increases, however, are not randomly assigned; they reflect district policy and philosophy. For example, faced with a teaching force characterized by higher levels of experience and education, some districts have felt financially constrained to refrain from hiring persons with advanced experience or education or to decrease the percentage or dollar awards to those beyond a certain number of years of experience or education. Yet other districts have adopted just the opposite policy and reward these individuals.

Knowledge- and Skills-Based Pay

Knowledge- and skills-based pay is one of the most popular alternatives to the single salary schedule and is a component of many of the alternative compensation plans today (Stronge, Gareis, & Little, 2006). Six states (Arizona, Delaware, Florida, Iowa, Minnesota, and New Mexico) have adopted knowledge- and skills-based pay systems (Olson, 2005). Knowledge- and skills-based pay is based on the premise that the more knowledge and skills employees possess, the better they can perform their jobs. Knowledge- and skills-based pay, also referred to as competency-based pay, rewards employees with salary increases as they acquire new knowledge or skills, demonstrate higher-level competence at existing abilities, or obtain additional endorsements or certification. Teacher groups have tended to view knowledge- and skills-based pay more favorably than merit pay plans, which they have staunchly opposed, because under competency-based pay plans potentially all teachers can earn salary increases. Districts also favor knowledge- and skills-based plans because there is some evidence that they have been a factor in a district's ability to retain highly qualified teachers (Reichardt & Van Buhler, 2003).

Knowledge and skills can be incorporated into the salary structure in several ways: (1) as a one-time bonus, (2) as an "add on" to the single salary structure, or (3) by restructuring the entire salary schedule around knowledge and skills benchmarks. Most districts have chosen either the bonus or the add-on approach. For example, over half the states and numerous school districts across the country provide salary supplements to teachers who receive NBPTS certification (see www.nbpts.org for a complete listing). Some provide a flat dollar amount, whereas others incorporate increases into the existing salary schedule. For example, in Florida, Palm Beach County pays teachers who receive NBPTS certification a one-time bonus of $2,000, while Duval County adds $2,500 to the annual base for the life of the certificate (NBPTS, 2006). And, in Denver, the highly publicized experiment with performance pay devolved into a plan with several components, including a knowledge and skills component where teachers can earn additional compensation by earning professional units by completing courses that increase their knowledge in an area of current or proposed assignment, then demonstrating their acquired skill and reflecting on the value of the knowledge gained to their work with students.

Districts often use knowledge- and skills-based pay to encourage teachers to take courses in subject areas of shortage, attain certification in needed areas (e.g., a bilingual certificate or endorsement), or otherwise engage in professional development to acquire knowledge and skills that advance specific school or district goals. Typically, districts identify knowledge and skills blocks which are assigned a value based on their relative difficulty of achieving or their value to the school or school district (Stronge, Gareis, & Little, 2006). Assessment of acquisition and application of the skills and knowledge are made against locally or externally determined standards.

Figure 9.2 depicts a knowledge- and skills-based model that uses both external (e.g., PRAXIS) and internal (e.g., the Danielson Framework for Teaching) assessments. Salary increases would be associated with moving from one competency level to another. Districts could decide any time limits for advancement. One or more of the assessments could be used for granting full professional licensure (accompanied by a salary increase of perhaps 10%); meeting the Danielson Proficient level or the INTASC could even replace the tenure process and would bring a sizable salary increase (Odden, 2000a).

Perhaps the greatest advantage of the knowledge- and skills-based salary plan is its focus on professional growth and development and its ability to promote the

Figure 9.2 Professional Benchmarks for a Knowledge- and Skills-Based Teacher Salary Structure

Year	Professional Benchmark
0	Graduation from college and initial licensure
1–2	PRAXIS II Content Test
1–2	PRAXIS II Test of Professional Teaching Knowledge
2–3	Danielson Basic
	PRAXIS III assessment
2–10	Danielson Proficient
	INTASC assessment
3+	Content master's
5+	Danielson Advanced
	State board certification
	Minor in second content area
	Second licensure in related field
6+	NBPTS certification
7+	Post-board-certification leadership

Source: A. Odden. (2000). New and better forms of teacher compensation are possible. *Phi Delta Kappan,* *81,* p. 364.

attainment of school and school district goals. Professional growth is one of the four key features of the increasingly popular Milken Family Foundation Teacher Advancement Program (TAP). Several hundred districts have implemented the TAP program, which involves all teachers in regular professional development sessions during the school day, multiple classroom observations of teachers, and expanded opportunities for new roles and responsibilities through multiple career paths. Fifty percent of salary bonuses in TAP are made on the basis of knowledge and skills, and the remaining 50% are tied to student performance.

Job Enhancement Pay

As discussed in a later section, extra pay for teachers (and some administrators) who take responsibility for extracurricular activities has been available for many years. This typically has been awarded only in relationship to activities that involve students (e.g., coaching, club sponsorship, and similar activities) and are covered in the teacher contract. As opposed to extracurricular pay, job enhancement pay rewards teachers for taking on additional professional responsibilities for non-classroom-related activities. These can include a variety of activities from serving as a mentor or lead teacher, to chairing a department or conducting a professional development workshop. Job enhancement "uses pay as a *facilitator* rather than an incentive, providing teachers the support they need to engage in extra tasks they find interesting and intrinsically rewarding" (Stronge, et al., 2006, p. 72).

Job enhancement programs can involve district-level responsibilities, site-based responsibilities, or both. In one of the more widely publicized compensation models in Douglas County, Colorado, faculty are eligible for several types of "bonus" incentive awards. The job enhancement component operates at two levels: district responsibility pay for those who take on responsibility at the district level and site-based responsibility pay which is awarded at the individual school level based on criteria and award amounts established by the school with minimal involvement from the district level. Salary enhancement pay goes up to $750.

Job enhancement compensation is attractive to teachers because of the autonomy it provides teachers in deciding how or how much to be involved and because compensation is directly linked to their effort. Job enhancement pay also helps alleviate the feeling of overload teachers often experience when they are required to be involved in sometimes competing activities outside the classroom (Stronge, et al., 2006). It is popular with school districts because it is easy to administer once the compensation associated with a particular role and responsibility have been established. In fact, the latter has proven to be the most challenging step in instituting a job enhancement pay program—determining what the equitable pay should be for such a wide array of roles and responsibilities.

Job enhancement pay promotes teacher leadership and involvement in more aspects of the school culture than just their own classroom. As a result, teachers have the opportunity to work with a wider array of students and staff and "to diversify their career experience. Moreover, because many of the roles . . . are leadership roles, the model encourages teachers in the development of leadership skills" (Stronge, et al., 2006, p. 73).

Group-Based Performance Pay

Group-based performance pay is a compensation strategy that has gained widespread use in business and industry. Group-based performance awards recognize that in most organizations the achievement of organizational goals is as much a result of group performance as individual performance. In education as in industry, the strategy is often seen as a natural complement to both knowledge- and skills-based pay or individual performance-based pay.

In education, group-based, or more accurately, school-based performance pay (SBPP) has also gained favor among policy makers. Experts in teacher compensation and many school administrators also favor school-based performance pay because it recognizes and encourages the collaborative work of teaching and encourages teachers to focus on goals that may be beyond their own classroom (Azordegan, Byrnet, Campbell, Greenman, & Coulter, 2005). Under SBPP programs financial rewards go to schools that meet certain prescribed standards or outcomes, such as increased student achievement, lower dropout rates, or reduced absenteeism. Some programs restrict the use of the funds to school improvement projects, whereas others allow the funds to be used for salary bonuses and/or school improvement projects. States such as California, Florida, Kentucky, North Carolina, and South Carolina, as well as numerous school districts, have developed some version of an SBPP program (Odden & Wallace, 2004).

One such program in North Carolina uses the results from state-mandated tests to place schools on one of 4 academic achievement levels. Employees in the two highest categories are eligible for bonus awards: awards of $1,500 per certificated staff (including administrators) and $500 per teacher assistants in schools in the highest category, high academic change, and $750 per certified staff and $375 per teacher assistant in schools classified as expected growth schools. Operating on top of the North Carolina state program in the Charlotte-Mecklenburg School District is the district's Local Accountability Bonus Program, which provides an award equal to the state award to certified and support staff of schools in two tiers: (1) schools that make AYP in all subgroups and achieve high academic change or expected growth with all applicable student subgroups, and (2) schools that make AYP in all subgroups but do not achieve high academic change or expected growth with all applicable student subgroups, or schools that make high academic growth or expected growth with all applicable student subgroups but do not make AYP.

Compensation researchers at the University of Wisconsin–based Consortium for Policy Research in Education have studied a number of SBPP and have enumerated the following seven factors that must be addressed by states or districts in designing such programs:

1. The most valued outcomes of the system must be identified. In states and districts that are administering SBPP student achievement typically constitutes 75% or more of the performance data, but other factors such as graduation or promotion rates, parent satisfaction, or student attendance may also be used.
2. Each element in the program must be measurable. Most states and districts use state tests if they exist.

3. Strategies for calculating changes in performance must be determined.
4. The measures and calculation of change for each school must be "made fair" by addressing such issues as the percentage of students who take the test, accommodations for students with disabilities, accounting for student mobility, dealing with students whose English proficiency is limited, and so on.
5. School systems need to determine the types and levels of awards. "Research in the private sector has found that in order to affect a worker's motivation, annual bonuses need to be at least 5 to 8 percent of salary—about $2,000 for a typical teacher" (Odden, 2001, p. 20).
6. The school system must develop and provide "system enablers" that schools and teachers need in order to become fully informed about school goals and to interpret the results of students assessments. Moreover, teachers will need substantial professional development.
7. The programs must be stable and sufficiently funded: when teachers meet their performance targets, the money must be there (Odden, 2000a, p. 365).

Group-based performance awards, like knowledge and skills programs, have been found to have a positive relationship with teacher retention (Reichardt & Van Buhler, 2003).

Individual Performance-Based Pay

Individual performance-based pay systems are designed to link teacher or administrator pay to performance, usually student achievement on standardized tests. As noted in Chapter 8, a number of states and districts have incorporated student performance in their teacher and/or administrator evaluation systems. Several of these (e.g., Arizona, Florida, Iowa, New Mexico, and North Carolina) have taken the next step and are experimenting with pay for performance. Individual performance-based pay plans establish achievement goals and then reward teachers and administrators to the extent they achieve these goals.

Many teacher groups are as concerned about performance-based pay plans as they were about merit pay systems in the past. Opponents contend that standardized tests are intended to broadly assess a child's academic skills and general intellectual development, not to evaluate the teacher's abilities, and that a student's performance cannot be attributed to one teacher. Moreover, the opponents point out, the scores are significantly influenced by factors outside the control of the teacher or the school, from how much time a teacher actually has with a child to the socioeconomic status and family background of the child (LaFee, 2000).

Despite these concerns and others, in addition to statewide plans, numerous individual school districts have adopted some form of pay for performance. Many of these emerging plans have adopted value-added approaches to assess student gains over time rather than a criterion-based reform in an attempt to address concerns about the influence of an individual teacher as opposed to the collective influence of several teachers over time (Stronge, et al., 2006). These plans typically use the single-salary schedule to establish the teacher's base pay and then provide performance awards to those teachers who attain established levels of performance. Normally the award is not added to the salary base but must be re-earned each period of the program (Strong, et al., 2006).

To address the concerns of teachers and others, Michael Allen of the Education Commission of the States suggests that states or districts considering the adoption of pay-for-performance plans ensure the following:

1. A vehicle to reasonably measure student learning gains against state education standards;
2. A method to collect and analyze data that can generate a "value added" correlation between individual teachers and student learning gains over time;
3. Appropriate appraisal of the data that emphasizes *patterns* of performance by students of individual teachers;
4. An initial corrective, but not punitive, approach to deal with teachers whose students show a pattern of poor learning; and
5. Buy-in from teachers and parents. (Gleason, 2000, pp. 82–83)

COMPENSATION FOR EXTRACURRICULAR ACTIVITIES

At one time extracurricular activities were considered normal duties that teachers had to assume as part of their work. In the 1950s, however, as teacher salaries began to lose ground in a rising economy, and as many teachers sought to supplement their incomes by working second jobs, teachers' organizations became more aggressive in seeking additional compensation for time spent in extracurricular activities (Greene, 1971). Today, districts generally compensate teachers with supplemental pay for the guidance and supervision of students engaged in extracurricular activities.

The methods used by school districts in scheduling supplements for extracurricular activities vary widely. The most common approach is to provide a fixed amount unrelated to teachers' salaries The fixed-amount approach, used by about two-thirds of the districts in the United States, can be a lump sum, multiple units of a specific amount, or a percentage of a fixed amount not on the teachers' salary schedule. The size of the fixed amount normally depends on some consideration of the various factors related to the activity involved. Typically, points are awarded to levels of each factor depending on the degree of time, effort, or responsibility involved. An example of the point-factor system for high school athletics from Bellingham, Washington, is summarized in Figure 9.3. As seen, the factors considered in this rating system included (1) length of season; (2) public relations (public exposure and expectations for interacting with the media); (3) equipment and facilities; (4) safety considerations (chance of injury and need to educate students); and (5) program coordination and preparation time, and number of evening and Saturday contests. Each activity is given a total point score, which is then multiplied by a board-established value for each point. In 2006–2007 this was Step 1—$151.67; Step 2 (head coaches only)—$166.84. Applying this system, the wrestling coach would get $4095.09 (27 pts × $151.67).

Figure 9.3 Bellingham, WA, Extracurricular Activity Points and Criteria: High School Athletics

1. <u>Length of Season</u> – Number of weeks in the regular season (one point per week).
   14 – Basketball (B & G)
   13 – Gymnastics
   12 – Swimming (B), Wrestling
   11 – Baseball, Football, Soccer (B & G), Softball, Tennis (G), Track
   10 – Golf, Volleyball, Swimming (G)
    9 – Cross Country, Tennis (B)

2. <u>Public Relations</u> – Public exposure and expectations; media coverage imposed by press; and crowd size.
   Rated on the following point scale:
   Exceptional – 4 points
   Average   – 3 points
   Low   – 2 points
   4 – Basketball (B & G), Football
   3 – Volleyball, Wrestling, Baseball, Gymnastics, Soccer (B & G), Softball, Track
   2 – Cross Country, Golf, Swimming (B & G), Tennis (B & G)

3. <u>Equipment and Facilities</u> – Ordering, inventory, repair, and facility/site preparation. Rated on the following point scale:
   Exceptional – 4 points
   Average   – 3 points
   Low   – 2 points
   4 – Football, Gymnastics, Track
   3 – Baseball, Softball, Soccer (B & G), Volleyball, Wrestling, Basketball (B & G)
   2 – Cross Country, Golf, Swimming (B & G), Tennis (B & G)

4. <u>Safety Considerations</u> – Chance of injury, nature of injury, responsibility for educating students and staff in area.
   Rated on the following point scale:
   Exceptional – 4 points
   High   – 3 points
   Average   – 2 points
   Low   – 1 point
   4 – Football, Gymnastics
   3 – Baseball, Soccer (B & G), Track, Wrestling
   2 – Basketball (B & G), Softball, Volleyball
   1 – Cross Country, Golf, Swimming (B & G), Tennis (B & G)

5. Program Coordination and Preparation Time
   a. This category includes preparation time and program coordination responsibilities outside the normal teaching day, which is assumed to encompass one-half (1/2) hour before and one-half (1/2) hour after the regularly scheduled teaching day for students.
   b. This category includes the following considerations:
      1. Budget planning time
      2. Pre/postactivity planning and preparation time
      3. Goal setting
      4. Establishing routines, rules, and procedures
      5. Scheduling events/contests
      6. Transportation and lodging coordination

c. This category is rated on the following scale:
Exceptional – 4
High   – 3
Average   – 2
Low   – 1
4 – Football, Track
3 – Baseball, Basketball (B & G), Volleyball
2 – Cross Country, Gymnastics, Softball, Swimming (B & G), Tennis (B & G), Wrestling, Soccer (B & G)
1 – Golf (B & G)

6. <u>Evening and Saturday Contests</u> – Number of regularly scheduled evening (after 6:00 p.m.) and Saturday contests in regular season.
Based on the following scale:
14-20 contests – 4 points
7-13 contests – 3 points
Less than 7 contests – 2 points
4 – Basketball (B & G), Volleyball, Wrestling
3 – Football, Gymnastics, Soccer (B & G)
2 – Baseball, Softball, Cross Country, Golf, Swimming (B & G), Tennis (B & G), Track

B. There will be an experience step included in the schedule for head coaches only. This step will be applied at the beginning of the fifth year as a head coach in that sport. Placement of the head coach is at the discretion of the district.

C. Assistant coaches will be paid a salary of 70% of the Step 1 head coaching salary for that sport.

Source: Bellingham, Public Schools, Bellingham, Washington. Reprinted with permission.

The second major approach to scheduling supplements for extracurricular pay is the ratio or percentage of a specific point on the teachers' salary schedule. The supplement is related to the teachers' salary schedule by the application of a ratio or percentage of a specific point on the schedule, commonly the BA with no experience. Here, again, the size of the percentage is normally determined by some consideration of the activity involved.

DIRECT COMPENSATION: ADMINISTRATOR SALARIES

Historically, principals and other school administrators had to negotiate individually for their salaries. This practice is still common in the hiring of superintendents and other top administrators. However, for most administrative positions and in most districts, salary schedules for administrators have been adopted. Three types of salary schedules for school administrators are typical: (1) ratio or index schedules related to teachers' salaries; (2) schedules based on add-ons to the teachers' schedules; and (3) schedules independent of teachers' schedules constructed on the basis of such variables as instructional level, scope of responsibilities, education, and experience (ERS, 1991). In addition, as was true in regard to the determination of teachers' salaries, the push for accountability in recent years has brought an increase in attempts to link administrative pay to performance and the addition of this variable to administrative salary structures. Another practice that is paralleling teacher salary is the awarding of signing bonuses. The shortage of qualified superintendents and principal candidates, especially high school principals, has led to the offering of signing bonuses. More common and larger for superintendents than for principals, the shortage of principals is beginning to turn the tide in principal perks, and enhanced health benefits, matching IRA retirement contributions, and signing bonuses are becoming more common (Shorr, 2006).

Index or Ratio to Teachers' Schedule

Indexing administrative salary schedules to teachers' schedules historically was the most common practice in determining administrative schedules. In this type of schedule the administrative salary is a ratio of some point on the teachers' schedule (e.g., lowest minimum salary, highest scheduled salary, or average salary). Each administrative position may be assigned a different ratio depending on school size, school level, number of staff supervised, or other variables that reflect the relative importance and complexity of the various administrative positions.

In the last quarter century there has been a growing trend away from the practice of relating administrators', particularly principals', salaries to teachers' salaries by ratio or index. Currently, very few school districts use a salary approach that indexes principals' salaries to the teachers' salary schedule.

Add-on to Teachers' Schedule

Even a smaller number of districts use the add-on approach to determine administrative salaries. Schedules that determine administrative salaries by making an addition to the teachers' schedule do so by adding either a specific dollar amount or a flat percentage to the point on the teachers' schedule at which the administrator would be classified on the basis of his or her preparation and experience. This method is more commonly used in determining salaries in lower-level administrative positions than in upper-level positions. It is not uncommon for the salary of a department chairperson or lower-level supervisor to be based on a bonus above a teacher's salary, but it would be rare to find a principal or superintendent whose salary is determined in this manner.

Administrator Salary Schedule Independent of Teachers' Schedule

The vast majority of salary schedules for administrators are established independent of teachers' salary schedules. Most salary schedules for administrators are constructed to reflect a number of factors related to the administrative function as well as individual competence. The two most commonly considered factors are number of students supervised and instructional level supervised. Most salary schedules for principals and assistant principals presume that greater responsibilities are inherent as size and grade levels increase. These schedules either provide a separate schedule for elementary, middle school/junior high, or senior high administrators or recognize instructional level as a factor in a single salary schedule. Among the factors that may be considered in constructing a salary schedule for administrators are the following:

Number of Contract Days. Perhaps the most important variable that affects administrative salaries is the length of the contract year. Many administrators serve beyond the normal school term. Indeed, many administrative positions are year-round positions. Because the number of contract days does vary among positions, the salary schedule should reflect the longer work period.

Scope of Responsibility. Obviously, administrative positions vary in responsibilities. Elements that influence the level of responsibility and consequently the points assigned each level include (1) number of adults supervised, (2) staff qualifications and experience, (3) number and types of special programs, (4) number and size of attendance centers, (5) size and number of budgets administered, (6) number and size of support programs (i.e., food services, transportation, etc.), and (7) student body and community characteristics.

Professional Experience. The types of experience that are generally recognized under this factor include (1) number of years in present position, (2) number of years in a similar administrative position, (3) number of years of other administrative experience, (4) number of years of teaching experience, (5) number of years of other educational experience, and (6) number of years of service in the school district.

Education and Professional Development. Most administrative positions require a certain minimum academic preparation. The administrative salary schedule may be constructed to recognize levels of academic preparation above the minimum or specified professional development.

Performance. As discussed earlier in this chapter, there is growing interest in linking compensation to performance and to the attainment of organizational goals. Accordingly, advancement on the administrative salary schedule may be based on the results of performance appraisal rather than simply gaining additional education or experience.

The Point-Factor Method. One approach to establishing administrative salaries that attempts to recognize the foregoing variables is the previously discussed point-factor method. The point-factor method, commonly used for salary determination in business and industry, is based on an evaluation of the position description for each administrative and supervisory position and the assignment of a point value to each position across a number of domains: e.g., supervisory responsibility, fiscal responsibility, program responsibility, formal education and experience requirements, contact with others in the school system and the community, and degree of independent judgment and consequences of errors. The total point value for each position is then calculated and a pay scale assigned commensurate with the position's total score and relationship to other positions on the organizational chart.

Table 9.2 presents 2005–2006 salaries for a number of administrative positions. Ultimately, each school district must decide which level and type of administrative salary structure it can best support. If a schedule is to be developed independent of teachers' salaries or other established bases, the district must decide what factors to include and the weight to be given to each.

Table 9.2 Mean Salaries Paid Personnel in Selected Administrative Positions, 2005–2006

Position	Salary
Superintendents	141,191
Deputy/Associate Superintendents	128,307
Assistant Superintendents	111,963
Administrators for:	
Finance and business	91,718
Instructional services	95,025
Public relations/information	77,121
Staff personnel services	94,761
Technology	81,809
Subject Area Supervisors	75,922
Principals	
Elementary school	82,414
Jr. High/Middle school	87,866
Sr. High school	92,965
Assistant Principals	
Elementary school	67,735
Jr. High/Middle school	73,020
Sr. High school	75,121

Source: Salaries & Wages Paid Professional and Support Personnel in Public Schools, 2006–2007 (Table 15), Educational Research Service, 2007, Arlington, VA: Author.

INDIRECT COMPENSATION: EMPLOYEE BENEFITS

Employee benefits are all the benefits and services other than salary and wages provided by an employer to employees. Employee benefits have become a fundamental component of the total compensation package of school employees and can play a major role in the ability of the district to recruit and retain quality employees. In the past these benefits were supplemental to the paycheck and of minor value, so they were referred to as fringe benefits. Although the term is still used, these benefits are no longer considered fringe: fringe benefits in the United States represented 30% of total wages and salaries of all workers in state and local governments (U.S. Department of Labor, 2000). They also represent a rapidly growing share of the school district budget. The growth of fringe benefit programs in school districts, as in other sectors of the economy, has been a result of union agreements as well as changing tax policies which have made them more advantageous and the financial constraints faced by many districts which have made the offering of fringe benefits an attractive alternative to increasing wages and salaries. The district can purchase the benefit cheaper than the employee, and in most cases the benefit is nontaxable to the employee.

In this chapter, employee benefits for public school personnel are discussed in terms of the following components: (1) legally required benefits, (2) health and welfare programs, (3) savings plans, (4) pay for time not worked, (5) income-equivalent payments, and (6) free and reduced-cost services (see Figure 9.4). In addition, one type of compensation packaging, the flexible benefit plan, is presented.

Legally Required Benefits

Both the federal and state governments have enacted laws to protect the welfare of employees. These laws require employers to provide certain benefits to employees whether they want to or not. These required benefits are described in the following sections.

Social Security. The Social Security Act of 1935 established the Old-Age, Survivors, Disability and Health Insurance System. The system is financed by contributions by the employee (based on a percentage of the employee's salary up to a maximum) and a matching contribution by the employer. Under the Social Security system, totally and permanently disabled persons may be eligible for disability payments, and retirement income is provided to workers retiring at the age of 62, or

Figure 9.4 Employee Benefits for School Employees

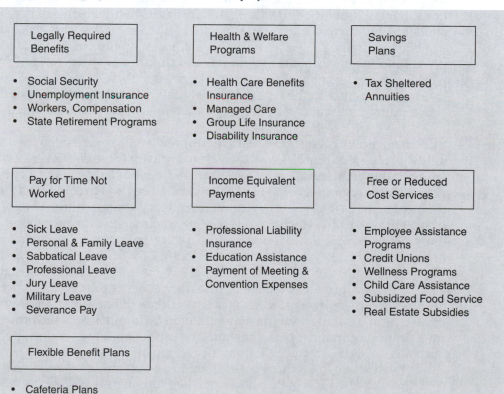

insurance benefits to those working until age 65 or longer. The actual amount the employee receives is based on the number of years worked, average earnings, and number of dependents at the time benefits begin. The Social Security Act provides health care services (Medicare) to those 65 and older and benefits to eligible survivors of deceased workers. The Social Security Act does not require government employers to participate in the program. As a result, many school districts do not include teachers and administrators in the Social Security program because they are usually included in the state retirement system.

Unemployment Insurance. The Social Security Act also requires states to provide unemployment compensation through state legislation that provides income payments to individuals who have become unemployed through no fault of their own. The employee must actively seek work to be eligible for benefits. Each state administers its own unemployment insurance program, and as a result, unemployment benefits vary from state to state and are a function of the employee's previous wage (up to a state maximum) and length of service. The costs of this program are paid by the employer.

Workers' Compensation. All states require almost all employers to pay medical expenses and provide employees with partial lost wages in the event of occupational injury, disability, or death. Each state has its own schedule of benefits that depend on the current and future wages of the employee and the extent of the disability sustained. Workers' compensation insurance also provides burial expenses and income benefits for widows and children. Districts can purchase private workers' compensation insurance, or if large enough, self-insurance. The cost of the insurance depends on the type of business or industry and can be kept down by an active safety program and by actively reviewing claims (Smith & Mazin, 2004).

State Retirement Programs. All states provide retirement benefit plans for public school professional employees. The vast majority of these employees (98%) are covered by state retirement systems (U.S. Department of Labor, 2000). State retirement systems vary regarding what kind of service can be used to compute a member's retirement benefits (i.e., prior service credit, military service credit, in-state public employment other than teaching, out-of-state teaching credit, and others). Most state retirement systems are "defined benefit" plans that use a set formula to determine the retirement benefit (e.g., years of services $\times$ 2.5%). State plans vary on such provisions as number of years to become vested, disability benefits (all states but Arizona and Iowa provide permanent disability benefits to members), provisions for borrowing, postretirement adjustments, work restrictions after retirement, and administration. Although administrators should be familiar with the provisions of the state or local retirement plan, they must be careful about rendering specific advice. Such advice should come only from the retirement agency.

In most states, retirement benefits are financed jointly by employee and public contributions. In a few states, however, the retirement plan is financed entirely by the state. In an attempt to increase compensation for public school employees while maintaining the present level of state aid to education, several states have passed legislation requiring local school districts to pay not only the employer's share toward retirement but also the employee's share. This benefit has great appeal to employees because it has a significant impact on net income without increasing gross taxable income. Consequently, in an increasing number of school districts, this provision has become a popular item for negotiations.

Health and Welfare Programs

The provision of private welfare and security programs for school employees was limited before 1960. School districts did not consider the added incentives of these benefits until they began to experience the frustrations of teacher shortages and growing competition with other districts, business, and industry (Greene, 1971). The principal private welfare and security programs provided by school districts include health and hospitalization insurance, health maintenance and preferred provider organizations, life insurance, long-term disability insurance, severance pay, tax-sheltered annuity plans, and professional liability insurance.

Health Care Benefits Insurance. Health insurance is the most costly benefit provided to employees and is growing in cost at an alarming rate. The aging teaching population and soaring prescription drugs and health care costs are key factors in the rising costs for health insurance that is breaking many school district budgets. In fact, the rising cost of health insurance has led some districts to self-insure or to join in a state-sponsored self-insurance program.

Health insurance premiums are completely paid by some districts, and in others the costs are shared with the employee. Health insurance premiums depend on the number of employees covered, type of coverage, deductible level, and claims history. The principal types of health care benefits found in school district compensation programs are (1) medical care, (2) dental care, (3) vision care, and (4) prescription drugs.

As the data presented in Table 9.3 indicate, 86% of all teachers participate in a district-sponsored medical care program for teachers. About half of these paid the full premium for single coverage and 75% paid the full premium for family coverage.

There has been a significant increase in the last few years in the number of districts providing dental, vision, and prescription drug insurance: 62% percent of teachers participate in district-sponsored dental care programs, 40% in vision care programs, and 82% participate in district prescription drug insurance (see Table 9.3).

Managed Care: Health Maintenance Organizations, Point-of-Service Plans, and Preferred Provider Organizations. The growing cost of health care and the growing need for health care at a reasonable price have led to a dramatic increase in enrollments in **health maintenance organizations** (HMOs), **point-of-service** (POS) plans, and **preferred provider organizations** (PPOs). The Health Maintenance Organization Act of 1973 requires employers covered by the Fair Labor Standard Act to offer an HMO as an alternative to health insurance if a federally qualified HMO is available in the community. HMOs provide comprehensive health care to members for a fixed monthly fee on a prepaid services basis. PPOs and POS plans offer

Table 9.3 Benefits Available to Public School Teachers

Type of Benefit	Percentage of Teachers Receiving Benefit
Medical care	86
Dental care	62
Vision care	40
Prescription drugs	82
Group life insurance	88
Long-term disability insurance	38
Severance pay	33
Tax-sheltered annuity plans	76.7
Professional liability insurance	65
Sick leave	97
Personal leave	35
Military leave	60
Sabbatical leave	69
Jury Duty	96
Education assistance	52
Employee Assistance Program	53
Wellness Programs	37

Source: U.S. Department of Labor Bureau of Labor Statistics (2000). *Employee Benefits in State and Local Governments.* Washington, DC: Author.

more choice to employees while still providing cost-effective health care. PPOs contract with physicians and hospitals to provide services to members at discounted rates. The employee has the option of going to a physician or hospital that is not a member of the PPO (i.e., out-of-network), but must assume a larger share of the associated costs. POS plans operate similar to PPOs except that under a POS plan the employee chooses a primary care physician who coordinates in-network care. Among managed care plans, PPOs have the largest enrollment (44%), followed by HMOs (28%), and POS plans (19%) ("HMO enrollment on the decline," 2001). The importance of HMOs, PPOs, and POS plans as health care providers for school district personnel has increased dramatically in recent years and is anticipated to increase as health care costs continue to rise.

Group Life Insurance. Life insurance is a relatively inexpensive but popular benefit. The group plan permits both the district and the employee to benefit from lower rates. Most group life insurance plans include all employees regardless of physical condition and provide for conversion to an identical policy without physical examination if the individual leaves the district. The standard policy provides for death benefits of one to five times the employee's annual salary. Two disadvantages of group life insurance plans are (1) they are term insurance policies, providing coverage during the employees' work years, and (2) they have no cash loan or paid-up value. As shown in Table 9.3, approximately 88% of school teachers are provided group life insurance coverage. And, 55% are provided the option of paying for increased coverage.

Disability Insurance. Disability insurance provides employees a percentage of their earnings if they are unable to work because of health-related problems. Disability insurance can be short term (usually considered up to 6 months) or long term. Disability insurance is a supplement to workers' compensation, which covers only work-related disabilities. Long-term disability plans may be provided in conjunction with a retirement plan or may be provided by separate coverage. Many group life insurance plans also have a total permanent disability feature. The definition of a disability must meet applicable state requirements and is generally more stringent under long-term plans than short-term plans (Smith & Mazin, 2004). Approximately 38% of districts provide long-term disability to teachers. In most of the others the insurance is offered as a payroll deduction.

Savings Plans

Tax-Sheltered Annuities. Tax-sheltered annuities (TSAs) provide a vehicle for employees to supplement their state retirement plan with additional retirement income. TSAs allow school personnel to invest part of their salaries in annuities that are not taxed as current salary. The payment to the annuity is made before any computation of taxes owed (i.e., it is *tax sheltered*). Thus, income tax payments are reduced at the same time that an investment is being accumulated. The annuity, or income from it, is paid to the employee upon retirement or at some future date. Income taxes are then paid on the amount received at a time when the employee's income presumably is lower. Annuities purchased by an employee fall under Section 403(b) of the Internal Revenue Code (IRC) and those purchased by the school district fall under Section 457 of the IRC. Because of their obvious attractiveness to employees, school districts are making an increased effort to design annuity programs that will be helpful in recruiting and retaining prospective or current employees, as well as in encouraging early retirements.

In most school districts, employees are allowed to choose a TSA from among a number of providers. Participation in TSA programs is voluntary. Currently, 30–35% of eligible employees in public elementary and secondary schools participate in 403(b) plans. Unfortunately, in many districts employees are given minimal education regarding basic investing concepts and the difference between the various choices (e.g., fixed annuity plans and mutual funds) in terms of expenses, transfer fees, redemption penalties, etc. As a result, many retire with significantly less than they could have earned had the district provided them with the appropriate investing education (Hauer, 2000).

Pay for Time Not Worked

For the employee, "possibly the most desired but frequently unrecognized benefit is time off with pay" (Henderson, 1994, p. 554). The most common time-off-with-pay provisions for public school personnel are sick leaves, personal/emergency leaves, vacation leaves, sabbatical leaves, religious leaves, family and bereavement leaves, civic and jury duty leaves, professional leaves, and military leaves. One other type of pay for time not worked, severance pay, is also offered by many districts.

Sick Leave. Virtually all school districts provide employees paid sick leave. In fact, statutory provision for sick leave has been made in most states. Included under this category are leaves for family illness and death in the immediate family. In most instances a set number of days per year is provided, with 14 being the average number of days per year for teachers (U.S. Department of Labor, 2000). In some systems the entire allotment of sick leave is made at the beginning of the school year, whereas in others the leave is accrued during the next 12 months. Districts are about evenly split between set and unlimited in terms of the maximum number of days employees can accumulate over the length of employment. The average number of days allowed to accumulate is 155 days. Some districts allow a sick leave pool, which is available under specified circumstances, to employees who have exhausted their own sick leave. And, 90% of teachers are allowed to use sick leave for other purposes (U.S. Department of Labor, 2000).

Personal and Family Leave. School districts also recognize that employees will, from time to time, need to take leave for a variety of personal and family reasons. Fifty-five percent of teachers receive personal leave and 4% family leave. The mean number of days allowed is four.

Sabbatical Leave. Provisions for sabbatical leaves for teachers are found in 69% of the school districts (ERS, 1995). Often the provision for sabbatical leave has come about as a result of collective negotiations. Professional study is the primary purpose for which sabbatical leave may be taken. The most common time periods granted, in which leave is provided, are 6 months (30%) and 2 semesters (58%).

Six years of satisfactory service is the typical prerequisite for a sabbatical leave. Most districts also require some justification in terms of the value of the proposed professional study program to the district and an assurance that the employee will either return to employment in the district for a minimum period of time, usually 2 years, or repay any salary received during the sabbatical. The district may also have a policy limiting the number of employees who may be on sabbatical leave at the same time.

About two-thirds of districts offering this benefit provided salary during the sabbatical. Full salary was paid by only 5% of these districts; however, a percentage of salary or some other salary provision was provided by 61% (ERS, 1995).

Professional Leave. Professional leave is granted to almost all teachers. Professional leave may be granted for a number of reasons, including (1) professional study, (2) attendance at professional meetings, (3) professional service, (4) research, (5) visits to other schools, and (6) educational travel.

Religious Leave. Leave for religious holidays not observed in the school calendar is granted by most school systems. In most districts the leave is charged against the teacher's or administrator's personal leave bank.

Jury Duty. Although in several states teachers are exempt from jury duty, leave for jury duty is granted to 96% teachers. This leave is normally considered as a separate paid leave category. In most jurisdictions any payment received for jury duty must be turned over to the school district if the employee is receiving full pay from the district. In other jurisdictions the jury pay is simply deducted from the employee's regular salary.

Military Leave. Although there is no legal requirement to pay employees for military or National Guard duty (usually 1 or 2 weeks), because school districts are particularly sensitive to the public duties and responsibilities of their employees, most districts make some provision for military leave for their employees. In fact, 60% of teachers are allowed military leave separate from personal leave (U.S. Department of Labor, 2000).

Severance Pay. Severance pay normally is a one-time payment to an individual upon severing his or her employment with the district. This severance can occur at retirement or at an earlier point in the employee's career. The size of the payment is often based in part on length of service before separation. Teachers' organizations have increasingly sought severance pay in addition to retirement benefits. When paid upon retirement, it is regarded as a bonus for long-term, loyal service and as an aid to bridging the gap between full service with pay and retirement on a reduced income. Severance pay is provided to about one-third of teachers (U.S. Department of Labor, 2000). Very often severance pay is based on the number of unused sick days, with a set maximum number that will be reimbursed.

Income Equivalent Payments

Income equivalent payments have been introduced into compensation programs in response to changes in the economic situation and to tax demands. They give the employee an opportunity for an improved, more enjoyable lifestyle. Income equivalent payments include in-kind benefits that, if purchased by the employee, would necessitate spending after-tax dollars. Discussions of some of the more common income equivalent payments available to school district employees follow.

Professional Liability Insurance. Lawsuits alleging misfeasance, malfeasance, nonfeasance, and malpractice are increasingly being filed against school districts and their employees. Because of their involvement with children, school teachers and administrators are particularly subject to increased liability. For this reason the major professional educational organizations provide professional liability coverage as a benefit of membership or at a nominal rate. School districts also often provide such coverage under a blanket provision in the board's policy. Professional liability coverage was provided to teachers by 65% of the districts included in the ERS study (1995).

Education Assistance. More and more school districts are offering tuition reimbursements or other educational assistance. This provides employees with as many educational opportunities as possible while upgrading the knowledge and skills of the district workforce. Education assistance is provided to 52% of teachers if job-related, and 18% of teachers can receive educational assistance, even if not job-related. However, educational assistance is often limited to graduate credits only.

Payment of Meeting and Convention Expenses. Attendance at professional meetings and conventions is a means of professional renewal and development. In recognition of these benefits, many school districts reimburse some meeting and convention expenses. However, this benefit is most often provided to administrators, not teachers.

Free or Reduced-Cost Services

Employee Credit Unions. Credit unions have been established by employees in many large school districts and by a cooperative arrangement of employees of several smaller districts to serve the financial needs of the employees. In some districts if a credit union does not exist specifically for school district employees, they are eligible for membership in a credit union established by other public employees. Credit unions are operated by employees under federal and state legislation and supervision. Credit unions enable employees to make savings or loan payments through payroll deductions. This not only encourages thrift by the employee, but deposits normally earn a higher rate of interest or dividends than those paid at commercial banks or savings and loans. Loans are also made to employees at a lower interest rate than that charged by commercial enterprises. In addition, credit union members are often eligible for a variety of other benefits ranging from no-charge purchase of travelers' checks to dealer discounts on the purchase of automobiles.

Employee Assistance Programs. It is estimated that at any given time 10 to 15% of employees are experiencing difficulties that interfere with their job performance (Martocchio, 2004). In an effort to help employees address their difficulties, many school districts offer **employee assistance programs.** In fact, 57% of teachers are eligible to participate in employee assistance programs (U.S. Department of Labor, 2000). Employee assistance programs (EAPs) provide "confidential evaluation, referral and outpatient counseling services for emotional and nervous disorders, marital and family distress, drug or alcohol problems, financial or legal concerns, stress related problems, and crisis intervention to employees and their families" (Martini, 1991, p. 10). EAP services may be provided internally by professionally trained staff or contracted to external organizations. In many instances employees may have access to psychological counseling through the district's health care policy or may be eligible to receive financial counseling from other sources.

District-sponsored EAPs focus on job performance and restoring employees to full productivity, not on their problems. Through self-referral or supervisor referral, employees consult with an EAP counselor who, depending on personal training, counsels with the employees or refers them to an outside agency or professional.

A good EAP will not only provide assistance to employees, but will train supervisors on how to identify and properly handle employees who show signals of problems such as domestic violence or substance abuse (Smith & Mazin, 2000). Districts using EAPs have found them to have a positive effect on employee morale, turnover, absenteeism, medical costs, unemployment and disability insurance rates, and productivity.

Wellness Programs. The health of its employees is of obvious concern to the district. Many districts require a preemployment physical. Some pay for periodic physical examinations. In addition, a number of districts have initiated **wellness programs** designed to improve the overall health of employees: 37% of teachers are covered by district wellness programs (U.S. Department of Labor, 2000). Such programs include not only health education and fitness programs and use of school fitness centers and sports facilities, but such affirmative steps as district-sponsored smoking cessation programs, cardiovascular fitness, stress reduction, nutrition and weight loss, and ongoing health-related assessment. Such wellness programs pay off not only in terms of increased employee health, but in a reduction in absenteeism and work-related injuries (Agulnick, 2001). This in turn leads to reduced health insurance premiums for the district. It has been established that "For every $1 invested in preventive health care programs, companies can expect to save as much as $6 in medical insurance costs" (Martocchio, 2004, p. 348). As a result, a few districts have followed the lead of some businesses and offer employees a waiver of the employee deductible payment or actual cash payments for reduced claims or for maintaining positive health goals (e.g., reduced cholesterol, reduced weight, reduced blood pressure).

Child Care Assistance. The growing demand for child care has led some districts to add this service to their employee benefits program. Such services may be provided through a child care center operated by the district that enrolls children of both employees and students. A popular alternative is to include child care as one of the benefits in a flexible benefit plan such as those discussed in a following section.

Subsidized Food Service. Most school districts operate a food service program that not only is nonprofit, but also is subsidized by both local and federal contributions. As a result, an adult meal purchased in the school cafeteria costs far less than a comparable meal purchased at a commercial establishment. In addition, vending machines are typically located in office areas, shops, and schools. The profits from these machines often go to some type of employee benefit or fund.

Real Estate Subsidies. As reported in Chapter 4, in an attempt to recruit and retain qualified employees, at least one state and a growing number of school districts are using various strategies to assist present or prospective employees in securing affordable housing. This has included not only working with banks and other businesses to secure affordable housing and low interest loans for employees, but actually providing funds toward the purchase of a home (e.g., Baltimore) or providing subsidized housing (e.g., San Francisco).

Flexible Benefits Plans: Cafeteria Plans and Flexible Spending Accounts

Because each individual has different needs, no fixed compensation plan will satisfy everyone. Young married workers are interested in maternity or paternity benefits and tuition reimbursements, whereas older employees are more interested in retirement benefits. Families with two wage earners do not require duplicated benefits and services from each employer. Recognizing the differing needs and interests of employees, many school districts now offer various forms of **flexible benefits plans**. One very popular flexible benefit plan called a *cafeteria plan* allows each employee to choose, within a fixed dollar allotment and legal requirements, the combination of benefits and services that best meets his or her needs and lifestyles. Many districts have found that the cafeteria plan allows them to provide employees with meaningful choices among an array of benefit options while controlling costs. Flexible benefit plans seem to particularly fit the culture of knowledge-work organizations such as schools, which are "staffed largely by highly educated professionals who like to make decisions for themselves" (Odden & Conley, 1992, p. 79).

Before involving the employee in the selection of benefits and services, the employer must identify which benefits and services will be made available, the cost of each benefit and service, and the total permissible cost for the entire program. Benefits required by the government must be included. In one of the most common flexible benefit plan arrangements, referred to as a *core-plus option plan*, a common core of benefits (e.g., retirement, health, group life, disability) is offered with a menu of optional benefits from which the employee may choose. Most plans allow the employee to choose among optional benefits and among several levels of coverage for the core benefits: e.g., 50% or 60% of pay for long-term disability; a $250 or $500 deductible PPO; or $50,000, $100,000, or $200,000 life insurance.

The best way to determine what other benefits or services to offer is by an employee preference survey that requires respondents to rank their benefit choices among a number of options. It is incumbent upon the human resources office to provide adequate information and counseling about each option, both at the time the preference survey is conducted and at the time employee selections are made, so that employees can make informed decisions in their own best interests. Informed decision making also reduces the desire or need to change selections and the associated administrative costs. In the movement toward the paperless office, benefit information is increasingly being communicated by the district's website or by an interactive phone system. Using the Internet, employees can review information about various aspects of the benefits program whenever they want. Interactive phone-voice response systems allow employees to make common transactions 24 hours a day, 7 days a week. Both systems virtually eliminate the need for employees to visit the benefits office (Martocchio, 2004).

The larger the school district, the more benefits can be included in the flexible benefit plan. Some employee benefits specialists maintain that flexible benefit plans are most effective for school districts with 500 or more employees.

While almost any benefit chosen by employees could be included in a cafeteria plan, among the more common, beyond the core, are vision coverage, accidental death and dismemberment, cancer coverage, and long-term care insurance. Other options that may be included on an after-tax basis are group homeowners and auto insurance, and, more recently, funeral/burial coverage and pet insurance (Meyer, 2000). Whatever benefits are offered, it is incumbent on human resources to ensure that they equitably address the interests of both single and married employees, older and younger employees, certificated and classified employees, and higher-salaried and lower-salaried employees.

Research has found that cafeteria plans typically result in improved employee morale and satisfaction. Most organizations have also found that their flexible benefit programs are less expensive to operate than most other options and that, because employees are involved in the selection process, they have a greater understanding and appreciation of benefits and their costs (Kushner, 2006).

A second type of flexible benefit plan found in school districts is the *flexible spending account*. This type of plan takes advantage of Section 125 of the Internal Revenue Code, which allows an employee to place a portion of pretax income into a special account, held by the employer, that can be used to pay for such allowable expenses as the employee's health, dental, or life insurance deductible or coinsurance payments, and child or elder care. Employees must decide at the beginning of the tax year how much will be placed in the account. Then as expenses are incurred, employees submit claims and are reimbursed.

As the example in Table 9.4 illustrates, the benefits of this plan are not only the flexibility it provides employees, but also the increased take-home pay. One drawback to the plan, at least from the employee's perspective, is that according to IRS rules, all funds in the account must be used by the end of the tax year or they are

Table 9.4 Savings with a Flexible Spending Assert (FSA)

	Without FSA	With FSA
Annual salary	$40,000	$40,000
FSA contribution (for health and dental insurance and child care)		8,000
Taxable income	40,000	32000
Federal income tax (18%)	7200	5760
State income tax (5%)	2000	1600
Social Security	3060	2448
Health and dental insurance	2000	
Child care	6000	
Net pay	20,260	22,192
Annual savings		1,852

forfeited. The amount forfeited, however, may still be less than what the employee would have paid in taxes. A second rule states that funds from one category cannot be used to pay expenses for another category. If, for example, near year end an employee has not used all the funds in the health care account but has used all the funds placed in the elder care account, funds cannot be transferred from the health care account to the elder care account.

When the school district operates a flexible spending account, it is the responsibility of the human resources office to cost each benefit and determine the total value of benefits. It must also ensure compliance with Internal Revenue standards and establish schedules for enrollment and changes. Perhaps most important, the human resources office must assume a greater role in employee benefit counseling and in assisting employees to estimate the amounts to be placed in the flexible spending account. Human resources administrators must help employees to move from being a passive recipient of their benefits to informed, educated consumers (Kushner, 2006).

SUMMARY

The compensation of personnel is the largest item in the school district budget. Traditionally the direct compensation of teachers has been accomplished through the use of the single salary schedule based solely on preparation and experience. However, with the renewed public interest in improved teacher quality and student performance, attention has focused on a number of compensation strategies designed to overcome the flatness of current compensation systems; attract and retain highly qualified teachers; promote the knowledge, skills, and competencies needed by the organization; and link student performance to compensation. Likewise, over the last two decades school districts have increasingly abandoned fixed salary schedules for administrators and adopted schedules that are based on factors such as responsibility of position, experience, professional preparation, length of contract year, and performance.

Employee benefits represent the fastest-growing area in the compensation of employees. The growth and strength of unions has contributed to this increase, as has the realization by employers that they must provide increased benefits to remain competitive in the labor market. Flexible benefit plans are an approach to the provision of indirect compensation that has gained popularity in business and industry and is making greater inroads in education. This approach allows employees to select, within a dollar limit, the mix of benefits best meeting their individual circumstances.

Through its compensation program the district aims to attract and retain competent personnel, motivate them toward optimum and specific performance, promote skills and competencies, reinforce organizational goals and structures, and maintain control of budgetary expenditures. These goals can be accomplished only if the district, and the human resources administrator in particular, recognizes and implements a compensation program that is well planned, internally fair and equitable, and externally competitive.

Discussion Questions

1. Discuss the factors that directly or indirectly determine the compensation program established by a school district. How has each factor affected the compensation program in your school district or a school district with which you are familiar?
2. How do knowledge- and skills-based pay and performance-based pay differ? Describe any such programs in operation in your area or state. How successful are they? If none are operating in your area or state, describe those you have read or heard about.
3. Survey three districts and compare their employee benefits programs. Also, determine which three elements have been the most recent additions to each program.
4. Compare the advantages and disadvantages of a flexible benefits plan with those of a fixed compensation program.

CASE STUDIES

—CASE 9.1

Comparable Worth

The Penzville High School Marching Band has won this year's regional band contest and has been asked to march in the Magnolia Bowl Parade on New Year's Day. Phil Smith has been the band director for 5 years and has given unlimited time and energy to transforming the band from a handful of stragglers to a full-size band and the pride of Penzville. Just before the Thanksgiving holiday Phil asks the principal to increase his extracurricular pay for serving as band director to equal that of the head football coach. He argues that he puts in as much or more time as Doug Jones, the football coach, and that his students have been more successful. From Phil's conversation and tone, it is clear that he has given this matter a lot of thought and that he is not going to take no for an answer.

Questions

1. Does Phil Smith appear to have a legitimate comparable worth claim?

2. To what extent, if any, should student success be an issue in this case?
3. How would you respond to Phil? How would you respond to the sponsor of the debate team who made a similar request after the team won in a national competition?

—CASE 9.2

Flexible Spending Account

The Rocky Point School Board has voted to implement a flexible spending account plan. A survey of employees has shown that employees' preferences are distributed among an array of possible benefits and services. To include all of them would result in high per person costs.

Questions

1. What process should be used to decide what benefits and services will be included?
2. Should specific benefits (e.g., health, medical, and dental insurance) be required in order to lower per person

costs for all employees, or should employees be allowed to choose whatever they please as long as they are willing to pay the cost from their flexible spending account?

3. Is it fair for the school district to keep the funds from an unexpended flexible spending account? How should these funds be used?

CASE 9.3

Incentives or Teachers?

Plainview School District No. 12 has adopted site-based management for its 15 schools. Authority for many curricular, instructional, budgetary, and personnel matters now resides with the administrator and a school council at each school. The school council is made up of parent representatives and representatives from the school staff.

Like most communities in the state, Plainview's economy has suffered during the current recession, and the school district is not anticipating any increase in funding for next year. Because of enrollment increases, however, Digrazzi Elementary School has been allotted two additional instructional positions for next year under the funding and staffing formula.

Digrazzi serves a lower socioeconomic neighborhood and in the last few years has experienced declining test scores and a high teacher turnover rate. During the last year the staff has been discussing a variety of measures to tackle these problems, including incentive pay plans that would reward teachers based on improvements in student achievement.

When the Digrazzi staff learns that funding has been authorized to hire two additional teachers, a formal proposal is made to the school council to forgo the hires. The proposal suggests that the money allocated for the hires be used to fund an incentive pay program that would reward teachers for increased student achievement.

Questions

1. How would you respond to the proposal if you were a member of the school council?
2. What are the possible positive and negative implications for students?
3. What is the possible impact or reaction of students and staff in the other schools in the district?
4. What alternatives to hiring two additional teachers might you propose that would improve the working conditions or welfare of the teachers at Digrazzi?

REFERENCES

Agulnick, S. (Septemper 2, 2001). Wellness plans good business for companies. *Arizona Republic*, p. D2.

Azordegan, J., Byrnett, R., Campbell, K., Greenman, J., & Coulter, T. (2005). *Diversifying teacher compensation. Issue Paper*. Denver, CO: Education Commission of the States and the Teaching Commission.

Bureau of Labor Statistics, U.S. Department of Labor. (2006). *Occupational outlook handbook, 2006–07 edition*, Teachers—preschool, kindergarten, elementary, middle, and secondary. Retrieved 1/4/2007 from http://www.bls.gov/ocu/olos069.htm.

Chambers, J. (1996). *Patterns of teacher compensation*. Washington, DC: U.S. Department of Education, National Center for Education Statistics.

Cohn, E., & Geske, T. E. (1990). *The economics of education* (3rd. ed.). New York: Pergamon.

Educational Research Service. (1987). *Methods of scheduling salaries for teachers*. Arlington, VA: Author.

Educational Research Service. (1991). *Methods of scheduling salaries for principals* (4th ed.). Arlington, VA: Author.

Educational Research Service. (1995). Fringe benefits for teachers in public schools, 1994–95. *National survey of fringe benefits in public schools* (Part 3). Arlington, VA: Author.

Equal Pay Act of 1963 (P.L. 88–38), 29 U.S.C.A. 206.

Firestone, W. A. (1994). Redesigning teacher salary systems for educational reform. *American Educational Research Journal, 31*, 549–574.

Foster, C. W. (1960). *Wage and salary administration: A handbook for school business officials*. Chicago: Research Corporation of the Association of School Business Officials.

Foulkes, F. K., & Livernash, E. R. (1989). *Human resources management: Text and cases* (2nd ed.). Englewood Cliffs, NJ: Prentice Hall.

Gleason, B. (2000). Pay for performance. *Educational Leadership, 57*(5), 82–83.

Greene, J. E. (1971). *School personnel administrator*. New York: Chilton.

Hauer, M. (2000). Tax sheltered annuities—403(b) plans: solving the mystery. *School Business Affairs, 66*(6), 26–27.

Henderson, R. I. (1994). *Compensation management: Rewarding performance* (5th ed.). Reston, VA: Reston.

Hill, P. T. (2006). The costs of collective bargaining agreements and related district policies. In J. Hannaway & A. J. Rotherham (Eds.), *Collective bargaining in education: Negotiating change in today's schools* (pp. 89–109). Cambridge, MA: Harvard Education Press.

HMO enrollment on the decline: PPOs, POS plans gain in membership and satisfaction ratings. (March, 2001). *Employee Benefit Plan Review, 17*, 20–21.

Hussar, W. J., & Bailey, T. M. (2006). *Projection of education statistics to 2015*. NCES 2006–084. Washington, DC: U.S. Department of Education, National Center for Education Statistics.

Johns, R. L., Morphet, E. L., & Alexander, K. (1983). *The economics and financing of education*. Englewood Cliffs, NJ: Prentice Hall.

Johnson, S. M., & Donaldson, M. L. (2006). The effects of collective bargaining on teacher quality. In J. Hannaway & A. J. Rotherham (Eds.), *Collective bargaining in education: Negotiating change in today's schools* (pp. 111–140). Cambridge, MA: Harvard Education Press.

Kushner, G. B. (2006). *Flexible benefits plans*. SHRM Information Center White Paper. Retrieved 1/2/2007 from http://www.shrm.org/hrresources/whitepaper/published/CMS 000025.asp.

LaFee, S. (2000). Linking teacher pay to student scores. *School Administrator, 57*(10), 14–20.

Martini, G. R., Jr. (1991). Wellness programs: Preventive medicine to reduce health care costs. *School Business Affairs, 57*(6), 8–11.

Martocchio, J. J. (2004). *Strategic compensation: A human resources management approach*. Upper Saddle River, NJ: Pearson.

McCabe, M. (2005). Salary adjustments. *Education Week*, 24–25.

McMahon, W. W. (1994). *Interstate cost adjustment*. Washington, DC: U.S. Department of Education, National Center for Education Statistics.

Meyer, J. J. (2000). The future of flexible benefit plans. *Employee Benefits Journal, 25*(2), 3–7.

Murray, J. E., & Brown, K. S. (2003). *Paying teachers for their worth: Policies on teacher compensation at the school district and regional level*. Paper presented at the annual meeting of the Mid-Western Educational Research Association. Columbus, OH. October 15–18, 2003. ED482 348.

National Board for Professional Teaching Standards (NBPTS). *Resources*. Retrieved 1/2/2007 from http://www.nbpts.org/resources/state_local_information/FL.

Nelson, F. H. (1994). *An interstate cost-of-living index and state poverty thresholds*. Washington, DC: American Federation of Teachers.

Odden, A., & Wallace, M. (2004). Experimenting with teacher compensation: Incentives piloted in districts include skills-based salary structures, school performance awards and incentives for higher assignments. *School Administrator, 61*(9), 24–28.

Odden, A. (2000a). New and better forms of teacher compensation are possible. *Phi Delta Kappan, 81*, 361–366.

Odden, A. (2000b). Paying teachers for performance. *School Business Affairs, 66*(6), 28–31.

Odden, A. (2001). Defining merit: Rewarding experience. *Education Matters, 1*(1), 16, 18, 20, 22, 24.

Odden, A., & Conley, S. (1992). Restructuring teacher compensation systems. In A. Odden (Ed.), *Rethinking school finance: An agenda for the 1990s* (pp. 41–96). San Francisco: Jossey-Bass.

Olson, L. (2005). Financial evolution. *Education Week, Quality Counts 2005: No small change, 24*(17), 8–14.

Plauny, L. (1994). Don't get compressed: The secret to compressing salary schedules. *School Business Affairs, 60*, 43–45. Aurora, CO: Mid-continent Research for Education and Learning. Retrieved 1/2/2007 from http://www.mcrel.org/PDF/TeacherPrepRetention/5021RR_RecruitingRetainingTeachers.pdf.

Protsik, J. (1995). *History of teacher pay and incentive problems*. Paper presented at the CPRE Conference on Teacher Compensation, Washington, DC, November, 1994.

Provasnik, S., & Dorfman, S. (2005). *Mobility in the teacher workforce* (NCES 2005–114). Washington, DC: U.S. Department of Education, National Center for Education Statistics.

Reichardt, R., & Van Buhler, R. (2003). *Recruiting and retaining teachers with alternative pay*. Aurora, CO: Mid-continent Research for Education and learning. Retrieved 1/2/2007 from http://www.mcrel.org/PDF/TeacherPrepRetention/5021RR_RecruitingRetainingTeachers.pdf.

Shoor, P. W. (2006). Money makers. *Scholastic Administrator, 5*(7), 31–35.

Sherman, A. W., Jr., & Bohlander, G. W. (1992). *Managing human resources* (9th ed.). Cincinnati, OH: South-Western.

Smith, S., & Mazin, R. (2004) *The HR answer book: An indispensable guide for managers and human resources professionals*. New York: AMACOM.

Stronge, J. H., Gareis, C. R., & Little, C. A. (2006). *Teacher pay & teacher quality*. Thousand Oaks, CA: Corwin.

U.S. Department of Labor, Bureau of Labor Statistics. (2000). *Employee benefits in state and local governments, 1998*. Washington, DC: Author.

Young, I. P., & Castetter, W. B. (2005). *The personnel function in educational administration* (8th ed.). New York: Macmillan.

Young, I. P., Dell, D. A., Miller-Smith, K., & Buster, A. (2004). An evaluation of the relative efficiency for various relevant labor markets: An empirical approach for establishing teacher salaries. *Educational Administration Quarterly, 40*, 388–405.

CHAPTER 10

Collective Bargaining and the Human Resources Function

After reading this chapter, you will be able to:

- Define employee union and collective bargaining.
- Describe the evolution of the empowerment of teacher unions.
- Identify the responsibilities of the human resources unit and human resources administrator in the collective bargaining process.
- Compare the distributive and integrative approaches to collective bargaining.
- Identify the roles and responsibilities of negotiation team members.
- Explain the four components of distributive bargaining in education.
- Describe the procedures for dealing with impass.
- Explain what is meant by good faith bargaining.
- List the major components of the collective bargaining agreement.
- Discuss the impact of collective bargaining on education.

Negotiations was a negative word in education less than 50 years ago. In 1960, for example, an attempt by the National Education Association (NEA) to pass a resolution at its national convention in Los Angeles stating that "representative negotiations are compatible with the ethics and dignity of the teaching profession" was soundly rejected by the association's representatives (1961). The use of such terms as *collective bargaining* and *teachers' union* was slow to be accepted by a profession that viewed them as applicable only to organized labor. Yet, by 2006 more than 34 states and the District of Columbia had passed legislation approving bargaining in the public sector, and collective bargaining between boards of education and employee groups had become routine. Today, the results of collective bargaining affects the direction school districts take in almost all areas of operation, including human resources and the instructional program.

This chapter examines the work of the human resources function in relation to collective bargaining. Attention is given to the implications of collective bargaining for the work of human resources administrators. The nature of the collective bargaining process, including both distributive and integrative approaches, is fully discussed. Special attention is devoted to mediation strategies and to grievance procedures as these relate to collective bargaining. The chapter concludes with a discussion of the impact of collective bargaining on education.

EMPLOYEE UNIONS AND COLLECTIVE BARGAINING: DEFINITIONS

The National Labor Relations Act (NRLA) of 1935 defines a union as any kind of a labor organization "in which employees participate and which exist for the purpose . . . of dealing with employees concerning grievances, labor disputes, wages, rates of pay, hours of employment, or conditions of work" (NLRA, 1935). Over 65 years later, Lunenburg and Ornstein (2000) defined a union as "an organization of employees formed for the purpose of influencing an employer's decision concerning conditions of employment" (p. 548). According to DeMitchell (2005) unions have the characteristics of both an outside special interest group and an integral part of the school district governance system by way of the collective bargaining agreement.

Collective bargaining is defined by Cunnigham and Cordeiro (2006) as "the process of negotiating an agreement between an employer and an employee organization, usually for a specific term, defining the conditions of employment, the rights of employees and their organization and the procedures to be followed in settling disputes" (p. 304). The process of collective bargaining is based on the position that employees have the right to form, join, and participate in the activities of organizations of their choosing for the purpose of representation on matters of employment relations. It also assumes that an association has the right to request exclusive representation in negotiations when the majority of the membership so authorizes, to meet with the board of education to negotiate on matters relating to salaries, fringe benefits, and working conditions.

In this chapter the terms *teacher union* and *teacher association* are used interchangeably as are the terms *collective bargaining* and *negotiation*.

EMPLOYEE UNIONS AND COLLECTIVE BARGAINING: HISTORICAL PERSPECTIVES

The National Teachers Association (NTA) was organized in 1857. At that time there were 15 state teachers' associations. In 1870 the NTA merged with the Normal Teachers Association and the National Association of School Superintendents to form the National Education Association (NEA). Twenty-seven years later, the Chicago Teachers Federation (CTF) was formed in an attempt to gain salary increases for Chicago teachers. Despite reprisal from the school board, the CTF aggressively pressed for other teacher benefits, including a pension program and a guarantee of employment following a probationary period of service. In 1916 the CTF and teacher organizations from several other states joined to form the American Federation of Teachers (AFT), which was granted a charter by the American Federation of Labor.

During the early years of their existence, both the NEA and the AFT were unable to leverage any significant political influence. The largely female membership was one contributing factor, but an even larger one was that teachers, as public employees, were considered outside the ambit of collective bargaining (Kahlenberg, 2006). The landmark National Labor Relations Act, passed by Congress in 1935, granted the right of private sector employees to form and join unions and to engage in collective bargaining. However, the latter right was limited to the private sector. Even the NEA opposed collective bargaining, and both the NEA and the AFT had policies opposing strikes.

By the 1950s, however, as teachers saw the gains made by unions in the private sector, and as their pay and working conditions continued to remain poor, they became increasingly militant. The AFT also saw collective bargaining as a way for teachers to gain respect because their salaries would be commensurate with their preparation (DeMitchell, 2005). The major breakthrough in teacher collective bargaining came in 1960 when the United Federation of Teachers (UFT) called a one-day strike for its members in the New York City schools. Among its leaders was Albert Shanker, who was to go on to become president of the AFT. As a result of the strike, New York City teachers were allowed to vote on whether they wanted to bargain collectively. An election was held the next year, and in 1962, when negotiations failed, the union called another strike. The strike was successful and the UFT negotiated the first formal collective bargaining agreement for teachers, one that awarded teachers a $1,000 raise and duty-free lunch.

The success of the AFT in New York in 1962, in Detroit in 1964, and in Philadelphia in 1965 not only led to an explosion in its membership, from 60,000 to 175,000 in 1968 (Kahlenberg, 2006), but prompted the NEA to change its policy on negotiations. In 1969 the NEA officially recognized the right to strike. In time the NEA came not only to act like the AFT—a labor union—but also adopted the industrial union model of collective bargaining which assumes an adversarial relationship exists between labor and management (DeMitchell, 2005). And, acting like industrial labor unions, teacher labor unions were willing to use strikes in an effort to achieve their objectives when negotiations failed: the number of teacher strikes exploded from 3 in 1960–1961 to 241 in 1975 (Hess & West, 2006).

Competition between the AFT and the NEA for membership led to a rapid spread of collective bargaining. In the ensuing years teachers and teacher groups became more sophisticated in the actual process of negotiations. As a result, not only did the number of strikes decline, but each successfully negotiated contract fueled the movement. The growth in the number of negotiated agreements in education had a "spillover" effect on non-negotiating districts and tended to cement the process as an expected practice.

Two decades after the first collective bargaining agreement for teachers, the practice of collective bargaining had become common in education and encompassed both professional personnel and support staff personnel. Even in those states with no legislative provision for bargaining, the "meet and confer" concept was well established. And, the process of bargaining has not been restricted to teacher groups. Principals, supervisors, middle management personnel, and staff in other classifications have negotiated agreements in a growing number of school districts.

Today teacher unions are the largest and among the most powerful organizations in local, state, and national politics (Hess & West, 2006). In 2007, membership of the NEA numbered 3.2 million and the membership of the AFT was estimated to be more than 1.4 million. The NEA is the largest employee union in the United States. Almost three-quarters of all teachers are members of unions. The growth of the teachers unions has not been without its criticism. One of the most common is that the unions have placed the desires of their members over the needs of students. Other critics assert that collective bargaining agreements stifle flexibility and block reform, promote inefficiency, and protect unqualified and incompetent teachers.

Attending to this criticism, several key leaders within both the NEA and the AFT have promoted what has been called the "new unionism" or "reform unionism." New unionism embraces the concept of professionalism, school choice, performance-based pay, and teacher accountability. However, the concept of new unionism has not been widely embraced. The industrial model remains entrenched in most state and local affiliates. Whether the new unionism or the traditional unionism will prevail remains to be seen. But what is certain is that, given the power of the teacher unions, the answer will have a significant impact on the future of public education in America (Kahlenberg, 2006).

THE HUMAN RESOURCES FUNCTION AND COLLECTIVE BARGAINING

The superintendent has the primary responsibility for representing the school board in the area of employee relations. It is the superintendent who is responsible for the development of viable human relations policies for the district, and it is the superintendent who serves as the primary liaison between the school board and employee groups, and between the school board and school administration on matters of employee relations. It is also the superintendent who is responsible for providing the instruction for school administrators and other personnel regarding the implementation of the master contract agreement and the administration of grievances related to the contract (Norton, Webb, Dlugosh, & Sybouts, 1996).

While the superintendent is ultimately accountable for each of these tasks, in the performance of each of these responsibilities, vital support is provided by the human resources unit of the school system and other human resources administrators. The superintendent and the human resources administrators in the district must assume responsibility for development of a positive working relationship with school employees and employee groups. The human resources administrators must work to develop mutual support and trust between the administrative staff and employees and in the performance of this task they become advocates of the district's employees. Efforts on the part of the human resources unit to gain optimal work conditions and appropriate salaries for employees promote cooperation, mutual trust, and a positive image of the school district.

One of the major areas of responsibilities of both the superintendent and the human resources administrators is collective bargaining also referred to as negotiations.

Figure 10.1 Collective Bargaining and the Human Resources Processes

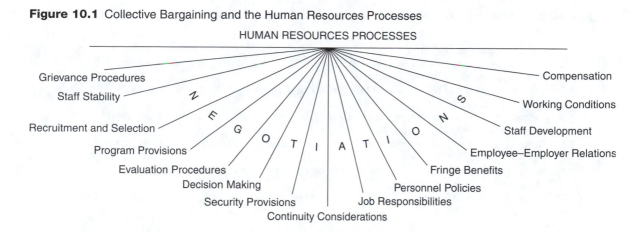

Collective bargaining has impacted virtually every process and activity within the human resources function. Figure 10.1 illustrates the influences and impacts of collective bargaining on the human resources function. Human resources administrators play a major role in three specific areas of collective bargaining: proposal development, strategy development, and negotiations at the table. A study of personnel administrators in one state found that almost 80% served on the district collective bargaining team and 54% served as chief spokesperson for the school board's negotiations team (Norton, 1999). The use of the human resources director as the chief negotiator or spokesperson for the board team varies among school districts. Smaller districts tend to use the school superintendent or a member of the school board more often than larger districts, which often use a negotiation consultant or the human resources director as the chief negotiator.

Not only do human resource administrators serve as spokespersons for the negotiations team, it is common practice for the human resources director or the director of employment relations to coordinate the entire collective bargaining process for the school board. In addition, the human resources unit serves a primary role in the fair and equitable implementation of the negotiated master agreement of the school district. The human resources director is also frequently delegated the responsibility of representing the school district in personnel matters such as contract grievances, affirmative action, litigation of employment matters, due process, and others.

Because human resources administrators play such a major role in the collective bargaining process, it is important that they be competent in a number of tasks related to negotiations. These tasks are summarized in Figure 10.2.

COLLECTIVE BARGAINING IN EDUCATION

The two primary approaches to collective bargaining described in the literature are typically referred to as traditional or **distributive bargaining** and **integrative** or **win-win bargaining**. Distributive bargaining is the process most commonly used in education and is patterned after the traditional labor-management model found in

Figure 10.2 Negotiations Competencies of Human Resources Directors

1.1   Ability to understand the nature of collective negotiations and the skills involved in the process.
1.2   Ability to make all necessary preparations for negotiations by gathering information, establishing priorities, and interpreting parameters.
1.3   Ability to contribute to the resolution of a collective negotiations agreement.
1.4   Ability to prepare news releases for the media.
1.5   Ability to interpret and communicate the negotiations agreement as it relates to the personnel function and employee contractual relations.
1.6   Ability to review and recommend revision of policies, regulations, and procedures as these relate to the "newly negotiated" agreement.
1.7   Ability to interpret, communicate, and evaluate the negotiated agreement as it relates to employer–employee relationships.
1.8   Ability to evaluate the negotiated agreements as these relate to future negotiations and school district policy development.

Source: Norton, M. S., & Farrar, R. D. (1987). *Competency-based preparations of educational administrators—Tasks, competencies and indicators of competency* (p. 109). Tempe, AZ: Arizona State University, College of Education.

the private sector. It is often adversarial and has as its basic purpose the removal of power from one party and the transfer of power to the other party. As described by Booth (2002):

> compromise and concession form the style in adversary bargaining based on de-mand from the union and counter proposals from management . . . The usual out-come of traditional bargaining is that both sides lose a little. Negotiating from a board perspective is a gradual process of losing as little as possible. Unions also feel a sense of loss because they don't get as much as they want. Rarely do both sides feel like winners unless they both gain something very important that overshadows their losses. (p. 1,2)

Dissatisfaction with the adversarial nature of distributive bargaining led a growing number of districts beginning in the 1980s to adopt alternative approaches to collective bargaining. *Integrative bargaining, win-win bargaining, collaborative bar-gaining, dual collaboration bargaining, creative bargaining*, and *joint problem solving* are all names for bargaining approaches designed to eliminate adversarial relationships and serve both parties in achieving their bargaining objectives, while at the same time feeling good about the results. Integrative bargaining involves a *quid-pro-quo*, give-and-take process of compromise and places emphasis on problem solving. It focuses on the interests and needs of both parties and is associated with the so-called "win-win" approach to collective bargaining.

In practice, approaches to collective bargaining being used in school districts across the United States fall along a continuum of traditional on one end to very nar-row versions of win-win on the other (Sharp, 2003). In many districts a combination of traditional and integrative bargaining, called **dual collective bargaining,** is used. Often wages, benefits, and working conditions are negotiated using more tradi-tional approaches, while win-win strategies are employed in the negotiation of all other issues (Sharp, 2003).

The decision as to whether to use a distributive approach or integrative approach to bargaining depends on the situation at hand. Some of the situations which might call for distributive bargaining include

- Your interests clearly conflict.
- You are much more powerful.
- You do not need or want a long-term harmonious relationship.
- You do not trust the other party.
- The agreement is easy to implement.
- The other party is pure bargaining.

On the other hand, integrative bargaining would be better for situations in which

- You have common interests.
- You are weaker or power is approximately equal.
- You need or want a continuing, harmonious relationship.
- You trust the other party.
- Implementing the agreement may be difficult.
- The other party is problem solving (Schoonmaker, 1989, pp. 12–13).

Before the actual bargaining process begins, two important decisions must be reached: what employee groups will be included in the bargaining unit, and what items will be negotiated (i.e., the scope of the negotiations). These are discussed in the following sections.

Determination and Recognition of the Bargaining Unit

Before collective bargaining can begin, the employee groups to be included in the bargaining unit and their official memberships must be determined. A school district consists of several different employee groups and clusters of employees within those groups. For example, teachers, librarians, nurses, counselors, and psychologists are among the professional staff personnel. Support staff personnel include employees such as clerks, secretaries, maintenance and custodial workers, transportation staff, and food service workers.

The determination of which **bargaining unit** each of these employee group belongs to is of paramount importance for the purpose of negotiations. A *bargaining unit* is a group of employees certified as the appropriate unit for collective negotiations. This unit is the one to which the negotiated contract will apply. It is not unusual for a school district to have several bargaining units, although a common practice is that one unit represents the combination of teaching and nonadministrative professional personnel.

Procedures to determine the appropriate bargaining unit often are established by state statutes which state that employees who share a "community of interests" (e.g., qualifications, training and skills, hours of work, supervision) may comprise an appropriate bargaining unit. Some statutes actually specify the specific bargaining units, such as teachers, support staff, maintenance, etc. ("Teacher unions/collective bargaining," 2003). In the absence of statute, the procedures for deciding which employees to include in the bargaining unit most often are determined by mutual agreement of the school board and employee groups. Less often the determination of the bargaining unit is made by an external agency such as a state public employment relations board or other outside authority or by the unilateral decision of the school board.

The National Labor Relations Board and court decisions have also provided guidance as to what would be considered an "appropriate bargaining unit." The appropriate unit for bargaining purposes meets at least one of the following criteria:

1. The unit is the one certified by the National Labor Relations Board.
2. The unit is the one the employer and union have historically recognized.
3. The unit is the one the employer and union agree to recognize as the appropriate bargaining unit (Loughran, 1992, p. 14).

The Bargaining Agent. The **bargaining agent** is the employee organization recognized as the official representative of all employees in the bargaining unit. Two types of recognition are generally found in education: exclusive representation and multiple representations. Exclusive representation is the certification of one particular employee organization to represent all employees in the unit. The general procedures for determining exclusive recognition include (1) the request by an employee organization to be the bargaining agent for all employees in the bargaining unit, (2) an election or other means of determining majority preference, and (3) certification by the school board that the organization has exclusive bargaining rights. One nonvoting method of determining the bargaining agent is that of recognizing the organization which for the last 2 or 3 years has enrolled a majority of the school employees as members.

Exclusive representation is widely used in education and is supported by both the NEA and AFT. In many states exclusive representation is mandated for the public sector and is also the form of recognition most generally accepted when statutes do not specify what form of recognition is to be given.

The less used multiple representation generally takes one of two forms: (1) the negotiation team has proportional representation based on the size of the membership of each employee group, or (2) each employee group conducts separate negotiations with the board.

Determining the Scope of Collective Bargaining

The **scope of bargaining** varies among the states and is frequently determined by state statute or court decisions. The most commonly negotiated items include salary and benefits, class size, the school calendar, hours of work, leave, tenure, performance evaluations, seniority, reduction in force, transfers, early retirement, grading frequency, use of teacher aides and substitute teachers, security, preparation time, classroom management, use of school facilities for union meetings, leaves of absence for union activities, and grievance procedures. Items considered as non-negotiable in most states include the number of days or total hours of school, nondiscrimination, special education placement procedures, First Amendment issues, federal programs, teacher discipline if a constitutional issue, and student discipline if a constitutional issue (Thompson, Wood, & Honeyman, 1994).

State laws concerning the scope of collective bargaining vary widely. In the absence of legal guidelines, precedence is most likely to determine what is negotiable. The obvious position of representatives of employee groups is that no limits should be placed on the items that are negotiable, that every matter has some influence on conditions of employment. Board of education representatives, on the other hand, argue that the public interest must be protected, and bargaining must not interfere with the board's right and responsibility to govern the school district.

Integrative Bargaining in Education

One operational model for integrative bargaining, the PRAM model, has been proposed by Reck and Long (1987). Their PRAM model for win-win negotiations is presented in Figure 10.3.

Step 1 of the PRAM model is the establishment of the win-win plans. In this step, parties agree on their own goals, anticipate the goals of the other party, determine probable areas of agreement, and develop win-win solutions to reconcile areas of probable disagreement. Most authorities emphasize the importance of the identification of common interests and shared goals to successful integrative bargaining. For example, a shared goal might be that no decision should be made that benefits teachers to the detriment of students, which would be the case if too much of the budget went for salaries and delayed the replacement of badly used and out-of-date science texts (Sharp, 2003). While exploring the interests of both parties often consumes a considerable amount of time, this is an essential step that should precede the development of specific proposals (Skopec & Kiely, 1994).

Step 2 of the PRAM model focuses on developing win-win relationships. Activities are planned that allow a positive personal relationship to develop; a sense of mutual trust is cultivated and the relationship is allowed to develop

Figure 10.3 PRAM Model

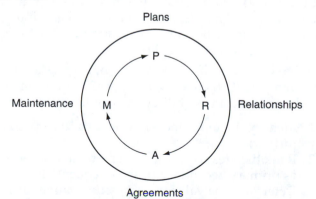

Source: *The Win-Win Negotiator* (p. 84) by R. R. Reck and B. G. Long, 1987, Kalamazoo, MI: Spartan. Copyright © 1987 by Spartan Publications. Reprinted by permission.

fully before business is discussed in earnest. Cooperation is emphasized over conflict. Building a positive relationship is essential for win-win bargaining; it provides a climate of trust in which the two parties more willingly share information and ideas. Economy (1994) used the term *to agree* as a primary attitude in achieving the goals of Step 2. According to Economy, such an attitude is most achievable when each party (1) recognizes and agrees to mutual objectives, (2) identifies and attacks key obstacles to agreement, (3) uses momentum to get through areas of disagreement, and (4) emphasizes the need for cooperative discussion. Information exchange and subsequent insight lead to win-win agreements only when a real sense of mutual trust exists and when each party believes that the other is truly concerned with its needs (Pruitt, 1981).

In the furtherance of developing a sense of trust and building positive relationships for the long term, some win-win approaches discourage the use of outside negotiators in the bargaining process except as observers or advisors; they do not sit at the table. This emphasizes that this is a local concern and lessens any fear of union empowerment (Sharp, 2003).

Step 3 In step 3 the win-win agreement is formed. The goals of the other party are confirmed, areas of agreement are identified, proposals are considered for win-win solutions to the areas of agreement, and the remaining differences are jointly resolved. It is essential that proposals address the underlying interests of the two parties, and that they are clearly written and easily understood. The bargaining parties meet over extended time periods to discuss and select those agreements that will be included in the contract. In some cases, subcommittees (negotiation teams in win-win bargaining are typically larger than those in traditional bargaining) representative of the two parties are selected to develop specific proposals for later examination, revision, and approval of the two teams. Intensive discussion is devoted to issues on which agreement has not been reached. In some cases, a neutral facilitator is included in the discussions for the purposes of keeping discussion moving in a positive direction and pointing out areas in which the parties have similar views. Pressure should not be used to finish the bargaining; rather, each area of agreement should be emphasized and the remaining areas of disagreement downplayed (Economy, 1994).

It has been said that the "real art of negotiation is in turning disagreement into agreement" (Economy, 1994, p. 132). Recommended procedures for resolving those areas of disagreement that remain are to

1. Identify the roots of disagreement and be prepared to discuss them further;
2. Rank the areas of disagreement in their order of importance and title them as primary, secondary, or inconsequential;
3. Determine the value of each issue relative to all other issues;
4. Resolve the disagreements by the give-and-take process; to be a winner make the other party a winner too;

5. Brainstorm alternatives for resolution; find alternatives that are acceptable to both parties; and
6. Give yourself and the other party time to work through an agreement; don't be pushed into an agreement that isn't acceptable to you or your counterpart.

Step 4 of the PRAM model addresses maintenance of the win-win agreement. Following the agreement and ratification of the written master contract, both parties assume a responsibility for providing feedback to others concerning agreement performance, and each party works toward keeping the agreement in force. By so doing contracts are maintained and mutual trust is reaffirmed.

Integrative bargaining often results in a widening of the scope of the negotiations agenda. In some cases, the bargaining sessions become a "forum" for the discussion of a broad spectrum of concerns of the school district (e.g., student discipline, curriculum, educational reform, decision making, etc.). Integrative bargaining also tends to change the decision-making model within the district itself. That is, integrative bargaining fosters collaboration in the decision-making process and thereby promotes site-based decision making.

Integrative strategies such as win-win bargaining can easily result in win-lose or lose-lose negotiations when there is only an appearance of mutual goal interest, compromises, and general sincerity relative to the procedural requirements of successful win-win bargaining. In such cases, bargaining sessions tend to disintegrate, as one party or the other soon recognizes that the pretense of cooperation is meant only to disguise the tactics of an adversarial mind-set (Economy, 1994). Although win-win bargaining models certainly can result in one party gaining more of its goals than the other party, when approached in good faith, neither party is denied some positive benefits from the activity (Edson, 2000).

Distributive Bargaining in Education

As previously noted, distributive bargaining is based on a quid-pro-quo, give-and-take approach in which the utilization of power and bargaining strategy plays a major role. In practice, most school districts do not use a pure distributive bargaining approach, but utilize a modified or quasi-distributive model. In fact, the quasi-distributive bargaining model is the model most frequently used in education. Quasi-distributive bargaining has four major components: (1) planning and preparation, (2) determination of the composition of the negotiation team and roles of members, (3) determination of the initial bargaining procedures and appropriate table strategies, and (4) administration of the contract agreement. These activities follow the initial activities common to any approach to collective bargaining in education: determination and recognition of the bargaining unit and determination of the scope of the negotiations. Figure 10.4 illustrates the various activities related to each of these areas, which are also discussed in the following sections.

Figure 10.4 The Negotiation Process

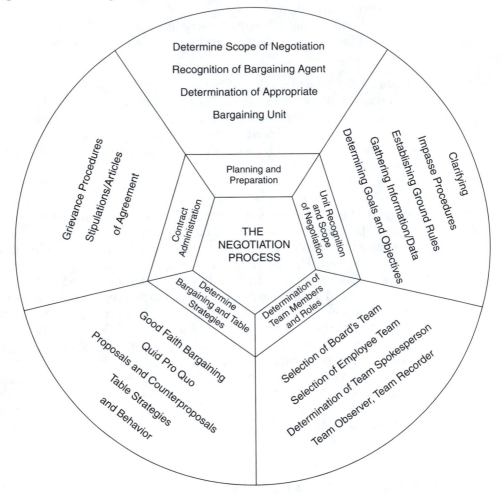

Planning and Preparation for Collective Negotiations. Authorities generally agree that the most important consideration for successful bargaining is careful planning. Unfortunately, this is often a neglected activity. Planning and preparation for collective negotiations include the following specific activities: (1) determining goals and objectives for negotiations, (2) gathering the information and data needed for decision making and cost analysis, (3) establishing ground rules for conducting negotiations, and (4) clarifying procedures for dealing with impasse.

Determining Goals and Objectives for Negotiations. An essential activity in planning and preparing for bargaining is the establishment of goals and objectives. They serve as the foundation for all bargaining activities and provide the necessary guidelines for the entire process. The school board team must understand the bargaining objectives of the school board and the level of importance of each item to be considered.

Anticipating the major negotiation topics and their relative importance is another important planning task. Although such a determination is difficult, there are numerous sources that can help, including items in newspapers, conferences and other presentations, and journals of state and national associations. Negotiation topics in other school districts that have recently been through the collective bargaining process can also provide important clues. Law firms may also offer sessions on current negotiation issues, and some school districts hold prenegotiation sessions "to discuss topics that are likely to arise at the negotiation table so the agenda isn't a surprise to the parties involved" (Zorn, 2006, p. 44).

Consideration of the school board's objectives and a careful anticipation of the objectives of the employee group allow the board team to be proactive rather than merely reactive at the table. Such knowledge is essential in determining what the team wants to accomplish in the negotiations and what strategies best serve these purposes. Attempting to gather this information during table negotiations handicaps the team and severely inhibits its ability to react intelligently to requests or to question adequately the information provided by the other party.

A team's objectives should be ranked in some manner, perhaps as primary, secondary, or tertiary. Such a ranking of objectives clarifies the expectations of the team and plays an important role in determining tactics and strategies during ongoing bargaining sessions.

Gathering the Information and Data Needed for Decision Making and Cost Analysis. At the outset of the planning and preparation activities the school board bargaining team must gather and analyze all data related to any problems with the current agreement as well as topics that most likely will be the focus of future bargaining sessions.

The data gathering process is key to the ultimate success of the negotiation process. If one or both sides is negotiating in the absence of data or with inaccurate data, they may be unwilling to settle for what may be in truth a favorable offer. Several information sources should be utilized in preparing for bargaining, including (1) comparisons with school districts with similar demographics; (2) information from the school district administrative staff about their concerns and needs; (3) troublesome areas in the present contract agreement; (4) publications, reports, press releases, and public statements by the respective professional groups; (5) data relating to budgets and the financial plans of the school district; and (6) information on the results of negotiations, arbitration, and/or court actions under present contracts in other school districts. Once gathered, information must be analyzed in terms of related problems and their potential significance in the bargaining process. Possible impact on the school program, employer–employee relationships, budgets, and any school district goals must be evaluated.

The process of costing out the contract is one of the most important preparation activities. Knowing how much each item will cost the district and what it is worth to employees will enable the district bargaining team to make decisions at the table that are based on facts rather than "guesstimates." Cost data would include data relative to salaries, fringe benefits, program expenditures, human resources needs, administrative expenses, maintenance and operations costs, and transportation expenses. Such information must not only be organized and properly recorded, but be easily retrievable for use during the planning and preparation phases of bargaining as well as during table negotiations. Thus, some form of negotiations "bargaining book" should be organized whereby information is organized by topic and labeled for convenient referencing and updating.

Establishing Ground Rules for Conducting Negotiations. Ground rules consist of the statements and agreements that govern the bargaining activities. Such rules include the clarification of the authority of the groups' representatives (e.g., who has the authority to sign the agreement), time and place of meetings, length of sessions, procedures for extending sessions, procedures for handling agenda items, number of members on the negotiation team and their roles, use of outside consultants, use of meeting minutes, use of open or closed meetings, quorum rules, use of a spokesperson, procedural rules, use of caucuses, use of press releases, ratification procedures, impasse provisions, and a time line for bargaining activities.

Ground rules can be an unnecessary addendum to bargaining activities if they become more important than primary issues of the negotiations and can inhibit later table bargaining processes if they cause major disputes. Because of the negative effects of ground rules, their use has decreased. As team members become more sophisticated in the process of bargaining and if prior relationships have established mutual trust, ground rules become less important to the process.

Clarifying Procedures for Dealing with Impasse. When good faith bargaining fails to resolve a difference or disagreement between the negotiating parties that has reached an irresolvable stage, an **impasse** occurs. At that point negotiations are usually suspended. School boards and employee groups must determine well in advance of table discussions how an impasse will be resolved. Collective bargaining legislation, where enacted by the state, generally sets forth the specific process for resolving any impasse. The first step is usually to attempt mediation, then fact-finding, and then arbitration. If none of these efforts are successful, the union may choose to strike in an effort to persuade the school board to meet its demands. Each of these methods is discussed below, including the advantages and disadvantages of each.

Mediation. **Mediation** is the most commonly used procedure for resolving impasses and is often required by state statue when impasse is reached. In mediation a jointly agreed-upon neutral third party, a mediator, serves as advisor and counselor for both parties. "The function of a mediator is to conciliate, counsel, persuade, dissuade, and assist the negotiating parties in any legitimate way so that they are able to reach an agreement. The function of the mediator is not to judge, decide, or arbitrate disagreements between the two sides" (Loughran, 1992, pp. 372–373). The seeking of an agreement on the part of the two parties is the sole objective of the mediator. By conferring independently with representatives of the employer and employee groups, the mediator seeks to determine the reasons for the disagreement, the issues that surround it, and, to the extent possible, what constitutes acceptability on the part of each group. Through a process of interpretation and advisement, the mediator attempts to bring the representatives back to the table to settle the issue at hand.

Specific recommendations and alternatives often are provided by the mediator but are not binding on either group.

Through mediation the parties continue to retain control of the negotiations process in that they ultimately have the opportunity to determine a solution of their own making. In fact, some states have mandated mediation before complainants go before the courts (Payne, Kohler, Cangemi, & Fuqua, 2000).

A primary disadvantage of mediation is the extreme difficulty of the procedure itself. Because the impasse centers on complex issues and problems, mediation activities demand exemplary personal competence on the part of the mediator.

Fact-Finding. **Fact-finding** also involves the selection of a neutral third party, a fact-finder, who serves as an investigator in analyzing all of the facts and circumstances that surround the impasse. As in mediation, fact-finding can proceed as a relationship between the fact-finder and the parties in dispute on an independent basis; however, arrangements often are made for a hearing in which both groups of negotiators present their cases.

In either the independent or formal hearing approach, the fact-finder prepares a report of the facts and recommendations for action based on the impartial findings. The representatives of each group study the findings and recommendations and respond with their acceptance or rejection. The fact-finder's recommendations are advisory only. However, the recommendations may influence public opinion regarding the appropriate resolution of the dispute, an important consideration to school board members who are elected officials ("Teacher unions/collective bargaining," 2003).

Voluntary Binding and Compulsory Arbitration. **Voluntary binding** and compulsory arbitration are procedures for resolving disagreements at impasse through the use of a neutral third party whose decision is binding on both parties. The third-party arbitrator might be an individual, a group of individuals, or a board or association (e.g., the American Arbitration Association). Either party may call for arbitration. Some states mandate binding arbitration often as an alternative to strikes ("Teacher unions/collective bargaining," 2003). In others the parties may volunteer to submit the dispute to binding arbitration. Specific procedures, including the arrangement for paying the costs of arbitration most often are set forth in the master agreement. Most commonly, costs are equally shared between the school district and the employee association. Following an in-depth study of the issue and all relative information, the arbitrator or panel of arbitrators render a decision that is final and binding.

The major advantage of compulsory arbitration is its potential to avoid a more disruptive event such as a strike. At the same time, the fact that compulsory arbitration places the settlement outside the jurisdiction of the bargaining parties, especially the governing board of education, is considered a disadvantage by many persons. Yet the removal of the two parties from the personally traumatic experiences of face-to-face table disputes and further professional alienation is an advantage in the minds of others.

Strikes. Strikes are actions that result in stoppage of work and services rendered by an employee group. The right to strike in the private sector is guaranteed by the

National Labor Relations Act. However, teachers have been given the right to strike by statute in only 12 states (see Figure 10.5), while in about half the states, the right of teachers to strike has been prohibited by law.

In those states where teachers have been given the right to strike, a strike typically takes place only after all other efforts have failed. When teachers strike in violation of state law or violation of court order, they are subject to various penalties, including fines and imprisonment.

When teachers do go on strike, it is typically for a shorter period of time than strikes in the private sector (Kearney in Sharp, 2003). And, the number of strikes nationwide has decreased significantly in recent years as states have passed mandatory collective bargaining, good faith bargaining, and mandatory mediation and arbitration statutes.

From the school board's point of view, contingency planning for a possible strike must be part of the preparation for collective bargaining. Essential activities included in such preparation are the following:

1. A comprehensive plan must be developed to obtain and retain the services necessary to keep the schools open. This consideration includes the identification of employees who likely would cross picket lines and others who would be employable on a temporary basis.

Figure 10.5 States Where Teacher Strikes Are Allowed

2. An effective means must be established for communicating important information to both internal and external constituencies. Alternative channels of communication (e.g., private, unlisted numbers or cell phones for key individuals) must also be identified in anticipation of an interruption of the usual communication channels (e.g., if regular phone lines become jammed).

3. Policies and procedures must be developed for dealing with the media. The union will undoubtedly attempt to present its position to the public as a reasonable one, so the board should demonstrate its openness to present its position, utilizing internal and external public relations personnel as necessary (Sharp, 2003). A straightforward approach for dealing with the media concerning developments and issues is always the best policy.

4. A central office or unit should be organized to serve as the coordination and control center for information gathering, decision making, and implementation procedures. Key personnel who will serve in the central office must be identified and their roles clearly delineated, including the designation of a spokesperson for the district.

5. Building administrators and supervisors should develop site plans for dealing with the strike situation. Responsibilities must be clarified and program alternatives that meet instructional goals should be identified. Guidelines for establishing the safety and welfare of students and other personnel must be stated and understood. Security personnel must be kept well informed of the ongoing conditions and potential problems that might occur.

6. Procedures must be determined for establishing meaningful communication with the employee group representatives. Serious efforts to keep talking in relation to the issues in dispute must be made. A well-organized, creative means for fostering ongoing internal discussions of the issues must be established in advance. Such communication must be positive and focus on a sincere attitude of resolution and possible agreement.

In addition to strikes, teachers' groups nationally have used other strategies to protest salary, working conditions, and other issues. For example, teachers have staged 3-day walkouts, 1-day "blueouts" in which all teachers call in sick, stacked contracts without signatures outside the central office, sponsored television commercials that portray their views of the state of education, and various other strategies to gain public support and influence state legislators and pressure school boards. Their primary purpose is to gain an advantage in the bargaining process by having the other party change its present position on a bargaining issue or issues.

Determine the Composition of the Negotiations Team and Roles of Members. The selection of the bargaining team is a critical decision for successful negotiations. Each party must have individuals at the table who can answer the questions that will arise and who can complete the process effectively. Neither the school board nor the union has any control over the selection of representatives of the other party (Ray, Candoli, & Hack, 2005). The size of the negotiations team will vary depending primarily on the size of the school system and the representations needed, but will usually be composed of three to five members. Multiple representation usually requires a larger team.

Experience in the collective bargaining process appears to be an important criterion for team member selection. Additional criteria that can be used to determine the selection of individuals for the bargaining team include the following:

1. *Time*. Does the individual's schedule and responsibilities allow the time required to serve on the team?
2. *Temperament*. Does the individual have the emotional stability and personal poise necessary to serve on the team?
3. *Tenacity*. Will the individual "stay with it" and work through the complex and tenuous collective bargaining process?
4. *Technical know-how*. Does the individual have the necessary understanding of the process of bargaining and knowledge of the content information required in the collective negotiations?
5. *Talent*. Does the individual have the talent for participating in the art of collective bargaining?

The inclusion of school board members, the school superintendent, the human resources director, the board attorney, or an outside professional negotiator on the board of education team will depend largely on the unique characteristics of each school district. The advantages and disadvantages in using each of these persons are summarized in Table 10.1.

Members of the negotiations team may have assigned roles. The *spokesperson* is the chief negotiator for the team and serves as team captain. A study in one state found that the school superintendent served as the chief negotiator in 56.8% of the school districts, a professional negotiator in 9.5% of the districts, and other school administrators in 12.2% of the districts (Norton, 2001). The role of the chief negotiator is central to the success of the collective bargaining process; this individual can greatly enhance or inhibit the realization of the bargaining team's goals (Kovach & Hamilton, 1997). The focus of unity for the team, the spokesperson generally serves as the single "voice" of the team's position.

Two other team roles are team observer and team recorder. The team observer listens and watches for clues and behaviors communicated by members of the other party. Verbal statements and body language are monitored for clues as to priority of issues, major concerns, closing arguments, and possible closure. The team recorder maintains written information concerning strategy and positions as well as facts, decisions, and events surrounding each negotiations session.

Determine the Initial Bargaining Procedures and Appropriate Table Strategies.
Once bargaining has been initiated and negotiation items have been submitted by the employee group, the school district and the union are required by the NLRA to bargain in "good faith." Good faith as specified by the NLRA has been interpreted to mean openness, fairness, and cooperation between the two parties. Some state

Table 10.1 Advantages and Disadvantages of Including Certain Individuals on the Board of Education s Negotiations Team

Position	Advantages	Disadvantages
School board member(s)	Participation can gain the confidence of the total board that their real interests are being protected; could facilitate acceptance of "final package." Participation may help the board understand the nature of the process and its complexity. Could provide a psychological advantage to the board's team. May have more time than other school district. Personnel who might represent the board's team.	Board members on the team are viewed as members of the board, rather than as members of the negotiating team; may tend to speak for the board instead of participating in the negotiations. May inhibit the effectiveness of the team's chief spokesperson; employee team tends to look to the board member as confirming the power of acceptance or nonacceptance. May not be skilled in the art of negotiation. Conditions surrounding the negotiations process may cause board members to lose objectivity; value of board member "as a board member" in evaluating, end product may be jeopardized; board members have to decide ultimately on ratification of the agreement.
Superintendent of schools	Most knowledgeable of the entire school system; expertise is invaluable at the negotiations table. School board generally views the superintendent as having the kind of competence required for successful negotiations. Because of responsibilities, superintendent is in best position to view school system as a whole and to conceptualize both organizational objectives and human resources needs.	Time commitment required may interfere with other major responsibilities. Although generally accepted that superintendent represents management, involvement in negotiations can promote poor attitudes and adversary relationships with employees. Employee representatives tend to want responses of administrative authority rather than negotiation strategy responses. Membership tends to place the superintendent in untenable position—an equal at the table on one day and chief administrator of the district the next.
Human resources director	Likely to have best understanding of employee relations in school district. Normally well trained and highly skilled in negotiations and school law. Has key information relative to primary agenda items in negotiations. Possesses experience and knowledge of human resource needs and their importance in fulfilling mission of the school district.	Role as an adversary at table conflicts with responsibilities of personal counselor and enhancer of positive human relationships in office. Time commitments detract from other major responsibilities. Although knowledgeable of employee relations and negotiations, might be utilized much more advantageously as primary resource and consultant to negotiation team.
School board attorney	Can provide important advice and counsel relative to statutes and court decisions that relate to negotiations process.	May not be knowledgeable of school system and its internal problems and needs. Legal expertise does not automatically translate into expertise in negotiation.

Continued

Table 10.1 (Continued)

	Can help develop language of the contract agreement in order to obviate unclear statements and possible problems of legal interpretations due to poor contract language. Can provide legal advice in ongoing negotiations at time of deliberations rather than after the fact.	May prove costly both in time and money.
Outside professional	Often can save time by understanding importance and/or unimportance of activities. Generally brings high level of expertise in negotiations to table. Allows internal personnel to concentrate on other educational matters. Has strong incentive to be highly effective in order to serve again and to build the reputation needed for expanded employment contracts.	Professional fees costly. Usually unfamiliar with school district. Does not remain to help implement contract agreement or to face possible grievances. Problems can arise concerning payment arrangements; hourly contract arrangement with outside negotiator carries certain disadvantages, whereas set fee can pose problems of performance. In lengthy negotiations that encounter impasse or work stoppage, district encounters problem of paying outside negotiator for other services or being without counsel and advice.

statutes define good faith, and some provide guidance as to what constitutes good faith bargaining as well as what constitutes bargaining in bad faith ("Teacher unions/collective bargaining," 2003).

Good faith bargaining requires that both parties respond to items submitted to them. Good faith bargaining does not require that one side make concessions or "give in," but it does require that they bring to the table a willingness to compromise. DeMitchell (2005) proposes the following rules for bargaining in good faith:

- Approach bargaining with a mind accessible to persuasion.
- Follow procedures that will enhance the prospects of a negotiated settlement.
- Be willing to discuss freely and fully your respective claims and demands; when such claims and demands are opposed by the other side, be prepared to justify your claims with reason.
- Explore with an open mind proposals for compromise or other possible solutions of differences; make an effort to find a mutually satisfactory basis for agreement. (p. 546)

The goal of collective bargaining is not to win a debate, but rather to reach an agreement on the proposals. The tactics that serve best are the ones that include a possible response to a proposal, or a solution to differences between the two parties. A reasonable proposal or counterproposal has the potential for resolving the issue or settling the existing differences.

Kennedy, Benson, and McMillan (1982) discussed compromise toward the goal of reaching agreement in relation to team movement and "distance between the two parties." They illustrated the distance in terms of movement and suggested that each team has a limit and "break point." The range of settlement lies between a team's most favorable position (MFP) and that break point or limit (see Figure 10.6). The final position is defined by the relative strength of the parties and their negotiating skills. If the teams' limits do not overlap, reaching agreement is highly unlikely. If the first team's range overlaps the second team's MFP, the first team holds a decided advantage in the negotiations process.

Movement in negotiations infers flexibility; flexibility requires compromise. The Latin term *quid pro quo* means something for something or, in negotiation terminology, get something for something. In negotiations each team moves closer to an agreement by giving something of value in return for receiving a desired goal. Thus, both teams use the tactics involving submission of proposals and counterproposals in a give-and-take process to try to reach a tentative agreement.

Although there is no one best way to negotiate, and bargaining is more art than science, a review of the literature suggests the following guidelines for successful bargaining:

- Always bargain from the viewpoint of the total contract amount. Never agree on economic items separately.
- Do not submit a proposal or counterproposal and then attempt to retract it. Do not "show your hand" before you need to do so.
- Be cautious about stating that your team is eager to settle early. When this becomes known, then the terms of settlement may become higher.
- Remember that collective bargaining is a process of compromise. Generally, it is not good in the long run to "win it all." Seasoned negotiators try to build long-term relationships that include mutual trust and respect. Any agreement must have mutuality of benefit. Do not bluff. A team must be prepared to carry out threats. Try to develop a high degree of credibility through a positive relationship.
- In bargaining, say what you mean and mean what you say. Be certain that you write what you mean in any tentative or final agreement.
- Do not present items for bargaining that are already within a group's jurisdiction (e.g., school board's legislative rights, administration's evaluation responsibilities, employees' academic freedom).

Figure 10.6 Range of Settlement

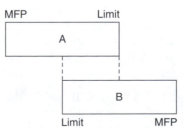

Source: Managing Negotiations by Gavin Kennedy, John Benson, and John McMillan, 1982. Upper Saddle River, NJ: Prentice Hall. Reprinted by permission of the publisher.

- Team representatives negotiate with team representatives. The board of education, for example, should not take its case directly to the employee association.
- Be a good listener. A good negotiator spends the majority of time listening to the other team's responses, rationale, key issues, and major concerns. Responses such as "Tell me more," "I didn't know that," and "Why?" help the negotiator learn more of the other team's position statements and closing arguments.
- Use closed-ended questions to bring issues into focus. Keep dialogue going. When teams stop talking, bargaining breaks down. The sophisticated negotiator wants to reach an agreement.
- Develop signaling techniques, such as cue-cards, that serve your team (e.g., OBS, return to original bargaining statement; CQ, state the closing question; etc.). Verbal signaling, sending an intended message to the other team, is a necessary tactic as well. But be careful about body language. Hesitation in responding, for example, sends a message that you might accept the proposal.
- Use reason rather than rhetoric to explain your stand. State your case and stay with the facts.
- Realize that timing is a major aspect of bargaining. At the outset, very little is agreed to. In the course of bargaining, teams tell each other their priorities and what they want.
- Use the term *we* for the team's position and never the personal *I* at the table. Team representatives do not have a position; they represent the larger group.
- Personal poise and behavior are of major importance. Self-control is essential. As presented previously, team members must be selected on the basis of their availability, temperament, tenacity, technical know-how, and talent.

Administration of the Contract Agreement

The **contract agreement,** or master contract, is the ratified document that specifies the terms of the negotiated contract and provides a framework for employee relations in the district. Because the agreement is used by all parties to guide contractual employee relations, the contract language is of primary importance. Contract language represents the final product of the negotiations. It is what both parties must live with for the contract period. Carelessness in the use of words can lead to serious problems, including arbitration. The phrase "you get what you write" applies directly to the written agreement. Consider each of the following contract statements:

Statement 1: Regular teachers will be hired for summer school teaching on a first preference basis.

Statement 2: This agreement becomes part of board policy and board policy becomes part of the contract.

Statement 3: Employees have the right to file a grievance at any time, in case of violation of this agreement.

Statement 1 tends to lock the school district into a summer school program. Also, how would the term *first preference* be applied? Is the contract agreement applicable to summer school as well? In the case of statement 2, board policy and contract agreements are two separate matters. Board policy can be changed unilaterally at any time. A contract agreement cannot be changed without mutual consent. Wording such as that in statement 2 tends to bind the board of education to no policy development without the approval of the employee group. In statement 3 a statute of limitations is needed. Such a limitation must stipulate the time period after the incident during which the grievance must be filed. With no such limitation, a grievance could be filed, withdrawn, and then refiled weeks, months, or even years later (Colon, 1989).

Content of the Written Agreement. The average length of teacher collective bargaining agreements on file at the Bureau of Labor Statistics in 2005 was 105 pages (Hess & West, 2006). The information included in these pages varies considerably. However, most agreements include (1) a statement of recognition; (2) the nature of the agreement, its scope, time considerations, and communication channels; (3) the specific stipulations or articles of agreement; (4) mutual understandings concerning the agreement, including the responsibilities of both parties; (5) grievance and impasse procedures; and (6) procedures for handling grievances related to the performance of the contract.

The statement of recognition stipulates the one specific organization or arrangement for the bargaining representation of the defined employee unit. The section centered on the nature of the agreement includes the curtailment of any further negotiations until the approved agreement has elapsed and provisions for ongoing communication between the two parties. The specific agreement stipulations or articles include the agreements reached concerning compensation, employee benefits, and other conditions of employment. Included in the section concerned with mutual understandings and responsibilities are the obligations of both parties for implementation of the agreement, the responsibilities to administer professional working relationships and thus to provide high-quality education, and, in some cases, a statement concerning strikes. As previously described, impasse procedures are significant considerations of any written agreement as well.

The ultimate success of the labor agreement is determined by the daily application and administration of what was signed:

> The climate of labor relations in any organizations will, to a large degree be determined by the extent to which the parties—the school district and whatever unions are involved—discharge their day-to-day understanding and application of the contract. The administration of the contract usually allows some flexibility on both sides, but flexibility can create problems. Problems are then handled and settled through the grievances procedures of the labor contract. (Ray, et al., 2005, p. 198)

Grievances. A **grievance** is a problem or complaint related to the contract agreement. It represents a violation, or alleged violation, or misapplication of the terms of the negotiated agreement. Most states have established procedures for handling grievances. These procedures usually require that a series of steps, such as those in Figure 10.7, be taken by the school district within a specified period of time after the grievance has been filed by an employee or group of employees in an attempt to resolve the dispute. In more than 20 states the district procedures may culminate in binding arbitration (Ray, et al., 2005). The following questions are typical of those addressed in the grievance procedures:

- What is the definition of a *grievance*?
- Who may initiate a grievance?

Figure 10.7 Operational Model for Grievance Procedure

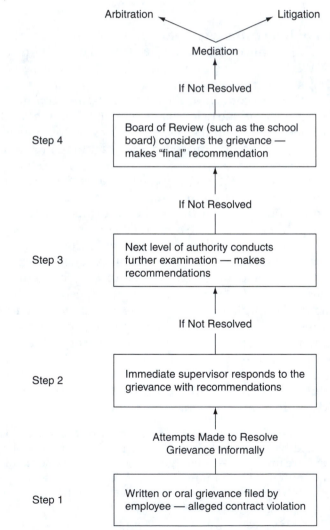

- How long does the grievant have to decide whether or not to file a grievance?
- What is the union's role in the process?
- Where should the grievance be filed?
- What are the procedural steps to follow?
- What are the time lines and deadlines?
- What is the final step? (Ray, et al., 2005, pp. 20–202)

A grievance procedure should be designed to ensure that legitimate grievances and problems are heard, reviewed, and resolved as efficiently as possible with minimal disruption to the school system. A properly designed procedure helps to place problems and complaints in the proper channels of the school system for possible solution at the most appropriate level of administration. Grievance procedures also provide the union with an inexpensive vehicle to enforce the contract.

IMPACT OF COLLECTIVE BARGAINING ON EDUCATION

The effects of collective bargaining on education have been the subject of much discussion. One of the topics of greatest interest has been the effect of collective bargaining on teacher quality. The research has provided varied results. On the one hand, the majority of research has found that collective bargaining leads to at least modestly higher salaries, which is important in efforts to attract and retain high-quality teachers (Johnson & Donaldson, 2006). On the other hand, contract provisions related to seniority, transfers, and other aspects of staffing have been said to be a factor in the disproportionate number of inexperienced and unqualified (teaching out of field) teachers in schools serving low-income and low-performing schools (Hill, 2006). And, while little evidence suggests that collective bargaining has improved the physical aspects of teachers' work (facilities, equipment, instructional materials), it does show that collective bargaining is associated with a 12%, on the average, decrease in pupil-teacher ratios and that unionized teachers have, on the average, 4% more preparation time than their nonunionized colleagues (Johnson & Donaldson, 2006). The conclusion reached by Johnson and Donaldson (2006) following an exhaustive review of data and reported studies was that

> no consistent evidence shows that the quality of the teaching force has either improved or diminished as a result of collective bargaining . . . the findings are inconclusive because collective bargaining practices and local teacher contracts vary widely. As a result, beliefs about the relationship between unions and teacher quality are shaped far more by rhetoric and ideology than disinterested, thorough inquiry. (Johnson & Donaldson, 2006, p. 138)

Another topic of great interest is the effect of unionization and collective bargaining on student achievement. Again, the limited evidence on this topic is inconclusive. Goldhaber (2006) concludes from his review of the literature on the topic that the conflicting results in the literature are largely a result of the fact that "the data necessary to do high-quality micro-level qualitative studies do not currently exist" (p. 158). While one might speculate that the effects of such things as teacher salary/quality and class size translate into improved student achievement, there is no real evidence to support this conclusion.

One of the reasons why much of the research on the effect of collective bargaining on education is unclear is that research which attempts to isolate the effects of collective bargaining on compensation has been confounded by the difficulty of controlling for the many other variables that influence the determination of salary levels. For example, the influence of bargaining districts on nonbargaining districts, sometimes termed *spillover*, is virtually impossible to measure. However, while the research on the effect of collective bargaining on education is limited, given the current interest in accountability and achievement, it seems safe to assume that it is a topic that will be more actively explored in the coming years.

SUMMARY

Collective negotiations is a process whereby matters of employment relations are determined mutually by representatives of employee groups and their employer within the limits of law or mutual agreement. The development of collective bargaining in education has been influenced historically by collective bargaining in the private and public sectors.

The human resources unit in education is involved in collective bargaining in two specific ways. First, the human resources administrator assumes many of the responsibilities in the negotiations process itself. Second, the process of bargaining affects virtually every other facet of the human resources function. In order to be effective in the role, the human resources administrator must have a complete understanding of the tasks related to the bargaining process and possess specific personal competencies appropriate for these tasks.

The two primary approaches to collective bargaining in education are distributive and integrated collective bargaining. The collective bargaining process includes (1) planning and preparation for collective negotiations and recognition of the bargaining agent, (2) determining the scope of bargaining, (3) establishing goals and objectives for bargaining, (4) gathering information, (5) establishing ground rules, (6) clarifying impasse procedures, (7) determining the composition of the bargaining team and their roles, (8) determining the initial bargaining procedures and appropriate table strategies, and (9) administering the contract agreement.

The tentative agreement reached by the negotiating parties must be ratified by the membership of each group. Once the agreement is ratified, steps must be taken to communicate the provisions of the agreement. Grievance procedures, which have been identified in the master agreement, are implemented in case of a violation or grievance related to the contract.

The impact of collective bargaining on education has been the subject of considerable debate. Little evidence exists to support a relationship between either teacher quality or student achievement and collective bargaining. In part this can be attributed to the difficulty in isolating the effect of collective bargaining.

Discussion Questions

1. Consider the distributive bargaining strategy as compared to the integrative strategy. What factors have influenced increases or decreases in the use of the integrative strategy?

2. Divide the class into triads that represent bargaining teams for the school board and for the teachers. Each of the teams has 20 minutes to consider the following situation:

   The teachers' organization bargaining team plans to request 3 personal-leave days as a negotiation item. Presently, teachers have 10 days of sick leave available each year, accumulative to 180 days. Professional leave is available with administrative approval for 3 days per year, and the teacher may take 3 bereavement days.

   a. During the 20-minute time period, each of the teacher teams should draft its version of the personal-leave proposal as it will be presented at the table.

   b. Board teams are aware of the general nature of the teachers' request as presented here, but have not seen the specific proposal that ultimately will be presented. Thus, during the 20-minute time period, each school board team should discuss the general proposal and consider its position relative to its provisions for compensation, approval authority, days such leave could be taken, limitation on the number of approvals, trade-offs, and so on.

   c. After the 20-minute individual team sessions, the triads meet as board and teacher teams. Each teacher team presents its proposal, and the board team reacts to it. Triads take another 20 minutes to "negotiate" a tentative agreement on this matter.

   d. Each bargaining triad reports its results to the class as a whole.

3. Consider the rationale and strategies associated with distributive and integrative bargaining methods. Discuss why an effective negotiator in one method may not be effective in the other method.

CASE STUDIES

CASE 10.1

A Win-Win End Run

Union School District had bargained with teachers on a meet-and-confer basis for 4 years. Because there were no state statutes to require collective bargaining between school boards and employee groups, negotiation practices varied widely throughout the state.

In the Union District, the human resources director had served as the school board's chief spokesperson for the last 4 years. Negotiations had gone well until last year when an impasse was declared and a mediator was called in to help resolve the matter relating to extra-duty assignments. Budget restraints in the district were such that an override election was necessary last year to meet this year's operating expenses. The possibility of receiving a favorable vote on a second override appeared highly questionable in the eyes of the school board.

"I think we should move to a win-win, problem-solving approach in our negotiations with teachers this year," offered Merlin George, human resources director. "In view of the current economics, I can't see our past approaches to negotiations effective this year. I would be glad to serve as a resource person this year, but I recommend that someone else serve as chief spokesperson this year."

In the final analysis, the school board and superintendent agreed to George's recommendations. Thelma Morton, the school business manager, was named as negotiations team leader for the school board. Overall, teachers were receptive to the proposal for win-win bargaining.

As bargaining for the year proceeded, Thelma spent considerable time giving facts and figures relating to a tight budget and lack of needed legislative financial support. She underlined the fact that 90% of the operations budget already was directed to staff salaries and benefits. She informed the teachers' team that the voters would not stand for another override election. "Such an attempt would bring down the wrath of the community on the schools," Thelma contended.

After several weeks of conversation between the school board and teachers' bargaining teams, Thelma met with the school superintendent and Merlin George to brief them on progress to date.

"I've spelled out the budget situation for the teachers," stated Thelma. "I think it's time to present the recommendation to the teachers that it would be the best win-win strategy for all of us to forgo any salary increases for next year; only salary increments based on experience or degree credits using the present salary schedule would be provided. I think that I've got the teachers' team convinced that we're in a dire situation. Timing is good; just last week the factory workers at Specialty Supply accepted a cut in hourly pay," she noted. "Are you both agreeable to my plan?"

Questions

1. Assume the position of Merlin George. How would you respond to Thelma Morton?
2. What evidence in the case justifies this situation as win-win bargaining?
3. Knowing the economic conditions prior to bargaining in this case, as a representative of the teachers union, what approaches and recommendations for bargaining might you have suggested?

—CASE 10.2————————

Legislative Alert!

Prior to the passing of S.B. 1008 (Negotiations for Public Employees), no state legislation had ever reached the senate floor in the area of collective bargaining. As passed, S.B. 1008 allowed boards of education to negotiate with teachers' groups on a permissive basis. That is, boards could negotiate with teachers' groups if they chose to do so. If the choice was made to negotiate, the bill stipulated that representative parties "must negotiate in good faith on topics of salary, benefits, and working conditions."

Teachers' groups were active during the discussion stages of the legislation and lobbied long and hard for its approval. Because the legislation was permissive, school boards took little active part in either supporting or opposing its passage. School administrators generally were passive about the bill and had no hand in its design.

During the time S.B. 1008 was in discussion stages, another bill, S.B. 1111, also was being considered. S.B. 1111 dealt with public employee benefits. On the day S.B. 1111 was passed, an amendment was approved on the floor. The amendment stipulated that "when the provisions of S.B. 1008 are exhausted, S.B. 1111 comes into force." In brief, the Board of Industrial Relations was authorized to intervene and authorized to decide ongoing negotiations issues between parties.

Early in the implementation stages of S.B. 1008, one local teachers' group approached its board of education and requested to negotiate salaries for the ensuing year. The school board, using S.B. 1008's permissive provision, refused the request. As a result, the court of appeals ruled that the provisions of S.B. 1008 had been exhausted and therefore S.B. 1111 would come into effect. The matter of teachers' salaries would be determined by the Board of Industrial Relations.

The school board appealed to a higher court, claiming that its legislative responsibilities had been usurped. The higher court ruled that the Board of Industrial Relations was created by the state legislature and indeed was an authoritative extension of the legislative branch of government. Thus, the decision by the Board of Industrial Relations on the matter of salaries would stand.

Questions

1. Discuss the implications of Case 10.2 generally. For example, what can be learned from the case concerning involvement in legislative proposals relating to education?

2. Why is it important for administrators, teachers, and school boards to be knowledgeable about the legislative process generally and pending educational legislation specifically?

REFERENCES

Booth, R. R. (January/February, 2002). Collective bargaining: Ready to play by new rules? *Illinois School Board Journal*. Retrieved 10/11/2006 from http://www.iasb/com/filesij2010203.htm.

Colon, R. J. (1989). Issues brought to grievance arbitration by Iowa Public School teachers: January 1982 through December 1986. *Journal of Collective Negotiations in the Public Sector, 18*, 217–227.

Cunningham, W. C., & Cordeiro, P. A. (2006). *Educational Administration: A problem-based approach* (2nd ed.). Boston Allyn & Bacon.

Demitchell, T. A. (2005). Unions, collective bargaining, and the challenges of leading. In F. W. English (Ed.), *The Sage handbook of educational leadership: Advances in theory, research and practice* (pp. 538–544). Thousand Oaks, CA: Sage.

Economy, P. (1994). *Business negotiating basics*. Burr Ridge, IL: Irwin Professional Publishing.

Edson, L. (April, 2000). *The negotiation industry: Across the board, 37*(4), 14–23.

Goldhaber, D. (2006). Are teacher's unions good for students? In J. Hannaway & A. J. Rotherham (Eds.), *Collective bargaining in education: Negotiating change in today's schools* (pp. 141–157). Cambridge, MA: Harvard Education Press.

Hess, F. M., & West, M. R. (2006). *A better bargain: Overhauling teacher collective bargaining for the 21st century*. Cambridge, MA: Pragenon.

Hill, P. T. (2006). The costs of collective bargaining agreements and related district policies. In J. Hannaway & A. J. Rotherham (Eds.), *Collective bargaining in education: Negotiating change in today's schools* (pp. 89–109). Cambridge, MA: Harvard Education Press.

Johnson, S. M., & Donaldson, M. L. (2006). The effects of collective bargaining on teacher quality. In J. Hannaway & A. J. Rotherham (Eds.), *Collective bargaining in education: Negotiating change in today's schools* (pp. 111–140). Cambridge, MA: Harvard Education Press.

Kahlenberg, R. D. (2006). The history of collective bargaining among teachers. In J. Hannaway & A. J. Rotherham (Eds.), *Collective bargaining in education: Negotiating change in today's schools* (pp. 7–25). Cambridge, MA: Harvard Education Press.

Kennedy, G., Benson, J., & McMillan, J. (1982). *Managing negotiations*. NJ: Prentice Hall.

Kovach, K., & Hamilton, A. (1997). Leveling the playing field. *Business & Economic Review, 1*, October-December, 12–18.

Loughran, C. S. (1992). *Negotiating a labor contract: A management handbook* (2nd ed.). Washington, DC: The Bureau of National Affairs, Inc.

Lunenburg, F. C., & Ornstein, A. C. (2000). *Educational administration: Concepts and practices*. (3rd ed.). Belmont, CA: Wadsworth.

National Labor Relations Act. (1935). 49 stat. 452, as amended, 29 U.S.C.

National Education Association. (1961). *Addresses and proceedings*. Washington, DC: Author.

Norton, M. S. (2001). *The school superintendency in Arizona*. Division of Educational Leadership and Policy Studies. Tempe, AZ: Arizona State University.

Norton, M. S. (1999). *The personnel administrator in Arizona*. Tempes, AZ: Arizona State University, Division of Educational Leadership and Policy Studies.

Norton, M. S., Webb, L. D., Dlugosh, L. L., & Sybouts, W. (1996). *The school superintendency*. Boston: Allyn & Bacon.

Payne, K., Kohler, P., Cangemi, J. P., & Fugua, Jr., H. (2000). Communication and strategies in the mediation of disputes. *Collective negotiations in the public sector, 29*(1), 29–47.

Pruitt, D. B. (1981). *Negotiation behavior*. New York: Academic Press.

Ray, J. R., Candoli, I. C., & Hsck, W. G. (2005). *School business administration: A planning approach* (8th ed.). Boston: Allyn & Bacon.

Reck, R. R., & Long, B. G. (1987). *Win win negotiator*. Kalamazoo, MI: Spartan Publications.

Schoonmaker, A. N. (1989). *Negotiate to win*. Englewood Cliffs, NJ: Prentice Hall.

Sharp, W. L. (2003). *Winning at collective bargaining: Strategies everyone can live with*. Lanham, MD: Scarecrow Press.

Skopec, E. M., & Kiely, L. S. (1994). *Everything's negotiable ... when you know how to play the game*. New York: AMACOM, a division of the American Management Association.

Teacher unions/collective bargaining. (2003). *Encyclopedia of everyday law*, S. Phelps (Ed.). Retrieved 10/21/2006 from http://law.endnotes.com/everyday-lw-encyclopoedia/teacher-unions-collective-bargaining.

Thompson, D. C., Wood, R. C., & Honeyman, D. S. (1994). *Fiscal leadership for schools: Concepts and practices*. White Plains, NY: Longman.

Zorn, R. L. (2006). Information-based bargaining for a new age. *School Administrator, 63*(7), 44.

CHAPTER 11

Legal Aspects of Human Resources Administration

After reading this chapter, you will be able to:

- Define and identify policies, regulations, and bylaws in relation to school governance.
- Describe the benefits of a viable set of governance policies and regulations for the school district and its stakeholders.
- Discuss the position of the courts in regard to certification, residency, health, physical, and testing requirements of teachers and other employees.
- Identify the basic elements of a contract.
- Differentiate between the due process rights of tenured and nontenured teachers and dismissal and nonrenewal of contracts.
- Distinguish between procedural and substantive due process.
- Discuss the conditions under which a school district may be liable for the sexual harassment committed by its employee.
- Describe the major personnel issues involved in dismissal for cause, suspension, and involuntary transfers.
- Identify the primary grounds for legal challenges to reductions in force.

The public schools, like all other institutions in society, operate within the framework of school board policies, state and federal statutes, and court decisions (case law). The operation of the schools is also subject to a multitude of ordinances, rules, and regulations promulgated by numerous federal, state, and local agencies and government entities.

All aspects of the employment relationship have been the subject of legislative and executive pronouncements and judicial interpretation. Although school administrators are not expected to be legal experts, they should be aware of the basic legal concepts in human resources administration and know when to seek legal counsel. It is imperative that school administrators understand their rights as well as their obligations under the law, and that these rights and obligations are translated into everyday personnel practices in their districts (Cascio, 1998).

The purpose of this chapter is to familiarize school administrators with the role of school board policies and regulations in the administration of human resources and the basic concepts of law as they relate to employment in the public schools. Although there is some variation in the application of these legal concepts from one state or locality to another, certain topics and issues are of sufficient similarity and concern to warrant consideration. These include (1) terms and conditions of employment, (2) due process, (3) discrimination, (4) sexual harassment, and (5) adverse employment decisions. Some of these topics also are discussed in other chapters of this text; here, attention is given to the legal considerations involved in each.

SCHOOL BOARD POLICIES AND REGULATIONS IN HUMAN RESOURCES ADMINISTRATION

A school district's personnel policies and regulations are a direct reflection of how it values its human resources. Governing board policies directly affect the work and life of school employees and school district clients and will determine in large part the extent to which the school system will achieve its goals. In addition, the formal adoption of policy by the board of education gives the professional staff the necessary support and direction for the implementation of program initiatives.

Policy and regulation are defined in various ways in the literature. Generally, a **policy** is considered a comprehensive statement of a decision, principle, or course of action that serves the local school system in the achievement of stated goals. Policies are local adaptations of stated goals; they are developed through the actions of the school board with the leadership of the professional staff. Governing board policies answer the question of what the school system is to do; essentially, they serve as guidelines for the administration of the school district. School personnel policies should provide guidelines for consistently fair and equitable treatment for all employees. Although policies must provide for the use of discretionary judgments on the part of the professional staff, they must not be so stated as to permit capricious interpretations.

An **administrative regulation** or **rule** is a precise statement that answers the question of how a policy is to be applied or implemented. Although administrative regulations most often are approved by the governing board, they are developed primarily through the judgments of the professional staff with representative community input and ultimately through administrative decision. For our purposes, the terms *regulation, rule*, and *procedure* are used interchangeably. Consider the following policy statement:

> The school superintendent and persons delegated by the superintendent are given the responsibility to determine the personnel needs of the school district and to recruit qualified candidates to recommend for employment to the board. The school board will employ and retain the best qualified personnel available. Concerted efforts shall be made to maintain a variation in staff relative to educational preparation, personal background, and previous experience. There shall be no discrimination against any candidate by reason of race, national origin, creed, marital status, age, or sex.

It is the responsibility of the school superintendent to certify that persons nominated for employment shall meet all qualifications established by law and by the school board for the position for which the nomination is made. The employment of any individual is not official until the contract is signed by the candidate and approved by the governing school board.

The above policy specifies *what* the board desires concerning practices for employment and sets forth what is to be done relative to employee qualifications. The policy represents a broad statement that allows the professional staff to use its judgment concerning specific recruiting and selection procedures. The policy is legislative in substance and is directly related to the question of what to do relative to the important matter of hiring school district personnel. Finally, although specific procedures regarding recruitment and selection might change, the guiding policy could remain as stated for a substantial period of time. That is, the question of "what is to be accomplished" could remain unchanged even though the question "how to do it" might be altered to improve current practices.

Next, consider the procedure illustrated in Figure 11.1 that sets forth steps for position application. This regulation relates specifically to the policy for personnel recruitment and selection; it is executive in nature, calling for specific procedures to be followed; it is possible to revise these procedures without having to change board policy; and it serves to answer the question of how selection of personnel is to be implemented.

Compliance with Policy

Governing board policies and regulations are subject to and must be in compliance with state and federal laws. It is not unusual for state laws and/or court decisions to mandate school policy; that is, state statutes and court rulings often specify what school systems must do relative to a specific matter. However, seldom is the specific law written verbatim in the school district's policy manual. Rather, a policy statement based on the requirements of the law is written as a school policy, followed by specific statute references or citations. Exceptions to this provision are policies and regulations concerning personnel dismissal which are often written verbatim from state statutes. The reason is that dismissals are frequently challenged in court and school districts want to make sure that their policies and regulations are in compliance with all applicable federal and state laws.

TERMS AND CONDITIONS OF EMPLOYMENT

Within the framework of state and federal constitutional and statutory protection provided for school district employees, the state has plenary power to conduct and regulate public education within the state. Accordingly, the state, through its legislature, state board of education, state department of education, local school boards, and in some instances school-based councils, has promulgated the rules and regulations for the operation of the schools. Among these rules and regulations are those that establish the terms and conditions of employment. These may vary considerably

Figure 11.1 Procedure for Position Application

Personnel: Certificated
Code: 4111 Recruitment and Selection

To aid in obtaining the best available personnel for school positions, the following criteria and procedures will be utilized:

Concerted efforts will be made to maintain a variation in staff relative to educational preparation, background, and previous experience through recruiting on a broad basis. All available sources of personnel supply, including college and university career placement offices, career-information-day programs, student-teacher information, advertisements in appropriate publications, and others that serve to identify a pool of qualified personnel for position openings will be used.

Written applications, official transcripts of college work, student teaching and teaching reports and recommendations, and personal interviews provide the primary data for personnel selection. The procedures for screening and selecting personnel for teaching positions are as follows:

1. Notices of position openings in teaching will be disseminated internally through the offices of school principals and externally through selected college and university teacher placement offices.
2. The central human resources office will collect and process applications; the official application form of the school district and other application materials, as required by the human resources office, must be completed and received before an applicant can be considered for a position.
3. The central human resources office will gather all evidence for purposes of screening applicants including the application form, evidence of certification or licensure for the position in question, teacher placement records of the applicant, official college transcripts, at least three professional references from former employers and/or supervisors, and other information of importance. In addition, the district's prescreening background-check form is to be completed and returned by the applicant.
4. Preliminary interviews of applicants who are best qualified will be conducted by the central human resources office, although other representatives may participate as interviewers as the case requires.
5. Finalists for the position, as determined by the human resources office, will be scheduled for interviews with appropriate building principals and/or supervisors. The human resources office, together with the appropriate building principal and/or supervisor, will decide if the position should be offered to a specific applicant.
6. When a position is offered tentatively and accepted pending school board approval, the human resources office will send its recommendation to the school superintendent. Upon the superintendent's approval, the nomination will be made to the school board for final approval.
7. All final applicants for a position will be notified of the decision reached by the school board.

from state to state, but the areas most often affected by state statutory and regulatory provisions are discussed in this section and deal with certification, citizenship and residency requirements, health and physical requirements, teacher competency testing, the employment contract, and tenure.

Certification

To qualify for teaching, administrative, and many other positions in the public schools, an individual must acquire a valid certificate or license. The certification or licensure requirement is intended to ensure that the holder has met established state standards and is qualified for employment in the area for which the certificate or license is required. The courts have held that states not only have the right but the duty to ensure that school district employees meet certain minimum qualifications for employment. The certificate does not constitute a contract or a guarantee of employment; it only makes the holder eligible for employment.

Certification requirements may include a college degree with minimum credit hours in specific curricular areas, evidence of specific job experience, "good moral character," a specified age, United States citizenship, the signing of a loyalty oath, and more recently, a minimum score on a job-related exam such as the PRAXIS examination (39 states require a test of basic skills of teacher education candidates). In determining whether candidates for certification meet state standards, the courts will generally interpret and enforce the standards quite literally and will intervene only if the denial of certification is clearly erroneous or unsupported by substantial evidence or if statutory or constitutional rights are violated.

Not only is the state empowered to issue certificates, it is also authorized to revoke or suspend certificates. Revocation or suspension of a certificate is a more severe action than dismissal, because the former forecloses employment opportunities within the state in the area of certification. As a result of their severity, the evidentiary standards and conformity to due process in suspension or revocation actions are usually more rigorous (Beckham, 1983). The procedures to be followed in the revocation or suspension of a certificate and the grounds for the revocation or suspension are normally stipulated in statute. In a number of states, a decertification charge must be job related (Valente & Valente, 2001).

A lesser penalty, nonrenewal of certification, can be imposed by the state when the individual seeking recertification fails to satisfy the requirements for recertification. In many states, teaching and administrative certificates expire every 5 to 10 years but can be renewed if the holder meets specific requirements which are usually related to professional growth (e.g., completion of a specified number of credits during a certain period of time or positive performance evaluations). More recently, a few states have imposed a test requirement as a precondition for recertification. The courts have upheld requirements for recertification if they are shown to be reasonably related to maintenance of standards or improved performance. If the requirement is found not to be reasonably related, or the school board exceeds its authority in establishing requirements, the decertification will be overturned.

Where certification requirements exist, lack of certification can result in dismissal of the employee. For example, in a case in Texas, a prospective teacher entered into a contract with a school district for a teaching position that required him to file his certificate with the personnel director no later than the issuance of the first payroll check (in this case, September 20). The prospective teacher failed the state exam that was a requirement for certification twice before the school year began, but eventually passed it and so informed the district on October 20. In the meantime the district had hired another teacher, and the prospective teacher was unsuccessful in his breach of contract suit against the district (*Grand Prairie Independent School District v. Vaughn*, 1990). If a school district knowingly employs a noncertificated individual, it may be subject to nonpayment of state aid. In fact, state laws usually provide that it is unlawful for a district to pay an uncertified teacher (*Flanary v. Barrett*, 1912). If an employee knowingly provides services without a certificate, some courts have viewed this service as voluntary and, as such, not demanding of compensation (see, e.g., *Floyd County Board of Education v. Slone*, 1957; *Sorenson v. School District No. 28*, 1966).

Citizenship and Residency Requirements

The courts have upheld both citizenship and residency requirements for certification and/or as a condition of employment. With regard to U.S. citizenship, the U.S. Supreme Court has held that education is one of those government functions that is "so bound up with the operation of the state as a governmental entity as to permit the exclusion from those functions of all persons who have not become part of the process of self-government" (*Ambach v. Norwick*, 1979, pp. 73–74). Further, the Court acknowledged a rational relationship between such a New York citizenship requirement and a legitimate state purpose. The Court found the requirement justified because of the critical part teachers play "in developing students' attitudes toward government and understanding the role of citizens in our society" (p. 78).

Where state statute permits, school districts may require employees to reside within the school district. Residency requirements have been upheld by the majority of state and federal courts when there is a rational basis for the requirements. For example, a residency requirement for all future district employees of the Pittsburgh school district withstood challenge by the Pittsburgh Federation of Teachers because the court agreed that the district's stated reasons for the requirement—namely, that employees would have an increased personal knowledge of conditions in the district, would feel a greater personal stake in the district, would pay taxes in the district, and would have reduced absenteeism and tardiness—were all rational, legitimate, and justifiable (*Pittsburgh Federation of Teachers v. Aaron*, 1976). Similarly, the Arkansas Supreme Court held that a school district's requirement that teachers reside within district boundaries or within 10 miles of city limits did not violate equal protection even though it did not apply to noncertificated personnel. The court determined that the policy was "rationally related to community involvement and district identity as it related to tax base in support of district tax levies, and [the] 10 mile limit was reasonable commuting distance and was not arbitrary" (*McClelland v. Paris Public Schools*, 1988, p. 908). And, an Illinois court held that a state statute prohibiting residency requirements for teachers did not serve to prohibit such requirements for administrators (*Owen v. Board of Education of Kankakee School District No. 111*, 1994). It should be noted that although school district residency requirements have been upheld in several states and at the federal level, other states have statutory provisions against school districts imposing such requirements (Cambron-McCabe, McCarthy, & Thomas, 2004).

Health and Physical Requirements

Most states and school districts have adopted health and physical requirements in an attempt to ensure that employees can meet their contractual obligations as well as to protect the welfare of students and other employees. The courts will uphold these requirements as long as they are not arbitrary and are appropriate for the specific condition and job. And they have supported the dismissal of employees whose condition posed a threat to the well-being of students or other employees. For example, a Michigan court upheld a school district that suspended a tenured teacher for 3 years and required that before returning to work the teacher undergo physical and mental examinations at the board's expense. The court found that the board had a legitimate concern, following numerous instances of misconduct and insubordination, that the teacher might be undergoing a breakdown (*Sullivan v. River Valley Sch. Dist.*, 1998). The courts have also upheld the authority of the school district to release or reassign employees whose physical conditions (e.g., failed eyesight or hearing) have made it impossible for them to meet their contractual duties. For example, the court supported the school board against a claim of violation of the Americans with Disabilities Act when it denied tenure to a teacher with attention deficit hyperactivity disorder (ADHD) noting that "the duty to supervise students is an essential function of any teacher's job" (*Hess v. Rochester Sch. Dist.*, 2005).

A major issue involved in the physical testing of school employees is mandatory testing of urine or blood for alcohol or drug use. Employees have challenged such tests as violating their rights of privacy and freedom from unreasonable search. In balancing the employees' rights against the government's interest, the courts have ruled that when employees occupy "safety sensitive" positions, where even a momentary lapse of attention could have serious consequences, mandatory testing for drugs and alcohol is justified without any individualized suspension (*Skinner v. Railroad Labor Executive Association*, 1989). Extending the "safety sensitive" rationale to school district employees, the mandatory, nonindividualized, suspicionless drug testing of employees in the transportation department (*English v. Talledega County Board of Education*, 1996) and custodians has been upheld (*Aubrey v. School Bd. of Lafayette Parish*, 1998). And, the U.S. Supreme Court has let stand a decision of the Sixth Circuit Court with potentially far-reaching consequences which allowed mandatory urinalysis of all individuals (including teachers and principals) who applied for positions or transfers in the school district (*Knox County Educ. Assn. v Knox County Board of Educ.*, 1999). Despite the lack of evidence that drug use was a problem among existing or potential employees, the court reasoned that the *in loco parentis* status of educators places them on the "frontline of school security," including drug interdiction, that teachers occupy safety-sensitive positions which, combined with the special interest of the government in protecting school children, justified the policy. Also important to the court's decision was that (1) the testing program was narrowly prescribed and not overintrusive (it was a one-time test with advance notice) and (2) that educators participated in a "heavily regulated industry" so their expectations of privacy were diminished.

In reviewing health and physical requirements, the courts have shown increasing concern that such requirements not be arbitrarily applied, be specific to the position, and not violate state and federal laws protecting the rights of the handicapped. For example, Section 504 of the Rehabilitation Act of 1973, which protects "otherwise qualified" handicapped individuals from discrimination, was used as the basis for the 1987 decision of the U.S. Supreme Court in a case involving a teacher with the contagious disease tuberculosis (*Arline v. School Board of Nassau County*, 1987). The court upheld a lower court decision that determined that the physical impairment associated with the disease justified the teacher being considered handicapped within the meaning of the Rehabilitation Act, and that discrimination based solely on the fear of contamination is discrimination against the handicapped. The lower court was instructed to determine if the teacher posed a significant risk of communicating the disease to others which would preclude her from being "otherwise qualified," and if her condition could be reasonably accommodated by the school district. And, the court said that the determination of whether a risk is significant should depend on "(a) the nature of risk (how the risk is transmitted), (b) the duration of the risk (how long is the carrier infectious), and (c) the severity of the risk (what is the potential harm to third parties), and (d) the probabilities the disease will be transmitted and will cause varying degrees of harm" (*Arline*, 1987, p. 288). The lower court ultimately found the teacher posed little threat of infection to others, was otherwise qualified, and ordered the teacher reinstated with back pay (*Arline v. School Board of Nassau County*, 1988).

The **significant risk standard** articulated in *Arline* has been relied on by teachers with AIDS and HIV to fight alleged discrimination in employment. For example, the Ninth Circuit Court applied the significant risk standard to a case involving a teacher of hearing-impaired children and determined that medical evidence regarding the nature and transmission of AIDS did not support the conclusion that the teacher posed a significant risk of transmitting the disease to children or others through casual social contact (*Chalk v. U.S. District Court*, 1988). A similar rationale was applied by the court in overturning a Racine, Wisconsin, school board policy which excluded from "regular school work" any staff member with AIDS or ARC (AIDS-Related Complex). While the court recognized the duty of the district to protect students and staff from contagious diseases, it found fault with the policy's presumption that all employees with AIDS or ARC were inherently incapable of performing their jobs, rather than reviewing each case on a case-by-case basis (*Racine Unified School District v. LIRC*, 1991).

A major federal statute affecting health and physical requirements for school employees is the Americans With Disabilities Act of 1990, which prohibits employment discrimination against an "otherwise qualified" individual with a disability. Such a person is defined as a person who "satisfies the requisite skill, experience, education, and other job-related requirements of the . . . position . . . and who, with or without reasonable accommodation, can perform the essential functions" of the position. This law, like Section 504, does not require that unqualified persons be hired or retained. But it does go further in prohibiting specific actions of the employer that adversely affect the employment opportunities of persons with disabilities (e.g., inquiry into disabilities before an offer is made, requiring a medical examination preoffer, classifying jobs or writing job descriptions on the basis of nonessential functions); it also requires employers to make "reasonable accommodation" for a known mental or physical disability unless the employer can demonstrate that providing such accommodation will constitute severe hardship.

Competency Testing

In recent years, in response to the emphasis on educational reform and the public's concern about the quality of education and the quality of the teaching force, the number of states involved in teacher testing increased dramatically. As of 2005 some form of testing for initial certification of teachers was required in 44 states. In over one-half the states, prospective teachers are tested in professional pedagogy and subject area competency. The No Child Left Behind Act requires that all newly hired teachers in schools that receive Title I funds be highly qualified. For new elementary teachers, this means they must pass a rigorous state test of the elementary curriculum and teaching skills. New middle and high school teachers must pass a rigorous state test in the academic subject they are to teach or complete an academic major in every subject they will teach. The most commonly used tests are the customized state tests developed by National Evaluation Systems and the PRAXIS series developed by the Educational Testing Service. In addition to testing for initial certification, a few states require testing for recertification.

The use of competency tests as either a prerequisite to initial certification or as a requirement for recertification of practicing educators has brought them under the same legal scrutiny as any other employment tests. The legal question is not whether tests can be used; the Civil Rights Act of 1964 specifically sanctions the use of "professionally developed" tests, as have the courts. Rather, the primary issues that continue to be litigated in regard to teacher testing involve allegations of discrimination in violation of Title VII of the Civil Rights Act of 1964 and unreasonableness in violation of the equal protection clause of the Fourteenth Amendment. In most instances where tests have been used in employment decisions, their use has disqualified disproportionately more minorities than nonminorities. In these instances the courts have upheld the use of tests if it can be shown that they are significantly related to "important elements of work behavior which comprise or are relevant to the job or jobs for which candidates are being evaluated" (*Albemarles Paper Company v. Moody*, 1975, p. 431).

For example, in a 2000 California case, *Association of Mexican-American Education v. State of California*, which challenged the use of the California Basic Education Skills Test (CBEST) as a requirement for certification for teaching and nonteaching positions (administrators, counselors, librarians) in California, the court of appeals determined that the state had established the validity of the test (e.g., that the test had a "manifest relationship to the employment in question" (*Griggs v. Duke Power Co.*, 1971, p. 432) by meeting the three-pronged test established in *Albemarie* (1975): (1) a particular trait or characteristic that the test is designed to measure has been specified—here "basic skills in reading, writing, and mathematics," (2) the particular trait or characteristic is an important element of work behavior—this was established by three different validation studies, and (3) that the test is predictive or significantly correlated with the element(s) of work behavior identified—"professionally acceptable methods," including testimony from Educational Testing Service (ETS) personnel, were used to establish that the test measured the types of skills it was designed to measure. The court also ruled that the challenged cutoff score on the reading section, which had been set at the point which all the external reviewers agreed was passing, did not violate the EEOC's Guidelines, which stated that where cutoff scores are used, they should "be set so as to be reasonable and consistent with normal expectations of acceptable proficiency with the workforce [*Association of Mexican-American Educators v. State of California*, 2000, quoting 29 C. F. R. Sec. 1607.5(H)].

In addition to testing for initial certification or recertification, in an isolated number of cases school districts have sought to test practicing teachers to determine their competency. The Massachusetts State Board of Education, for example, enacted a regulation requiring math teachers at low-performing schools and teachers teaching math but not certified in math to take a math assessment test. It used the results in developing professional development plans. On challenge by the Massachusetts Federation of Teachers, the court upheld the regulation finding it was a reasonable way to assess poor student achievement and identify teacher deficiencies that might be addressed by professional development and that it did not violate teachers' rights of due process and equal protection (*Mass. Federation of Teachers v. Bd. of Educ.*, 2002).

The Employment Contract

The general principles of contract law apply to the employment contract. That is, in order for the contract to be valid, it must contain the basic elements of (1) offer and acceptance, (2) legally competent parties, (3) consideration, (4) legal subject matter, and (5) proper form (see Figure 11.2). In addition, the employment contract must meet the specific requirement of applicable state law.

Offer and Acceptance. In order to be valid, a contract must contain an offer by one party and an acceptance by another. "For a communication to be an offer, it must create a reasonable expectation in the offeree that the offeror is willing to enter a contract on the basis of the offered terms" (Sperry, Daniel, Huefner, & Gee, 1998, p. 4). Often the form the acceptance is to take is specified in the offer. Typically, the offer also indicates that acceptance must be made within a certain period of time of the offer of employment. Until the party to whom the offer is made accepts the offer (e.g., acceptance cannot be made by a spouse or other relative), the contract is not in force. For this reason it is good practice to require that acceptance be made in writing and within a specified period of time. And, until acceptance has been received, unsuccessful candidates should not be notified that the position has been filled.

Legally Competent Parties. The statutory authority to contract lies exclusively with the school board. The superintendent or other authorized employee may recommend employment, but only the school board may enter into contract. There are cases every year in which prospective employees, vendors, or contractors have relied on the presumed authority of a principal, superintendent, or other employee, only to discover the person lacked the authority to enter into a binding contract. Moreover, a school board can enter into contract only when it is a legally constituted body. That is, contracts issued when a quorum of the board was not present or at an illegally called meeting of the board (e.g., adequate notice was not given) are not valid. In these instances the board is not considered a competent party because it lacks legal status. By the same token, a teacher or other employee who lacks the necessary certification or other requisite conditions is not considered to be a competent party for contractual purposes, nor are individuals who are

Figure 11.2 Elements of a Contract

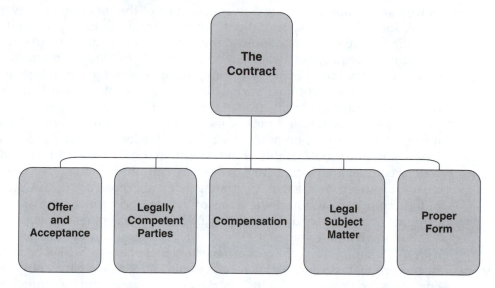

mentally ill, impaired by drugs or alcohol, or under duress at the time of entering into the contract.

Consideration. Consideration is something of value or importance that persuades a contracting party to enter into a contract. The consideration offered by the school district must be clear and definite. Although school boards have considerable latitude in the matter of employee compensation, they must abide by any state statutes regarding minimum salary levels, and they must abide by the terms of any negotiated contracts. In the absence of any incentive pay program, salaries must be applied uniformly to individuals or groups of individuals who have the same preparation and experience and perform the same duties.

Legal Subject Matter. In order to be valid, a contract must pertain to legal subject matter. That is, a contract for the commission of a crime (e.g., the purchase of illegal substances or the performance of illegal services) is not enforceable. Nor can the terms of the contract violate state or federal requirements or public policy. For example, districts cannot contract with employees to pay less than the state or federal minimum wage.

Proper Form. To be enforceable, the contract must be in the proper form required by law. Most states require that the employment contract be signed and in writing. Some states also specify the provisions that are to be included in the contract.

Terms of the Contract: Duties and Responsibilities. The employee's rights and obligations of employment are derived from the employment contract. It is important, therefore, that the contract be specific in stating the terms and conditions of employment, be unambiguous, and include those rules and regulations of the school district applicable to employment conditions. Even when rules and regulations of the school board have not been specifically included, the courts have held that they, as well as all applicable state statutes, are part of the contract. However, the school board does have the responsibility to inform employees of its rules and regulations, including those in effect not only at the time of initial employment or at the time of awarding of tenure, but also on an ongoing basis as they are revised. This point is especially important because the courts have held that even though a teacher has tenure, each yearly contract is considered a new contract and includes whatever rules and regulations are in effect at the time of the new contract.

In most states certain terms of the contract are controlled by state law and are not subject to negotiation or the discretion of the local school district. For example, tenure and due process rights granted by state statute could not be modified by the contract offered by a local school district. In a number of states, state statutes require that certain terms (e.g., salary, beginning and end of contract, duties, etc.) be detailed in the contract. In addition, the terms of the contract cannot conflict with the terms or rights of employees detailed in any collective bargaining agreement.

Although it is desirable that the contract be specific in stating the terms and conditions of employment, the courts have held that employees may be required to perform certain tasks incidental to classroom activities regardless of whether the contract specifically calls for their performance. These implied duties have included such activities as field trips; playground, study hall, bus, and cafeteria duty; supervision of extracurricular activities; and attendance at open houses. Teachers cannot, however, be required to drive a bus, perform janitorial duties, or perform duties unrelated to the school program. The courts also have found that the types of duties that may be permissibly required of school employees vary by position. That is, administrators may be expected to perform a broader range of implied duties than teachers; coaches, different implied duties than classroom teachers; etc. The primary considerations of the courts in reviewing duty assignments are whether the duty has been expressly provided for in the contract and whether the duty in question can be considered part of normal school operations and reasonable (Valente & Valente, 2001). If an employee refuses to perform extracurricular duties required as a condition of employment, regardless of whether the duties are specified under contract, the court may construe such refusal as an illegal strike or as insubordination justifying removal (Beckham, 1983). For example, in an Alabama case a guidance counselor was dismissed for refusing to perform his assigned rotational supervision duty before school. He maintained that counselors should be exempt from such supervision. The court upheld the dismissal (*Jones v. Alabama State Tenure Commission*, 1981).

Because of the importance of the employment contract, and because it is a legally binding document, it should be prepared and periodically reviewed by the school board attorney. If the district is a party to a negotiated labor agreement, the terms of the contract must be reviewed to ensure the contract's compliance with the terms of the negotiated agreement.

Tenure

Tenure is "the status conferred upon teachers who have served a probationary period . . . which then guarantees them continual employment until retirement, subject to the requirements of good behavior, financial necessity, and in some instances, good periodic evaluations" (Sperry, et al., 1998, p. 1041). Tenure is said to benefit the state by helping to create a permanent and qualified teaching force. It benefits teachers by providing them greater rights than those held by nontenured teachers. Tenure has been a fixture of American public education. However, there have been attempts in several states to do away with tenure. Given that few other workers enjoy the benefits of tenure, "it is not surprising that they begrudge their own employees a guarantee of lifetime employment" (Hess & Maranto, 2000, p. 54).

Because the tenure status (referred to in some states as "continuing" status) is created by state statute, specific provisions vary from state to state. Most statutes specify the requirements and procedures for both acquiring tenure and for dismissing a tenured teacher (dismissal of both tenured and nontenured teachers is treated in a later section). Generally, tenure can be acquired only in the area of certification. In addition, tenure is not transferable from one school district to another, even within the same state. Because tenure is created by the state, the terms of its acquisition and the requisites for dismissal cannot be altered by the local school board.

Tenure statutes normally require the successful completion of a probationary period before the awarding of tenure, usually 3 years. During the probationary period, the probationary teacher is usually issued a 1-year contract that, subject to satisfactory service and district finances, is renewable at the end of each of the probationary years. Renewal of the contract at the end of the term is at the discretion of the school board.

Legal issues surrounding the probationary period primarily have involved questions of what constitutes service during the probationary period and what protections are afforded probationary teachers. Most tenure statutes require "regular and continuous" teaching service during the probationary period. When teachers have spent a part of the probationary period as guidance counselors, administrators, homebound teachers, social workers, or other positions outside the classroom, questions have arisen as to their eligibility for tenure under the "regular" service requirement. Similar issues have arisen when service was as a substitute teacher, was for less than full time, was less than the full school year, or was interrupted by a leave. In deciding each of these cases, the courts have attempted to interpret the state tenure statutes to protect the teachers' rights while maintaining the discretion and flexibility of school officials in the administration of personnel matters. However, since the requirements of the probationary period have been strictly enforced by most courts, it is important that school administrators be aware that in asking or assigning individuals to "other" positions during the probationary period, they could in fact be jeopardizing those individuals' eligibility for tenure.

In the absence of a statute to the contrary, school boards may decide not to renew the contract of probationary teachers without giving cause or providing a hearing. However, in about two-thirds of the states, school districts are required to give nontenured teachers a statement of reasons for nonrenewal. And, as shown in Table 11.1, in half the states, nontenured teachers being nonrenewed have the right to meet with administration.

Even successful completion of the probationary term does not entitle a probationary teacher to continued employment. In an Alabama case where a probationary

Table 11.1 Nonrenewal Rights of Nontenured Teachers

	Right to Know Reasons for Nonrenewal	Right to Meet with Administration		Right to Know Reasons for Nonrenewal	Right to Meet with Administration
Alabama			Nebraska	✓	✓
Alaska	✓	✓	Nevada	✓	
Arizona	✓		New Hampshire		
Arkansas	✓	✓	New Jersey	✓	✓
California		✓	New Mexico	✓	
Colorado	✓		New York	✓	
Connecticut	✓	✓	North Carolina	✓	
Delaware	✓	✓	North Dakota	✓	✓
Fed. Ed. Assn.			Ohio	✓	✓
Florida			Oklahoma	✓	✓
Georgia	✓		Oregon	✓	✓
Hawaii		✓	Pennsylvania	✓	✓
Idaho	✓	✓	Rhode Island	✓	✓
Illinois	✓		South Carolina		✓
Indiana	✓	✓	South Dakota		
Iowa	✓	✓	Tennessee		
Kansas			Texas		✓
Kentucky	✓		Utah		
Louisiana	✓		Vermont	✓	✓
Maine			Virginia	✓	✓
Maryland			Washington	✓	✓
Massachusetts			West Virginia	✓	✓
Michigan			Wisconsin		✓
Minnesota	✓		Wyoming	✓	
Mississippi	✓	✓			
Missouri	✓				
Montana					

Source: From "NEA Examines the Rights of Nontenured Teachers. Rights Watch," May 2001, *NEA Today.*
http://www.nea.org/neatoday/0105/rights.html

teacher who had received a positive evaluation each of her 3 years and had been recommended for retention was not continued, the court said that the district's adoption of an evaluation policy for nontenured and tenured teachers did not create a right of employment for nontenured teachers who received a favorable evaluation under the policy (*King v. Jefferson County Board of Education*, 1995). However, most states do require that the school board give timely notice (usually no later than April 1) that the contract will not be renewed. And in no state can the contract be broken during the term of the contract without, at a minimum, a notice of dismissal and a hearing on the causes.

In some states, tenure is automatically awarded at the end of the probationary period unless the school board notifies the teacher that he or she will not be rehired.

In other states the school board is required to take some affirmative step to award tenure. When school officials fail to follow applicable state laws, the courts will attempt to balance the public policy interests of employing competent and qualified teachers against the rights of the individual. As a result, in a number of cases in which the school board did not give timely notice of nonrenewal, the courts have ordered the teacher rehired, but still as a probationary teacher, until the proper evaluation and notification takes place. In an equal number of other cases in which the school board failed to follow state tenure laws, the courts have said "it is the school district, not the teacher, that must bear the consequences," and the teacher has been granted tenure status (*Nixon v. Board of Cooperative Educational Services*, 1990, p. 905). However, *de minimis* (trifling, insignificant) violations of policy or state statutes have typically been decided in favor of school boards.

Another issue related to tenure is what positions are eligible for tenure. A number of states do identify in statute the areas in which school personnel may acquire tenure. For example, in some states personnel can acquire tenure as an administrator. However, unless provided by statute, the courts have generally interpreted administrative and supervisory positions to be outside the scope of tenure. On the other hand, the courts generally recognize such nonadministrative positions as guidance counselor, librarian, homebound teacher, or resource room teacher as within the scope of the tenure statutes. There has also been a question of whether teachers whose salaries are funded totally or in part by federal funds fall under teacher tenure statutes. The courts have generally held that they do unless specifically waived in the contract.

The supplementary service appointment most often the subject of efforts to acquire tenure is that of athletic coach. However, the courts have been almost unanimous in declaring supplementary service positions such as coaching separate from teaching and not eligible for tenure status. In many cases the courts have noted that tenure rights accrue only to employment in certified areas, and thus the lack of a certification requirement for coaching negates the tenure claim (Cambron-McCabe, et al., 2004). In other cases, even when state certification was required, the courts have noted the extracurricular nature of coaching, the awarding of supplementary pay, and the issuance of a separate contract for the coaching assignment as distinguishing it from the teaching assignment (see, e.g., *Lagos v. Modesto City School District*, 1988).

Employees with supplementary service appointments serve at the pleasure of the board and can be dismissed from these positions at any time without any procedural or substantive due process. By the same token, these employees may resign these positions and still maintain the primary teaching contract unless the offer of the teaching contract had been made contingent on the individual performing specific supplemental duties (e.g., coaching). School administrators who consider offering contingency contracts should consult state statues to determine the status of such contracts in their state. They should also ensure that by combining teaching and coaching positions they are not eliminating the most qualified teachers or unlawfully discriminating against female applicants.

The awarding of tenure does not guarantee permanent employment. As discussed later in this chapter, a tenured teacher may be dismissed for disciplinary reasons or as a result of declining enrollments or financial exigencies. Nor does the granting of tenure guarantee the right to teach in a particular school, grade, or subject area. Teachers may be reassigned to any position for which they are certified as long as their due process rights are not violated. In a case in which a school board informed a teacher on July 5 of the board's intent to transfer her from a high school to a middle school, the court ruled the board had violated state procedural requirements by not notifying the teacher by July 1 (*Estill v. Alabama State Tenure Commission*, 1994).

DUE PROCESS

The term *due process* is found in the Fourteenth Amendment of the U.S. Constitution, which provides that no state shall "deprive any person of life, liberty, or property without due process of law." The two aspects of due process are procedural, which guarantees fair procedures, and substantive, which protects a person's liberty or property from unfair government seizure or interference. The essence of due process is to protect against arbitrary and unreasonable action.

Procedural Due Process

Procedural due process is not an absolute right. An individual is entitled to procedural due process only if he or she can show that the government's actions denied "life, liberty, or property." Presuming that life issues are not involved in school district personnel issues, the employee must show a property or liberty interest in order to be constitutionally entitled to procedural due process. In school district employment decisions, the courts have defined a property interest to be a "legitimate entitlement" to continued employment, not merely the desire to remain employed. A legitimate entitlement to continued employment can be obtained by the granting of tenure or by an employment contract. Thus, teachers or other employers who have tenure or who are operating under an employment contract are said to have a **property right** or property interest to that position that cannot be abridged without due process. This would mean, for instance, that a tenured teacher could not be dismissed, or that a probationary teacher could not be dismissed during the contract year, without being afforded due process of law.

A liberty interest or **liberty right** can become a factor in education employment cases if government actions create such a stigma or cause such serious damage to the employee's reputation or integrity that it forecloses future employment opportunities. That is, simply because a person is demoted or even dismissed for reasons that are made public would not be reason enough to support a violation of a liberty interest. The courts have noted that almost any reason that is given for an adverse employment decision is going to cast negatively on the affected employee. The two-part question that is asked to determine if a liberty interest has been violated is (1) did the employee actually suffer a loss of benefit, such as employment, and (2) did this happen as a result of publicly made charges by the board that resulted in the employee becoming the object of public ridicule or public scorn? (Charges made in a private meeting of the board cannot be said to hold the employee up to public scorn.) A liberty interest can also become involved if governmental actions violate the employee's constitutionally protected rights or if they infringe on the employee's fundamental rights related to marriage, family, and personal privacy.

Once it has been established that a property or liberty interest is involved and that an action requires procedural due process, the central issue becomes what process is due. In arriving at its decision, the court will look to standards of procedural due process embodied in state statutes, state agency or school board regulations, employment contracts, and collective bargaining agreements to determine both their propriety and the extent to which they were followed. In one case a nonprobationary cook was terminated without notice or hearing. The Supreme Court of Arkansas held that although the board had the right to terminate the employee at any time for any reason, to do so without notice or a hearing violated the terms of the Arkansas Public School Employees Fair Hearing Act (*Gould Public School v. Dobbs*, 1999).

In determining what due process should be provided in those cases not covered by statute, the courts have noted that no fixed set of procedures is applicable in all situations. Rather, the courts must decide what due process is due in light of the following guidelines:

> (1) the private interest that will be affected by the official action; (2) the risk of an erroneous deprivation of such interest through the procedures used, the probable value, if any, of additional procedural safeguards; and (3) the Government's interest, including the fiscal and administrative burdens that the additional or substitute procedural requirement would entail. (*Mathews v. Eldridge*, 1976, p. 321)

Applying this standard, it would appear that where limited interests are involved, only minimal procedures are required, whereas the deprivation of more serious interests requires a more extensive, formal process. Generally, the courts have held that an employee facing a severe loss, such as termination of employment, must be ensured the following procedural elements (Cambron-McCabe, et al., 2004):

- Notice of charges
- The opportunity for a hearing
- Adequate time to prepare a rebuttal of the charges
- The access to names of witnesses and evidence
- A hearing before an impartial tribunal
- The right to representation by legal counsel
- The opportunity to introduce evidence and cross-examine witnesses
- A decision based solely on the evidence presented and findings of the hearing
- A transcript or record of the hearing, and
- The opportunity to appeal an adverse decision. (p. 326)

Notice must not merely be given; it must be timely (on or before an established date) and in sufficient detail to enable the employee to attempt to remediate or to prepare an adequate defense (see, e.g., *McDaniel v. Princeton City Sch. Dist. Bd. Of Educ.*, 1999). Although a full evidentiary hearing conforming to all the rules of procedure and evidence is not required, the Supreme Court has ruled that if termination of an employee with property rights is a consideration, a hearing is required prior to termination at which the employee is given oral and written notice of the charges, an explanation of the school board's evidence, and an opportunity to respond orally and in writing to the charges and evidence (*Cleveland Board of Education v. Loudermill*, 1985). Testimony is given under oath and a written record of the hearing made by a reporter paid by the board of education. The purpose of such a hearing is to determine if there are reasonable grounds to believe the charges are true and support dismissal (Fischer, Schimmel, & Stellman, 2007). Lastly, although the ability of the school board (the employer) to act as an unbiased hearing body when it is a party to the action has been frequently challenged, the Supreme Court has held that school boards are presumed to be impartial and that those challenging their actions have the burden of proving otherwise (*Hortonville District v. Hortonville Education Association*, 1976). However the same school official cannot act as both the prosecutor and the hearing officer (*Board of Education v. Lockhart*, 687 P.2d 1306 Colo. 1984).

Substantive Due Process

Substantive due process is somewhat more difficult to ensure than procedural due process. Substantive due process is meant to protect the employee from arbitrary, unreasonable, and discriminatory governmental action as well as vague and unclear policies and guidelines. Substantive due process is often equated with the concept of "just cause." Substantive due process also means that school officials cannot deprive an employee of "life, liberty, or property" unless to do so is necessary to accomplish a legitimate state objective. In the employment context, the provision of substantive due process requires a rational balancing of the individual's right to a position or to pursue other positions against the government's interest in the improvement of the educational system (Sperry, et al., 1998). The Supreme Court has not articulated precise guidelines for properly balancing these interests; rather, the guidelines are constantly being refined by the courts and decisions are made on a case-by-case basis.

EMPLOYMENT DISCRIMINATION

Discrimination on the basis of race, religion, national origin, sex, age, or handicapping condition is prohibited under both federal law and the laws of most states. Allegations of arbitrary and unreasonable actions, not overt discriminatory actions, form the basis of most discrimination suits in education. Most cases involving allegations of discrimination are brought under Title VII of the Civil Rights Act of 1964, as amended by the Civil Rights Act of 1991, or under other federal laws modeled after Title VII, such as the Age Discrimination in Employment Act of 1967, Section 504 of the Rehabilitation Act of 1973, the Americans With Disabilities Act of 1990 and the Immigration Reform and Control Act. Other statutory guarantees against discrimination in employment are found in the Pregnancy Discrimination Act and the Equal Pay Act and, to a lesser extent, Title IX of the Education Amendments of 1972, all of which prohibit sex-based discrimination. Title VII, the most used statute, prohibits employers from discriminating against employees on the basis of race, color, religion, sex, or national origin. It covers many areas of human resources administration including recruitment; hiring; promotion; compensation; and other terms, conditions, or privileges of employment. The Equal Employment Opportunity Commission is responsible for enforcing Title VII.

Two types of employment discrimination claims have traditionally been brought under Title VII. The first claim, **disparate treatment**, places the burden of proof squarely on the plaintiff. The plaintiff must first demonstrate a *prima facie case* of discrimination. This requires that the plaintiff show that he or she (1) was a member of a group protected by Title VII, (2) is qualified for the position in question, and (3) was treated less favorably than others by a particular employment practice. If the claimant can establish the foregoing facts, the employer can still rebut the claim by articulating a nondiscriminatory reason for the practice. This means the employer must show that the challenged practice is job related and justified by a legitimate business goal. If the employer meets this burden of proof, the burden of proof shifts back to the plaintiff to show that the articulated reason is a mere pretext for intentional discriminatory intent. Intent is very difficult to prove. In 1982 the Supreme Court said discriminatory intent can only be established by demonstrating actual motive and cannot be presumed from employment data that show something less than intent (*Pullman-Standard v. Swint*, 1982).

The other type of discrimination claim that may be brought under Title VII is based on employment practices that appear facially neutral but have a **disparate impact** on protected groups. Proof of intent is not necessary to prove discrimination based on disparate impact. According to the Supreme Court decision in *Griggs*, which was strengthened by the Civil Rights Act of 1991, if the claimant can show that an employment practice or policy results in a disparate impact on a protected class, the burden shifts to the employer to demonstrate that the challenged practice or policy is job related and is consistent with business necessity. Even if the employer does offer a business necessity for the discriminatory practice, it is still possible for the claimant to prevail by showing that the district could serve its interests by means that are not discriminatory. For example, a female applicant for a high school biology teaching position in Arizona filed a sex discrimination suit against the school district on the basis that its requirement that applicants for the teaching position also have the ability to coach varsity softball had a disparate impact on women (*Civil Rights Division v. Amphitheater Unified School District*, 1983). Although the board admitted the coupling of the two positions did have a disparate impact on women, it defended the practice by maintaining that it was a business necessity. In considering this defense, the court maintained that to be successful the district must show compelling business purposes and that there were no acceptable alternative practices or policies available that would better accomplish the business purpose advanced. Because the board was unable to demonstrate that less discriminatory alternatives had been attempted when, in fact, there was substantial evidence that alternatives were available, the appellate court held for the plaintiff and remanded the case to the lower court for a determination of damages.

If an employee is successful in a discrimination complaint, the court may order a stop to the discriminatory practice and order any "such affirmative action as may be appropriate, which may include, but is not limited to reinstatement or hiring of employees, with or without pay," as well as any other "equitable relief" the court may deem appropriate to rectify the situation [42 U.S.C. 2000e-5(g)]. However, remedies may be limited if the complainant is able to show discrimination was a factor in the employment decision, but the employer is able to prove it would have made the same decision even if discrimination were not a motivating factor.

Sexual Harassment

Sexual harassment is considered a form of sex discrimination and as such is prohibited under Title VII of the Civil Rights Act of 1964, as well as state fair employment statutes in most states. Sexual harassment in the workplace occurs when unwelcome advances or requests for sexual favors are made a condition of employment **(quid pro quo harassment)**, or when verbal or physical conduct is sufficiently severe or pervasive as to unreasonably interfere with an individual's work performance or creates an intimidating, hostile, or offensive work environment **(hostile environment harassment)**.

Sexual harassment can occur even when the people involved are of the same gender. Same-sex harassment claims do not require a gay or lesbian context. The crucial issue is whether members of one sex are exposed to disadvantageous terms or conditions of employment to which members of the other sex are not exposed. Actionable same-sex harassment might be motivated by sexual desire, but could also be based on other sex-related motivation. However, a plaintiff must prove that the conduct was not merely tinged with offensive sexual connotations but actually constituted discrimination because of gender.

Under the legal principal of agency, in cases involving *quid pro quo* harassment, school districts will be held liable for the sexual harassment committed by a school employee in a position of authority, such as a teacher or administrator. In cases of hostile environment harassment, the school will not be held liable for the harassment if it can prove (1) it exercised reasonable care to prevent harassment (e.g., had a sexual harassment policy in place) and acted promptly to correct any allegations of sexual harassment, and (2) the complaining employee did not take advantage of the protective or preventative safeguards provided by the employers to prevent the harm that could have otherwise been avoided (e.g., did not follow the policies dictated by the sexual harassment policy) *(Burlington Industries v. Ellerth*, 1998; *Faraghar v. Boca Raton*, 1998).

In sexual harassment situations involving employment, the courts see whether

- The conduct was verbal or physical or both;
- The conduct was physically threatening or humiliating;
- The conduct was repeated;
- The inappropriate remark was an isolated incident;
- The conduct was hostile and patently offensive;
- The alleged harasser was a coworker or supervisor;
- Others joined in perpetrating the harassment; and
- The harassment was directed at more than one individual. *(Harris v. Forklift Systems*, 1993; *Clark County School District*, 2001)

Courts use all of these factors in combination to make a determination; the facts of each situation are very important in determining whether sexual harassment has occurred. If found liable for sexual harassment, the school district may be required to pay monetary damages and attorney fees, as well as reinstate or promote the harassed employee.

ADVERSE EMPLOYMENT DECISIONS

It is almost inevitable that school administrators will become involved in adverse employment decisions. These decisions include dismissals, suspensions, involuntary transfers and reassignments, demotions, and reductions in force. Not all cases involve disciplinary actions. Decisions may result from declining enrollments or other needs of the district that require the shifting of personnel. Whenever adverse employment decisions are contemplated, it is important that the employee be assured due process in the conduct of the action. In fact, the adequacy of the due process procedures provided by school officials is one of the major issues in the litigation involving adverse employment decisions (Cambron-McCabe, 1983).

Dismissal for Cause

Possibly the most undesirable task of a school administrator and/or school board is the dismissal of an employee. A dismissal is defined as the termination of employment during the term of a contract. A dismissal may occur at any time and may be applied to tenured or nontenured employees. The impact of a dismissal on an employee's personal and professional life can be devastating. Lengthy proceedings may become costly both to the employee and the district. In controversial cases, morale and relationships among staff, administration, and the school board may be negatively affected. Nonetheless, from time to time it seems in the best interest of the school district to dismiss an employee. All states have some statutory provisions that specify the grounds for teacher dismissal. Collective bargaining agreements also typically set forth the reasons why teachers may be dismissed. The statutory reasons specified for dismissal vary from the very general (e.g., "good cause") to the very specific. The reasons most frequently cited in statute are immorality, incompetence, and insubordination. Other commonly cited reasons are neglect of duty, unprofessional conduct or conduct unbecoming a teacher, unfitness to teach, and the catchall phrase, "other good and just cause." Although traditionally the courts have left the application and definition of each of these reasons to the discretion of the school board, the burden of proof in justifying a dismissal for cause rests with the school board and must be supported by sufficient evidence to justify the dismissal. In addition, as previously discussed, in all cases of dismissal the school board must provide the employee all the due process to which the employee is entitled by law, policy, or negotiated agreement. If not, even though the cause may be sufficient to justify a dismissal, the dismissal most likely will not be upheld. A review of some of the most frequently cited grounds for dismissal will provide some insight into those conditions or behaviors that have sustained judicial scrutiny, as well as the judicial requirements to support a charge.

Immorality. Immorality is the most cited ground for dismissal in state statutes. Nonetheless, legislatures often have been reluctant to define the term immorality or to discuss its application to specific conduct. Consequently, these tasks have been left to the courts. Among the definitions of immorality provided by the courts is that immorality is "such a course of conduct as offends the morals of the community and is a bad example to the youth whose ideals the teacher is supposed to foster and elevate" (*Horton v. Jefferson County-Dubois Area Vocational Technical School*, 1993, p. 183). Dismissals related to immorality generally are based on one or more of the following categories of conduct: (1) sexual conduct with students; (2) making sexually explicit remarks or talking about sex unrelated to the curriculum; (3) distribution of sexually explicit materials to classes; (4) use of obscene, profane, or abusive language; (5) possession and use of controlled substances; (6) criminal misconduct; (7) public lewdness; and (8) dishonesty.

Because it would be impossible to list in state statutes all the behaviors that might be considered "immoral," the courts apply certain standards that have evolved from case law to cases involving a dismissal for immorality. First is the *exemplar standard*. Although this concept is not as universally accepted today as in the past, the courts do recognize that "there are legitimate standards to be expected of those who teach in the public schools" (*Reitmeyer v. Unemployment Compensation Board of Review*, 1992, p. 508). A significant percentage of the public also believes that teachers should be good role models for their students, both in school and out of school (Imber, 2001). Second, while not true in all jurisdictions, the vast weight of contemporary judicial decisions in employee dismissal cases says that in order to justify a charge of dismissal there must be a *nexus* or connection between the personal conduct of the employee and the teacher's job performance.

However, because the facts of no two cases are exactly the same, this connection may be said to exist in one case involving a particular conduct but not in another, school administrators cannot expect to find definitive lists of impermissible or immoral behavior in case law.

Homosexuality is an area in which the circumstances of the particular case very much dictate the ruling of the courts. With the exception of the 1977 Washington Supreme Court ruling in *Gaylord v. Tacoma School District No. 10*, most courts have ruled that homosexuality *per se* is not grounds for dismissal. To support a dismissal, there must still be a nexus between a teacher's private sexual orientation and the performance of his or her duties as a teacher to justify dismissal. For example, in *Weaver v. Nebo School District*, 1999, the court overturned a teacher's dismissal as a girls' volleyball coach based only on her public discussion of her lesbian sexual orientation. The court found that the principal's decision not to continue the teacher's contract as volleyball coach because of her sexual orientation was unconstitutional. It stated that there was no evidence to indicate an inability to coach solely because of sexual orientation.

Although cases involving alleged immorality must often be settled on a case-by-case basis, the courts have agreed on the factors to be considered in determining if a teacher's immoral conduct renders the teacher unfit to teach. These factors include (1) the age and maturity of the teacher's students, (2) the likelihood that the teacher's conduct will have an adverse effect on students or other teachers,

(3) degree of anticipated adversity, (4) proximity of the conduct, (5) extenuating or aggravating circumstances surrounding the conduct, (6) likelihood that the conduct would be repeated, (7) underlying motives, and (8) the chilling effect on the rights of teachers (*In Re Thomas*, 1996, pp. 165–66).

Incompetency. Those conditions or behaviors that have been most successfully sustained as constituting incompetence fall into six general categories: (1) inadequate teaching; (2) lack of knowledge of the subject matter; (3) failure to maintain classroom discipline or unreasonable discipline; (4) failure to work effectively with colleagues, supervisors, or parents; (5) physical or mental disability; and (6) willful neglect of duty. In reviewing dismissals for incompetency (referred to in some state statutes as "unprofessional conduct") the court will presume that a teacher certificated by the state is competent unless the district can prove incompetency by the quality and quantity of its evidence. As with dismissals for alleged immorality, in dismissals for incompetence the courts require that there be an established relationship between the employee's conduct and the operation of the school. In addition, the standard against which the teacher is measured must be one used for other teachers in a similar position, not the standard of the "ideal teacher," and that the dismissal be based on a pattern of behavior, not just a single incident. And, although testimony of students and parents is important, the courts pay closest attention to classroom observations by superiors (e.g., principals, curriculum supervisors, etc.) (Alexander & Alexander, 2001).

Before any action is taken to dismiss an employee for incompetency, a determination should be made as to whether the behavior in question is remediable, a notice of deficiency must be given, a program designed to remediate the difficulty developed, and a reasonable opportunity to correct the behavior must be provided. If remediation fails, then dismissal becomes the only alternative to eliminate the teacher's incompetent performance.

Insubordination. Insubordination is the persistent, willful, and deliberate disregard for disobedience of a reasonable school rule, regulation, or official order. Regardless of whether it is specified in state statute, insubordination is an acceptable cause for dismissal in all states. Among the meanings of insubordination that have been upheld by the courts are (1) refusal to follow established policies and procedures, (2) refusal to obey the direct and lawful orders of school administrators or school boards, (3) refusal to meet or cooperate with superiors, (4) encouraging students to disobey school authority, (5) unauthorized absence from duty, (6) abuse of sick leave, (7) inappropriate use of corporal punishment, (8) refusal to accept a school or teaching assignment, and (9) failure to acquire approval for use of instructional materials. Unlike the charge of immorality, the school district is not required to show a relationship between the alleged insubordinate conduct and the teacher's fitness to teach. For example, an industrial arts teacher was terminated for refusal to submit lesson plans even though he had received positive performance evaluations (*Vukadinovich v. Board of School Trustees of North Newton School Cooperation*, 2002).

In order to sustain a charge of insubordination, the school district must demonstrate a persistent, willful, and deliberate violation of a lawful rule or order emanating from a school authority. While typically the courts require that there be a pattern of insubordination, a single insubordinate act, if sufficiently serious, can justify dismissal. However, if the violation involves an order that is not within the legal right of the school official or school board to issue, the dismissal for insubordination will not stand. In addition, the rule or order must be reasonable, clear, and unambiguous. Insubordination charges also may not be supported if "the teacher tried, although unsuccessfully, to comply with the rule or order . . . the teacher's motive for violating the rule was admirable . . . (or) no harm resulted from the violation" (Alexander & Alexander, 2001, p. 679). Finally, school employees cannot be dismissed for insubordination for failing to follow rules that violate their constitutional rights. For example, rules that prohibit teachers from using certain materials in the classroom may interfere with their right to academic freedom, or rules limiting what they can say or write may also violate their right to free speech under the First Amendment (Fischer, et al., 2007).

Suspension

The power of the school board to suspend an employee, with or without pay, is inherent in the power to discipline employees (see, e.g., the judgment of the court in *Daily v. Bd of Ed. of Morrill County Sch. Dist. No. 62–0063*, 1999, upholding the authority of the school board to suspend a teacher for 30 days without pay for hitting a disobedient student on the head and restraining the student by his arms). The types of conduct that can give rise to suspension are generally the same as those for dismissal, though less serious in nature, although in some cases employees may be suspended pending the outcome of a due process dismissal hearing. A few states have statutory provisions related to suspension, but more often they do not. For this reason it is more difficult to define what procedural due process must be provided. For example, in a case where an industrial arts teacher was suspended for 4 days without pay and then transferred after fighting with a student, the court said the teacher had a property interest in continued employment because of his tenure status, as well as a liberty interest because of the potential stigmatization resulting from a charge of child abuse, both of which warranted the granting of a due process hearing before the school board, notwithstanding the fact that during the course of the investigation into the matter he had been given the opportunity to give his version of events and notwithstanding the fact that he had been granted an administrative review by the superintendent (*Winegar v. Des Moines Independent Community School District*, 1994). One thing that does appear clear from case law is that if the suspension is longer than 5 days the employee should be afforded a hearing with an opportunity to respond to charges.

Involuntary Transfers, Reassignments, and Demotions

The authority to transfer and reassign personnel is an implied power of school boards. Employees have no common law rights to a specific classroom, building, grade assignment, or position and may be transferred to any assignment for which they are qualified by certificate. Whereas the school district has the power to transfer, this power may not be exercised arbitrarily, capriciously, discriminatorily in retaliation for the legitimate exercise of a constitutionally protected right, or in violation of proper statutory or board procedures. For example, when teachers in a Kentucky school district who supported a candidate opposed by the superintendent for the school board were transferred with the sole explanation that the transfers were for "the betterment of the schools," the court determined the transfers to be punitive in nature and ordered the teachers reinstated (*Calhoun v. Cassady*, 1976).

A major legal issue in transfer and reassignment cases is whether the transfer constitutes a demotion. Depending on state statutes, a transfer or reassignment may be considered a demotion if it (1) results in a reduction in salary; (2) results in the loss of professional rank, reputation, or prestige; or (3) requires a teacher to teach a grade of subject for which he or she is not certified or has not had significant experience in the last 5 years (*Singleton v. Jackson Municipal Separate School District*, 1970). Restrictions relative to demotion are often contained in statute. Generally, such laws require proper notice, a hearing, and that the demotion be supported by substantial evidence and not be arbitrary or discriminatory. This does not mean that transfers or reassignments that are in fact demotions cannot be affected. Demotions may be lawfully accomplished for two purposes: (1) nondisciplinary reasons (e.g., reductions in force or financial exigency) and (2) discipline of the employee (Valente & Valente, 2001). Disciplinary transfers and demotions that are not arbitrary, capricious, or in violation of the employee's statutory or constitutional rights will be upheld.

The transfer or reassignment of administrators is somewhat different from that of teachers. Since administrators generally serve at the will of the board, in most states their transfer can be made arbitrarily, with no notice, reason, or hearing afforded.

Principals and other administrators who have challenged transfers from larger to smaller schools, from senior high schools to junior high schools, or from one administrative position to another (e.g., transfer from assistant superintendent to principal, *Barr v. Clarendon*, 1995) or to the classroom have generally been unsuccessful. They might get a favorable judgment if (1) there has been a reduction in salary, (2) state statute provides for tenure as an administrator, (3) there are contractual provisions to the contrary, (4) state or locally mandated due process procedures were violated, or (5) there has been an abuse of discretion.

Reduction in Force (RIF)

Declining enrollments, school reorganizations or consolidations, financial exigencies, elimination of positions or programs, and other reasons often result in a reduction in the total number of employees needed by the district and the release of excess employees. Forty-six states have statutes that address RIF (Hartmeister & Russo, 1999). Typically, they address the proper reasons, the order of release, and the order of reinstatement. Some statutes also provide detail as to the procedures to be followed and the protections afforded teachers. These same issues are often addressed in school board policies and collective bargaining agreements. Usually, these statutes, policies, and agreements require the employee be given adequate and timely notice of impending RIF and the right to an appropriate hearing (Hartmeister & Russo, 1999).

The legal challenges to reductions in force usually involve three issues: (1) whether the abolition of the position is justified; (2) whether the release of the particular individual is justified; and (3) the retention, reassignment, and call-back of employees. As a general rule, an employee has no right to a position no longer deemed necessary by the district. However, the reasons articulated by the district must be reasonable and supported by adequate justification to support the RIF decision. For example, a school business manager was terminated on the basis that the district needed to reduce the number of administrative positions. The business manager appealed, claiming religious discrimination: he was the only Catholic in a workplace where the superintendent and most of the other administrators were Mormon. In finding in his favor the court noted that (1) although the purported goal of the reorganization was to save money, it actually resulted in higher costs; (2) the person who replaced him was less qualified but paid more; and (3) the financial condition of the district was sound and did not require any reduction in force (*White v. Blackfoot School Dist. No. 55*, 2001).

Unlike other terminations, the burden of proof for an RIF is on the plaintiff to show the stated reason to be a subterfuge for an impermissible basis (e.g., discrimination, retaliation for union activity, or the exercise of a constitutionally protected right). The board need not prove that it made the perfect decision in regard to a particular set of circumstances, only that the relevant evidence supports the board's decision as being rational, not arbitrary or capricious (*Palmer v. Board of Trustees*, 1990). In the absence of evidence to the contrary, the courts presume that the board acted in good faith and with permissible motives (Cambron-McCabe, et al., 2004). For example, a tenured drafting teacher alleged that the school board discriminated against him on the basis of age when it refused to transfer him to positions in social studies or industrial arts after his position was eliminated. The court rejected his allegation because he was not tenured in either of these areas (*Davis v. School Dist. of City of Niagra Falls*, 2004).

The RIF process may not be used as a means to circumvent state tenure laws. When an Oklahoma school board dismissed an elementary librarian, citing declining enrollments and budgetary constraints, and then rehired nontenured teachers for positions for which the librarian was certified and had previously taught, the court ruled that the district could not "manipulate job assignments in a manner that defeats the rights of tenured teachers and circumvents the purpose and spirit of the tenure law" (*Babb v. Independent School Dist. No. I–5*, 1992). On the other hand, a Connecticut court upheld the elimination of a nurse-teacher position even though the elements of the job, clinical nursing and health education instruction, were maintained. The court ruling was based on the fact that no one employee was assigned both the clinical nursing duties and the health education (*Ballanto v. Board of Education of Stronington*, 1993).

The second issue, who should be released, involves questions of preference and has been the subject of the majority of litigation related to "RIFing." State statutes, school board policies, and employment contracts often specify the order of release in terms of tenure, seniority, or other criteria, as well as the procedures to be followed (notice, appeal, etc.). When preference and due process requirements are articulated, the courts will require that they be followed. When statutes, policies, or agreements are silent or ambiguous about order of release, the courts almost unanimously have accorded qualified tenured teachers priority over nontenured teachers in similar positions. Certification has been the major, but not the exclusive, criterion considered by the courts in determining the "qualifiedness" of teachers. Between tenured teachers holding similar positions or between nontenured teachers holding similar positions, seniority has been the primary, but not the exclusive, factor in determining order of release. Absolute seniority preference may be qualified by other factors such as performance evaluations, years of teaching experience in the subject matter (see *State ex rel. Melchiori v. Board of Educ.*, 1992), and collective bargaining agreements (see *Underwood v. Henry County Sch. Bd.*, 1993).

The order of reinstatement, reassignment, and recall of RIFed employees should be roughly the inverse of the order of release. That is, qualified tenured teachers would be called back before qualified nontenured teachers, in the order of seniority rank within each group. The courts have been fairly unanimous in affirming that neither tenure nor seniority provides an absolute right to recall over certification or other evidence of qualification. For example, a New York court held that a tenured guidance counselor whose position was abolished was not entitled to reemployment as a school social worker. While some of the duties of the two positions were similar, the positions were sufficiently dissimilar to require a separate certification, which the guidance counselor did not hold (*Brown v. Board of Education, Morrisville-Eaton*, 1995).

SUMMARY

Perhaps no other aspect of public school administration is subject to the plethora of rules, regulations, and legal mandates that govern human resources administration. Every aspect of the employment relationship has been subjected to legislative pronouncements and judicial interpretation. The courts have upheld the right of state governments and local school districts to specify terms and conditions of employment. One of these conditions, the passing of a competency test, has generated substantial controversy as the practice has spread to almost every state. Whereas the testing of teachers has been upheld by the courts, in those situations in which the tests have not been job related or test scores have been used arbitrarily or used to create unreasonable or arbitrary classifications, the courts have disallowed their use.

The major issue litigated in adverse employment decisions is the extent to which adequate due process was provided. The more severe the action and the more serious the individual interests involved, the more extensive and more formal is the due process required. The procedures to be followed in the dismissal of a tenured employee are more extensive than those required for the dismissal of a nontenured employee. However, employees who are RIFed are generally not entitled to a hearing, because the courts consider their dismissals to be impersonal, in no way impugning the teacher personally and therefore outside the scope of teacher termination statutes.

Although the specific laws related to personnel administration vary somewhat from state to state, the basic legal concepts, especially those designed to protect individual rights and ensure fairness and reasonableness, are common to all jurisdictions. A failure by the school district to adhere to these concepts leaves it vulnerable to a charge of arbitrary and capricious conduct.

Discussion Questions

1. List the terms and conditions of employment that are most often affected by state statutory and regulatory provisions. For each area, discuss the basis and/or the purpose for the requirement.
2. There are two elements of due process. Define each element and discuss what protection it affords school district employees.
3. All states have some statutory provisions regarding teacher dismissal or revocation of a certificate. What are the statutory provisions in your state? How do these compare with those most frequently cited in other states' statutes?
4. What policies has your district adopted regarding RIFing of teachers and administrators?

CASE STUDIES

—CASE 11.1—

I Prefer Whiterock, but . . .

The Whiterock School District has had a great deal of trouble securing a permanent, certified teacher of the severely mentally disabled. The district advertised in the major educational publications in circulation in the state and attended the recruitment "round-ups" at the six institutions in the state that prepare special educators. Nonetheless, only two people applied for the position. Of the two, by far the most attractive was Mark Thompson, a graduating senior at State University. His grades were excellent, as were his references. Mark had not passed the state certification exam but was scheduled to take the exam in late May.

An invitation to interview was extended to both Mark and Susan Lewis, the other applicants. Susan interviewed on May 3 and Mark on May 16, the Monday after his graduation. Following Mark's exit meeting, James McGee, the director of human resources, and Nancy Kirch, the principal of the school at which the vacancy existed, informed Mark that they would recommend at the next school board meeting that he be offered the position. They reminded him, however, that the offer would be contingent on his passing the exam and becoming certified. Mark was excited by their announcement and assured them he would pass the exam and would be sending them a copy of the test results and certificate as soon as they arrived. He said he wanted the position and would be looking forward to getting the board's offer. On June 3 the school board met and voted to extend an offer to Mark.

On June 6 Mark called Mr. McGee to say that he had not been able to take the exam because he had broken his foot 2 days before the exam while playing softball in a church-sponsored softball league. The exam would not be offered again until July 15, but Mark assured Mr. McGee that he had already made application to take the exam at that time. Mr. McGee asked Mark if he had received the board offer yet, and Mark said yes and that he would return it along with his test result. Mr. McGee told him he did not need to wait for the test results, that in fact he should notify the board of his acceptance within the next couple of weeks.

When Mr. McGee had not received the written acceptance by July 1, he called Mark and was assured by Mark that he would put it in the mail that very day. On July 6 Mark called Mr. McGee and told him that he had just received an offer from another district for $4,000 more than the Whiterock offer. Mark shared that he really prefered Whiterock but that the additional $4,000 would make a big difference in his ability to pay off his student loans.

Questions

1. Balancing the district's need and Mark's actions thus far, what should Mr. McGee do? What options are there for making the Whiterock offer more competitive?
2. Is there a breach of contract if Mark accepts the second offer or if Whiterock withdraws its offer to Mark and makes one to Susan?
3. Suppose you offer the position to Susan. Would you be honest with her regarding the circumstances that have led to the belated offer? If Susan rejects the offer, how should the district proceed?
4. Is there an issue of professional ethics that should be reported to the state certification board or state board of education?
5. Some districts send a prospective teacher an "intent to hire" letter. How binding is this type of offer on a school district? On the prospective teacher?

—CASE 11.2—

Lot's Wife

Phil Harris, principal of Eastwater High School, received the following anonymous note: "You should see what goes on in the coaches' showers after swim practice. Jim Murphy and Elaine Lorenzo are sinners. Fornicators and adulterers have no place in this district." Within the next 2 weeks several more notes arrived alleging the same thing. The last one added, "If you don't do something about this, you are as much a sinner as they are and I will see that the school board destroys you as surely as God destroyed Lot's wife for looking upon the evil of Sodom." The notes had all been delivered through

school mail, so Mr. Harris assumed the sender was someone within the school system.

Before the matter went any further, Mr. Harris felt compelled to meet with Jim and Elaine to share the essence of the letters with them. They both vehemently denied the allegations. However, they did admit that on three occasions they had both used the female coaches' showers after practice because of building repairs where the male coaches' showers are located.

Questions

1. Should Mr. Harris have confronted Jim and Elaine based on anonymous allegations? How else might he have responded? What type of investigation, if any, should take place now?
2. Based on the evidence thus far, what disciplinary action, if any, should be taken on Jim Murphy and Elaine Lorenzo?
3. If you were Jim or Elaine, how would you respond to the allegations? Would you hire an attorney? Have their rights to privacy been violated?

—CASE 11.3—

A Gun in Class

On January 25, 1988, Robert T., a sixth-grade student, brought a loaded revolver into the class of Mr. Chaddock, a language arts teacher. Mr. Chaddock asked Robert to give him the gun and Robert refused. He then opened a drawer and asked Robert to put the gun in the drawer, but Robert again refused to give up the gun. Mr. Chaddock then decided to go on with class. He felt he knew Robert well enough to know that Robert would not deliberately do anything to hurt his classmates, and that violence would occur only if Robert felt threatened. Toward the end of the class, the principal, who had heard that Robert had a gun, sent for him to come to her office. When she demanded that he give her the gun, Robert aimed it at her and told her to get away from him, and then he ran from the school.

At a dismissal hearing stemming from the incident, Mr. Chaddock defended his actions by stating that because there was no school policy on handling such situations, he had to rely on his instincts. West Virginia statute states that dismissal must be reasonable based on one of the just causes listed: immorality, incompetency, cruelty, insubordination, intemperance, or willful neglect of duty, none of which are defined.

Questions

1. How should Mr. Chaddock have acted? Should Mr. Chaddock be dismissed? Under which clause could he be dismissed?

2. What about the principal? To what extent did the action taken by the principal in calling the student from the class to come to her office endanger the safety of others? What, if anything, might she be charged with? What disciplinary action, if any, should be taken in regard to her conduct?

3. Who is responsible for ensuring that the school district has a policy covering the now all-too-common situation of students bringing guns to school? Had someone been injured, what parties should be held responsible?

This case study is based on an actual court case, *Board of Education of County of Gilmer v. Chaddock*, 398 S.E.2d 120 (W. Va. 1990).

REFERENCES

Albemarles Paper Company v. Moody, 422 U.S. 405 (1975).

Alexander, K., & Alexander, M. D. (2001). *American public school law* (5th ed.). Belmont, CA: West/Thompson Learning.

Ambach v. Norwick, 441 U.S. 68 (1979).

Arline v. School Board of Nassau County, 772 F.2d 759 (11th Cir. 1985), aff'd, 480 U.S. 273 (1987).

Arline v. School Board of Nassau County, 692 F. Supp. 1286 (M.D. Fla. 1988).

Assoc. of Mexican-American Educators v. State of California, 231 F.3d 572 (9th Cir. 2000).

Aubrey v. School Bd. of Lafayette Parish, 148 F.3de 559 (5th Cir. 1998).

Babb v. Independent School Dist. No. I-5, 829 F.2d 973 (Okl. 1992).

Ballanto v. Board of Education of Stronington, 663 A. 2d 323 (Conn. App. 1993).

Barr v. Clarendon County School Board District 2, 462 S.E.2d 316 (S.A. Ct. App. 1995).

Beckham, J. (1983). Critical elements of the employment relationship. In J. Beckham & P. A. Zirkel (Eds.), *Legal issues in public school employment* (pp. 1–21). Bloomington, IN: Phi Delta Kappa.

Board of Education v. Lockhart, 687 P. 2d 1306 (Colo. 1984).

Brown v. Board of Education, Morrisville-Eaton Central School District, 621 N.Y.S.2d 167 (A.D. 3 Dept. 1995).

Burlington Industries v. Ellerth, No. 97–5695 S.Ct. (1998).

Calhoun v. Cassady, 534 S.W.2d 806 (Ky. 1976).

Cambron-McCabe, N. H. (1983). Procedural due process. In J. Beckham & P. A. Zirkel (Eds.), *Legal issues in public school employment* (pp. 78–97). Bloomington, IN: Phi Delta Kappa.

Cambron-McCabe, N. H., McCarthy, M. M., & Thomas, S. B. (2004). *Public school law: Teachers' and students' rights* (5th ed.). Boston: Allyn & Bacon.

Cascio, W. F. (1998). *Applied psychology in personnel management* (5th ed.). Reston, VA: Reston.

C.F.S. v. Mahan, 934 S.W.2d 615 (Mo.Ct. App. 1996).

Chalk v. U.S. District Court Central District of California, 840 F.2d 701 (9th Cir. 1988).

Civil Rights Division of the Arizona Department of Law v. Amphitheater Unified School District No. 10, 680 P.2d 517 (Ariz. 1983).

Clark County School District v. 532 U.S. 268 (2001).

Cleveland Board of Education v. Loudermill, 470 U.S. 532 (1985).

Daily v. Bd. of Ed. of Morrill County Sch. Dist. No. 62–0063, 588 N.W.2d 813 (Neb. 1999).

Davis v. School Dist. of City of Niagra Falls, 772 N.Y.S.2d 180 (N.Y. App. Div. 2004)

English v. Talledega County Board of Education, 938 F. Supp. 775 (N.D. Ala. 1996).

Estill v. Alabama State Tenure Commission, 650 So.2d 890 (Ala. Civ. App. 1994).

Faragher v. City of Boca Raton, 524 U.S. 775 (1998).

Fischer, L., Schimmel, D., & Stellman, C. (2007). *Teachers and the law* (7th ed.). New York: Longman.

Flanary v. Barrett, 143 S.W. 38 (Ky. 1912).

Floyd County Board of Education v. Slone, 307 S.W.2d 912 (Ky. 1957).

Gaylord v. Tacoma School District No. 10, 559 P.2d 1340 (Wash. 1077), *cert. denied*, 434 U.S. 879 (1977).

Gould Public Sch. v. Dobbs, 993 S.W.2d 500 (Ark. 1999).

Grand Prairie Independent School District v. Vaughn, 792 S.W.2d 944 (Tex. 1990).

Griggs v. Duke Power Co., 410 U.S. 924 (1971).

Harris v. Forklift Systems, 510 U.S. 17 (1993).

Hartmeister, F., & Russo, C. J. (1999). "Taxing" the system when selecting teachers for reduction-in-force. *Education Law Reporter, 130*, 989–1007.

Hess V. Rochester Sch. Dist., 396 F. Supp. 2165 (D. N. H. 2005).

Hess, F. M., & Maranto, R. A. (2000). Tenure's tenacious tenure in public schools. *Education Digest, 65*(5), 51–55.

Horton v. Jefferson County-Dubois Area Vocational Technical School, 630 A.2d 481 (Pa. Commw. Ct. 1993).

Hortonville District v. Hortonville Education Association, 426 U.S. 482 (1976).

Imber, M. (2001). Morality and teacher effectiveness. *American School Board Journal, 188*(4), 64–66.

In re Thomas, 926 S.W.2d 163 (Mo. App. 1996).

Jones v. Alabama State Tenure Commission, 408 So.2d 145 (Ala. Civ. App. 1981).

King v. Jefferson County Board of Education, 659 So.2d 686 (Ala. Civ. App. 1995).

Knox County Educ. Assn. v. Knox County Board of Educ., 158 F.3d 361 (6th Cir. 1998), *cert. denied*, 120 S.Ct. 46 (1999).

Lagos v. Modesto City School District, 843 F.2d 347 (9th Cir. 1988).

Mathews v. Eldridge, 424 U.S. 319 (1976).

McClelland v. Paris Public Schools, 742 S.W.2d 907 (Ark. 1988).

McDaniel v. Princeton City Sch. Dist. Bd. of Educ., 72 F. Supp. 874 (S. D. Ohio 1999).

Massachusetts Federation of Teachers, 629. 436 Mass.763, 767 NE 2d 549 (2002).

Nixon v. Board of Cooperative Educational Services of Sole Supervisory District of Steuben-Allegheny Counties, 564 N.Y.S.2d 903 (App. Div. 1990).

Owen v. Board of Education of Kankakee School District No. 111, 632 N.E.2d 1073 (Ill. App. 1994).

Palmer v. Board of Trustees of Crook County School District No. 1, 785 P.2d 1160 (Wyo. 1990).

Pittsburgh Federation of Teachers Local 400 v. Aaron, 417 F. Supp. 94 (Pa. 1976).

Pullman-Standard v. Swint, 456 U.S. 273 (1982).

Racine Unified School District v. Labor and Industry Review Commission, 476 N.W.2d 707 (Wis. App. 1991).

Reitmeyer v. Unemployment Compensation Board of Review, 602 A.2d 505 (Pa. Com-wlth. 1992).

Singleton v. Jackson Municipal Separate School District, 419 F.2d 1211 (5th Cir. 1970).

Skinner v. Railway Labor Executives Association, 489 U.S. 602 (1989).

Sorenson v. School District No. 28, 418 P.2d 1004 (Wyo. 1966).

Sperry, D. J., Daniel, P. T. K., Huefner, D. S., & Gee, E. G. (1998). *Education law and the public schools: A compendium* (2nd ed.). Norwood, MA: Cristopher-Gordon.

State ex rel. Melchioro v. Board of Educ. 425 S.E.2d 251 (W. Va. 1992).

Sullivan v. River Valley Sch. Dist., 20 F. Supp. 2d 1120 (W.D. Mich. 1998).

Underwood v. Henry County Sch. Bd., 427 S.E.2d 330 (1993).

Valente, W. D., & Valente, C. M. (2001). *Law in the schools* (5th ed.). New York: Macmillan.

Vukadinovich v. Board of School Trusties of North Newton School Cooperation, 2002, 47 Fed. App. 417 2000 Wk 311593 (2000 WL 31159318 7th Cir. 2002).

Weaver v. Nebo School District, 29 F. Supp. 2d 1279 (1999).

White v. Blackfoot School Dist. No. 55, No. 99–35820 (9th Cir. 2001).

Wingegar v. Des Moines Independent Community School District, 20 F.3d 895 (8th Cir. 1994).

CHAPTER 12

The Support Personnel Program

After reading this chapter, you will be able to:

- Identify the most common approaches to job analysis.
- Describe the process used to establish salary schedules for classified personnel.
- List the most common preemployment conditions for classified personnel.
- Discuss the goals of the employee induction program.
- Distinguish between the training approaches used in on-the-job training and off-the-job training.
- Describe the objectives of the classified personnel appraisal system.

The major focus of any discussion of school human resources administration in education is on the certificated personnel, those individuals who are required to have some certificate of qualification from the state in order to teach, supervise, counsel, or administer. These individuals constitute the numerical majority of people in a school system, and their salaries account for about two-thirds of the school district budget, so the attention given to them seems justified. Nevertheless, a very important group of employees cannot be overlooked in any consideration of the administration of human resources in education: the 3.5 million employees known as classified, noncertificated, or support personnel. This group of employees makes up about one-third of the full-time staff in the public schools and is composed of such employees as secretarial and clerical personnel, teacher and library/media aides, security officers, transportation staff, food services employees, plant operation and maintenance workers, and health and recreational staff (U.S. Department of Education, 2007). More important than simply their numbers, in recent years support staff have increasingly assumed responsibility for complex tasks (Zepeda, 2000) and have become essential to the successful operation of the school district and to the maintenance of a positive, safe, and productive school environment. The school bus driver is often the first school employee the child sees each day. Secretaries, aides, and other support staff can make students feel significant and wanted, or scorned and rejected (Welch & Daniel, 1997).

The status of classified or support personnel varies widely among the states. Some states recognize certain groups of support personnel for such purposes as tenure or retirement. State or local civil service arrangements cover all noncertificated personnel in some states. In yet other states, local school districts are given complete authority and responsibility for the establishment and administration of the support personnel system.

Whatever plan is in operation for the administration of the support personnel program, certain human resources functions and activities must be performed. Some of these functions (e.g., recruitment, selection, and employee benefits) have been discussed elsewhere in this text, primarily in regard to certified personnel. This chapter will discuss these functions as they differ from those in the certificated personnel system and will discuss other activities and problems specific to the support personnel program. The first section presents the development of a classification system, the necessary first step in establishing and maintaining a classified personnel system. Other sections include salary determination, recruitment, selection, staff development, and performance appraisal.

DEVELOPMENT OF A CLASSIFICATION SYSTEM

Unlike certificated personnel, who represent a more limited range of job categories (i.e., teachers, administrators, counselors, nurses, librarians), classified personnel represent a broad spectrum of employees with varying levels of skills and responsibilities. For this reason, in all but the smallest districts, it is necessary to differentiate among positions on the basis of duties and responsibilities. This can be done only after a job analysis. Following the job analysis, positions with similar duties and responsibilities can be grouped into common classes. This classification plan, as it is called, provides the foundation for the entire support personnel program. The information about positions used to develop the classification plan and the classes subsequently established provide the basis for employee recruitment, selection, assignment, and evaluation, as well as salary determination.

Job Analysis

The development of the classification system begins with **job analysis.** As noted in Chapter 4, job analysis is the systematic process of collecting, organizing, and evaluating information relating to the responsibilities and tasks associated with the successful performance of a specific job. The data collected serve a number of human resource functions such as recruitment, selection, and performance appraisal. Job analysis describes job duties, the personal requirements necessary to perform a job, and the job context or working conditions (Martocchio, 2004).

The U.S. Department of Labor (1991) job analysis procedure suggests that the following four dimensions be included in a job analysis: (1) *worker functions*—what the worker does in relation to Data, People, and Things (see Table 12.1); (2) *work fields*—the

Table 12.1 Department of Labor Worker Functions

Data	People	Things
0 Synthesizing	0 Mentoring	0 Setting Up
1 Coordinating	1 Negotiating	1 Precision Working
2 Analyzing	2 Instructing	2 Operating–Controlling
3 Compiling	3 Supervising	3 Driving–Operating
4 Computing	4 Diverting	4 Manipulating
5 Copying	5 Persuading	5 Tending
6 Comparing	6 Speaking–Signaling	6 Feeding–Offbearing
	7 Serving	7 Handling
	8 Taking Instruction and Helping	

methodologies and techniques essential to the performance of the job; (3) MPSMS—the *materials* being processed, the *products* being made, the *subject matter* being dealt with, and the *services* being rendered; and (4) *worker characteristics*—the worker attributes that contribute to successful job performance (education, specific vocational preparation, aptitudes, temperaments, interests, physical demands and strength, and environmental conditions). The analysis of the physical demands and environmental conditions is particularly important in meeting the challenge of the Americans With Disabilities Act (ADA). An example of a data collection form used to make an analysis of physical demands and environmental conditions is provided in Figure 12.1.

The three most common approaches to collecting the data needed for job analysis are (1) questionnaires, (2) observation, and (3) interviews. A job analysis questionnaire is designed to elicit the job incumbent's and supervisor's descriptions and perceptions of the job. Typically, experienced job incumbents provide the most details and insights, while supervisors provide detailed information but with a different focus. That is, "supervisors are most familiar with the interrelationships among jobs within their department" and "are probably in the best position to describe how employees performing different jobs interact" (Martocchio, 2004, p. 200). Specifically, the job analysis questionnaire seeks information relative to

- The type and number of tasks performed;
- The frequency with which the task is performed;
- The level of skill required;
- The position(s) from which supervision is received and over which supervision is given;
- The equipment or tools operated in the position;
- The experience required;
- Any formal education, training, or license requirements; and
- Contacts with other departments or external agencies or organizations.

Questionnaires provide an inexpensive way to gather large amounts of data in a short period of time. However, they also provide no opportunity for follow-up and clarification. And, because they are often very long, employees often delay returning or fail to return the questionnaire.

Figure 12.1 Data Collection Form for Physical Demands and Environmental Conditions

ID NO._____

Physical Demands		Comments	Environmental Conditions	Comments
Strength			1. Exposure to Weather	
Position			2. Extreme Cold	
Standing _____ %			3. Extreme Heat	
Walking _____ %			4. Wet and/or Humid	
Sitting _____ %			5. Noise Intensity Level	
Weight/Force			6. Vibration	

Weight/Force

	N	O	F	C
Lifting				
Carrying				
Pushing				
Pulling				

Controls: Hand-Arm____Foot-Leg___
Strength Level: _____

Climbing _____
Balancing _____
Stooping _____
Kneeling _____
Crouching _____
Crawling _____
Reaching _____
Handling _____
Fingering _____
Feeling _____
Talking _____
Hearing _____
Tasting/Smelling _____
Near Acuity _____
Far Acuity _____
Depth Perception _____
Accommodation _____
Color Vision _____
Field of Vision _____

Environmental Conditions:

1. Exposure to Weather
2. Extreme Cold
3. Extreme Heat
4. Wet and/or Humid
5. Noise Intensity Level
6. Vibration
7. Atmospheric Conditions
8. Moving Mechanical Parts
9. Electric Shock
10. High, Exposed Places
11. Radiation
12. Explosives
13. Toxic/Caustic Chemicals
14. Other Environmental Conditions

Protective Clothing or Personal Devices

Analyst_____ Date_____
Field Center Reviewer_____ Date_____
Additional Reviewer_____ Title_____

Source: U.S. Department of Labor. (1991). *The Revised Handbook for Analyzing Jobs.* Washington, DC: Government Printing Office.

One popular questionnaire, the Position Analysis Questionnaire (PAQ) (McCormick, Jeanneret, & Mecham, 1989), is concerned with the type and level of human behavior and activities rather than the tasks and technologies of the job. The PAQ consists of 195 job elements, which are categorized as (1) information input (where and how the employee gets the information used on the job); (2) mental processes (the reasoning, planning, decision making, and information processing involved in the job); (3) work output (the physical activities performed and the tools or devices used); (4) relationships with other persons required to perform the job; (5) job context (the physical and social environment in which the work is performed); and

(6) other job characteristics. The PAQ provides quantitative data which can be computer analyzed to create a job profile. The job profile created can then be compared to standard job profiles of job families and similar jobs assigned to the appropriate job family. A substantial body of research exists on the PAQ and has shown it to have reasonably good reliability estimates.

A second approach to collecting job-related data, *observation*, involves the observation of the job incumbent by a trained observer who records incumbent activities and interactions. Observation allows the job analyst to collect first-hand data that cannot be obtained by other job analysis methods such as questionnaires or interviews. Observation as a method of job analysis is most appropriate for jobs in which activities or behaviors are readily observable rather than ones involving primarily intellectual or cognitive processes (Pynes, 1997). Observation should include a representative sample of job activities. And it should be made clear to the employee being observed that the job is being assessed, not the person. Observation may be done in person by a trained, inconspicuous observer, or the observation may be videotaped and reviewed at a later date by the job analyst or by the job analyst and the employee. The latter provides the opportunity for the analyst to ask the employee questions about various aspects of the job.

One observation technique, known as Function Job Analysis (FJA), builds on the Department of Labor (DOL) methodology by adding functions to the worker functions (things, data, and people) and by including several additional scales: the *scale of worker instructions*, which identifies the levels of discretion exercised by the employee and the extent of instruction necessary for the employee to perform the job; and scales of *reasoning development, mathematical development*, and *language development*, which measure the extent to which these abilities are necessary for the worker to perform the job (Fine, 1995). A functional job analysis distinguishes between the essential and marginal job functions and identifies the physical and mental characteristics necessary to perform the essential functions. Such an analysis helps both the district and the potential applicant to determine if the applicant can perform the essential job functions with or without reasonable accommodation, and can be critical in ensuring ADA compliance (National School Boards Association, 1996).

Another common approach to job analysis is the *interview*. Either an individual interview, in which one or more job incumbents are interviewed extensively, or a group interview, in which a number of job incumbents are interviewed simultaneously, can be used. Interviews provide the opportunity for the reporting of activities and behaviors that would often not be observed, as well as those that occur over long time periods. Interviews also have the advantage of being flexible and therefore usable to collect different kinds of information from a range of positions. It is also the only technique that provides for the interaction of the analyst and the job incumbent. This interaction allows the interviewer to learn more about the problems, challenges, and limitations associated with the position than might not otherwise be available. However, the danger does exist that incumbents describe what has been done rather than what should have been done or may inflate the importance of particular tasks. To mitigate against these distortions, more than one incumbent or a supervisor familiar with the job should be interviewed. One example of a worksheet used by interviewers to obtain information about a job is provided in Figure 12.2.

Figure 12.2 Job Analysis Worksheet

1. Job title _____
   Department _____
   Date of interview _____
   From what information secured _____
2. Briefly describe the primary functions of
   the job: _____
3. Types of duties performed (check):
   ( ) Accounting.
   ( ) Answering telephone.
   ( ) Bookkeeping.
   ( ) Calculating.
   ( ) Checking work.
   ( ) Composing letters.
   ( ) Computing.
   ( ) Confidential work.
   ( ) Contact with others.
   ( ) Decision making.
   ( ) Duplicating.
   ( ) Filling.
   ( ) Opening mail.
   ( ) Posting.
   ( ) Supervising others.
   ( ) Tabulating.
   ( ) Transcribing.
   ( ) Typing.
   ( ) Serving as receptionist.
   ( ) Report writing.
   ( ) Routing materials.
   ( ) Taking shorthand.
   ( ) other _____
4. Description of the individual duties:

Duty	Time Spent	Description (material and information handled)

   (NOTE: This part of the form would be
   expanded to full page depth.)
5. Minimum educational requirements of the job. State
   what you think is required:
   ( ) High school diploma preferred.
   ( ) High school diploma necessary.
   ( ) Business or technical.
   ( ) College degree.
   ( ) Graduate degree.
6. On-the-job experience required for full proficiency in
   this position:
   ( ) Two weeks.
   ( ) One month.
   ( ) Two months.
   ( ) Three to six months.
   ( ) One year.
   ( ) More then one year.

7. Does the work of this employee's position require
   the use of any machines or equipment?
   ( ) Yes ( ) No If yes, indicate kind of machines
   and equipment and extent of use.
   Kind:_____
   _____
   ( ) Occasional use   ( ) Frequent use
   ( ) Continuous use
8. Does this position require working with confidential
   data?
   ( ) Yes ( ) No If yes, list data by type.
   For example, salary data, personnel record, etc.
   _____
   _____
   _____
9. Contact with others
   ( ) Contacts with peers and supervisor within
       department only.
   ( ) Routine contacts with other departments.
   ( ) Contacts with other departments requiring tact
       and judgment.
   ( ) Routine contacts with public.
   ( ) Contacts with superintendent and/or board,
       presenting data that may influence important
       decisions.
   ( ) Frequent contacts involving the carrying out of
       programs and schedules, requiring the
       influencing of others to obtain the desired results.
10. Supervisory responsibilities
   ( ) Assigning work.
   ( ) Checking work.
   ( ) Disciplining.
   ( ) Establishing methods.
   ( ) Setting grievances.
   ( ) Hiring.
   ( ) Planning.
   ( ) Setting quality standards.
   ( ) Setting quantity standards.
   ( ) Routing.
   ( ) Scheduling.
   ( ) Training others.
11. To what extent are judgments and initiative required
    to perform this job?
   ( ) Job requires close immediate supervision and
       detailed instructions.
   ( ) Job requires frequent guidance with all
       questions referred to supervisor.
   ( ) Job holder follows established practice on
       most duties, makes some decisions, and
       infrequently refers questions to supervisor.

Continued

Figure 12.2 (Continued)

( ) Job holder plans objectives, makes many decisions, infrequently refers specific cases to supervisor.	( ) Could lead to considerable waste of time and money.
( ) Job holder works independently under general board policies.	( ) Could be critical to the well-being of the organization.
12. Effect of errors by job holder	13. Remarks _____
( ) Of minor inconvenience or consequence to organization.	_____
( ) Could lead to moderate waste of time and money.	_____
	Date _____
	Signature of interviewer _____

Source: The Job Analysis Work Sheet, *The School Personnel Management System*, National School Boards Association (Alexandria, VA), 1996: p. 144. Reprinted with permission.

The interview itself should be conducted in private with a minimum of distraction or interruption. The interview will typically last at least one hour. Some suggestions for conducting a successful job analysis interview come from Henderson (1994, pp. 165–166):

1. When only a select group or small number of incumbents are to be interviewed, ask the supervisor responsible for the job to select as an interviewee the individual who knows most about the job. (The supervisor should be careful not to select a self-serving flatterer. Another danger here is that the worker singled out by the manager may feel that social interactions with the work group are jeopardized. In that case, why not let the work group make the selection?)

2. Establish immediate rapport with the interviewee, introduce yourself, know the incumbent's name, speak in easily understood language, briefly review the purpose of the interview, and explain how the selection was made and what opportunity the incumbent will have to review the final report for accuracy and validity. Do not exhibit impatience if the interviewee is nervous or ill at ease.

3. When possible, use structured outlines (or forms) to obtain job information . . . It may be helpful to give the interviewee a copy of the form to be completed and explain what is meant by a responsibility and duty and how you would like to have the task information presented. In most cases, the employee will soon recognize what is desired and will provide the information by using a verb and an object and stating the effect of the action and even the work aids used.

4. If possible, confine questions to one area at a time when asking more than one question. Always focus the discussion on what the incumbent does and the processes, work aids, materials, devices, tools, machines, and so on required in the work activities. Differentiate between what the incumbent does and what the equipment produces. If the interviewee begins to stray from the subject, summarize the data collected to that point and then return to the subject.

Give the incumbent sufficient time to ask additional questions to stimulate thought about infrequent assignments. At this point, it may be a good idea to give the interviewee an opportunity to complain. In this manner, the interviewer may discover hidden job issues. Always close the interview on a friendly note and express appreciation for the time and the effort spent on the interview.

5. After completing the interview, verify the job data. Normally, the interviewee's immediate supervisor is the best person to ask about accuracy. The supervisor will probably be able to interpret the interviewee's comments or clarify certain hazy terms or phrases.

In practice, no one approach to job analysis will be appropriate for analyzing all jobs in the district. Accurate and sufficient data for some positions may be generated by observation. For other positions this is not the best approach. Because no one approach is superior or applicable to the analysis of all positions, districts often use a combination approach. For example, the DOL's job analysis process combines observation and interview. Often the questionnaire, observation, and interview are used together. It is also common to use group interviews to clarify or reach consensus on points that emerged following the survey or observation of multiple incumbents.

The actual analysis of the data collected may be performed by a qualified district personnel specialist, or it may be necessary for the district to hire a personnel consultant specializing in job analysis. Regardless of who performs the analysis or the approach employed, ultimately what is most important is that the job analysis be reliable and valid. "A reliable job analysis yields consistent results under similar circumstances, whereas a valid job analysis accurately describes each job's duties" (Martocchio, 2004).

It is important that the job analyses be periodically reviewed if they, and the job descriptions that emanate from them, are to remain valid. Jobs do not remain stable, but change to meet current demands. In some cases technological advances have reduced once difficult jobs requiring higher levels of education to jobs that can be performed by workers with only limited formal education but with specific technical training. Numerous court decisions have emphasized a concern that job requirements be relevant and not unrealistically high. Over time, job activities may also shift somewhat dramatically. These shifts should be reflected in job descriptions and job specifications.

Job Classification

After all jobs have been analyzed, jobs with similar work requirements may be grouped into a common **job class.** Typical classes involving support personnel in school districts are custodial, clerical, technical, paraprofessional, professional, and managerial (NSBA, 1996). Positions within any one class may differ in experience and skill requirements, or in degree of responsibility. For example, the custodial class might include a custodian I, custodian II, and head custodian. A good classification system "provides supervisors with a convenient basis for comparing employee performance . . . [and] helps administrators identify overlapping duties, unnecessary levels of supervision, unclear delegations of authority, and inefficient separation of tasks or duties" (NSBA, 1996, p. 145).

The final classification plan must be adopted by the school board. If support personnel are covered by civil service arrangements, however, the classification plan may require the approval of the civil service commission prior to presentation and adoption by the board.

Because school districts and the jobs they support are rapidly changing, the classification system should be reviewed about every 5 years. Such a review will help identify which positions should be upgraded, downgraded, or left unchanged. Obsolete classes may be abolished and new ones created. The review may also reveal any misclassifications. Unfortunately, because classification studies are both labor intensive and expensive, it is not uncommon for school districts to go years without a thorough review of the classification system (Mosley, 1998). And, for misclassified or underpaid employees, even 1 year is unacceptable.

Job Descriptions

As discussed in Chapter 4, job descriptions are the most immediate products of the job analysis process and provide a written, detailed outline of the duties, qualifications, and responsibilities of a specific job. Job descriptions provide the details needed for the recruitment and selection processes, as well as the performance expectations included in the appraisal processes. The job description should describe the job, not the person who holds, or will hold, the position. Job descriptions assist human resources administrators, potential employees, and present employees in understanding existing positions and role expectations. They also enhance employees' understanding of their roles by providing a statement of the duties, responsibilities of the position, the qualifications required, the situation of the position within the organization, and the interactions and relationships expected with other employees.

The descriptions of the essential job functions and the skill sets required to execute them, as well as the physical requirements of the job, are the most important sections of the job description in terms of compliance with the federal Americans With Disabilities Act (ADA) and related state statutes and the determination of whether these can be accomplished with reasonable accommodation by the district. According to the ADA, the essential functions of the job are those that are intrinsic to the position. That is, the reason the position exists is to perform these functions. In determining the essential functions, the focus should be on the desired end rather than the means to accomplish it. The reason is that a person with a disability may be able to achieve the desired outcome with or without a reasonable accommodation, but in a manner different from a nondisabled person (Pynes, 1997). In one suit that was lost by the employer, the employer had required that each employee be able to use both arms when performing a particular task. One employee could not meet this requirement because his disability caused limited mobility in one arm. However, the court found that the essential function of the job was the ability to lift and carry a particular article (which he could do), not the ability to use both arms (Greenberg & Bello, 1992).

What happens to the job descriptions after they have been prepared depends in part on the existence, if any, of any union agreements or civil service contracts. That is, in areas of high unionization, agreements may call for union agreement of initial job descriptions or any alteration of existing job descriptions (Ray, Candoli, & Hack, 2005). Ultimately, of course, it is the school board that must approve all job descriptions and classifications.

WAGE AND SALARY DETERMINATION

Once the classification plan has been established, the district is ready to develop the salary schedule for its support employees. As discussed in Chapter 9, the salary schedule should be an expression of the district salary policies. In some cases support personnel may be paid an hourly wage. The principles involved in the establishment and maintenance of hourly wages are the same as those involved in the establishment and maintenance of a salary schedule. The following principles should be followed in the development of the salary schedule:

1. School district salaries should reflect prevailing wages in the community.
2. Benchmark positions should be established for each class.
3. The salary schedule should be equitable: placement of positions on the salary schedule should reflect accepted indications of difference.
4. The salary schedule should be internally consistent.
5. All classified positions should be on the schedule.
6. The salary schedule and all adjustments to it should be public and accessible.
7. Fringe benefits should be considered.
8. Provisions should be made for periodic review.

Basic to the development of the support employee salary schedule are the principles that school district salaries should be fair and competitive. A fair salary structure emphasizes unbiased decisions and justice. Competitive pay is central to the district's ability to attract, retain, and motivate qualified and competent employees. In the past, school districts often assumed that the value of regular employment, vacations, and fringe benefits entitled them to pay somewhat less than business and industry. For most districts this is no longer a viable assumption. The security and protection offered by unions, combined with the expanded benefits programs offered by many businesses, are equal or superior to that offered by most school districts. If the district is to attract and retain qualified, competent support personnel, it must be competitive with both the private sector and other public agencies in its compensation program.

Wage and Salary Studies

The determination of the prevailing wages and salaries in the community may be accomplished in several ways. In smaller communities the human resources administrator may contact the major employers in the district and solicit wage and salary information. This may be supplemented with data from public and private employment agencies and from state and federal departments of labor. In larger communities and districts, a more formal *wage and salary study* involving the solicitation of wage and salary information from other districts, agencies, industries, and professional organizations may be conducted. Whatever data are being used for comparison should take into consideration indirect compensation (employee benefits and services).

It is important that support personnel representatives be involved in the wage and salary study. Agreement must be reached as to which jobs will be compared and which districts, agencies, or industries will be contacted. Clearly, balance must be maintained between any attempts by administration to contact primarily employers known to pay lower salaries and attempts by employees to suggest only those employers known to pay higher salaries.

The most common sources of wage and salary data are questionnaires, telephone interviews, and survey data compiled by others. A major concern related to the use of surveys is designing a suitable form and, if using a mailed survey, the time lost waiting for responses, and the low rate of return. Internet surveys can be an effective alternative to mail surveys and offer the advantages of not only instant transmission and easy follow-up, but, if desirable and appropriate, districts can share salary data files. Telephone interviews can also be an effective approach if care is taken to ensure the most appropriate person is being interviewed, if sufficient time has been allotted for the interview, and if opportunity for preparation has been provided by scheduling the telephone interview in advance (Levesque, 1993). The use of survey data compiled by others, such as that compiled by the Educational Research Service (see Table 12.2), can be useful supplements (if current) but should not be used as the only source of data. Whatever approach is used, it is also important that the results of the salary study be made available to employees for their response and reaction before any recommendations are made to the board.

Table 12.2 Mean Salaries and Wages Paid Support Personnel in the Public Schools, 2006–2007

Position	Mean Annual Salary/Hourly Wage Rate
Central Office Positions	
Secretaries	35,629
Accounting/payroll clerks	35,991
Typists/data entry clerks	28,940
School Building Level	
Secretaries	27,398
Library clerks	19,806
Teacher Aides	
Instructional	12.32/hr
Noninstructional	12.19/hr
Custodians (not engineers)	13.78/hr
Cafeteria Workers (not supervisors)	11.16/hr
School Bus Drivers	15.48/hr

Source: Educational Research Service (ERS). (2007). *Salaries and Wages Paid Professional and Support Personnel in Public Schools*, 2006–2007, Arlington, VA: Author.

It is generally not possible to determine the prevailing wage or salary for each position in the district. It is necessary, therefore, to identify at least one position in each class as a **benchmark position.** A benchmark position is one whose duties and responsibilities are sufficiently common that it will be found in other districts, as well as in many businesses and industries. Once the prevailing wage or salary has been determined for the benchmark position, it becomes the basis for pay determinations for the other positions in the class in terms of their relationship to the benchmark position.

Job Evaluation

Establishing the proper relationship between the benchmark positions and all other positions in a class is primarily a consideration of equity and contributory worth. A process of *job evaluation* is used to "systematically recognize differences in the relative worth among a set of jobs and establish pay differentials accordingly" (Martocchio, 2004, p. 214). Among the factors typically considered in a job evaluation are (1) education or training requirements, (2) license requirements, (3) experience requirements, (4) skills requirements, (5) number of employees supervised, (6) number and range of responsibilities assigned, (7) decision making allowed and required, and (8) working conditions.

Various techniques, both quantitative and qualitative, can be used to conduct the job evaluation. One popular quantitative technique used in business and industry, as well as some larger school districts, is the point method. The point method evaluates jobs by assigning a point value to each component of a job. The magnitude of the point total for the position determines its placement on the pay grade. Qualitative methods include simple ranking plans, paired comparisons, and classification plans such as the federal government's classification system, which classifies federal jobs into 15 classifications, GS-1 through GS-15 (Martocchio, 2004).

Establishing the Salary Schedule

Ultimately, each position is assigned to a specific hourly, weekly, or monthly wage (the flat-rate pay approach) or, more commonly, for nonexempt positions (positions subject to overtime provisions), to a specific pay grade with a predetermined number of steps within the grade. Within each grade there is a salary minimum, maximum, and midpoint. A variety of jobs can be at the same pay grade. As in the pay-grade example in Table 12.3, while separate salary schedules have been created for the various classes of employees within the overall pay plan for classified employees, some pay grades (ranges) are found in more than one class. There are no rules about how many grades a district should have: the number depends primarily on the size of the district, the number, and the range of jobs (Smith & Mazin, 2004).

The establishment of differentials between the grades and the steps in each grade is a matter of internal consistency. The benchmark position for each salary grade should be within one step (on a five-step schedule) of the average. A common salary differential between steps in a grade is 4–5%. The differentials between grades should also be uniform. The 4–5% differential is also the common differential used between grades on school district salary schedules for support personnel.

Table 12.3 Avondale Elementary School District Classified Salary Schedule 2007–2008

Step Position	A	B	C	D	E	F	G	H	I	J	K	L	M	N	O
District Office															
Accountant	13.03	13.38	13.74	14.11	14.49	14.88	15.28	15.69	16.11	16.54	16.98	17.43	17.89	18.36	18.84
Accounting Clerk	11.32	11.62	11.93	12.25	12.58	12.92	13.27	13.63	14.00	14.38	14.77	15.17	15.58	16.00	16.43
Instructional Materials Assistant	8.99	9.24	9.50	9.77	10.05	10.34	10.64	10.95	11.27	11.60	11.94	12.29	12.65	13.02	13.40
Instructional Materials Manager	10.22	10.52	10.83	11.15	11.48	11.82	12.17	12.53	12.90	13.28	13.67	14.07	14.48	14.90	15.33
Migrant Community Liaison	10.22	10.52	10.83	11.15	11.48	11.82	12.17	12.53	12.90	13.28	13.67	14.07	14.48	14.90	15.33
Purchasing	13.03	13.38	13.74	14.11	14.49	14.88	15.28	15.69	16.11	16.54	16.98	17.43	17.89	18.36	18.84
Secretary/District	11.98	12.33	12.69	13.06	13.44	13.83	14.23	14.64	15.06	15.49	15.93	16.38	16.84	17.31	17.79
Food Services															
Assistant Manager	10.22	10.52	10.83	11.15	11.48	11.82	12.17	12.53	12.90	13.28	13.67	14.07	14.48	14.90	15.33
Baker	8.99	9.24	9.50	9.77	10.05	10.34	10.64	10.95	11.27	11.60	11.94	12.29	12.65	13.02	13.40
Cashier	8.55	8.79	9.04	9.30	9.57	9.85	10.14	10.44	10.75	11.07	11.40	11.74	12.09	12.45	12.82
Clerk	8.99	9.24	9.50	9.77	10.05	10.34	10.64	10.95	11.27	11.60	11.94	12.29	12.65	13.02	13.40
Cook/Cafeteria Worker	8.22	8.42	8.69	8.94	9.20	9.47	9.75	10.04	10.34	10.65	10.97	11.30	11.64	11.99	12.35
Manager	13.03	13.38	13.74	14.11	14.49	14.88	15.28	15.69	16.11	16.54	16.98	17.43	17.89	18.36	18.84
Part-time Cafeteria Worker	8.17	8.39	8.62	8.86	9.11	9.37	9.64	9.92	10.21	10.51	10.82	11.14	11.47	11.81	12.16
Secretary/District	11.98	12.33	12.69	13.06	13.44	13.83	14.23	14.64	15.06	15.49	15.93	16.38	16.84	17.31	17.79
Transporter/Warehouseman	10.22	10.52	10.83	11.15	11.48	11.82	12.17	12.53	12.90	13.28	13.67	14.07	14.48	14.90	15.33
School-Instruction/Office															
Health Aide	10.22	10.52	10.83	11.15	11.48	11.82	12.17	12.53	12.90	13.28	13.67	14.07	14.48	14.90	15.33
Library Manager	9.66	9.96	10.27	10.59	10.92	11.26	11.61	11.97	12.34	12.72	13.11	13.51	13.92	14.34	14.77
Paraprofessional I, Bilingual, and Spec. Ed.	8.99	9.24	9.50	9.77	10.05	10.34	10.64	10.95	11.27	11.60	11.94	12.29	12.65	13.02	13.40
Paraprofessional II (A.A. degree/60 hrs. college credit)	10.22	10.52	10.83	11.15	11.48	11.82	12.17	12.53	12.90	13.28	13.67	14.07	14.48	14.90	15.33

Position														
Paraprofessional Spec. Ed ED/Moderate/Severe and Alt Ed	10.22	10.52	10.83	11.15	11.48	11.82	12.17	12.53	12.90	13.28	13.67	14.07	14.48	14.90	15.33
Secretary/School	10.82	11.13	11.44	11.76	12.09	12.43	12.78	13.14	13.51	13.89	14.28	14.68	15.09	15.51	15.94
Technology															
System Support Technician	14.08	14.43	14.79	15.16	15.54	15.93	16.33	16.74	17.16	17.59	18.03	18.48	18.94	19.41	19.89
Technology Assistant	11.98	12.33	12.69	13.06	13.44	13.83	14.23	14.64	15.06	15.49	15.93	16.38	16.84	17.31	17.79
Maintenance															
Custodian	8.99	9.24	9.50	9.77	10.05	10.34	10.64	10.95	11.27	11.60	11.94	12.29	12.65	13.02	13.40
Custodian, Lead	11.98	12.33	12.69	13.06	13.44	13.83	14.23	14.64	15.06	15.49	15.93	16.38	16.84	17.31	17.79
Groundskeeper	10.22	10.52	10.83	11.15	11.48	11.82	12.17	12.53	12.90	13.28	13.67	14.07	14.48	14.90	15.33
Maint. Foreman/Leadman	14.08	14.43	14.79	15.16	15.54	15.93	16.33	16.74	17.16	17.59	18.03	18.48	18.94	19.41	19.89
Maintenance Worker I	10.82	11.13	11.44	11.76	12.09	12.43	12.78	13.14	13.51	13.89	14.28	14.68	15.09	15.51	15.94
Maintenance Worker II	14.08	14.43	14.79	15.16	15.54	15.93	16.33	16.74	17.16	17.59	18.03	18.48	18.94	19.41	19.89
Transportation															
Bus Driver	12.88	13.13	13.39	13.66	13.94	14.23	14.53	14.84	15.16	15.49	15.83	16.18	16.54	16.91	17.29
Bus Driver Trainee	8.55	8.79	9.04	9.30	9.57	9.85	10.14	10.44	10.75	11.07	11.40	11.74	12.09	12.45	12.82
Crossing Guard	8.17	8.39	8.62	8.86	9.11	9.37	9.64	9.92	10.21	10.51	10.82	11.14	11.47	11.81	12.16
Mechanic	14.08	14.43	14.79	15.16	15.54	15.93	16.33	16.74	17.16	17.59	18.03	18.48	18.94	19.41	19.89
Spec. Ed Transp. Aide	8.55	8.79	9.04	9.30	9.57	9.85	10.14	10.44	10.75	11.07	11.40	11.74	12.09	12.45	12.82
Transp./Maint. Coordinator	13.03	13.38	13.74	14.11	14.49	14.88	15.28	15.69	16.11	16.54	16.98	17.43	17.89	18.36	18.84
Warehouse															
Distribution Center Supervisor	14.08	14.43	14.79	15.16	15.54	15.93	16.33	16.74	17.16	17.59	18.03	18.48	18.94	19.41	19.89
Distribution Center Worker	10.22	10.52	10.83	11.15	11.48	11.82	12.17	12.53	12.90	13.28	13.67	14.07	14.48	14.90	15.33

Source: Avondale (AZ) Elementary School District (2007). *Classified Salary Schedule 2007–2008.*

The salary schedule should also recognize length of service. One way this can be accomplished is by adopting a schedule that has five or more steps for each grade or range. The employee advances from one step to another after predetermined periods of service. Another technique is to award longevity increments based on years of continuous service (e.g., after 10 years of continuous service, 2.5% per month; and after 20 years of continuous service, 7.5% per month).

Since exempt positions are normally paid on a flat weekly, biweekly, or monthly basis, and are often paid more than nonexempt hourly employees, many districts use a separate salary schedule for salaried employees. This schedule may also be constructed with salary steps that recognize length of service or merit advancements (Levesque, 1993).

All support positions should be included on the wage or salary schedule. No position should be considered too high or too low, and no differential treatment should be given. Authority on final adoption of the salary schedule is given to the school board. The salary schedule adopted should not only be made public, as is required in most jurisdictions, but also be distributed and made easily available to employees and other interested parties.

Finally, provision should be made for periodic review of the salary schedule. Such review should consider not only data obtained from salary studies, but also data relative to the cost of living. In periods of inflation the cost of living can rise quite rapidly, and unless consideration is given to periodic adjustments based on some indicator of price inflation, school district employees can fall behind their counterparts in other agencies and businesses. Whereas annual review of the master salary schedule would be most desirable, it is not uncommon for salary negotiations to fix salaries for periods of 2 years or more, making formal annual review unnecessary.

RECRUITMENT

The goal of any school district support personnel recruitment program, as with any personnel recruitment program, is the identification of sufficient qualified applicants to meet the personnel needs of the district. Since the classified service requires a staff with more varied skills and background than the certificated service, their recruitment is more varied and can often be more difficult. The importance of establishing and following the types of sound recruitment policies and practices discussed in Chapter 4 cannot be overemphasized. Not only are they critical in maintaining employee morale and faith in the board's and administration's commitment to equity and fairness, but, given the costs associated with the high turnover rate that inevitably follows poor recruitment, they are necessary cost-saving measures.

As was true for certificated personnel, prior to the actual solicitation of applications, an announcement of vacancy must be prepared following Equal Employment Opportunity Commission (EEOC) guidelines. In addition, the announcement of vacancy should be as detailed as possible to allow potential applicants to determine if they are interested in the position or qualified for it. Sufficient copies of the announcement of vacancy should be prepared so that one is available to each potential applicant and so that some can be posted in each school or building and in other public locations in the district.

Recruitment for any support position may involve both internal and external sources. For some openings, qualified individuals, or individuals who can be made qualified, may already be employed in the district and may welcome the opportunity for transfer or promotion. Personnel records can be used to identify employees who have the qualifications for a specific vacancy. Limiting initial recruitment to current employees is also not uncommon. If current employees know that they will receive consideration for vacancies that are of higher salary and status, the effects will often be reflected in increased performance and morale and a reduction in staff turnover.

For some vacancies, the district may lack the capacity to "grow their own" or may find it desirable to recruit from external sources. In these instances the various recruiting sources described in Chapter 4 are available. As described, the specific source(s) utilized by the district will depend on such factors as district size, district resources, the number of vacancies, and the type of position. As previously noted, certain recruitment strategies, such as using private agencies, have proven to be successful in recruiting administrative or technical personnel, whereas others, such as advertisement in local newspapers, have proven more effective in recruiting for lower-level positions. Employee referrals have also proven to be a favored and effective strategy for recruitment of support personnel.

SELECTION

The selection process is essentially a series of activities designed to gain information about the job applicant that can be compared to the selection criteria and, ultimately, result in the best match of person and position. As was true in regard to the selection of certificated personnel, prior to the initiation of the selection process selection criteria based on the job analysis and job description should be established. The actual selection process for support personnel typically includes (1) completion of an application form, (2) a preliminary interview, (3) employment tests, (4) reference and background checks, (5) an employment interview, and (6) final selection and assignment. The extent to which a particular district includes each of these steps will depend primarily on the size of the district, the position(s) to be filled, and the policies and procedures in force in the district. The larger the district and the higher the level of the position being filled, the more comprehensive and formal the process is likely to become. However, whatever procedures are used should be "detailed and available for review as part of general school board policy and procedures" (Ray, et al., 2005, p. 181). Specific aspects of the selection process as they relate to support personnel are discussed in the following sections.

Application Form

Virtually every district requires all applicants for classified positions to complete an application form as a part of the hiring process. As noted in Chapter 5, application forms provide the district with an easy and systematic method of obtaining a variety of factual information about the applicant. In addition to the factual information obtained, the application form can tell a lot about prospective employees—their neatness, their accuracy, their attention to detail (Woodward, 2000). As a general rule, other than biographical data, information solicited on the application form should be limited to that pertinent to success on the job. The areas of impermissible inquiry for the application form were noted in Chapter 5.

Preliminary Interview

As noted in Chapter 5, the primary purpose of the preliminary interview is to screen out applicants who are obviously unqualified. For example, some applicants may not meet the size, legal age, or intellectual ability for the position. In addition, whereas some basic data have been obtained on the application form, most application forms do not solicit the type of detailed information relative to knowledge and experience that can be determined in an interview. Nor can the application form generate data relative to attitude and conduct. The preliminary interview also provides the applicant the opportunity to obtain answers to questions about the position and the school system. As was also noted in Chapter 5, the preliminary interview is usually conducted by personnel in the human resources department and is usually short in duration.

Employment Tests

Following the initial interview, for certain jobs applicants may be required to take certain tests or submit validated scores from previous tests. The extent to which tests are used and the importance given them may vary from school district to school district. Employment tests are used primarily for entry-level positions where most applicants will not have enough acquired experience to assess their performance. Employment tests allow employers to identify work-related attitudes and job skills that they cannot identify in an interview because the types of questions they would need to ask would be too complex (Tyler, 2000). Moreover, when properly designed and utilized, "employment tests possess the unique ability to fairly, objectively and efficiently compare and contrast job candidates' qualifications" faster and more accurately than any other screening method (Tyler, 2000, p. 76).

Tests for most support personnel positions are normally either written general intelligence/aptitude tests or skills assessment tests. The former is often short and similar to a school achievement test for reading and math, with perhaps a few items common to those found on intelligence tests. They may be developed by the district or purchased commercially, taken at the district office, or administered online. As discussed in Chapter 5, if such tests are used, it is important that the school district take care to ensure that the tests are valid and nondiscriminatory. Valid "means that there is a demonstrated correlation between people's performance on the test and their performance on the job to the standard measured by the test" (Smith & Mazin, 2004, p. 22).

The written general intelligence/aptitude test may be followed by a skills assessment. Applicants for secretarial or clerical positions may be asked to take a test to assess typing and computer abilities. A performance test for a bus driver may include starting, stopping, backing, turning, and parking the bus under specified conditions. It is important when designing any skills assessment that the test developers examine the job description and understand what the job entails so that the test will, in fact, assess what it needs to be assessing (Tyler, 2000) and that the skill being assessed is an actual job requirement.

Reference and Background Checks

After the interview and employment test, the references, previous employment, and other information provided on the application form and in the interview by those applicants still under consideration may be checked. As noted in some detail in Chapter 5, the purposes of such checks are to gain additional information about the applicant, to clarify questions or inconsistencies, and to verify the accuracy of information provided by the applicant. Often candidates will have secured letters of reference; however, they typically lack the detail needed for the decision-making process and are not a substitute for good reference checks (Smith & Mazin, 2004). In checking references, the district is not limited to those supplied by the applicant. While those checking references cannot go on a "fishing expedition," they are authorized to contact persons who are in a position to have knowledge about the applicant's past employment. Figure 12.3 provides an example of a telephone reference check form used by the Kyrene, Arizona, Unified School District in the screening of support staff.

Employment Interview

Whereas the purpose of the preliminary interview is to screen out unqualified or overqualified applicants, the purpose of the employment interview is to "provide the opportunity to ask applicants about their abilities to perform job functions" and allow interviewers "to determine whether the personal traits and preferences of the applicant make a good match with the situation" (French, 2003, p. 67). Much of what was said in Chapter 5 relative to interviewing certificated staff applies to interviewing support staff. Perhaps the most important considerations are that the interview adhere to all EEOC guidelines, that the interview of each candidate be conducted using the same set of questions, and that each candidate be evaluated on the basis of the criteria enumerated on the job description.

The employment interview for support staff will normally involve the immediate supervisor for the position, an employee with the same or a similar position as the one being filled, and the human resources representative. For supervisory or administrative positions, the central office administrator responsible for that function as well as a human resources officer may be on the interview committee. For certain specialized positions, persons from business or industry may also be asked to serve on the selection committee. In districts in which site-based management has delegated personnel selection to the local site, the principal or other administrator may well be on the selection committee. Depending on the position, a teacher, counselor, librarian, other education professional, parent, or community representative may also be on the committee. Regardless of who serves on the committee, it is the responsibility of the administrator in charge of the selection process to provide interviewers with the selection criteria and guidelines and strategies for conducting the interview.

Figure 12.3 Support Staff Telephone Reference Check

Guidelines to follow:
- Speak with current or most recent supervisor if possible.
- State: "We are considering candidate for _____ position"
- Remarks will be kept confidential and not available to candidate.
- Appreciate your candid honest appraisal.

Name of Candidate: _____   Date: _____

Position applying for: _____   Employer: _____

Name of Reference: _____   Title: _____

Phone: _____

Name of person acquiring this information: _____

Check of company policy prohibits release of information _____

Employed from _____ to _____ Position _____

1) In general, how would you rate this person:
    - Outstanding_____   Good_____   Poor_____
2) How would you rate employee's work quality and quantity? Interpersonal skills?
    -
    -
3) What are the candidate's most outstanding qualities?
    -
    -
4) What qualities of the candidate could interfere with success in this position?
    -
    -
5) Is there anything else we should know before we hire this person?
    -
    -
6) Would you re-employ him/her?
    -
    -
7) Is there anyone else you would recommend that we contact?
    -
    -

_____   _____
Information taken by   Date

Source: Kyrene (AZ) Unified School District.

Final Selection and Assignment

In most government entities, including school districts, the final selection of individuals to fill job openings must come from lists of eligible candidates who have passed all the foregoing steps in the selection process. In some urban districts, the eligibility list for some positions is a civil service list that has been generated from tests and personal records and must be used by all governmental units in the city (Ray, et al., 2005). The use of eligibility lists is intended to increase the objectivity of the selection process. When a vacancy occurs, typically the names of the three individuals who ranked highest on the selection criteria are referred to the individual(s) authorized to make the final selection. For many support personnel positions, this will be the building principal. Unless the requesting party can provide sufficient justification as to why none of these individuals should be selected, selection must be made from among those referred. Eligibility lists are normally declared invalid after a few months.

Before a new employee is assigned to a vacant position, consideration should be given to providing an existing employee the opportunity to make a lateral transfer to the vacancy. For example, if the vacancy is in what is considered the most desirable school in the district, policy might provide the opportunity for an employee in what is considered a less desirable school to transfer to the vacant position and assign the new employee to the opening created by the transfer. The opportunity for transfer is essential to staff motivation and morale. However, this consideration must be balanced against the district's interest in finding the right person for each job and in what best serves the needs of the district and its students. The human resources administrator should provide leadership in the development of policies that will govern transfers and assignments.

Preemployment Conditions

Once the final selection has been made, and before the employment can be finalized, a number of preemployment conditions must be satisfied. The listing that follows is not exhaustive of all preemployment conditions placed by school districts. Nor do all districts place all these conditions on employment. However, the following list does include the most commonly found preemployment conditions.

Loyalty Oaths. Many states require prospective employees at the time of employment to sign an oath affirming support for both United States Constitution and the state constitution. Although the practice has been challenged many times, the courts have upheld the right of school districts to have such a requirement.

Completion of Immigration and Naturalization Information. As required by the 1986 Immigration Reform and Control Act, in order to be eligible to work, all new employees, not just aliens, must complete Part I of the U.S. Immigration and Naturalization Service (INS) I-9 form. The form asks the employee to provide evidence of his or her identity and employment eligibility from a list of preapproved documents, including birth certificates, Social Security cards, and green cards. The school district must review the material provided by the employee and verify that the documents appear genuine. Unfortunately, in some areas fake documents are easy to obtain. Nonetheless, under penalty of federal law, school districts must make a good faith effort to ensure the validity of these documents. And, the INS form must be completed within 3 business days of the hire.

Selective Service Registration. It is a requirement in some states that all new male employees born in 1960 or later show proof of Selective Service registration as a precondition to employment.

Fingerprint Checks. It has become common for states and school districts to require persons to be fingerprinted if they are to be employed in the public schools. Very often this will have been done for teachers, administrators, and other positions requiring licenses at the time they applied for the license. Since many applicants for support positions do not hold positions for which a professional license is required, they may not have satisfied this condition and will have to do so as a precondition of employment. The cost of the fingerprinting is normally borne by the employee. If the fingerprint check reveals convictions for certain criminal offenses, or if the employee has lied about convictions on his or her application or in the interview, the employee will be terminated.

Drug Testing. As discussed in Chapter 11, testing for alcohol and drug use may be required of school employees who occupy "safety sensitive" positions in the schools. This designation could potentially apply to a number of classified positions, and has specifically been held by the courts to apply to employees in the transportation department and custodians. When drug testing is required, it is important that a reputable company be used and that established procedures are followed.

Immunization Requirements. Most states require that prospective employees provide proof of immunization for measles and/or rubella and mumps prior to employment.

Vehicle Driving Licenses. Persons being considered for employment for a position which requires them to drive district vehicles must have the appropriate driver's license to operate the vehicle in question. In most states school bus drivers are required to hold a commercial driver's license.

Physical Examination. The preemployment physical examination is required by many school districts and, if required, should be paid for by the district. The Americans With Disabilities Act places limits on the use of medical exams in the employment process. A medical examination cannot be required before a conditional offer of employment is made. And, because they are costly and time consuming, they should be used only for positions that require "specific information related to performance and the potential need for reasonable accommodation" (Smith & Mazin, 2004, p. 23). Applicants cannot be screened out for a position unless the physical examination determines that, even with reasonable accommodation by the school district, they cannot perform the essential functions of the job (as detailed in the job description) safely and efficiently and without posing an unduly high risk to themselves, other employees, or the public.

Any information obtained from the physical examination must be kept on a separate form and in a separate medical file; it should not be placed in personnel files. The results of the exam cannot be disclosed except in very limited circumstances such as to make a work accommodation.

TRAINING AND DEVELOPMENT FOR SUPPORT PERSONNEL

According to the American Society for Training and Development (2006), organizations in the United States spend more than $100 billion annually on employee learning and development. Unfortunately, training and development programs for support personnel in education have traditionally lagged behind not only those in other organizations, but also those provided certificated personnel in education. Only in recent years have school districts come to recognize that staff development should include all employees and that the time and expense invested in development programs for support personnel are small compared to the inefficiency and ineffectiveness resulting from the lack of such programs. Research has shown that staff development can result in improved morale, an increased sense of professionalism, higher levels of job satisfaction, and reduced staff turnover. As a result of the growing recognition of the importance of training and development for support staff, some states have mandated and supported staff development for support personnel. And, in many school districts, staff development for support personnel is included in collective bargaining agreements.

In most school districts, development programs for support personnel are concerned with either (1) orienting employees into the district and the position or (2) providing them with job skills. These activities are discussed under the major programs in which they fall: orientation and professional development and training.

Induction

As discussed in some detail in Chapter 6, the primary goals of the induction program are to help the new employee or newly assigned employee to adjust to both the social and job-related aspects of the work environment, to reduce the anxiety associated with beginning a new job, and to help the new employee feel positive about having accepted the position. Initial impressions and information are important to later attitudes toward the job, coworkers, and the district. The time and resources spent recruiting employees are wasted if an employee does not remain with the district. An effective induction program can do much to reduce employee turnover, as well as to ensure that employees reach their maximum efficiency as soon as possible.

In certain respects the induction needs of support personnel are greater than those of certificated personnel. Most new certificated personnel have been oriented to various aspects of schools during their teacher or administrator preparation programs. They also have some understanding of the role of the school and of education as a process. Many support personnel, on the other hand, come to the job with certain skills or training but without a clear understanding of the role of the school and the workings of the educational system, as well as how they fit into the total picture.

Induction is most effective when approached as a cooperative activity of the human resources department and supervisors. It consists of four phases. The human resources department is normally responsible for coordinating the induction and for the first phase of the induction process: the provision of information about the district and the particular school (if applicable), and about personnel policies, salaries and benefits, promotion opportunities, time recording and absences, sick leave, holidays, grievance procedures, health and safety requirements, and other regulations. Much of this information can and should be provided in an employee handbook, which should also include an organizational chart clarifying lines of authority and communication. When the district presents this information to new employees, it is best to be honest and to present a realistic preview of what can be expected in working for the district.

It is important that the words used in the handbook be carefully chosen. Attempts to "sell" the district or the benefits of working for the district should not be overstated. The courts have held that statements made in the employee handbook may be binding on the employer.

The second phase of the induction program is conducted by the immediate supervisor, who, for many support personnel, will be the principal. The supervisor introduces the new employee to other employees and describes the relationship of the new employee's position to other positions in the school or department, gives a tour of the school or department, and provides information about department and school rules and regulations, safety requirements, and the detailed duties and responsibilities of the job. The supervisor also provides information about such details as the location of lockers, restrooms, and lunchrooms; use of telephones and computers; parking; supply procedures; hours of work; and call-in procedures. Also addressed at this phase are expectations for personal behavior, where the importance of behavior as a positive or negative source of public relations is stressed (Weller & Weller, 2000).

A third phase of the induction process is a form of mentoring or on-the-job training similar to that provided new teachers. That is, the new employee will be assigned to a first-level supervisor or to an experienced employee, who will provide support and instruction regarding any specific skills required of the job. This mentoring or on-the-job training for support personnel is much shorter than that for teachers and typically lasts for only a few days.

A follow-up interview several weeks after the new employee has been on the job constitutes the fourth phase of the induction program. The interview may be conducted by either the supervisor or a representative of the district human resources office. The purposes of the interview are to determine employee satisfaction with the job, answer any questions the employee might have, review important information, and appraise the employee of the perceptions of his or her performance thus far.

Staff Development and Training

Staff development and training for all employees is needed to meet the challenges presented by the rapid changes in technology, and the pressures to improve efficiency, academic achievement, and employee performance and to restructure organizational delivery systems. Yet other development and training needs are created by employee transfers or promotions, changes in district requirements or procedures, and legal and government mandates. Employee training may be used to provide information to employees about new programs, mandates, laws, or policies, as well as to provide opportunities for the acquisition of new or improved skills. This includes the training and development of both hard skills, the technical knowledge or requirements of the job, as well as the soft skills related to personal, individual development (Smith & Mazin, 2004).

If staff development and training programs for support staff are to be meaningful experiences for participants, they must be seen as relevant and important. Relevance and the other principles of adult learning discussed in Chapter 7 in regard to certificated staff apply equally to support staff. Moreover, if staff development and training programs are to be successful, they must have the support of school and district administrators.

The most effective way for school districts to create meaningful staff development programs for support personnel is to engage in a systematic process such as that depicted in Figure 12.4. As seen, the model is cyclical in nature and envisions a continuous process of needs assessment, planning, implementation, and evaluation. Each of these elements is discussed next.

Needs Assessment. The specific development and training activities provided by the district should be determined by a needs assessment. This can be conducted internally or by an external expert. Data gathering might include a review of district employment needs or the job analyses which describe the appropriate knowledge and skills required in various areas, as well as performance appraisals which indicate how successfully the requirements are being met (Ray, et al., 2005). Other important indicators of staff development and training needs are changes in legal requirements and information from school district records such as accident reports and grievance reports. However, the most important sources of information about training needs are the target

Figure 12.4 Steps to Develop a Professional Growth Program for Noncertified Staff

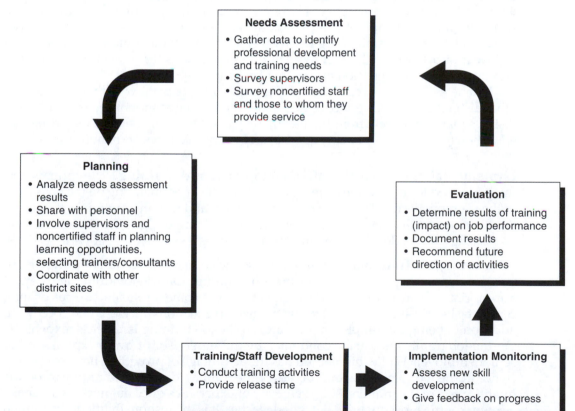

Source: S. Zepeda. (2000). Needed: Professional growth opportunities for non-certificated support staff. *School Business Affairs, 66*(6), 41.

employee groups and the supervisors of the target groups. Depending on the training being contemplated, it may also be helpful to contact those to whom the employees provide services inside the school system or those with whom they interact outside the school system. Input can be collected through surveys, interviews, or focus groups.

Planning. The information and data generated during the needs assessment process must be analyzed and the results shared with staff and used to determine exactly what needs and issues might be addressed by the district development and training program, as well as what district goals will be advanced. Equally important, the analysis should seek to determine if the need the training seeks to address is really due to lack of skills or knowledge or some deeper issue: "Training is not a quick fix for problems caused by management apathy, bad morale, or an unqualified workforce" (Smith & Mazin, 2004, p. 65). Representative staff and supervisors should be involved in planning the training activities, as well as in identifying potential trainers or consultants.

Many school districts outsource some or the entire development program using external trainers or consultants. Other districts rely more heavily on internal expertise. Using district trainers can not only save money, but provides the opportunity for the district to highlight the skills and talents of employees. It also has the advantage of a trainer who can more easily relate to the audience and is familiar with the work situation. If the use of external trainers is desired or necessitated, the district should take care to identify a trainer with expertise with the topic and the potential trainee group. Check with other districts or organizations that have used the trainer and never make the selection of a trainer based on cost alone.

Planners may also want to consider entering into cooperative arrangements with other districts or regional service centers to deliver training to support personnel. School districts may also benefit from the free training conducted by the state department of education (or other government agencies) and various vendors or manufacturers.

Implementation: Conduct Staff Development and Training. The formats and methods used to conduct the training activities will vary depending on the objectives of the training, the availability of qualified trainers and training materials, the size of the district, and the size of the school district's training budget. The more common approaches to staff development and training are discussed in the following sections.

On-the-Job Training. A commonly used training method for support personnel development programs is **on-the-job training**. On-the-job training is most appropriate when employees are "expected to become proficient in performing certain tasks or using equipment found at their work stations" (Pynes, 1997, p. 209). In addition to being the simplest to operate, on-the-job training is the least expensive. On-the-job training is usually conducted by the supervisor or by an experienced or senior employee. While this method has the advantage of providing hands-on experience in the work location, the success of the training depends in large part on the qualification of the trainers. More seniority or experience does not necessarily make a coworker the most qualified or a good teacher. It is the responsibility of the human resources department or on-site supervisor to identify potential trainers and to provide them with instruction on how to train new employees.

Off-the-Job Training. In addition to on-the-job training, most school districts find it necessary to provide some training to support personnel away from their normal work location. Workshops lasting one day or more for all employees within a certain department are typical off-the-job training techniques used by school district personnel programs. Off-the-job training provides for the maximum number of trainees with the minimum number of trainers and lends itself to instruction in areas in which information and instruction can be imparted by a variety of instructional methodologies, including lectures, demonstrations, video instruction, teleconferencing or video conferencing, and online instruction. Online instruction has become increasingly popular for teaching basic concepts and skills primarily because of its convenience—it can be delivered at the employee's work station or a district computer site—and the self-paced nature of most online learning (ASTD, 2006) is especially suited for technology topics. Many districts have found a hybrid of online and face-to-face instruction to be a highly successful method for delivering staff development and training. And, technology is increasingly evident in all delivery methodologies.

There is no one preferred approach to staff development and training. An effective staff development and training methodology is one that is the best fit for the topic, is the best match with the preferred learning styles of participants, and provides the desired results. And, in all cases it is just as critical that the principles of adult learning and adult education discussed in Chapter 6 guide the staff development and training program for support staff as it is for certificated staff.

Off-the-job training may be provided at a central location in the school district, in another district, or at a site selected by the state department of education or other provider. It is common for manufacturing and business concerns to provide training in the use of their materials and equipment. School district personnel may be sent to a training facility operated by the business, or the provider may send trainers to the local school district. Companies also normally will provide materials that may be used by the district in its training efforts. Even when training related to the use of specific materials and equipment is not needed, companies often have persons available to give presentations on a variety of topics.

Scheduling. By whatever approach training is provided, it is important that it be scheduled so as to avoid conflicts with established school or district schedules. Suggestions for scheduling staff development for support staff include

- Extending the contract by a few days immediately before or after the school year.
- Adding district-wide staff development days, workdays, or both to support staff contract days.
- Adding "shift" hours to the school day and offer staff development or training before or after school. (Zepeda, 2000)

Evaluation. The evaluation of the staff development program, while important to its continued success, is often the most neglected aspect of the program (Pynes, 1997). The school district will certainly need to know if the goals of the program have been met. It may also want to know if a training program, or certain parts of it, was worth the investment, or if one program worked better than another, was more costeffective, or worked better with some groups than others. To answer these questions, some form of evaluation must take place. The evaluation can be anything from a simple pretest and posttest to an elaborate set of experiments with trainees randomly assigned to various treatments (training) and a control group. While some aspect of the evaluation may address employees' reactions to the training and be concerned with the improvement of the training program, the focus of the evaluation should be on the success of the program in meeting the previously identified goals of the activity. "Some data will be more readily obtainable, including reduction in errors or cost savings that are a direct result of the training. Others, such as reductions in turnover or cost per hire, will take longer to evaluate" (Smith & Mazin, 2004, p. 74). Whether short-term or long-term evaluation is employed, the staff development and training program should be the subject of ongoing evaluation. And, the results of the evaluation should be summarized and disseminated to participants, supervisors, and central office personnel (Welch & Daniel, 1997). Most importantly, the results of the evaluation should provide direction for future staff development and training activities and serve as a key ingredient in the development of an annual staff development plan.

PERFORMANCE APPRAISAL

Performance appraisal is an organization's way of telling employees what is expected of them and how well they are meeting those expectations (Martocchio, 2004). The guidelines and principles for successful personnel appraisal systems articulated in Chapter 8 apply equally to the appraisal of support personnel. The objectives of the support personnel appraisal system also closely parallel those of the certificated personnel appraisal system: to give employees the opportunity to discuss their performance in comparison to district standards and in relation to district goals and to give supervisors the opportunity to identify employee strengths and challenges (Kilbourne, 2007) with the primary goal being the promotion of high-quality outcomes.

Swan, Holmes, Brown, Short, and DeWeese (1988) have developed a Generic Performance Appraisal System for Classified Employees (GPASCE) that can be adapted by most school districts to meet individual district needs and can be used for periodic or annual review. According to its developers, the purposes of the GPASCE are to (1) encourage and facilitate improvement in the performance of employees, (2) provide a documented record of the employee's job performance, (3) provide an opportunity for communication between supervisor and employee on the subjects of job requirements and work expectations, (4) specify direction for work improvement, (5) assure employees that objective criteria are used in performance appraisal, (6) demonstrate that exceptional or unsatisfactory performance will be noted, and (7) exemplify the supervisor's and school's continuing interest in performance improvement.

The sequence of actions to be followed in GPASCE are as follows (Swan, et al., 1988):

1. The supervisor and employee meet at the beginning of each year and discuss the employee's job in detail, including the criteria that will be used to appraise the employee's performance on each factor on the job description and any factors unique to the position (e.g., for bus drivers, maintaining discipline on the school bus).

2. The supervisor monitors the employee's performance throughout the appraisal period to obtain first-hand knowledge for the appraisal.

3. If any concerns develop during the appraisal period, the supervisor meets with the employee to provide encouragement, assistance, and direction for improvement. If necessary or appropriate, an improvement plan may be developed and negotiated with the employee and reviewed and approved by the supervisor's superior (the reviewer).

4. Within 2 weeks of the end of the appraisal period, the supervisor completes the performance appraisal rating form (see Figure 12.5). For any factor rated "1" or "5," the supervisor must provide narrative description. The supervisor must also provide a narrative justification for any overall performance rating of "outstanding" or "unsatisfactory." The average score across all factors is used as a guide for determining the overall rating: 5.0–4.3, outstanding; 4.2–3.4, superior; 3.3–1.9, satisfactory; 1.8–1.0, unsatisfactory.

5. The supervisor shares the completed appraisal form with the reviewer, who may provide recommendations for appropriate action for any "unsatisfactory" rating or provide supplementary information relative to any rating, but may not change the appraisal.

6. Within 2 weeks of the end of the appraisal period, the supervisor meets with the employee to share and discuss the approved appraisal with the

Figure 12.5 Performance Appraisal Form for Classified Employees

Employee's Soc. Sec. #		Name (Last, First, Middle)		Position Title (& Series/Grade)	
School	Rating Period From: To:	Check One:	__Probationary __Mid-Year __Annual	Appraiser's Signature	Reviewer's Signature

1. Factor Appraisal System

Directions: Each employee is appraised on the common factors according to the contents of the job description (provide reference). An employee is rated on unique factors if contained in the job description. Provide narrative comments on separate page for all factors appraised "5" or "1" and for unsatisfactory, outstanding, or postponed overall rating.

Explanation on Appraisal Categories
5 = Exceeded requirements to exceptional degree
4 = Exceeded requirements, not to exceptional degree
3 = Met and sometimes exceeded requirements
2 = Usually met, but rarely exceeded minimum
    requirements
1 = Did not meet requirements
N = Irrelevant or no opportunity to observe employee's
    performance

A. *Common Factors—For All Employees*	Job Description Reference	5	4	3	2	1	N
1. *Demonstrates knowledge of job* (Includes technical, procedural, and regulatory knowledge)		‖ ‖	‖ ‖	‖ ‖	‖ ‖	‖ ‖	‖ ‖
2. *Plans, organizes, and sets priorities* (Time scheduling, orderly arrangement of procedures, and systematic planning)		‖ ‖	‖ ‖	‖ ‖	‖ ‖	‖ ‖	‖ ‖
3. *Produces expected quantity of work* (Amount of work produced/accomplished according to goals, objectives, and activities)		‖ ‖	‖ ‖	‖ ‖	‖ ‖	‖ ‖	‖ ‖

Continued

Figure 12.5 (Continued)

4. *Meets schedules/time lines* (Accomplishes work on schedule/on time)	‖	‖	‖	‖	‖	‖	
	‖	‖	‖	‖	‖	‖	
5. *Communicates in written form* (Degree of completeness, clarity and conciseness, and organization of material)	‖	‖	‖	‖	‖	‖	
	‖	‖	‖	‖	‖	‖	
6. *Communicates in oral form* (Appropriateness of organization of material; clarity, conciseness, impact of presentation)	‖	‖	‖	‖	‖	‖	
	‖	‖	‖	‖	‖	‖	
7. *Informs/consults appropriately* (Provides information/seeks information when needed)	‖	‖	‖	‖	‖	‖	
	‖	‖	‖	‖	‖	‖	
8. *Makes judgments/decisions effectively* (Sees problems, chooses, and implements solutions)	‖	‖	‖	‖	‖	‖	
	‖	‖	‖	‖	‖	‖	
9. *Demonstrates positive interpersonal relationship* (Effective in working with others individually and in teams)	‖	‖	‖	‖	‖	‖	
	‖	‖	‖	‖	‖	‖	

B. *Unique Factors for Employees*

10.	‖	‖	‖	‖	‖	‖
	‖	‖	‖	‖	‖	‖
11.	‖	‖	‖	‖	‖	‖
	‖	‖	‖	‖	‖	‖
12.	‖	‖	‖	‖	‖	‖
	‖	‖	‖	‖	‖	‖
13.	‖	‖	‖	‖	‖	‖
	‖	‖	‖	‖	‖	‖
14.	‖	‖	‖	‖	‖	‖
	‖	‖	‖	‖	‖	‖

II. *Overall Performance Rating for Employee*

_____ Unsatisfactory _____ Satisfactory _____ Superior _____ Outstanding _____ Postponed

Acknowledgement of Receipt of Appraisal (Not Concurrence): _____

Employee's Signature   Date

Narrative Comments

Factor.#   Appraisal Category   Comment _____

Note:

Appraiser's Signature   Date

Source: "A Generic Performance Appraisal System Classified Employees," by W. W. Swan, C. T. Holmes, C. L. Brown, M. L. Short, and L. DeWeese, 1988, *Journal of Personnel Evaluation in Education, 1,* pp. 297–298. Copyright © 1988 by Kluwar Academic Publishers. Adapted by permission.

employee. At this meeting both the supervisor and the employee share perceptions, and the employee has the opportunity to present additional information of which the supervisor may be unaware.

7. Within 1 week of this meeting, the supervisor completes and signs the finalized appraisal form and submits it to the reviewer for approval.

8. Within 4 weeks of the end of the appraisal period, the employee receives the final performance appraisal. The employee acknowledges receipt of the appraisal by his or her signature and, if necessary and appropriate, may work with the supervisor to develop an improvement plan.

9. The final performance appraisal is filed in the employee's personnel file.

10. If the employee considers the final appraisal unfair or unreasonable, he or she may appeal directly to the reviewer for reconsideration. If reconsideration does not resolve the issue to the satisfaction of the employee, he or she may pursue the established grievance or appeal procedure of the school district.

While the GPASCE relies heavily on the supervisor as the source of appraisal information, many school districts are attempting to include additional input from the employee, coworkers, or clients in an attempt to provide a more complete perspective on the employee's performance. Whatever process is used to evaluate support personnel, it is important that it be conducted on a periodic and established basis, and, as with certificated employee evaluation, it is important that classified employees be involved in the development and implementation of the performance appraisal system. Equally important, the evaluation effort "should be viewed as a constructive effort toward the improvement of the performance of the particular staff member and toward the betterment of the supervisory process under which that staff member operates" (Ray, et al., 2005, p. 187).

SUMMARY

Because of the number and importance of support staff, it is mandatory that sound personnel policies and practices relative to support employees be in operation in all school districts. Districts need to conduct job analyses and prepare written job descriptions, after which they must develop a comprehensive classification plan. After the classification plan has been developed, the district is in a position to prepare salary schedules in which all support positions are included. Because school district funds are public monies, information related to the schedule should be made public and accessible to employees and the public. The salary schedule should be subjected to periodic review, and indirect compensation should be considered in any discussion of the compensation program.

The goal of the school district recruitment program goes beyond merely recruiting the individuals needed to fill existing vacancies. Ideally, sufficient numbers should be recruited so that the district has the opportunity to select the very best employee from a number of qualified applicants. Given the investment made in recruiting, selecting, and training employees, it is incumbent that the district have an established systematic selection process that not only is equitable and nondiscriminatory, but also will generate the kind of data on which informed decisions can be based.

Following the lead of business and industry, in recent years school districts have placed new emphasis on the development and expansion of training and staff development programs for support personnel. There has also been an increased emphasis on the performance of education personnel, including support personnel. The performance appraisal system for classified personnel, like that for certificated personnel, should be objective and based on job-related standards, effectively communicated to employees, and subjected to an ongoing analysis of results.

Discussion Questions

1. As a newly appointed human resources director, you have been asked by the superintendent to revise the salary plan for support personnel. What information will you require, and what activities must you perform to accomplish this task?
2. You are to hire a dietician, a maintenance supervisor, and a secretary. How will you design your recruitment program for these positions? What is your rationale for selecting these various recruitment methods?
3. It has come to your attention that 30% of the support employees leave the district prior to completing 1 year of service, and 60% of those who leave do so within 6 months. What programs might you consider implementing in order to reduce the turnover rate?
4. Describe the relationships among job descriptions, recruitment, selection, performance appraisal, and staff development.

CASE STUDIES

CASE 12.1

Ruth or Roy?

The Maryvale School District has an opening for a Data Processor II. By advertising the position in the local newspapers and throughout the school system, the district has been successful in attracting 11 applicants. Of these, two candidates have emerged as having the best qualifications. The two candidates, Ruth Owens and Roy Evans, were equally ranked by the selection process. Ruth Owens was referred by Nancy Kraft, a valued and long-time employee in the same unit in which the vacancy exists. The unit is currently all female. Roy Evans, a newcomer to the community, responded to an advertisement for the opening.

Questions

1. What are the advantages of hiring Ruth? Of hiring Roy?
2. What impact, if any, would hiring Roy have on the prospect of future employee referrals? What could you do to mitigate any negative effects?
3. What, if any, underlying legal issues are present in this case?

CASE 12.2

Ready to Work

Jacqueline Armstrong has been an employee of the Hartford School District for 23 years and currently is director of computing services. While driving back from a computing conference last spring, Jackie was injured in an accident that has left her permanently confined to a wheelchair. After many months of recovery, she is ready to return to work. Her office is on the second floor of the district administration office, where all the computer equipment is located. The district office was formerly a high school, built in 1933, and it does not have an elevator or any wheelchair access. Architectural estimates of the cost to make the necessary renovations to the building to provide Jackie access total $163,000. The district is what would be considered a "poor" district and cannot make the renovations without either asking voters for a special assessment or making serious cuts in personnel and programs.

Questions

1. What legal obligations does the district have to Jackie? What moral obligations?
2. If you were the human resources director or superintendent and had the opportunity to talk to Jackie about the situation, what would you say?
3. What are the alternative solutions for the district? Which would you choose?

—CASE 12.3

Harried Hank

Hank Sloane has been a bus driver for Hopeville School District No. 1 for 8 years. His on-time and safety record has consistently been one of the best in the district. Beginning in early February, his supervisor, Mike Thompson, began to receive complaints that Hank was being verbally abusive to students on his bus. After receiving a third parent complaint, Mike met with Hank to see what was going on. During the meeting Hank denied making the alleged statements to students but did admit that he was having marital problems and wasn't sleeping well.

Within the next 10 days, two more parents called. One complained about Hank's abusive language. Another reported that Hank had pulled away from the bus stop without her son even though he had to have seen the boy, who was half a block away and yelling for the bus to stop. The boy had to walk back home a half mile in the snow, and his mother had to cancel an important business meeting to drive him to school.

Again, Mike called Hank in, and again Hank basically denied the charges. In the case of the first complaint, Hank said that the child in question was being disruptive on the bus and needed some sharp language to settle him down. As for the second situation, Hank claimed he did not see the child.

When asked how things were going with his wife, Hank broke down and tearfully admitted that she had left him, taking his 3-year-old daughter. Mike warned Hank that his behavior must change and suggested he seek counseling through the employee assistance program. Hank seemed reluctant to do this, saying he could handle it by himself.

Questions

1. Should Mike have required Hank to seek assistance rather than just suggest it?
2. Should Hank be moved from driving the bus to some other position in the transportation department where he is not in contact with students, even if some retraining might be involved?
3. To what extent should the district involve itself in the emotional problems of its employees? What is Hank's responsibility to the district to solve his personal problems?

REFERENCES

American Society for Training and Development (ASTD). (2006). *2006 state of the industry*. Alexandria, VA: ASTD.

Andreson, K. M., & Durant, D. (1997). Classified staff developers unite! *Journal of Staff Development, 18*(1), 18–21.

Fine, S. A., & Getkate, M. (1995). *Benchmark tasks for job analysis: A guide for Functional Job Analysis (FJA) scales*. Mahwah, NJ: Lawrence Erlbaum.

French, N. K. (2003). *Managing paraeducators in your schools: How to hire, train, and supervise non-certificated staff*. Thousand Oaks, CA: Corwin Press.

Geber, B. (September, 1995). Producing deeper levels of training evaluation. *The Developer, 7.*

Greenberg, S., & Bello, R. (1992). Rewrite job descriptions: Focus on functions. *HR Focus, 69*(7), 6.

Henderson, R. I. (1994). *Compensation management: Rewarding performance* (6th ed.). Englewood Cliffs, NJ: Prentice Hall.

Kilbourne, S. (2007). Performance appraisal: One step in a comprehensive staff supervision model. *Exchange: The early childhood leaders magazine since 1978.* No. 174, 34–37.

Levesque, J. D. (1993). *Manual of personnel policies, procedures and operations* (2nd ed.). Englewood Cliffs, NJ: Prentice Hall.

Martocchio, J. J. (2004). *Strategic compensation: A human resources management approach* (3rd ed.). Upper Saddle River, NJ: Prentice Hall.

McCormick, E. J., Jeanneret, P. R., & Mecham, R. C. (1989). *Position Analysis Questionnaire*. Palo Alto, CA: Consulting Psychologists Press.

Mosley, S. (1998). How to survive a classification study. *Library Journal, 123*(17), 48–49.

National School Boards Association (NSBA). (1996). *The school personnel management system*. Washington, DC: Author.

Patrick, J. (1992). *Training: Research and practice*. New York: Academic Press.

Pynes, J. E. (1997). *Human resources management for public and nonprofit organizations*. San Francisco: Jossey-Bass.

Ray, J. R., Candoli, I. C., & Hack, W. G. (2005). *School business administration: A planning approach* (8th ed.). Boston: Allyn & Bacon.

Sherman, A. W., Jr., & Bohlander, G. W. (1992). *Managing human resources* (9th ed.). Cincinnati, OH: South-Western.

Smith, S., & Mazin, R. (2004). *The HR answer book: An indispensable guide for managers and human resources professionals*. New York: American Management Association.

Swan, W. W., Holmes, C. T., Brown, C. L., Short, M. L., & DeWeese, L. (1988). A generic performance appraisal system for classified employees. *Journal of Personnel Evaluation in Education, 1,* 293–310.

Tyler, K. (2000). Put applicants' skills to the tests. *HRMagazine, 45,* 75–80.

U.S. Department of Education, National Center for Education Statistics. (2007). *The condition of education 2007.* Washington, DC: Author.

U.S. Department of Labor. (1991). *The revised handbook for analyzing jobs*. Washington, DC: Author.

Welch, F. C., & Daniel, C. (1997). Staff development for classified staff: One school district's approach. *Journal of Staff Development, 18*(1), 12–15.

Weller, L. D., Jr., & Weller, S. (2000). *Quality human resources leadership: A principal's handbook*. Lanham, MD: Scarecrow Press.

Woodward, N. H. (2000). The functions of forms. *HRMagazine, 45*(1), 67–73.

Zepeda, S. (2000). Needed: Professional growth opportunities for non-certificated support staff. *School Business Affairs, 66*(6), 37–43.

Glossary

Administrative regulation/rule. A precise statement that answers the question of how a policy is to be applied of implemented.

Alternative certification. State provisions for awarding a teaching license to persons with a baccalaureate in a teaching field who have not completed a traditional teacher education program.

Applicant tracking system. A computer-based system designed to process and analyze applicant data.

Assessment center. A center in which various activities and exercises are conducted to assess the administrative performance and skill levels in such areas as organizational ability, judgment, leadership, and human relations.

Bargaining agent. The employee organization designated as the official representative of all employees in the bargaining unit.

Bargaining unit. A group of employees certified as the appropriate unit for collective negotiations.

Behavioral interview. An employment interview characterized by a set of job-related questions that seeks to examine a candidate's past job behaviors.

Benchmark position. A position whose duties and responsibilities are sufficiently common to be found in most organizations and thus serves as a basis for making comparisons.

Closed climate. A school climate that is characterized by low staff morale, limited and inadequate communication, and limited socialization.

Closed question. Question that seeks specific responses without providing the opportunity for opinion, explanation, or elaboration.

Cohort survival method. A method of forecasting future school enrollments; it is based on certain assumptions, such as the stability of birthrates, death rates, student migration, population mobility, and others.

Competency. The ability to accomplish a task at a satisfactory level of performance.

Knowledge- and skills-based pay/Competency-based pay. An approach to compensation of employees that rewards employees for the acquisition of new knowledge and skills or the demonstration of greater competency in existing abilities.

Contract agreement. The ratified document that specifies the terms of the negotiated contract.

Cost-of-living adjustment. Increases made to salary schedules based on increases in the consumer price index (a measure of the costs of goods and services).

Disengaged climate. A school's climate characterized by negative relationships and the fact that teachers are not engaged in the important tasks of the school.

Disparate impact. Discrimination that occurs when a facially neutral employment practice has an unequal impact on a member of a group protected under Title VII.

Disparate treatment. Discrimination that occurs when a qualified employee who is a member of a group protected under Title VII is treated less favorably than others by a particular employment practice.

Distributive bargaining. A bargaining process exemplified by a labor-management model of power-based, quid pro quo strategies. Considered to be adversarial in nature and designed to realize maximum gain through the use of authority, power, or withdrawal of services.

Duel collective bargainin. A form of collective bargaining that represents a combination of traditional and integrative bargaining.

Electronic document management system. A software system that provides for the storage, retrieval, and manipulation of the various documents received and generated in the personnel recruitment and selection process.

Employee assistance program. A program established by an employer to provide confidential psychological, financial, and legal services to employees.

Engaged climate. A school climate characterized by the fact that teachers ignore the principal's attempts to control their behavior, attention to tasks is high, and the faculty is professionally responsive in spite of the principal's restrictive behaviors.

Environmental scanning. An examination of the school's internal and external environments that identifies the system's strengths and weakness and its opportunities and threats. Scanning information supports the development of a rationale for operating assumptions.

External recruitment. Recruitment of personnel from outside the organization using such recruitment techniques as media advertising, employment agencies, educational institutions, computerized data banks and electronic bulletin boards, and professional organizations and unions.

Evaluation criteria. The job-related behaviors expected of the person being evaluated, which serve as the basis for what will be evaluated.

Fact-finding. Synonymous with advisory arbitration. However, it is most often associated with impasses in table negotiations involving a future contract agreement.

Flexible benefits plan. A benefit plan in which employees select benefits and services within a fixed dollar allotment.

Formative evaluation. Ongoing evaluation that is designed to provide continuous feedback to the person being evaluated for the purposes of self-improvement and professional development.

Grievance. A problem or complaint related to the contract or master agreement. It represents an alleged violation of the agreement.

Grow-your-own-program. A strategy for increasing the pool of qualified teachers and administrators. It involves a collaborative arrangement between a college or university and a local school district to provide the necessary coursework to a cohort of employees under a flexible scheduling arrangement, with the district providing some level of financial or other support to participants.

Halo effect. The tendency of an evaluator using a rating scale to form a strong general impression of the evalutee and then give basically the same rating to every item on the scale.

Health maintenance organization. An approach to health care management whereby comprehensive health care is provided to members for a fixed monthly fee on a prepaid services basis.

Hostile environment harassment. Sexual harassment that occurs when verbal or physical conduct in the workplace is sufficiently severe to create an intimidating, hostile, or offensive environment.

Human resources administration. Processes that are planned and implemented in the organization to establish an effective system of human resources and to foster an organizational climate that enhances the accomplishment of effective teaching, student learning, and other primary educational goals.

Impasse. A situation in which two parties become steadfast in their bargaining positions on one or more agenda items and a stalemate takes place.

Indicators of competency. Products or behaviors that illustrate one's capacity to perform effectively; a performance specification.

Induction. The process designed to introduce a new or a newly assigned employee into the social and performance-related aspects of the job.

Integrative bargaining. A process that centers on efforts to resolve mutual problems of interest to the school district as a whole. Emphasis also is given to attempts to improve school board and employee relations.

Internal recruitment. Recruiting of current and previous part-time employees within the organization and through employee referrals.

Job analysis. The process by which knowledge, skills, abilities, and other characteristics are identified with conditions under which job functions are performed.

Job class. A group of jobs with similar work requirements.

Job description. A formal description of a job, which includes the job title, code required and desired qualifications, person(s) supervised, person(s) to whom the employee reports, and the terms of employment.

Job sharing. Two or more employees each working part-time to fill one position.

Liberty right. The right to a fundamental constitutional liberty (speech, press, due process, etc.)

Line administrator. School officers in the hierarchical line of authority.

Mediation. A situation in which a third party serves as an advisor and counselor for both parties in an attempt to keep the bargaining process in place during an impasse.

Mentor. An experienced professional who guides the personal development of a less experienced individual by serving as a role model; a wise and faithful advisor or tutor.

On-the-job training. Instruction regarding the knowledge and skills provided in the work setting, typically by a supervisor or experienced employee.

Open climate. A School climate in which the staff enjoys extremely high morale, works well together, enjoys friendly relations, but does not engage in a high degree of socialization; possesses the incentive to work things out and to keep the school moving.

Open-ended question. A nonleading question that is not designed or intended to elicit an obvious or preferred response.

Organizational climate. The collective personality of a school or school system; the atmosphere that prevails in an organization that is characterized by the social and professional interactions of the people.

Organizational culture. The set of important beliefs, values, and assumptions that members of the school or school system share.

Planning. An effort to anticipate and shape the future; its aim is to focus the energies and resources of the school system on the right results.

Point of service plan. A health care plan by which members choose a primary care physician who coordinates their health care within a network of physicians and hospitals who contract with the plan to provide services at a discounted rate. Members who go outside the network pay a higher percentage of the cost of services.

Policy. A comprehensive statement of a decision, principle, or increase of action.

Portfolio. A collection of artifacts related to an individual's professional practice selected to reflect growth over time.

Preferred provider organization. A health care plan by which members choose their health care providers, but pay a lower percentage of the cost of services if they use a provider who has contracted with the plan to pay services at a discounted rate (in-network).

Preliminary interview. An interview to determine the correctness and completeness of the information provided on the applications, to eliminate candidates who do not meet the qualifications that the district is seeking, and to provide information for the employment interview.

Procedural due process. The process by which individuals are provided fair and equitable procedures in employment practices.

Property right. The right to specific real or personal property, tangible and intangible (e.g., the right to continue employment).

Quid pro quo harassment. Sexual harassment that conditions employment or terms of employment on the granting of sexual favors.

Reliability. The consistency of measurements across evaluators and observations.

Scope of bargaining. Those items considered as negotiable by statute, law, or mutual agreement.

Significant risk standard. Standard applied by the courts in reviewing cases involving alleged discrimination against employees with contagious diseases; to support a change in employment status or locale, the employee must pose a significant risk of transmitting the disease.

Similarity attraction. The attraction to those who are most similar to oneself: a pitfall to be avoided in employee selection.

Single salary schedule. A salary schedule designed to include all teachers in a district and based on equivalent pay for persons with equivalent education and experience.

Staff administrator. A school administrator who is not in the direct line of authority and whose position is created expressly to serve the major line functions of the organization.

Strategic human resources planning. A procedure concerned with the effective utilization of human resources and their contributions toward the accomplishment of educational goals.

Strategic planning. A document that gives direction to all operational planning activities for the school system.

Substantive due process. Guidelines and procedures designed to ensure the objectivity and equity of standards, evidence, actions, and results.

Summative evaluation. Evaluation that is conducted at the end of an activity or period that is designed to assess terminal behaviors or overall performance.

Syntality. As an individual has a personality, an organization is said to have a syntality that reflects its group personality.

360-Degree feedback. The systematic solicitation of feedback from the full circle of an employee's supervisors, subordinates, clients, and others with whom the employee interacts.

Task. A specific responsibility, obligation, or requirement associated with a professional position or function.

Teacher center. An enriched environment of resources, personal involvement, and peer communication in which the teacher participates for purposes of professional growth.

Teacher Identification Clearinghouse. National database of all teachers who have been denied certification or have had their certificates suspended or revoked for moral reasons.

Teacher institute. A 19th-century teacher training activity, typically conducted by the county superintendent, to provide teachers with the latest techniques of professional practice.

Validity. The extent to which an assessment instrument or system measures the performance that it is intended to measure.

Voluntary binding and compulsory arbitration. Procedures for resolving disagreements through the use of a neutral third party whose decision is mandated for both parties.

Wellness program. A program designed to improve the overall health of employees, which may include health and fitness programs, use of school fitness and sports facilities, and health-related assessments.

Win-win bargaining. Integrative approaches of collective bargaining designed to achieve agreement between the two parties and at the same time make both parties feel good about the agreement and one another.

Author Index

Subject Index